THE BRUSH AND THE COMPASS

The Interface Dynamics of Art and Science

Paul Z. Hartal

UNIVERSITY
PRESS OF
AMERICA

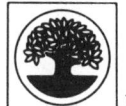

Lanham • New York • London

Copyright © 1988 by

University Press of America,® Inc.

4720 Boston Way
Lanham, MD 20706

3 Henrietta Street
London WC2E 8LU England

British Cataloging in Publication Information Available

Library of Congress Cataloging-in-Publication Data

Hartal, Paul.
The brush and the compass.

Bibliography: p. Includes index.
1. Art and science. 2. Visual perception. I. Title.
N72.S3H37   1988   701'.05   87–34627 CIP
ISBN 0–8191–6848–3 (pbk. : alk. paper)
ISBN 0–8191–6847–5 (alk. paper)

TO MY FAMILY

IV

ACKNOWLEDGEMENTS

In preparing the present volume I benefited from the works of many authors. I would like first to express my great indebtedness to them, including those with whom I entirely disagree.

This book is based on my doctoral thesis in interdisciplinary studies. But it also transcends the framework of my academic work.

It is my privilege and pleasure to acknowledge the help of numerous experts from several disciplines and from different countries. They provided me with information, read my manuscript, made illuminating comments, or acted as catalysts of insight and inspiration.

I owe particular debt to Professor F.G.W. Adams, Concordia University, Professor Alexander Altmann, Harvard University, Professor Gabriel Altmann, University of Western Ontario, Dr. Aage Bohr, Niels Bohr Institute of Copenhagen, Dr. Bernard Grad, McGill University, Professor P.R. Halmos, University of Santa Clara, Professor L.D. Henderson, The University of Texas, Dr. C.J. Kellersmann, Columbia Pacific University, Professor J.G. Kemeny, Dartmouth College, Dr. A.E. Koenig, Institute for Advanced Philosophic Research of Boulder, Colorado, Dr. Roy Lowe, University of Birmingham, Sir Nevill Mott, Cambridge University, Sir Rudolf Peierls, Oxford University, Professor Yacov Rabkin, University of Montreal, Dr. Svein Rosseland, University of Oslo, Professor Rosalie Staley, Concordia University, Dr. Heather Thompson, Columbia Pacific University, Professor Walter Van Nuss, Concordia University, and Dr. Victor Weisskopf, MIT.

I am also grateful to the Adelbert Ames Family; to S. W. Campbell, Clark University Library, K.C. Cramer and Barbara Krieger of the Dartmouth College Library; as well as to Scott Meredith, Madeleine Partous and Dr. David Pearson for their help.

I wish to express my gratitude to the writer Arthur Koestler; as well as to the architect Moshe Safdie for the stimulating exchange of ideas. I am also indebted to Dr. Vladimir Bonacic, a computer specialist concerned with programmed permutative light spectacles that he installed in Zagreb, Yugoslavia. It was through him that I learnt about Professor Gyorgy Kepes, a pioneer of the fusion of art and science, and the Founder of the Center for Advanced Visual Studies in Cambridge, Massachusetts.

As a practising painter and theoretician, I developed a keen interest in the relationship of art and science during the later 1960s. In 1975 I published *A Manifesto on Lyrical Conceptualism* that marked the genesis of a new element on the periodic table of art. It envisaged art in dialectical terms as the totality of the biotic and the geometrical, the unity of the Apollonian and the Dionysian. In this model, science is both a counterpoint as well as a complementary constituent of art. From the beginning lyrical conceptualism was concerned with the crossdisciplinary infrastructure of creativity as a synergic process. The origins of the holistic paradigm of inclusive knowledge discussed in this volume are firmly related to the idea of lyrical conceptualism.

Artists from various continents shared with me their concerns, and experimented with the lyrical conceptualist creative process. My special thanks go to Ryosuke Cohen, Billy Curmano, Ilana Isehayek, Ian Lark, Gertrud Nasri, Bernard Re, Jr., S.C. Richardson and Kara Szathmary.

I am highly beholden to Dr. Janos Ambrus, Director of the Psycho-Social Centre of the University of Lausanne at Montreux–the organizer of my one-man show in Switzerland–for his stimulating conversations, support and friendship.

I would like to express my appreciation of the gallery directors, of the museum curators and the critics who gave me their engaging feedback, critical analysis, encouragement, and moral support. My special thanks go to Ligoa Duncan of New York and Paris, to Irene Lazar and Joyce Yahouda Meir of Montreal; to Tom Konyves of the Vehicule Living Art Museum and the Art Montreal television program, to Professor Italo Faldi, Galleria Nazionale D'Arte Moderna, Rome; to Roger Delneufcourt of the Parisian *Le Nouveau Journal,* as well as to Francois Perche, *Revue Moderne,* also of Paris.

My grateful esteem is also due to the artists George Brett, 'Orgroup', USA; Ursula Meyer, City University, New York; Cho Sang-Hyun, Seoul International Fine Art Center, Korea; and Victor Vasarely, Fondation Vasarely, Aix-en-Provence, France.

My special thanks go also to Deb Martinez, and last but not least, to James E. Lyons, The Publisher and his Team at University Press of America.

Paul Z. Hartal

VII

TABLE OF CONTENTS

PREFACE   X

INTRODUCTION   XV

Chapter One
THE CREATIVE PROCESS:
NEWTON AND CONSTABLE   1

Chapter Two
MATHEMATICS AS APPLIED SCIENCE AND
AS SUBJECT MATTER IN THE VISUAL ARTS   45

Chapter Three
VISUAL PERCEPTION AND PAINTING   90

Chapter Four
BEYOND TECHNOLOGY:
THE AESTHETICS OF THE SUBWAY   165

Chapter Five
ARTIFICIAL INTELLIGENCE AND AESTHETICS:
COGNITIVE MACHINES, CONSCIOUSNESS AND
COMPUTER ART   217

Chapter Six
THE 'TWO CULTURES' AND THE
PROBLEM OF INCLUSIVE KNOWLEDGE   260

CONCLUSION   273

REFERENCES   283

BIBLIOGRAPHY   319

LIST OF ILLUSTRATIONS   332

INDEX   333

PREFACE

We live in a compartmental era in which the cultural gaps between the various intellectual disciplines are growing wider at an accelerated pace. These cultural gaps are not only utterly unaesthetic but also downright dangerous. They involve a super abundance of specialization which leads to the loss of the sense of direction.

We lack adequate blueprints of comprehensive development, coordinated attempts of planning and control. Often it is difficult for us to pick out the essentials from the surrounding mass of details. Thus, we lose sight of the main issues. The investigation of a particular problem produces proliferating particulars even when generalization is needed. By paying too much attention to the parts we can find ourselves in a situation of being unable to see the wood for the trees. It is a perilous situation which results in misconstrued premises, in wrong judgments, and in failing operational strategies.

Well within the mainspring of this problem lies the widely accepted but erroneous assumption that science and art are entirely different and severed polarities. This is a focal contemporary fallacy.

The purpose of this interdisciplinary study is to show through selected case histories that art and science interact in the conscious and extraconscious levels, and that they can be integrated into a synergistic whole. In my opinion the rise of a comprehensive culture is not only possible but necessary for the sake of human survival.

In terms of methodology this study primarily can be characterized as analytical and synthetic. It is also comparative as well as descriptive. Empirical evidence to be found in the history of art and science supports its edifice. Retrodictory inferences played a central role in its development. On the other hand, the conjecture concerning the growing interaction, and possible convergence, of art and science is predictory.

Certain projective aspects of this study are supported by phenomenological introspection. They, in part, rely on my own uneven experience in laboratory work, in scholarly research, in creative writing and painting. I also used some of my drawings and collages to serve both as empirical evidence and as illustrations to the text.

The interaction of art and science is an interdisciplinary theme. It has an extremely wide scope and range. In order to undertake a feasible investigation of this topic one must narrow it down and define its parameters. The central thread which I bring forward to serve as a vertical coordinate throughout this study is consciousness. For, the epistemological aspect seems to be the cardinal common denominator of art and science. It is the creative process whereby the yawning gap between art and science can be bridged and the centre of their interface dynamics located. The horizontal coordinate of the study is provided by selected case histories from the domains of art and science.

This book offers new ways to look at these focal human endeavors, and corrects numerous ficticious views with regard to their character and rapport.

Pivotal to the subject matter of the book is the premise that art and science are complementary symbolic systems through which humanity structures and interprets reality. Although these two realms cannot refute one another, they can lend mutual support to each other. There is science in art and art in science. A synergistic collaboration between artist and scientist is possible. There are already institutions where artists and scientists work together as equal partners; and there should be more.

Before and during the Renaissance there was no sharp separation of science from art as we know it nowadays. This categorical differentiation occurred in the modern age. However, the world is changing. The need for new ideas, the cybernation of society, the rise of a holistic science point to the possibility of a renewed alliance between art and science, which was violated by the Industrial Revolution and its aftermath.

My conceptual framework incorporates the holographic principle. This paradoxical concept is concerned with the ancient idea that just as the whole contains the part, the part also contains the whole. This apparently absurd notion represents a testable hypothesis which can be validated through infinitesimal calculus, and by holography. The latter is a method of making three dimensional photographic images by using coherent light for illumination.

As a mediating and unifying idea, the holographic principle manifests itself in both art and science. It reveals itself in their common infrastructure; in such aesthetic qualities as the dialectical combinations of variety and uniformity, conflict and harmony, chaos and order.

This volume is divided into six basic chapters. In each of them different kaleidoscopic aspects of cultural osmosis are investigated. The first chapter is concerned with the creative process. It offers probably the first available comparative study of the creative process of the physicist Isaac Newton and of the painter John Constable; and suggests that Newton was no less an artist than Constable was a scientist.

The second chapter deals with various aspects of mathematics as applied science and as subject matter in the visual arts. It advances the notion that extraconscious historical connections exist between the

Pythagoreans, Villard de Honnecourt, and Paul Cézanne's approach to painting. Another theme of this chapter involves the investigation of the Golden Section, Dürer's contribution to geometry, the Fibonacci series, and Birkhoff's aesthetic measure. One of the original findings of this unit is related to the mathematical conception of infinity. In my view, the historical roots of Georg Cantor's theory of infinite sets can be traced back to Leonardo da Vinci's thought.

The third chapter explores the relationship of visual perception as a psychological problem to art. It seems that both scientists and artists are concerned with the investigation of the reciprocal effects and processes of seeing and knowing. A central feature of this unit is the visual experiments that I developed for this project. They eventuated in the discovery of an original solution for the Müller-Lyer illusion.

The fourth chapter discusses the aesthetic dimensions of a technological system, the Montreal subway as an urban environment. An important aspect of my theoretical paradigm is based on the assumption that the problem of urban transportation transcends the field of science based technology: it is a problem which is intertwined with the quality of life.

The fifth Chapter is about cybernetic intelligence, machine consciousness and computer art. A salient bearing of this unit is the Aesthetic Cybernetic Test (ACT) which I have devised as an advanced Turing Test. By means of a conversation about a visual anagram it challenges the cognitive faculty of the computer. The development of advanced thinking machines is not merely a mathematical or logical problem. It is an interdisciplinary problem concerned, among other things, with feelings, emotions, and aesthetics.

The sixth chapter deals with "The 'Two Cultures' and the Problem of Inclusive Knowledge." It rejects C.P. Snow's contention that artists and scientists do not interact. Instead, it evolves a holistic model of culture based on inclusive knowledge.

The need for the rise of a holistic culture arises from several considerations. Art and science represent midmost pillars of contemporary western culture, but unlike scientists, artists are neglected and deprived of community leadership. This is a dangerous and paradoxical situation. For, we constantly need new ideas. Science alone cannot solve such conspicuous problems as unemployment, environmental pollution, stress, crime, alienation, mass education, population explosion, hunger and war. It is not flexible enough. It inclines to reduce the complexities of reality into simple formulas. In its method oriented approach the dynamic fluidity and wholeness of life turn to attenuated abstract and static concepts.

The accidents in the nuclear power plants at Three Mile Island and at Chernobyl reinforced my conviction that the monopolization of science-based technologies involves intrinsic dangers. These accidents result from an undemocratic, profit oriented science which ignores the reality of human errors, and the imperfectness of technological systems. Today the domineering influence of established science deprives us democratic alternatives. The idea of inclusive knowledge represents such an alternative. We need comprehensive approaches for the solution of comprehensive problems. Our survival depends on adaptability. And adaptability is bound up with lateral thinking, with artistic creativity and imagination. Science in its present condition is not only inflexible, it is simply not scientific enough.

Passionate defenders of the prevalent hypothesis testing, mathematical and experimental methodology of science, often belittle the importance of art as a fundamental form of human wisdom. They ignore the fact that mathematicians, for instance, are guided not only by logical considerations but also by aesthetic decisions. Although the observation that emotions play a principal role in art is absolutely correct, to conclude from it that art is an incommensurate tool for the investigation of reality is totally wide of the mark.

For, artists are propelled not only by emotions but by critical reasoning as well. Moreover, the commonly held belief that emotions are the enemy of sound judgment is a misconstrued premise. In actuality emotions often synergistically combine with reason. Thus, under appropriate conditions, they can enhance understanding and generate meaningful new insights.

XIV

INTRODUCTION

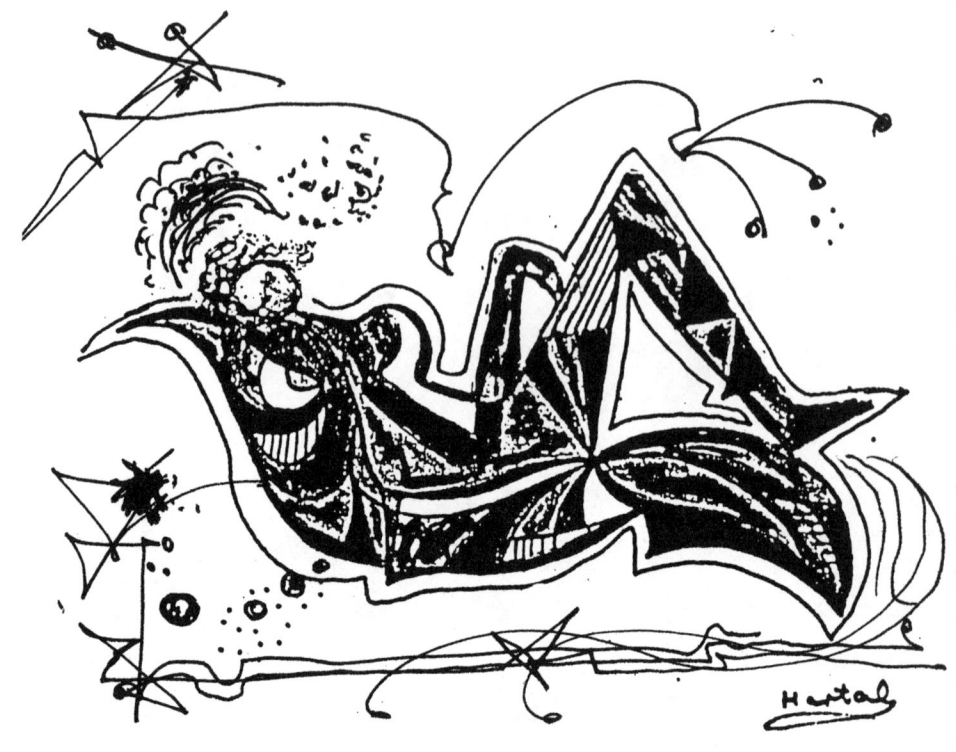

TROPICAL BIRD AS RECLINING GIRL

A stylized image can be perceived in various ways. An object can be more than just one thing. This geometrical abstraction is a metaphor of the relationship of art and science. In a sense, both art and science are complementary endeavors to structure and interpret an enigmatic reality through symbols (mathematics, words, and images). They are both poetic systems that involve observation, intuition, abstraction, analysis, imagination, and inference. They both wonder about the magic of existence, and stand in awe in the face of the great mystery of the universe. Of course, they are also different. Science is more concerned with the repeatable, the predictable, and the general than art. Science constructs generalized hypotheses, tests them by experiments; whereas art asserts concrete sensations, and expresses the unique vision of the mind's eye.

Hypotheses

Art and Science appear to be the two basic domains through which humankind relates and structures reality. The fundamental difference between these two domains seems to be not in the realm of facts or in the empirical determinants of reality, but in the realm of system properties. In other words the difference between art and science lies in the conceptual framework, in the method by which the artist and the scientist approach the world.

According to Arthur Koestler,

> . . . Einstein's space is no closer to reality than Van Gogh's sky. The glory of science is not in a truth more absolute than the truth of Bach or Tolstoy, but in the act of creation itself. The scientist's discoveries impose his own order on chaos, as the composer or painter imposes his; an order that always refers to limited aspects of reality, and is based on the observer's frame of reference, which differs from period to period as a Rembrandt nude differs from a nude by Manet.[1]

The precise relationship of art and science transcends definition. Their reciprocal status is elusive and ambiguous. Victor F. Weisskopf, a former president of the American Academy of Arts and Sciences and a Professor of Physics at MIT says in this regard:

> What could be more different than science and art? The former is considered as a rational, objective, and cool study of nature; the latter is often regarded as a subjective, irrational outburst of feelings and emotions. One may also consider scientific discoveries as the products of imagination, of sparks of sudden insight, whereas art could be viewed as the product of painstaking work, carefully adding one part to the other by a rational thinking process. Surely art and science have something in common: both are ways to deal with our experiences and to lift our spirits from daily drudgery to universal values. But the roles of art and science in society are very different.[2]

One of the fathers of quantum theory, Werner Heisenberg pointed out that science is an integral part of the human experience. Science is an endeavor which "rests on experiment" but "its results are attained through talks"[3]. According to Heisenberg, "science is rooted in conversations"[4], and it is quite inseparable from general human, political and philosophical problems.

Heisenberg wrote *Physics and Beyond,* among other things, in order to reduce "the gap between the two cultures, between art and science."[5] It seems that C.P. Snow's *Two Cultures* has convinced many that indeed a great schism exists in contemporary Western society, and that the humanities are not fertilized by the exact sciences. However, Michael Polanyi, Professor of Physical Chemistry and of Social Studies at the University of Manchester, disagrees:

> Sir Charles Snow complains about the gap between science and the rest of our culture . . . But I see the problem in a different perspective. I don't agree that the influence of science on the rest of our thoughts is too feeble. On the contrary, the claims made today on the minds of men in the name of science are comprehensive. Freud and Marx–little of modern culture is unaffected by the teachings of one or both of these two, and both derived their authority by speaking for science.[6]

Physicist like David Bohm and Roger S. Jones, argue that consciousness is an integral part of the world, that reality is not and cannot be external to the human mind. Reality is an unbroken whole of the matter-mind continuum. Thinking and reality are intertwined. "As careful attention shows", says Bohm, "thought itself is in an actual process of movement. That is to say, one can feel a sense of flow in the 'stream of consciousness', not dissimilar to the sense of flow in the movement of matter in general."[7]

According to R.S. Jones, the exclusion of the so called subjective realm from the domain of science does not make the latter more objective. In his view, space, time, matter and number constitute the four pivotal pillars of physics and these pivotal pillars are in fact cardinal metaphors. "I have never been able to separate matters of philosophy, belief, aesthetics, and ethics from the study of physics", explains Jones. "Within physical and mathematical ideas, it is always the philosophical, the aesthetic, the psychological that I savor and which excite me most."[8]

As Thomas S. Kuhn has shown in *The Structure of Scientific Revolutions* (1962), progress in science is tied to paradigm shifts. Accepted concepts (paradigms) are replaced in the history of science by others in a manner that is very similar to a gestalt switch. The objectivity of science is a very relative percept. The system properties of scientific theories are non-empirical entities; paradigms on the rise can compete with established ones, and authority can prevail over observed facts (particularly if these are unique facts which cannot be tested, are not predictable and repeatable).

In contrast to the rigid conception of science as an immutable and precise system that preoccupies the highest terrain in the hierarchy of disciplines, one can also view it as a dynamic process; an interface of form and content resulting from the dialectical interaction of paradigms, styles, schemata, and sensibilities.

According to Judith Wechsler, "the search in science for models that illuminate nature seems to parallel certain crucial processes in art." Aesthetics in science can be viewed as a way of knowing "concerned with the metaphorical and analogical relationship between reality and concepts, theories and models."[9]

Although an established science of mathematical aesthetics hardly exists, Henri Poincaré thought that mathematical processes are guided by intuition. A mathematical theorem, for example, can be examined in the light of various proofs. The selection of the best proof out of an existing set of competing and valid proofs can be the result of aesthetic considerations.[10]

Scientific progress seems to be a non-cumulative process. Paradigm mutations involve the conversion of the scientific community to new conceptual configuration as well as to new experimental procedures. In the various stages of these transformations the aesthetic dimension of the creative process can play a central role.

The theoretical models that the physicists construct, e.g., in order to study the behavioral aspects of nature frequently defy ordinary descriptive language. "We must be clear that, when it comes to atoms, language can be used only as in poetry", explained Niels Bohr in 1922 to the young Werner Heisenberg at Göttingen: "The poet, too, is not nearly so concerned with describing facts as with creating images and establishing mental connections."[11]

An intriguing aspect of the creative process concerns the problem of visualization. To what extent was Bohr, for example, influenced in his model building by his well known interest in modern art? The corpuscular and electromagnetic properties of light, its dual nature, had evolved in Bohr's sytem of quantum mechanics into an inevitable relationship which he called complementarity. The Danish physicist was a philosophically oriented scientist who often used the idea of complementarity to account for a variety of phenomena beyond the limits of science. In his views opposites could supplement each other like the Chinese symbols of Yin and Yang which represent synthesis and complementarity. Bohr was the friend of painters and musicians. His personal collection of paintings consisted of examples of Scandinavian and French art. It included a Cubist canvas, the work of Jean Metzinger, 'Lady with Horse'. Bohr liked his work particularly because the "painting could create illusions . . . for example giving the impression that planes were intersecting in a manner that is impossible in the real world."[12]

Could it be that Bohr's idea of complementarity was prompted by Cubism? Both cubism and quantum mechanics represent new ways of looking at the world. They both redefine the nature of reality. Bohr was well aware of the fact that in cubism "an object could be several things, could change, could be seen as a face, a limb and a fruitbowl."[13] Let us compare these words with Bohr's own statement:

> No sharp separation between object and subject can be maintained, since the perceiving subject also belongs to our mental content. From these circumstances follows not only the relative meaning of every concept, or rather of every word, the meaning depending upon our arbitrary choice of view point, but also that we must, in general, be prepared to accept the fact that a complete elucidation of one and the same object may require diverse points of view which defy a unique description . . . The necessity of taking recourse to a complementary, or reciprocal, mode of description is perhaps most familiar to us from psychological problems. In opposition to this, the feature which characterizes the so called exact sciences is, in general, the attempt to attain to uniqueness by avoiding all reference to the perceiving subject.[14]

The parallels between cubism and Bohr's words are easily discernible. His familiarity with modern art, his friendship with artists lend additional support to the hypothesis that indeed quantum mechanics has been influenced by the avant-garde.[15]

Although Bohr's concept of complementarity was an important contribution to the development of quantum physics, it could not provide a mathematical solution describing the relationship between particle and wave. The connection between these dual phenomena was the clue in the evolution of quantum theory. Eventually it was Erwin Schrödinger, a professor at Zurich, who on the basis of Prince Louis Victor de Broglie's equation, advanced his own triumphal wave equation. It became the fundamental mathematical formula expressing the behavior of a subatomic particle moving in a field of force.

While Bohr's creative process seems to be related to the visual aspects of aesthetics, Schrödinger's reasoning can be linked to music. This is an intriguing hypothesis on two accounts. It concerns the relationship of subject-object, that is to say the problem of the mind-matter continuum. On the subjective level Schrödinger's mental imagery appears to be audile in character; a man whose sense of hearing, auditory modality and musical education put him into tune with the reverberations of nature. This is not just a poetic conjecture. For, "atoms turn out to have definite electron energies as a result of a phenomenon similar to that which makes musical instruments sound definite tones."[16] The Greek philosopher Pythagoras already in antiquity discovered an intriguing relationship between music and number. "It had long been known that the vibrations of strings and organ pipes, of kettledrums, jellies, and light waves, were governed by wave equations . . ."[17] Unlike in Bohr's model in which the electrons may jump from one orbit to another, in Schrödinger's conception frequency differentiation is compatible with the beat frequency of music. The musical infrastructure of the cosmos finds its expression in atomic vibrations.

The Scientist As Artist

Was Leonardo da Vinci an artist who contributed also to the development of science, or was he a scientist who contributed also to the development of art? The question itself seems to be emerging from the dichotomic nature of our culture characterized by a sharp differentiation between art and science. During the Renaissance, the ideal of universal man had been crystallized in the archetype of the hybrid intellectual. For the universal man of the period art and science represented the same quest and passion.

It is rather intriguing that today we consider Leonardo as primarily an artist, whereas we regard Galileo Galilei as a scientist. Yet it is much more accurate to see Galileo as an outstanding humanist of the

Italian Renaissance, who had a long standing curiosity about natural phenomena. He had also a lifelong interest in poetry, music and painting. The painter Ludovico Cardi da Cigoli (1559-1613), and a friend of Galileo, said that it was the latter who taught him everything he knew about perspective. In 1612 Cigoli made a painting in Rome into which he incorporated Galileo's sketch of the moon. In his youth Galileo himself was an active painter whose work evoked the admiration of connoisseurs.

Sir Isaac Newton also excelled in painting. According to Albert Einstein, "in one person he combined the experimenter, the theorist, the mechanic and, not least, the artist in exposition."[18] Although Newton was an empiricist, the poetic qualities of his thought found their expression in his lifelong interest he took in alchemy and religion. Besides, if one approaches him from a historical perspective, it is not absurd to view his achievement as part of the English Romanticist movement. For Newton's preoccupation with nature, with alchemy, with the search for the infinite and the eternal are salient Romanticist traits.

The most famous scientist of the twentieth century, Albert Einstein was also a great musician. He was six years old when he took up violin playing. However, enthusiasm and inspiration for music did not come to him easily. At the beginning there was discipline. Delight came later. When he was a teenager he began to grasp the mathematical structure inherent of Mozart's music. For Einstein's part music was more than a psychological safety valve, more than a sanctuary to shelter from the hardships of life. For him, music was a subconscious force guiding his stream of consciousness and stimulating his thought. "Music has no effect on research work", Einstein said, "but both are born of the same source and complement each other through the satisfaction they bestow."[19]

Mogens Andersen, a painter and a friend of Einstein's great rival in science, Niels Bohr, had recorded the delight that the Danish physicist showed when he heard Picasso's aphorism: "I do not look for things, I find them." For, "Bohr knew that it was an art to be a scientist and that there is a science in creating art."[20]

The Artist As Scientist

The great English landscape painter John Constable (1776-1837) regarded painting as a profession which is scientific as well as poetic. He emphasized that imagination alone is never enough in order to produce realistic images. His work was founded on intensive research supported by detailed observation and meticulous knowledge of the small geographical area of South-Eastern England that served him as subject matter.

Lecturing in 1836 at the Royal Institution of London, the artist said:

> Painting is a science, and should be pursued as an inquiry into the laws of nature. Why, then, may not landscape be considered as a branch of natural philosophy, of which pictures are but experiments?[21]

The impressionist learnt a great deal from Constable. But the most scientific painter of the nineteenth century across the English Channel appears to be Georges Seurat. His neo-impressionism had been inspired by the color theories of the physicists E. Chevreul and N. O. Rood, by the artist Delacroix, by the writings of Baudelaire and by investigations into the aesthetic properties of the mathematical concept known as the Golden Section. Seurat rejected the impressionist spontaneity of the creative process. Instead of Monet's maxim that the painter paints just as birds sing, he wanted to paint according to scientifically supported theories. As the founder of the artistic techniques of divisionism and pointillisme, Seurat applied opposites and similarities, complementary colors, luminous and darker tones, optical mixtures, in order to create harmony which he considered the essence of art.

The painter Adelbert Ames, Jr. (1880-1955) was educated at Harvard University and during 1910-14 he studied art at Boston. The Indian head, a scup lture which became the trademark of the Shawmut Association Banks in 1910, was created by him.[22] At certain stage of his artistic career, the young visual artist became interested in physiological optics as a result of his consideration of the painter's need to see the world in an objective manner, and to investigate the relationship of that need to the nature of perception.[23] According to Hadley Cantril, it was Ames who practically established and pioneered the science of physiological optics. The best known apparatus that the artist devised is a distorted room in which a person of normal height appears to be a dwarf.[24] During the 1920s when Ames was associated with Dartmouth College, he discovered a visual deficiency which he named aniseikonia. It describes a condition in which the retinal images formed by the two eyes differ in size and shape.

Since 1956 artists began to experiment with the computer as a new creative tool. The characteristic properties of the computer are enormous speed, phenomenal memory and versatility to relate and structure information according to the specificities determined by the program. In a sense, the computer represents not merely an extension of the human nervous system, but also a new matter-mind relationship. In the new environment of man and machine the cybernetic interface facilitates a new stage of artistic evolution: The extra-organic or out of the body creative process. Machine and man become interacting partners in the act of creation. The computer eliminates "the necessity for hand-eye coordination on the part of the artist. With the computer, everyone can draw."[25]

Myron W. Krueger is a computer scientist at the University of Connecticut who combines aesthetics and technology as a new art form. His aim is to set up environments in which computers sense and interpret the participants' actions and needs and respond intelligently. The resulting art form is a sensitive cybernetic environment in which stimulating interaction between human and machine occurs. This interaction is mediated by the artist. According to Krueger,

> We will live in . . . a Responsive Environment
> where human behavior is perceived by a computer,
> which interprets what it observes and responds
> through intelligent visual and auditory displays.
> Since many kinds of displays, including discrete
> lights, video, computer graphics, and electronic music
> are amenable to computer control, a rich repertoire of
> relationships can be established between an
> individual and the Environment . . . Humanity's
> relationship to technology can be a positive
> experience . . . [26]

The Integration Of Art And Science

During the Italian Renaissance an extraordinarily gifted battery of men had been involved in the development of perspective, a field which belongs to both art and science. The Florentine painter and biographer Giorgio Vasari (1511-1574), had recorded the lives of such central figures as Brunelleschi, Alberti, Piero della Francesca, Masaccio, Leonardo and Uccello–all of whom were pioneers of the new aesthetics.

However, it was already clear to Vasari himself that a line of demarcation must be drawn somewhere to mark the difference between art and science. Writing on Paolo Uccello, "the most captivating and imaginative painter to have lived since Giotto", he exhorted:

Artists who devote more attention to perspective
than to figures develop a dry and angular style because
of their anxiety to examine things too minutely; and,
moreover, they usually end up solitary, eccentric,
melancholy, and poor, as indeed did Paolo Uccello
himself.[27]

There is a growing number of scientists who believe that in the
future science will be metamorphosed into a knew form of human
knowledge. For, mechanistic materialism, orthodox science is too
narrow and limited to function as a comprehensive philosophy.
Orthodox science is not an exclusive edifice for the discovery of truth,
not the only reliable path to knowledge. The scientific method cannot
deal with a huge array of problems simply because, as Abraham
Maslow had pointed out, it is not problem but method oriented: "It is
tempting, if the only tool you have is a hammer, to treat everything as
if it were a nail."[28]

According to Max Planck, the father of quantum mechanics:

Science . . . means unresting endeavor and
continually progressing development toward an aim
which the poetic intuition may apprehend, but which
the intellect can never fully grasp.[29]

In the holistic conception of human knowledge art and science are
incorporated into a grand synthesis. Through the confluence of beauty
and concept, through the fusion of the subjective and the objective
worlds a new synergic human experience will emerge which transcends
quantification. This synergic whole cannot be reduced to quantity. It is
more than the sum total of its parts.

Emotion and subjectivity are not necessarily the enemies of truth.
On the contrary. The artist's depiction of a beautiful woman, for
instance, can give us more truth about femininity, than any scientific
description can. Even when art is seen as a deception it carries the
dialectical side of actuality. Or as Picasso said: "We all know that art
is not truth. Art is a lie that makes us realize truth."[30]

The convergence of art and science in the twentieth century, as a
tendency, can be seen through the rise of abstraction. As it has been
pointed out above, art and science are two specific avenues to structure
and interpret reality. In this century they both became increasingly
abstract. For the world of the modern scientist is intrinsically tied to
the abstract language of mathematics, whereas the defining property of

XXV

modern art is visual abstraction. Another example can be found in the parallel development of quantum mechanics and surrealism.

For, the subjective world of the surrealist artist and the objective world of the quantum physicist are not far apart from each other. Take, for instance, Salvador Dali's painting, *The Persistence of Memory* (1931). It is set in a barren landscape inhabited with incongruous elements. The flabby watches hanging from the branch of a dead tree, from a rectangular form and a third limp watch placed over an amorphous figure, can be seen as a haunting allegory of temporal relativity. The three limp watches depicted in the painting show different, non-synchronized times and the fourth watch appearing in the foreground is seen only from its back side as it covered by a group of ants.[31]

In the bizarre world of quantum physics the ordinary space-time environment vanishes. Sub-atomic particles behave in a manner which is entirely unfamiliar to us. Quantum physicists believe that in the microscopic world of the atom causation collapses and particles can travel back into past time instead of moving into the future. They also suppose the existence of parallel worlds and overlapping realities. In the surrealist world of quantum mechanics Schrödinger's cat is simultaneously alive and dead.[32]

It is noteworthy that quantum physics is not a marginal domain of physics. It is central in fact to all modern sciences, including nuclear physics, lasers, television and computers.

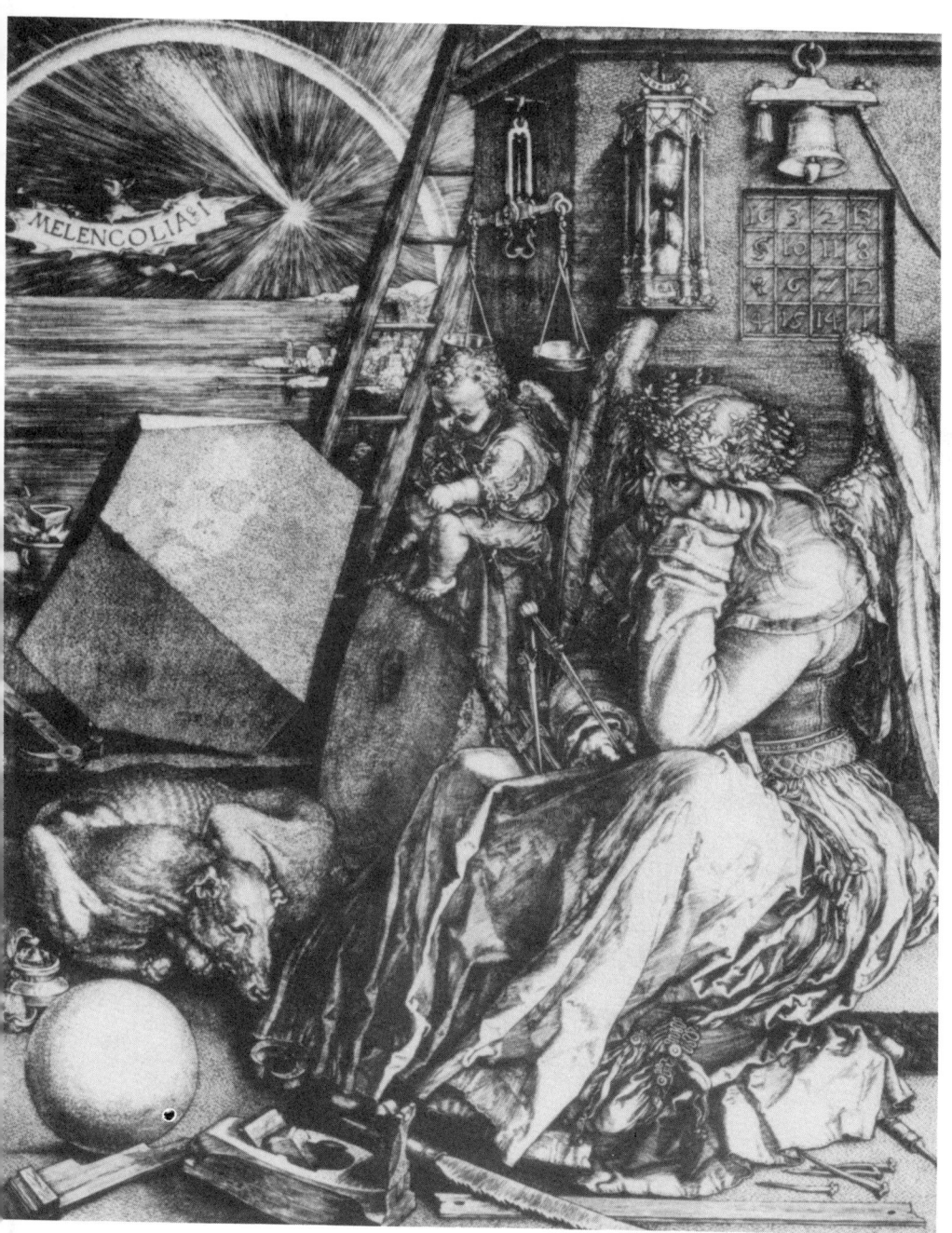

Dürer, MELANCOLIA I, 1514, Engraving, approximately 7.5'' x 9.5''

XXVII

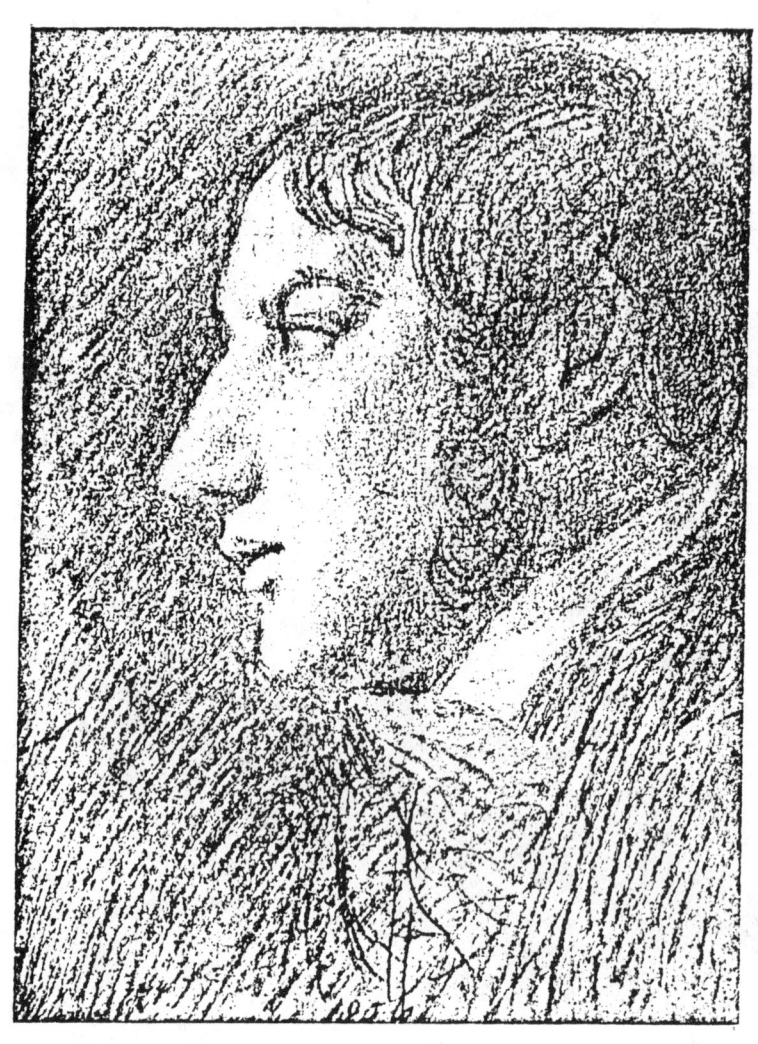

SELF-PORTRAIT OF CONSTABLE
Pencil, 1806

XXVIII

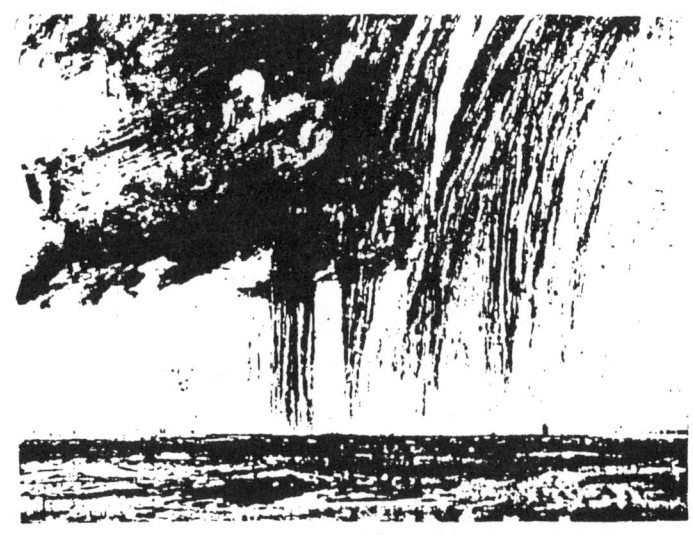

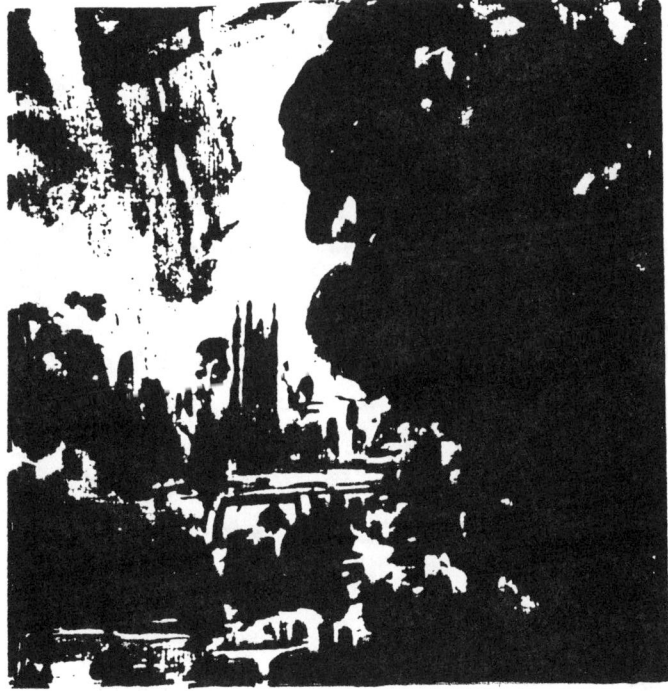

Top: *Seascape Study with Rain Clouds* by Constable; c. 1824-8, Royal
Academy of Art, London
Bottom: *View on the Stour; Dedham Church in the Distance* Sketch by
Constable; after 1830.

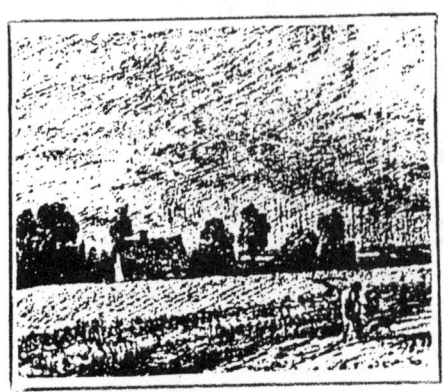
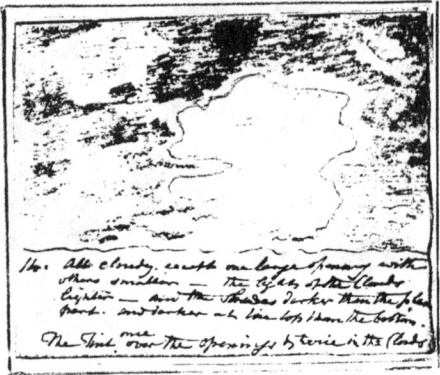

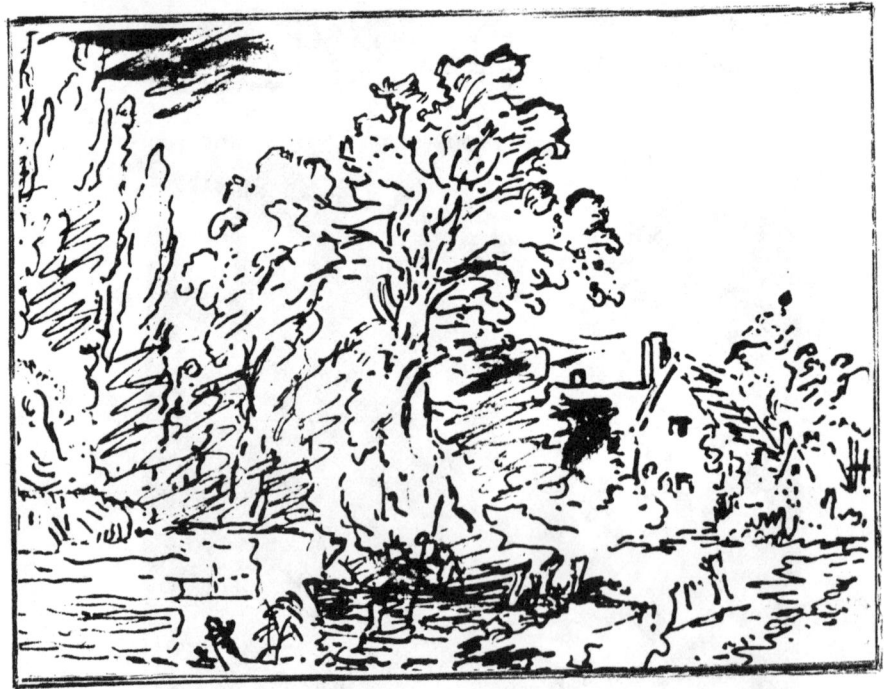

Drawings by Constable
Top left: *A Cottage near a lane at East Bergholt,* 1817 (Detail)
Top right: Inscriptions and sketch after the sky types included in Alexander Cozen's *A New Method of Assisting the Invention in Drawing Original Compositions of Landscape* (9.3 x 11.4 cm)
Bottom: *The Farmhouse by a River,* 1829

XXX

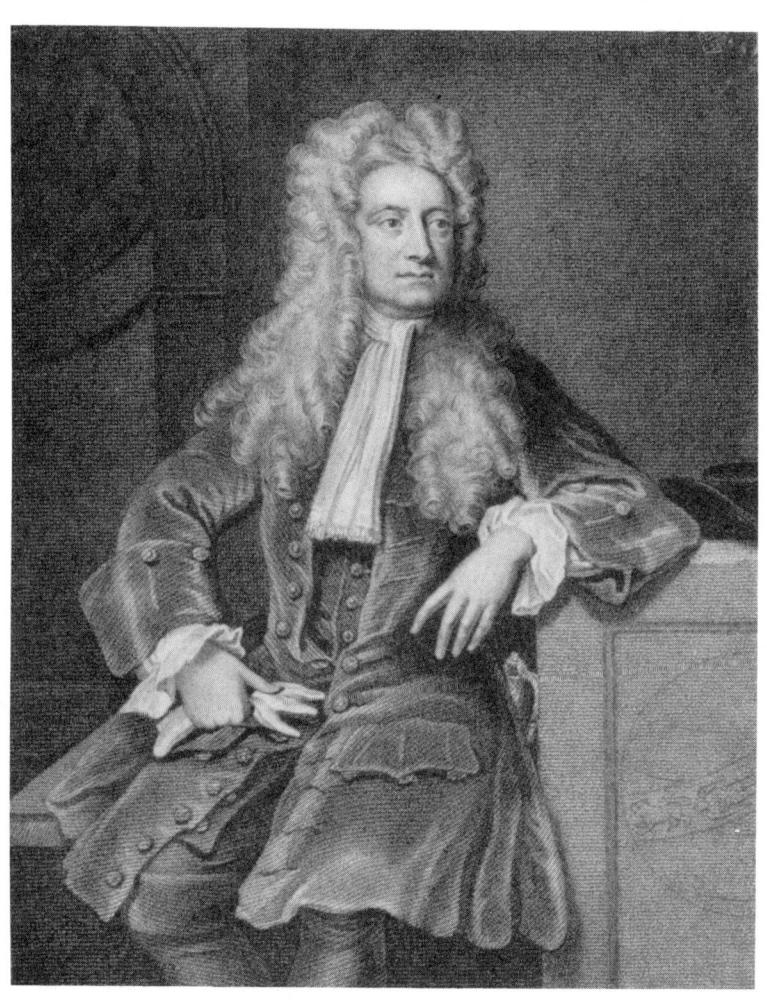

Sir Isaac Newton
Engraving by W. T. Fry

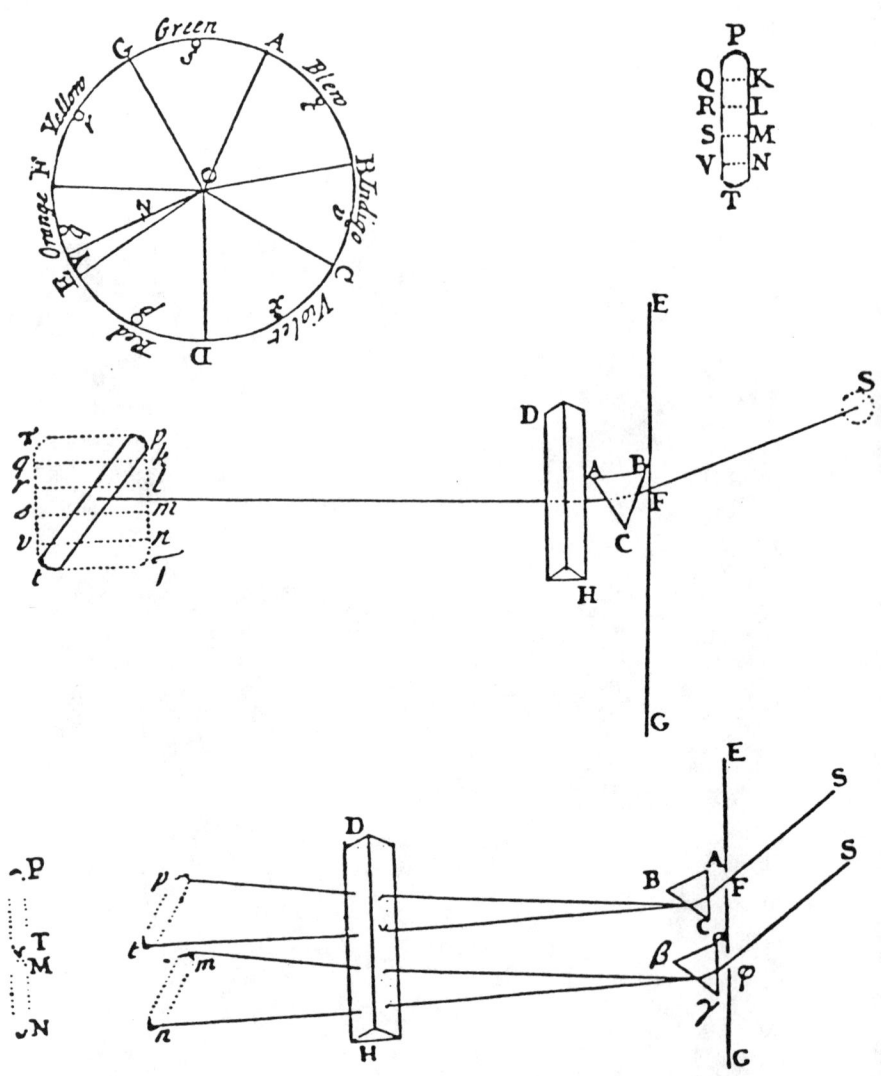

Illustrations from Newton's *Opticks* (1730) showing color wheel and refractive prisms in experimental schemes. According to the author, the seven color parts on the wheel are "proportional to the seven musical tones or intervals of the eight sounds" (sol, la, fa, . . .). Newton's theory of color exerted great influence on the development of modern art.

Chapter One

THE CREATIVE PROCESS: NEWTON AND CONSTABLE

This study is an investigation of the conceptual schemes and the creative processes of Isaac Newton and John Constable. It explores the peculiar method of the scientist and the specific approach of the artist as two distinct avenues in the human relationship to nature. Although Constable was born one hundred and thirty four years later than Newton, and they practised entirely different disciplines, they also had much in common.

For Constable's part painting was a science. His method of observation and his visual analysis represent essential scientific components. Moreover, the artistic elements in Newton's creative process and the scientific constituents in Constable's method of painting form a unique phenomenological palindrome. Their respective creative processes are structured in a particular symmetrical configuration of crystallized cognition. Newton's scientific method was based on the intricate lattice work of logic and intuition; Constable's painting rested on the unique combination of restrained imagination and the fiber of reason.

History is not a precise science. The reconstruction of the lives of people is always an extremely complicated endeavor and it is never accurate. The portrayal of Newton's life, for example, was undertaken by various biographers but their attempts might have been yielding rather different accounts. Thus, R. S. Westfall, for instance, suggests that it is highly unlikely that the Great Civil War, which raged through England during Newton's childhood, had any impact on his psyche. In Westfall's opinion, before Newton was a year old, the forces of Oliver Cromwell had been in complete control of Lincolnshire. Although,"troops may have passed up and down the Great North Road within sight of the manor house", they would have been only "bodies of men without meaning to the tiny boy."[1]

However, B. Tannenbaum and M. Stillman offer a different view of Newton's childhood. They say that

> Lincolnshire was a constant battlefield. The King's men had their stronghold at Nottingham, thirty miles to the West of Woolsthorpe. The forces of Cromwell were stationed at Cambridge, seventy miles southeast. Small pitched battles might occur at any time.[2]

When Isaac Newton started to attend day school the Civil War still continued. Every morning before he left for school, he heard the warning words of his grandmother: "Watch out for the soldiers, Isaac.

If you notice them coming, run and hide in the bushes."[3]

Newton was born on Christmas night, December 25, 1642. In the same year the great Italian scientist Galileo Galilei died. And it was in August 1642 that King Charles I raised his standard at Nottingham and the English Civil War began. Seven years later his crown had fallen together with his head, and Oliver Cromwell became the uncrowned ruler of the realm.

Hannah Newton lay in her bed as the two midwives on that Christmas night were helping her to deliver the prematurely born baby. The midnight bells had long finished tolling and the candles flickered in the chilly bedroom of the old manor house of Woolsthorpe in Lincolnshire. Isaac was born so tiny that the midwives did not believe that such a weak and small infant would live more than a couple of hours. However, the child did not pay much attention to the women's talk. In fact Isaac Newton grew into a healthy lad and died in 1727, at the old age of eighty five.

Isaac's father died before his son was born. Hannah Newton had to raise her son on a tiny income. The manor house was surrounded by lands cultivated by tenant farmers. The Newtons were a family of yeomen, freeholders farming their own land. The financial situation improved when Hannah married in 1646 the Reverend Barnabas Smith, a fifty years old bachelor and quite a well to do man. After her second marriage, she moved from the manor house to the nearby vicarage at North Witham. Isaac was three years old and left behind in the old family nest under the care of his grandmother.

Woolsthorpe was a splendid place to grow up. Isaac Newton especially enjoyed the summers. The gardens were filled with fruits, and vegetables. The pink apple blossoms were gradually replaced by tempting red apples in the orchards.

Isaac attended grammar school at Grantham. The town was the county seat of Lincolnshire, located seven miles from Woolsthorpe. He studied Latin, Biblical exegesis, ancient history, logic and mathematics. Yet he was an indifferent student who was frequently dreaming. Classes were a burden for him. But he liked to watch and study the operation of machinery. When a new mill was constructed he inspected each piece of it. Isaac lived with the Clarke family in Grantham and in the same household he befriended Catherine Storey who was several years younger than him. Isaac built a small scale model of the windmill he saw in town. To the great astonishment of the Clarke family and of Catherine the toy windmill was working. The secret was based on a trick. The maker of the model windmill put a small mouse inside which was turning the wheel.

3

Isaac also liked to make colorful kites. He was fascinated by the interplay of lights and shadows. He made also sundials to show the time. The old manor house at Woolsthorpe not only survived the storms of the centuries and the vicissitudes of history, but still features two of these sundials on its worn out walls. Isaac also constructed a clepsydra or water clock for the Clarke family. Clocks were still a luxury in those days, and the Clarkes were glad to have one. Since minute hands were not used on clocks in that period, Isaac installed a single hand to point to the hour.

In the years that followed Isaac Newton found himself in Cambridge. Since he could not afford to study at the university without supporting himself by work, he became a sizar. A sizar was a student who worked up himself through college as servant to tutors. For several years Newton earned his bread as a sizar. The job allowed him to pay tuition fees and to purchase books as well.

At Cambridge he studied arithmetic, rhetoric, logic, and astronomy. At nights he was learning over his candlelit books, and tried to ignore the disturbing noise which his roommate and his friends were making. Newton immersed himself in the study of the heliocentric thesis of Copernicus, according to which the sun, not the earth, was the centre of the universe. The previous geocentric tenet of Ptolemy taught that the sun and the planets were revolving around the earth. Copernicus, on the other hand, claimed that the earth was moving around the sun, and that the planets did the same thing. Newton also learnt about Galileo and Kepler.[4] He was interested not only in Kepler's laws of planetary motion, but also in the German scientist's optical theories, including the telescope and "the celebrated phenomena of colors".

One of Newton's tutors at Cambridge was Dr. Isaac Barrow, the most distinguished mathematician in England in those days, who held the position of the Lucasian Professor of Mathematics at Trinity College. The same chair is in existence even today. It has recently been occupied by Paul Dirac whose work in quantum mechanics concerned the mathematical investigation of atomic and subatomic matter, and predicted the existence of antimatter.

In contrast to Barrow, who liked to undertake detailed, meticulous investigations of everything, Newton concerned himself only with carefully selected fields of research that particularly interested him. History has recorded that King Charles II, who was restored to the English throne in 1660, once complained about Barrow. According to his majesty, due to the profound perfectionism of Dr. Barrow nothing was left to others on the subjects he dealt with. Charles II apparently was a playful monarch who enjoyed to invite the members of the Royal

Society and to pose deliberately embarrassing questions to them. For instance, he could ask the learned gentlemen to be so kind and explain "why a live fish placed in a full bowl of water does not cause it to overflow, while a dead fish does cause it to overflow." The philosophers did not dare to criticize their monarch's question. Instead, they produced preposterous answers.[5]

Charles II liked to dabble in science. He frequently amused himself in scientific 'magic' in his Whitehall Palace. It was in 1645 that a group of enthusiastic men interested in the advance of 'experimental philosophy' had founded in London a club from which the Royal Society emerged. In 1662 Charles granted the Society its first Royal charter. The basic outlook of the experimental philosophers was very different from the old philosophical approach. They adopted the radical idea of Francis Bacon (1561-1626) that theories and laws must be based on observations and experiments. At the same time they rejected the traditional philosophical method which started with the hypothesis or the theory and then searched for evidence to prove it. Thus Bacon laid down the foundations of the empiricist school that became the prevalent philosophical system in England.

At the time that Newton arrived in Cambridge University, mathematics was divided into two major branches: arithmetic and geometry. Arithmetic concerned itself with the study and manipulation of numbers. Algebraic symbols, such as: +, -, ÷, x, and =, which became integral part of contemporary life, were introduced by the French mathematician and philosopher René Descartes (1596-1650). Geometry concerned itself with the study of plane and solid figures. Descartes also invented a sort of shorthand arithmetic by applying algebra to the solution of geometric problems. This new field of mathematics became known as analytic geometry. Newton liked it more than traditional Euclidean geometry, and Dr. Barrow found his student's knowledge of Euclid falling short of his expectations.

Similarly to Euclid, Descartes and Barrow, Newton did not study mathematics for mathematics sake. Like his predecessors, he plunged into the study of mathematics in order to understand the universe.

But the old mathematics was static. Newton wanted a new tool which could be applied to a dynamic conception of the universe, to a cosmos in constant motion. The new mathematics was supposed to be used for measuring changes in motion, acceleration or diminishing speed.

In the winter of 1664 a great comet appeared in the sky. Its path was curved and its velocity was perpetually changing. Both Euclidean geometry and Cartesian algebra were useless to calculate the swerving orbit of the celestial phenomenon. Newton, however, gradually found a solution to the problem. He called the new mathematical method fluxions, from the Latin word 'fluxus' which means change. But the new mathematics had to be improved. It took several years of work for Newton until he indeed was capable of using it as a tool to calculate changing velocities and alternating slopes of curves. Nowadays this type of mathematics is called calculus.[6] Integral calculus is concerned with the variable of location and speed as functions. It predicts the position of the object when its velocity is known. On the other hand, differential calculus figures the velocity of the object when its position is known.

The friendship between Isaac Newton and Catherine Storey had deepened into a romantic bond. However, if Newton wanted to stay at Cambridge and take up a teaching position, he must relinquish his plans to marry Catherine. For, according to the rules of the university, professors could not marry. These rules originated in the middle ages when scholars were members of the Catholic Church. Cambridge University did not change these rules, although the right to marry has been granted to clergymen in the aftermath of the English Reformation back in the sixteenth century. The authorities of the university perhaps feared that family life would distract scholars from their academic work.

Eventually Catherine married another man. Nevertheless, she and Isaac Newton remained good friends for the rest of their lives.

Newton continued to prepare himself for the Master of Arts degree. But on August 8, 1665 Cambridge University closed its gates and all students had been sent home. The Black Death, the dread bubonic plague swept over England and killed thousands of people. All those who could afford to flee to the countryside left the towns and the cities in order to take refuge in the relatively safe rural environment.

Thus Newton returned to Woolsthorpe. In the pastoral atmosphere of his early childhood his creative energies bursted into epoch-making scientific breakthroughs. In the period of eighteen months that followed he worked out his three great contributions to the edifice of science: the law of gravitation, the theory of light and color, and the mathematics of calculus.

Thoughts concerning the secret of the planets preoccupied a great deal of Newton's time.[7] Kepler's laws gave mathematical determinations concerning the position of the planets in the sky at the various periods of the year. The first law said that every planet moves in an elliptical orbit with the centre of the sun as one focus. The second law stated that the radius vector of a planet moves over equal areas of the ellipse in equal time intervals. The third law concerned the ratio of orbiting time and the planet's distance from the sun: a direct relationship exists between the square of the time which is necessary for a planet to complete its path around the sun and the cube of its mean distance from the sun. In simpler words this means that as the distance of the planet from the sun increases, it needs proportionally more time to complete its orbit. Kepler's laws form the foundations of modern astronomy.

However, these laws could not answer Newton's fundamental question: What was the secret of the planets? What made them move around the sun? Why did not they fall out of the sky? Why was the moon revolving around the earth, instead of flying off at a tangent?

Kepler's explanation was that spirits held the planets in orbit. Descartes, on the other hand, maintained that tiny invisible particles in constant motion were responsible for the orbiting of heavenly bodies. He called these little particles 'vortices'. According to him there was no empty space in the universe. Vortices filled every part of empty space. They circled the sun and carried the planets around with them. Each planet had its own system of vortices. These lesser vortices carried with them the moon round the earth and the moons round Jupiter, like driftwood is carried by flowing water.

Newton was not satisfied with these explanations. It was a hot summer day and he was drinking tea beneath an apple tree in the garden of the old manor house at Woolsthorpe. Suddenly an apple dropped to his feet. Why, wondered Newton, does an apple always fall straight down? Why does not it fall on a slant? Why not up? Why not sideways? The accidental observation generated a sudden realization, and a brilliant but simple idea crossed his mind. The discovery came with spontaneous spur and he was overwhelmed with the joy of enlightenment. Perhaps it is the earth which attracts the apple. Furthermore, perhaps the apple attracts the earth as well. All objects seems to attract each other. A universal force of gravitation binds all objects in the cosmos together. The force of attraction depends on the mass, that is to say the quantity of matter contained in each body, and the distance between the bodies involved. The bigger is the mass, the greater is the force of gravitation. The earth attracts a large rock with more gravitational force than a small piece of stone, because the first contains more matter than the latter. Body weight is stemming from the earth's pull, the force of gravitation. And the same gravitational force keeps the sun and the planets in their orbits. Celestial bodies orbiting in space fall just like an apple does. They do not fly off at a tangent to their orbit because they fall exactly just as an apple does. Planetary motion is the end result of two different momentums: the flying off and falling of celestial bodies compensate and neutralize each other. Thus the interplay of the two motions eventuates in an elliptical movement of the planets round the sun.

Newton had concluded that the force of gravitation is inversely proportional to the square of the distance between two object. The sun attracts the planets to its centre. The earth attracts the moon similarly. The force of gravitation is directly proportional to their masses and does not let the moon fly off into space. The attracting force can be compared to a string tied between the earth and the moon, or between the sun and the planets. Had the earth ceased even just for a moment to pull the moon towards its centre, the latter would fly off at a tangent to its elliptical orbit.

Newton told the story of the falling apple, as the clue to the discovery of the force of gravitation, to his friend Dr. Stukeley. However, some people found the discovery so simple that they decided to view it merely as a metaphor, or a tale for naive laymen. They are wrong. For great ideas must not be complicated. Furthermore, the creative process of the scientist is based not only on conscious reasonig; but to a considerable extent on unconscious intuition. The story of the dropping apple is a salient example of the interaction which takes place between a creative genius and the physical environment. Thought processes are not isolated events occurring only in the brain. Newton observed the falling apple. The trivial event triggered a simple but extremely important and meaningful association of thought. The serene beauty of the garden and a single apple had been sublimed into a serendipitous inference which represents one of the greatest breakthroughs in the history of science.

During the year of 1667 the epidemic of the bubonic plague ended in England. Cambridge University re-opened its gates. Newton continued his work on mathematics and completed several papers on fluxions. His interest in astronomy led him to experiment with Kepler's telescope. It was a large instrument and around its field of vision colors appeared which distorted clear observation. This sort of optical faultiness is technically termed as chromatic aberration. In toy binoculars, for instance, chromatic aberration is still a problem. Large Kepler style telescopes in Newton's days had an additional problem: spherical aberration, i.e., blurred image in the field of vision. This could be corrected by making the telescope longer. The Dutch scientist Christian Huygens eliminated spherical aberration by building a twelve feet long telescope. On March 5, 1656 he aimed this instrument at Saturn, and for the first time in history he was able to observe clearly the rings of the planet. Huygens later made an immensely long telescope. Its length exceeded two hundred feet. Other scientists tried to surpass him. Some of them boasted that they constructed four hundred, five hundred and even six hundred feet long telescopes.

Obviously these huge instruments were very impractical. Newton plunged himself into the investigation of the problem. He read the work of James Gregory and became convinced that the way to improve the telescope was by means of mirrors. Gregory himself never made a reflecting telescope because of technical difficulties. The same technical difficulties faced Newton and hindered his progress. Yet Newton was not only a scientific genius but also an excellent mechanic. He made the various parts of the reflecting telescope all by himself, including the difficult process of grinding a concave mirror. He completed the production of the reflecting telescope in the year of 1668. It was only fifteen centimetres long. Nevertheless, it was as powerful as a twelve times longer ordinary telescope. Through his short reflecting telescope Newton was able to see from the darkness of Trinity College the moons of Jupiter as well as the phases of the planet Venus.

Three years later the Royal Society asked Newton to build a telescope for them. The short reflecting telescope that he produced for the Society was an immediate and huge success. In 1672 Isaac Newton had been elected to membership in the Royal Society. Among those most illustrious members who were immensely impressed by the invention were King Charles II, the architect Sir Christopher Wren, and the scientist Robert Hooke.

Already before this great accomplishment Newton was experimenting with prisms. He darkened his chamber and made a small hole in the window-shuts in order to let a beam of sun light penetrate the room. The set up refracted the beam through a prism to the opposite wall. After passing through the prism the light appeared on the wall as a spectrum of rainbow colors. Newton expected this result. The rainbow colors effect produced by a prism was described by Kepler. Newton was familiar with Kepler's optics from lectures he attended at Cambridge.

But Newton went farther in his experiments than Kepler did. He wanted to learn more about the nature of light. He was curious to find out whether the various parts of the spectrum could be broken into further optical phenomena.

He discovered that by adding a second prism to the first one the spectrum of rainbow colors disappeared. Instead, a beam of white light appeared on the chamber wall. Newton was also able to isolate various colors. He found that light of a single color passing through a prism produces only itself. An isolated beam of red for instance did not change even when it passed a second prism. This rule applied to the other colors of the spectrum as well. Thus orange, yellow, green, blue, indigo, and violet -- just like the red color itself -- could not be

9

decomposed or broken into further optical phenomena.

During the summer of 1668 Newton completed his Master of Arts degree at Cambridge. The examination placed him twenty third in a class of one hundred and forty eight students. In the following year Isaac Newton, A.B., M.A., Fellow of Trinity College, was appointed Lucasian Professor of Mathematics. The former occupant of the Lucasian Chair, Dr. Barrow, Newton's tutor, resigned his position in order to devote all his time to religious studies.

Professor Newton held two weekly conferences for students and delivered one weekly lecture throughout one semester of each academic year. He lectured in Latin, and informed his audience also about his latest discoveries of light and color. However, he was not a popular teacher. He often had to face an empty classroom because none of his students bothered to attend his lectures.

On February 6, 1672 Newton submitted a paper to the Royal Society. It dealt with his theory of light and color. Yet, rather unexpectedly for Newton, the paper had been rejected. His theory of light was adversely reviewed by Hooke, who clung to a different theory -- his own version of the substance of light. Besides, from the Continent, Huygens sent his objections to Newton's theory, and was very critical of the paper. Light became an issue of long controversy. So, no wonder, that even in a century later the English polemicist Samuel Johnson remarked: "We all know what light is; but it is not easy to tell what it is."

By the turn of the century Newton summed up the lessons of his experiments concerning light. The first edition of *Opticks: or, A Treatise of the Reflexions, Refractions, Inflexions and Colours of Light,* appeared in 1704. It was written in English. The author had pointed out at the outset of the book that his intention was "not to explain the properties of light by hypotheses, but to propose and prove them by reason and experiments." Neither Hooke, nor Huygens debated Newton's observations based on his experiments. They both accepted, for example, the experimental finding of the author of *Opticks* that "colour cannot be changed by reflexions and refractions." The controversy was about theory. Hooke claimed that light travels as waves. Newton, on the other hand, said that light was made of little particles, or corpuscles. However, his firm empiricism yielded a fascinating side-effect. Since he put the horse where it belongs; before the cart; the theories in the *Opticks* were based on observations, and not vice versa. The book shows that as a result of the empirical method and because of its author's scientific genius, the writer from time to time was unable to unequivocally decide which theory represented the truth; the corpuscular or the undulatory one. Thus, the *Opticks* essentially advocates a corpuscular theory of light but it also contains many of the fundamental principles of the contradictory wave theory. It seems then that Newton adopted a combination of the two conflicting theories at once. By doing so he violated a central conception of nineteenth century physics which maintained that whenever there are two rival theories a crucial experiment must be performed in order to decide uniquely in favor of one of them.

In the beginning of the nineteenth century Dr. Thomas Young had presented papers to the Royal Society in which he tried to raise the wave theory of light into the level of an unassainable principle. The corpuscular theory which Newton espoused fell into disgrace. His *Opticks* was considered chiefly of interest to the historian rather than to the scientist.[9]

But Einstein's photon theory vindicated Newton. Einstein asserted that light was a rain of particles consisting of light quanta or photons, that is to say very small units of definite energy. According to him both Newton and Hooke had made important contributions to the progress of science.

Furthermore, Newton's brilliant intuition concerning the dual nature of light was confirmed in the 1920s by quantum theory. Louis de Broglie espoused the idea that light manifests itself as both wave and particle, whereas Niels Bohr advanced the tenet that these dual aspects constitute a joint phenomenon of complementarity.

In 1684 Sir Christopher Wren, Edmund Halley and Dr. Hooke met in London. During their conversation the theory that the force of gravity is inversely proportional to the square of the distance was mentioned. They said that it was possible to explain the orbit of a planet by this theory. However, they could not produce mathematical proof for their contention.

It was at this stage that Halley decided to consult Newton. He took the trouble and made a trip to Cambridge. He did not leave disappointed. Newton, indeed, produced the required mathematical proof. Halley convinced him to write a paper explaining his ideas of motion.

Newton's great scientific work, *Philosophiae Naturalis Principia Mathematica*, grew out of a shorter treatise, "De Motu Corporum" (Of The Motion of Bodies), which he wrote following Halley's encouraging words. The *Principia* was written in Latin. In 1729 it appeared in English, translated by Andrew Motte. In our common earthly setting, the physical laws advanced in the *Principia* are as valid as they were in 1678, the year of its publication. Modern space science is based on Newtonian physics. Thus, the landing of the Apollo II lunar module, on July 20, 1969, on the moon became possible due to Newton's pioneering scientific work. Neil Armstrong and Edwin Aldrin, the two United States astronouts who were first to set foot on the moon, had to escape first the earth's gravity in accordance with Newton's laws. In order to escape earth's gravity, a spacecraft ought to be launched at seven miles per second (25,000 miles per hour). A spacecraft that develops this range of escape velocity goes into an orbit around the sun, under the influence of the sun's gravity. But in order to reach the planet Mars, or the planet Venus, a greater escape velocity is needed, and the spacecraft must be launched at 7.4 miles per second.

The *Principia* deals with the laws of motion. The first law is the law of inertia: "Every body continues in its state of rest, or of uniform motion in a right line, unless is is compelled to change that state by forces impressed upon it." The second law states that "the change of motion is proportional to the motive force impressed; and is made in the direction of the right line in which that force is impressed." Accordingly, "if any force generates a motion, a double force will generate double the motion, a triple force triple the motion." The third law says that "to every action there is always opposed an equal reaction; or the mutual actions of two bodies upon each other are always equal, and directed to contrary parts." Therefore "if you press a stone with your finger, the finger is also pressed by the stone. If a horse draws a stone tied to a rope, the horse will be equally drawn back towards the stone."

Nowadays a spacecraft can be sent, in accordance with the law of inertia, along a course of a so called 'minimum energy flight trajectory,' which is the path that requires the least power. Newton's third law, which asserts that "to every action there is always opposed an equal reaction", implies the essence of the secret why a rocket works.

Einstein rejected the Newtonian theory of universal gravitation but not the practical usefulness of its mechanical commonsense aspects. He stressed that Newtonian science "is even today still guiding our thinking in physics."

Despite Einstein's rejection of the idea of universal gravitation, Newton's conception of gravitation and the three laws of motion described in the *Principia* became the essential theoretical tools for twentieth century space scientists.

Newton's laws have also explained how the moon brought about the phenomenon of the tides, and allowed to calculate the orbit of comets. Halley used Newtonian formulas to calculate the periodical return of the comet which is named after him. He figured that Halley's comet as it travels on its parabolic orbit reappears in the earth's sky every seventy six years.

After the publication of the *Principia* Hooke claimed that he was the real inventor of the law of gravitation.[10] However, Hooke could only claim that he shared some similar ideas with Newton. Unlike Newton, he was a poor mathematician, unable to provide mathematical proofs for his points. Indeed, Newton on purpose overcomplicated the *Principia* in order to take the wind out of the sails of usurpers. Even well known mathematicians, like Abraham De Moivre, were of the view that Newtons's mathematical proofs were extremely difficult to be followed.

The empiricist philosopher and physician John Locke (1632-1704) frankly admitted that his mathematical knowledge was not adequate to read the *Principia*. He asked Christiaan Huygens for help. After that the Dutch scientist assured him that Newton's mathematical proofs were sound enough, Locke satisfied himself with the philosophical tenets and corollaries that he drew from the *Principia*. Yet Locke was not truly satisfied. He wanted to know the essential principles of the universe, or at least to find out what was the cause of gravity.

Newton was an introvert person, very reluctant to participate in any public debate. But in spite of his determination to stay aloof of scientific controversies, he found himself involved in the mathematical polemics concerning the primacy of the calculus. For, members of the Royal Society were very upset when news arrived in England from the Continent that the German philosopher and mathematician Gottfried Wilhelm Leibniz figured out a similar mathematical system to Newton's fluxions. Leibniz called the new mathematical method calculus, and the Royal Society wanted to claim the honor of its discovery for England. In the course of the bitter debate both Newton and Leibniz were accused of plagiarism.[11]

Newton was a royalist. During the interregnum when it was quite dangerous to show royalist sympathies, the young Isaac Newton drew a picture of King Charles I, and wrote a poem glorifying the beheaded monarch. However, at some point in his life he had to take a stand against his king. This happened many years later. In 1685 Charles II died, and his brother, James II ascended the throne. James was an absolutist monarch who believed in the divine right of kings. Besides, he wanted to re-catholicise England and packed his strong army with Catholic officers.

James interfered even with the affairs of Cambridge University. For example, he ordered the academic authorities to confer on the Benedictine monk Alban Francis a Master's degree without taking the required Anglican oath. Cambridge refused, and the king was furious. A group of Cambridge University representatives that included

Professor Newton was sent to the royal hearing in London. They believed that the University should stand firm concerning the issue of academic freedom. Eventually Cambridge University came out victorious from the clash with the monarch, and Alban Francis did not receive his Master's degree.

In the Glorious Revolution that followed James fled abroad. Mary Stuart, James's daughter, and her husband William of Orange ascended the throne of England. The crown which Parliament offered them was safeguarded against unconstitutional reign by the Bill of Rights of 1689. In the same year Newton was elected as member of Parliament representing Cambridge University. Yet he never rose to deliver a speech. In fact, he spoke only once in the House of Commons, and even then he just asked the janitor to close the window. Nevertheless, he was a faithful and active member of the Whig Party. He worked hard behind the scenes in order to guard the interests of Cambridge.

It was in this period that Newton's mother died. With the dissolution of Parliament in 1690 his membership ended and he returned to the university. But it was a very difficult period for him. His health deteriorated. He was unable to sleep and unable to eat. He also suffered from fever. There were rumors circulating in Cambridge that Newton had gone mad. But he stuck to his position firmly and eventually completely recovered.

In the years that followed Isaac Newton faced new challenges and became the recipient of great honors. In 1696 he was appointed to the position of Master of the Mint. His role was charged with the issuance of England's new coinage.[12]

A few years later he was re-elected as Member of Parliament representing again Cambridge University. His financial position was well established, and he resigned as Lucasian Professor of Mathematics. Newton was a philanthropist who supported not only his nieces and nephews and friends but contributed also sums for various worthy causes. Among other things, he had donated funds for the erection of a new library at Trinity College. The building was designed by his friend, Sir Christopher Wren. It is still in use today.

On April 16, 1705 Queen Anne came to visit Cambridge. She came to honor Newton for his life-long scientific achievements. People stood everywhere along the old buildings leading from Emmanuel College to Trinity College. Newton, who entered Cambridge University as a servant to tutors, now knelt before the Queen. And when he rose he was Sir Isaac Newton, a knight of the Kingdom of England.

Fifteen months prior to his ennoblement, Isaac Newton was elected

President of the Royal Society. The white haired scientist with his deep-toned voice and piercing eyes was a man of less than medium height, sensitive and modest. He frequently smiled. He spent more time studying alchemy, theology and Biblical chronology than dealing with mathematics and physics, a fact which is quite contrary to one's expectations. But, as I have pointed out above, Newton did not take up science for science's sake. For him science was a means to understand the cosmos.

According to John Maynard Keynes, Newton became convinced that the traditional Christian belief in the Trinitarian doctrine was the result of a misunderstanding of the Gospel. Newton devoted a great deal of his time to the study of Jewish customs, the mystical writings of the Kabbalah, and at some point of his life he embraced a form of religious belief which can be viewed as Judaic Monotheism. He was particularly influenced by Maimonides,[13] the medieval Jewish philosopher who in the *Guide of the Perplexed* tried to reconcile Biblical and Rabbinic teaching with Aristotelian rationalism.

Newton was also swayed by astrological superstitions and by the magic of alchemy. As a Fellow of Trinity College he made extensive alchemic investigations. Among other things, he studied the hidden face of reality through the encoded messages and symbolism inherent in such alchemical writings as "The hunting of the Greene Lyon." Although Newton's scientific method integrated ancient and new mathematics with the empiricism of Bacon, Galileo's phsyics with Kepler's laws of planetary motions, the legacy of alchemy comprised one of its supporting pillars as well. Modern scholars, biased by the overwhelming impact of rationalism, tend to ignore the religious and mystical traits in Newton's personality. He was not the first modern scientist, but an extraordinary genius who combined the old with the new. He belongs not only to the age of reason, but to the ancient world of the Sumerians and the Babylonians as well.[14]

Newton approached the universe as a riddle; as an encoded secret, a cryptographic enigma created by God. He believed that it was possible to find the clues scattered in the world, and to decipher the cryptogram.

Modern chemistry denies its ancient ancestry, its descent from millenia old patterns of thought, the womb of alchemy. The alchemists paved the way for the rise of modern chemistry. Their objectives might have been to find the elixir of life and to transcend the actuality of existence with the enigmatic philosopher's stone. But in the process they discovered many chemical elements, from antimony to phosphorus, as well as introduced techniques and tools, from flasks to water baths, which form part of the standard in modern laboratories.

15

Newton conducted many alchemical experiments. Like other alchemists, he was fascinated by the prospect of transforming one metal into another, transmuting lead into gold. The transformation of base metal into gold for the alchemist was more than just a materialist goal. Gold was the symbol of the untarnishable essence of life, the symbol of grace, loftiness, order and eternity.

Modern chemists saw in alchemy a delusion, or at best, a pseudo-science. Yet the last laugh belongs to the alchemists. For modern atomic scientists are capable of producing gold from other elements by means of nuclear fission. The high cost of the technique is prohibitive, of course, to turn this method into an economically feasible process.

Voltaire, Diderot, d'Alembert and other eighteenth century philosophers of the Enlightenment deified reason and progress. They were ardent believers in the idea that the day will come when mankind will know everything about life and the universe. Newton did not share their optimism. He understood that the universe is infinite and that human knowledge is limited. The philosophers of the Enlightenment were Deists. They believed that God did not interfere with human affairs. For them God was the Creator of the World, but at the moment that He completed the act of creation, He became a Retired Old Gentleman. Newton was not a Deist. For him the God of the Bible was real. For his part God was not a divine watchmaker who wound up the cosmic machine of the universe but the omniscient and benevolent Supervisor of his own creation. Thus, from time to time God intervened in wordly affairs and safeguarded the proper functioning of the laws of nature.

Newton's lifework evoked the muses. The poets were inspired by his scientific discoveries. The romanticist William Wordsworth portrayed Newton as a man "with his prism and silent face", a "mind forever voyaging through strange seas of thought alone". Alexander Pope wrote the famous epigram:

Nature and nature's laws lay hid in night
God said 'Let Newton be!' and all was light.

Pope belongs to the generation of the Enlightenment.[15] Like the philosophers of the Age of Reason, he also believed that God was a perfect mathematician whose calculations, although infinitely complex and subtle, were accessible to human intelligence. His epigram implies the hope that through scientists like Newton the human race will eventually know everything and discover all the secrets of the universe.

16

But Newton saw things in a different light. At the end of his long life he said of himself:

> I do not know what I may appear to the world, but to myself I seem to have been only a boy playing on the seashore, and diverting myself in now and then finding a smoother pebble or a prettier shell than ordinary, whilst the great ocean of truth lay all undiscovered before me.

He also said that if he could see further than his predecessors, it was because he stood on their shoulder.

Newton was an empiricist. The purest and most absolutist formulation of empiricism is probably Locke's *Essay Concerning Human Understanding* (1690), in which he rejected the idea of innate knowledge. According to him the mind is a tabula rasa, or a white paper, on which knowledge accumulates as a result of experience through the senses. However, when Locke wanted to read the *Principia* he was forced to rely on the judgment of Huygens, because he could not follow Newton's mathematical argumentation. This hardly can be viewed as a consistent demonstration of what empiricism is about. Besides, mathematics itself is not the purest incarnation of the empiricist idea either. Mathematical symbols, the manipulation of numbers, geometrical notions, algebraical devices and so on, are not the products of sense experiences. They are not to be found in nature. Rather, mathematics is an invention of the human mind. Prior to Locke, Francis Bacon suggested an inductive and empirical method of discovering truth. Bacon, who died sixteen years before Newton was born, had been inspired by the Renaissance, and revolted against the petrified logic of Scholasticism. Baconian induction was supposed to proceed through several stages eventuating in the discovery of truth. It started with empirical observation. The next step was the analysis of observed data. This was followed by inference and the construction of hypotheses. The hypotheses in turn were tested, either verified or rejected; and the process continued through additional observations and experiments. René Descartes sympathised with Bacon's aims, but thought that it was wrong to start with the empirical facts and with induction. He was very impressed by the mathematical method and advocated deduction instead of induction. In other words Bacon suggested to start with details, to proceed from the particular to the general; whereas Descartes's aimed at proceeding from the general to the particular. Unlike Locke, Descartes believed in innate ideas. Newton opposed the Galilean and Cartesian method of founding scientific experiments upon supposedly infallible concepts. Newton treated such concepts as hypotheses. According to him such concepts were useless in experiments. In his *Opticks* scientific speculations were separated from the section dealing with the description of experiments, and placed at the end of the book. Nevertheless, Newton's discoveries were the result of a unique combination of intuition, mathematical calculation, cognitive analysis and synthesis; rather than the result of Baconian induction based on scientific experiments.

The validity of classical Newtonian physics was brought into question several times in the course of the nineteenth century. Young and others assaulted the corpuscular theory of light. The law of universal gravitation came under attack as well. In 1781 William Herschel discovered a previously unnoticed object in the sky: the planet Uranus. It turned to be a trouble maker. For, its path of motion failed to follow the celestial orbit determined by the law of universal gravitation. The obvious inference drawn from the fact that Uranus moved on an irregular path amounted to the inescapable necessity to revise the Newtonian law of universal gravitation. Yet there appeared to be another possibility; namely, that not Newton was wrong but those who suggested so. Indeed, in 1843 John C. Adams, a young British astronomer and mathematician, came forth with the conjecture that the exceptional behavior of Uranus was perhaps the result of the gravitational pull of an unknown celestial object. He calculated that this unknown object would be about one billion miles farther from the sun than Uranus. Adams sent his calculations to Sir George B. Airy, the Astronomer Royal in England. However, Airy was so sure that Adams was wrong that he even did not bother to aim his telescope at all at the suggested area of the sky. Fortunately, Urbain Leverrier, a young French Astronomer and mathematician was working, independently of Adams, on the same project. By the summer of 1846 Leverrier also predicted the existence of an unknown celestial object attracting Uranus. He sent his intuitive extrapolations to the German astronomer Johann G. Galle. From the Urania Observatory in Berlin, Galle searched with a telescope for the object described by Leverrier. And he found it! It turned to be a planet, much larger than the earth, but it could not be seen without a telescope. The newly discovered planet was named Neptune. Its discovery is treated in the history of science as a great triumph for celestial mechanics and the power of the deductive method based on mathematics. But it is also a triumph of the intuition.

Science is an attempt to make the world comprehensible. Newton's science was charged with astonishing consistency and as the case of the discovery of Neptune illustrated, for instance, it was loaded with surprising predictive power as well. Although it was esoteric, obscure and complex, on the whole it seemed to be in accord with a commonsense view of the world.

Newton maintained that space and time are independent, separate entities, that there is no connection between them. He imagined both space and time as infinite substances. He thought that absolute time and absolute space form the matrix of the universe, and that they are entirely independent of the observer. Indeed, it appears to be entirely logical to assume that neither a car, for example, nor a watch will be affected by our observation, whether we are looking at them or we are not. Everyone who has some common sense would agree with this. The car continues to travel on the road, and the hands of the watch keep move, regardless of one's perceptions.

However, post-Newtonian modern science holds different views. Newton's rival, Leibniz already claimed that space and time are merely sets of relations between things and events. Time, according to him, cannot be independent of events, because time is created by events and relations among them. In contrast to Leibniz, Newton said that time "flows equally without relation to anything external," and it is independent and prior to events.

Time is an idea which appears to be one of the deepest mysteries known to man. It is invisible, amorphous. Unlike space which we can perceive through our senses, time transcends our sense perceptions. We simply do not have anything in our organism with which we can grasp physically its existence. Thus time remains a very elusive thing. Although we cannot explicitly define what is time, we can do something else. We can invent a metaphor for it, an analogous spatial machine which is commonly called 'clock'. The clock is a time machine only in the sense that it transforms an abstract concept into a visual object. It is, of course, an indispensably useful invention, and if everything goes well, it does show the time as well.

But according to contemporary philosophers and mathematicians, among them Kurt Gödel and D.C. Williams, the passage of time is an illusion. The conception of time as a flowing river is a myth. The assumption that time is passing by incorporates the belief in the existence of a hypertime. For, if time is a flowing river, the question is, at what speed does it flow? The equation of velocity contains the time factor, because motion is measured by distance units per time intervals: miles per seconds, kilometers per hours, etc. So what is the speed of time? Seconds per hours? Hours per days? It is an absurdity to define or to measure time by itself; because it leads to the analogue of a rose is a rose is a rose . . .

The enigma of time finds a partial solution in the assumption that time is a relationship between before and after. As a matrix of change it does not flow but stands still. In other words, it is not time which goes by; we are passing through time. Time is a cosmic womb, the invisible theatre of everlasting performances. Time is change.[16]

And time is also duration. It is more than a scientific concept. Time transcends the domain of logic and science. It is a very subjective phenomenon. It is also an extremely relative experience. When the experience is a pleasant one, we would like to prolong its duration. When it is not, we would like to shorten it. And time is also a strange pool where memories dwell and yearnings grow.

Contemporary science has contradicted Newton's postulate that we do not influence the objects of our observations. Man's perceptions constantly influence the objects of perceptions. In the realm of subatomic particles, for instance, each observation can yield a different result. The observer is not an independent agent, but an integral part of the process of observation and interacts with the objects of the experiment. In 1927 the physicist Werner Heisenberg discovered a serious limitation imposed on the observer to penetrate into the secrets of the microscopic world. He found by means of experiments that one can precisely measure either the momentum of an electron or its position. It is impossible to determine exactly the simultaneous momentum and position of a particle. This uncertainty principle became one of the fundamental postulates of quantum mechanics.

Furthermore, the brain organizes, alters and selects the incoming information.[17] What we observe is not the retinal image but a modified picture projected to consciousness by the most sophisticated computer that we know: the human brain. Let us take an example to illustrate the interplay between fact and observation. A three dimensional object, such as a ball, appears from a short distance as a sphere to the observer. If we place the same ball at a great distance, eventually it will shrink into a point until it finally disappears from our eyes. In other words, the ball, i.e. the same fact, metamorphosed itself through observation from a three dimensional object into a thing of one dimension (point), and into zero, or nothingness.[18] Now, let us apply this lesson to the field of astronomy. The astronomer is not in a position that he can examine celestial objects from a short distance from the stars. If he could conduct his observations from different vantage grounds, the gathered facts would crucially change his state of knowledge. But until then, most stars will be observed only as one dimensional points. Optical instruments are the extensions of our eyes. Through their development the observed face of the world is changing. The Milky Way dissolves through the telescope into a multitude of stars. A tiny mosquito grows into a giant monster under the microscope.

According to Albert Einstein there is no absolute rest to be found in nature. The laws of classical physics are only valid within the mechanical system established by Galileo and Newton. In the decade between 1905 and 1915, Einstein's papers, his special and general theories of relativity have revolutionized the texture of scientific thought. Einstein postulated that mass and energy are interconvertible entities. His famous equation, $E = m \cdot c^2$, that energy equals mass times the velocity of light squared, became a corner stone of atomic science and led to the actuality of nuclear fission. In a sense, the equation is both a metaphor and the epitome of relativity: it represents the gates of the most terrible collective image of horror, and at the same time it is also a symbol of hope.

Unlike in Newton, space and time are not separated in Einstein. In fact, according to the theory of relativity, time is an integral ingredient of space, and they form a four dimensional space-time continuum. Classical physics implies that the universal force of gravitation is scattered evenly throughout the infinity of space. The theory of relativity asserts that since mass is distributed unevenly in space, the gravitational forces in the universe are uneven as well. The velocity of light is a limited constant: light cannot travel faster then 300.000 kilometer per second; and, in fact, nothing can travel faster than the speed of light. Newton implies that universal gravitation is a force which is distributed by infinite velocity. The theory of relativity contradicts this assumption. Newton said that time is absolute and it flows independently of the observer. However, according to Einstein, time is not independent of the observer at all. In a fast moving train, which travels about the speed of light, clocks would slow down in comparison to the clocks of stationary observers. Einstein explained planetary motion rather differently from Newton. He said that enormous masses generate huge gravitational forces and these in turn give rise to large gravitational fields. Due to the existence of vast gravitational fields, those regions of space which are in the vicinity of great gravitation-generating-masses become curved. On the other hand, in those areas where the forces are small, the surface of space is flat. Light moves throughout space in accordance with the features of its surface: it travels along straight lines where it is flat, whereas if the surface is spherical light glides in warped paths. The planets move

21

around the sun in a four dimensional space-time continuum. The immense gravitational field of the sun deforms its surrounding space. The planets move around the sun along their curved paths because, like light itself, they choose the shortest possible distance for travel. The shortest way to bridge the distance between two points on a spherical surface is a rounded line. Airplanes flying along intercontinental routes also travel in curved paths.

Although the theory of relativity has contradicted certain aspects of classical physics, on the whole it seems more to expand, explain and complement its range and scope than to refute Newton's system.

In 1905 Einstein laid down the foundations of a new branch of science: quantum mechanics. In a paper published in that year, he explained the photoelectric effect on the ground of the material properties of light. It was known even before 1905 that a beam of light can cause metals to release electrons and turn them into an electric current. But since scientists advocated in those days the wave theory of light, they could not account for the photoelectric effect. Then Einstein came and suggested that light could be viewed as tiny pockets of energy or quanta. He demonstrated that when quanta of light energy is streamed at a metal, the atoms in the metal react by releasing electrons. The invention of the photoelectric cell, or electric eye, became possible through Einstein's work. A long series of other inventions which form indispensable props in our technological culture, including sound motion pictures, television and laser, resulted from quanta theory.

Einstein had been indebted to Newton with regard to the idea of light as matter. Newton postulated a corpuscular theory of light. The conception of light as particles or quanta generated a renewed interest in Newton's work. His *Opticks* had been republished in 1931. In the foreword of this edition, Einstein wrote that to the

> great Newton . . . nature was an open book, whose letters he could read without effort. The conceptions which he used to reduce the material of experience to order seemed to flow spontaneously from experience itself, from the beautiful experiments which he ranged in order like playthings and describes with an affectionate wealth of detail. In one person he combined the experimenter, the theorist, the mechanic and, not least, the artist in exposition.[19]

The romanticist visionary William Blake saw Newton in a very different light.[20] Blake was born in England in 1757 and he died in

1827. He was a brilliant poet, a painter and engraver, a recluse and a mystic. He illustrated "The Book of Job" and the works of Dante. His "Songs of Innocence", "Songs of Experience", "Milton", and "Jerusalem" are characterized by their lofty lyricism and profound symbolism. For Blake, Newton -- together with Bacon and Locke -- became the symbol of worshipping the "Goddess Nature, Mystery, Babylon the Great." For his part the school of empiricism represents a group of experimental philosophers who "deny a conscience in man."

The salient quality of Blake manifests itself in his unequivocal rejection of the ideals of the Age of Reason. Blake revolted against the deification of reason. He saw in reason an ultimately destructive force because it suffocates vision and inspiration. The truth revealed by the inner eye was more significant and meaningful for him than the truth of the visible world around him.

According to Blake, we can merely catch a glimpse of the arcane vessel of reality. Our access to knowledge is restricted by our senses, however we concern ourselves with scientific truth. In order to gain insight into a more profound domain of reality we must trust our instinct, imagination and energies.

> To see a World in a Grain of Sand
> and Heaven in a Wild Flower,
> Hold Infinity in the palm of your hand
> And Eternity in an hour.
> ("Auguries of Innocence")

Perhaps the strangest thing about Blake's visionary message is that it is so valid. Not only in the philosophical sense; or from an angle of the human condition. It is valid in the scientific sense as well. The words of the "Auguries of Innocence" form a beautiful, poetic expression of the scientific idea of relativity. The infrastructural parallel in a few lyrical lines conveys a metaphor of the Alice in Wonderland mindscape of contemporary science.

Now let us turn our attention to Constable. In certain respects he represents the reverse of Blake. Although, like Blake himself, Constable was a painter, he operated with a mind-set which was quite parallel and in tune to a considerable extent with the conceptual framework of Newton. Both Newton and Constable considered themselves natural philosophers. Nowadays scientists do not regard themselves natural philosophers any longer. Their aspiration is to become the unrivalled masters of nature. Newton tried to reconcile science with religion.

John Constable was born in the year of 1776, about half a century after Newton's death, and he died in 1837 as a God fearing man. Yet religion in the Victorian age was not the same as it used to be. At some point during the nineteenth century Nietzsche had concluded that God was dead.

The celebrated English landscape painter was born in East Bergholt,[21] a village in Suffolk County. His father was a well-to-do mill owner. Similarly to Newton, Constable also spent the formative years of his youth in the countryside. The art schools in London taught him important lessons and skills. But as a natural painter, he learnt the most important things from nature itself. Above all, he developed the acuity and shrewdness of making precise observations in the open air. As a country lad he watched the skies, the slow climb of the sun, the gorgeous sunsets, and the flickering stars. He noted the changing directions of the wind, its play with the leaves, its gentle whisper turning into the roar of storm. His eyes followed the growth of the trees, the flow of the rivers meandering amidst gently undulating hills, the greenery of the meadows and the changing of seasons. The foundations of Constable's originality rested on nature. He himself said that the sceneries of the Suffolk countryside made him a painter.

Constable developed a profound interest in painting quite early in his life due to his friendship with John Dunthorne, a plumber and glazier of East Bergholt, who was also an amateur painter.[22] His interest was further encouraged by Sir George Beaumont and Dr. John Fisher, who later became Bishop of Salisbury.[23] Sir George Beaumont was a connoisseur. His collection of paintings included "Hagar in the Wilderness" by the great French landscape painter of the seventeenth century, Claude Lorrain. Constable admired Claude. He was also influenced by the works of Jacob van Ruisdael, the Dutch master of landscape painting, who shared the same century with Claude. Constable regarded Titian's "Peter Martyr", Poussin's "Deluge", Rubens' "Rainbow", and Rembrandt's "Mill" as the four outstanding landmarks in the history of landscape painting.

In February, 1799, Constable arrived in London, resolved to become a professional artist. He enrolled as a student at the Royal Academy in the following year. His studies included anatomical drawings, the nude model, and copying the works of the old masters.

Constable was well aware of the existing difference between copying from nature and rendering an artistic composition in accord with academic rules: the conflict between observed fact, and the canons of aesthetics; the conflict between Nature and Art. In a letter to Dunthorne, dated May 29, 1802, he wrote:

'There is no easy way of becoming a good painter': It can only be obtained by long contemplation and incessant labour in the executive part. And however one's mind may be elevated, and kept up to what is excellent by the works of the Great Masters -- still Nature is the fountain's head, the source from which all originality must spring.[24]

Constable wanted to be a natural painter; to acquire truth, not from the artificial setting of the studio but from first hand, from the source itself, which is nature. However, landscape painting was an underdeveloped field of art, the Cindarella of painting. Thus, Constable was preparing himself for a career in which the prospect of making a living by his brush was gloomy. Indeed, prosperity came late to him, only in the last decade of his life, and even then it did not stem from his brush but from an inherited fortune.

His first exhibition was held in London in 1802, at the Royal Academy. He spent the summer and the autumn of the same year at East Bergholt, and purchased a studio near the house of his parents. Sir George Beaumont came to visit. The conversation revolved around painting. He asked Constable whether it is difficult to determine where to place a brown tree? "Not in the least", replied the painter, "for I never put such a thing into a picture." Apparently there was a tradition in academic circles to paint the trees in brown color. In the studios art students learnt to copy into their canvases the brown trees painted by the old masters. Yet Constable's tutor was nature. He realized that trees might have different colors. And it was equally evident for his part that spatial relations, the location of the various elements in the composition should not be determined by the artist but by nature itself.

Once Sir George Beaumont suggested that the color of an old fiddle was the dominant tone of everything to be found in a natural environment. Instead of plunging into a heated debate with his friend, Constable chose the art of convincing through the method of empirical observation. He took an old fiddle and laid it on the green grass. The contrast between the grass and the fiddle was remarkable. It was obvious that Beaumont was wrong.

In the year 1819, Constable exhibited at the Royal Academy a six-foot canal scene, "The White Horse", and was elected as associate to the same institution. His celebrated large canal scene, "The Hay Wain", [25] was first displayed at the Royal Academy in 1821. Three years later, this painting became part of Constable's exposition in the French capital. The visitors at the Salon in Paris could see, in addition to "The Hay Wain", also his "View on the Stour near Dedham", and a "View of Hampstead Heath". The works aroused great interest and exerted a considerable influence on the development of French painting. They made a remarkable impact on Eugéne Delacroix (1798-1863), the leading painter of the French romanticists. Jean François Millet, Thédore Rousseau, and other members of the Barbizon School were swayed by Constable as well. Their aims included to portray an unprettified and exact reflection of peasant life and scenery painted in the open air. In the sense that Constable and the artists of the Barbizon group painted directly from nature, they can be regarded as precursors of the impressionists. Painting under the open sky became the vogue in France after Constable's oeuvre had been exposed in the Paris Salon. Constable was awarded with a gold modal. But the landscape painter himself did not attend the exhibition. In fact, he never left his native England. This is another similarity which the artist shares with Newton. Neither Newton nor Constable ever crossed the English Channel in order to visit the Continent.

On the other hand, J.M.W. Turner (1775-1851),[26] the romanticist landscape and seascape painter and the sole great English rival of Constable, traveled a great deal abroad. Due to his frequent visits to Italy, Turner's work increasingly became more luminous and poetic. The magical effects of luminosity achieved an Impressionist quality, a stage of colored light which Constable called "tinted steam." Two central figures of the Impressionist movement Claude Monet and Camille Pissarro, arrived in London before Monet's *Impression, Sunrise* -- a painting that gave its name to the trend -- launched a new artistic era. It was exhibited in the first impressionist show in 1874. Both Monet and Pissarro came to England following the outbreak of the Franco-Prussian War in 1870, and while in London they went to see the works of Turner and Constable in the National Gallery and in the Victoria and Albert Museum. Interestingly enough, Constable's friend Sir George Beaumont was an influential critic as well, and he conducted a raging campaign against the merits of Turner's art. On the other hand, the leading art critic of nineteenth-century-England, John Ruskin supported Turner. In the first volume of *Modern Painters*, which was published in 1843, after Constable's death, Ruskin claimed that Turner was superior "in the art of landscape painting to all the ancient master", and that his work was the incarnation of the "true, the beautiful, and the intellectual." Ruskin did not like Constable's painting.

Unlike Turner, Constable did not desire to thrill the spectator. He did not want to paint exotic sceneries, violent and ecstatic pictures. He was not a visionary romanticist but a natural painter. Wild mountains oppressed his spirit. He felt home at Suffolk alone, in the pastoral, tranquil countryside of south-east England where men were growing crops and feeding cattle.

Constable liked to read the Bible as well as good poetry. He also read Leonardo's *Treatise on Painting* (Trattato della Pittura), Hessner's *Essay on Landscape*, and Howard's *Climate of London*. He was a practical, humble man, dominated by one central idea: the painter is a scientist who must learn directly from nature, and not from derivative sources, such as the painting of other painters. In a lecture delivered in London on June 16, 1836, Constable said:

> It appears to me that pictures have been over-valued; held up by a blind admiration as ideal things, and almost as standards by which nature is to be judged rather than the reverse; and this false estimate has been sanctioned by the extravagant epithets that have been applied to painters, as the 'divine', the 'inspired', and so forth. Yet in reality, what are the most sublime productions of the pencil but selections of some of the forms of nature, and copies of a few of her evanescent effects; and this is the result, not of inspiration, but of long and patient study, under the direction of much good sense . . . Painting is a science, and should be pursued as an inquiry into the laws of nature. Why, then, may not landscape he considered as a branch of natural philosophy, of which pictures are but experiments? [27]

While viewing Constable's painting in the Paris Salon, a spectator remarked: "Look at these landscapes painted by an Englishman: the ground appears to be covered with dew." [28] His paintings, indeed, represented new, fresh and arresting images because he refused to accept the academic rules what the artist should see and how to paint. Instead, he used his own eyes and painted directly from nature. Constable was a precise observer. His biographer and friend, C.R. Leslie, had recorded that the artist wrote on the back of his studies data concerning the physical conditions under which they were made. For example, on one of them Constable wrote this:

> Fifth of September 1822. Ten o'clock morning, looking south-east, brisk wind at west. Very bright

and fresh, grey clouds running fast over a yellow bed,
about half-way in the sky. [29]

His meticulousness enabled him to create accurate photographic transcripts of pleasant English sceneries in a period prior to the invention of the camera. Some of Constable's painting are visually so accurate and convincing that their inherent illusionism is of trompe l'oeil quality. The French term denotes the deception of the eye by refined artistic techniques which generate the illusion of reality. In order to deceive the eye, artists throughout history applied visual devices, such as: perspective and foreshortening. The photographic realism of the twentieth century is also a trompe l'oeil style of painting.

Constable's landscape painting was founded on intensive research supported by detailed observation and meticulous knowledge of the small area that served him as subject matter. From his sketch books of 1813 and 1814 it is evident that the artist had recorded the changes occurring in nature. If a fir tree, for instance, lost one of its branches the artist duly indicated the event. This is an example of his preoccupation with individual form. It represents the rejection of eighteenth century aesthetic theory which advocated generalization. According to the old theory the artist should find the essence of things and depict them as abstractions of ideal entities and events.

The acuity of the painter's vision stemming from the accuracy of observation is related to his emotional attachment toward his subject matter. Obviously, Constable was very fond of the landscape portrayed in his work. However, this sort of emotional attachment to the subject matter of inquiry is not an isolated phenomenon characterizing artists alone. Emotional attachment to research field plays a pivotal role in science as well. Professor Seymour Papert's *Mindstorms,*[30] a book which was published in 1980, supports this assertion. Papert, a mathematician at the Artificial Intelligence Laboratory of the Massachusetts Institute of Technology, is the inventor of LOGO: a symbolic and quantitative computer language. His book conveys compelling insights concerning the relationship of understanding and affection, cognition and sensory motor activity. The author recalls a crucial experience in his early childhood. Before he was two years old, he developed a special relationship with automobiles. He particularly liked to play with the differential gear. In the years that followed this special combination of understanding and affection towards the gearbox yielded rather unexpected results: It has been transferred to the field of mathematics. Thus the understanding and the fondness of a mechanical system enabled Papert to illustrate or visualise an array of complicated mathematical problems.

This sort of experience is very much in accordance with earlier theories to the same effect. Plato in the *Republic* put forth the assertion that compulsion in teaching is useless and harmful. Educators must not exercise any form of compulsion, because "compulsory learning never sticks in the mind." Instead, "let your children's lessons take the form of play." Learning through play in Plato is tied with "sympathy and conformity with beauty and reason." Aesthetic training, art, beauty and goodness ought to form the basis of education. So the child "when reason comes he will recognize and welcome her as a familiar friend because of his upbringing."

Friedrich von Schiller (1759-1805) espoused Plato's theory of education. According to him, "man plays only when he is truly human, and he is truly human only when he is at play." He maintained that man's intellectual development rests on aesthetic foundations. The capability of reasoning is bound up with the sense of beauty. The aesthetic percepts allow the physical and sensuous aspects of man's existence to reach the cognitive hierarchy of perceiving truth and goodness, of making moral judgments and of acquiring spiritual liberty.

In effect, the educational philosophy of Rousseau, of Pestalozzi, Froebel, Montessori, Read and Piaget rely, to various extents, on Platonian thought. Papert collaborated with Piaget in the investigation of learning as an unconscious process. He was particularly motivated by the "idea that children learn so much without being taught." His LOGO language is a conceptual tool designed specifically for children. It enables the learner to program and master the computer. The interaction with the machine occurs through the natural process of play and as an aesthetic experience.

It is noteworthy that Galileo took great pleasure in mechanical labor, as well as in working in the garden and observing the beauty of the growth of flowers. He also concerned himself with the mathematical investigation of music, and established a reputation as a gifted painter. Isaac Newton took also delight in playing with mechanical gadgets already at a tender age, and revealed considerable artistic talent. The five years old Albert Einstein was fascinated by the secret of the magnetic needle which he saw in a pocket compass that his father gave him. Later he took pleasure in playing the violin and he talked about the aesthetic beauty of mathematics.

But let us return to Constable. It seems that topographical accuracy is more characteristic of his earlier work than of his later painting. It is still possible today to identify the georgraphical site of the bucolic scene depicted in *The Hay Wain* (1821).[31] Although the elms that once grew there disappeared, and have been replaced by firs, sycamores and shrubs, the house seen in the painting (the Cottage of Willy Lott) as well as the broad meadowlands look to be the same as in the days of Constable. Nevertheless, the painting is a mixture of fact and imagination, of observation and interpretation. The artist made many sketches of the scene, but completed the painting in his London studio. The final image that evolved into *The Hay Wain* was more a summing up, a generalized essence of Willy Lott's Cottage at Flatford Mill, than an isomorphic mirror image. Thus, the painting represents an imaginative composition: an actual view combined with the crystallized memories of the artist's experiences in Suffolk. It is an interesting feature of this work that the painter shortened the roof of the cottage in order to allocate more vertical space for the composition. This in turn, allowed him to accomodate the chimney of the house within the pictorial frame of the canvas.

In October 1827 Constable's pencil rendered *Men loading a barge on the Stour*. The drawing is topographically accurate, although the artist displaced the location of Dedham Church in the image.[32] In other works, he compressed or concentrated the observed physical features in the process of the pictorial rendition, in order to make room for them in the composition. Another form of visual interpolation resulted from the artist's desire to emphasize the slope of the hill, or other topographical elements.

The artist is not a neutral observer. His aesthetic impulse and conceptual framework interact with his subject matter in terms of its spatio-temporal selection and conditioning. In other words, the compositional elements to be included in the picture are determined by the artist, and so is the timing; the hour, the weather conditions and the season. Constable liked to paint sceneries lit by the bright mornings of sunshiny days. The intrinsic realism of his work reveals itself in all its grace, serenity, and harmony only if it is measured against appropriate weather conditions and timing. On a dull afternoon, for instance, the same place which is depicted in the painting can be disappointing and hardly distinguishable.

The conflict between the scientist and the artist, between observed fact and the aesthetic impulse, finds also its expression in Constable's tendency for vertical exaggeration. In contrast to him, the camera conveys views which are more horizontally spread in space. However, it is not evident at all that the camera view is more realistic than that of the artist. For, the camera itself distorts. The objects close to the lens appear much larger than they are seen by the human eye. So whose reality is more valid? Whose world is truer, the one made by the artist or that which has been taken by the camera? Furthermore, reality even among human beings varies. The world of a color blind person is different from the world of another person with ordinary color vision. However, this does not mean that the world of the color blind is not real. It is as real as anyone's else, although it is, of course, different.

Not only the camera distorts. The human eye distorts too. The perceived image reflected on the retina is altered by the brain. Perception is not a mechanical process. It is affected by our expectations and experience, by our mental and emotional condition. To a great extent we see what we know. It is quite easy to demonstrate this by placing, for instance, two identical pencils before our eyes: Let us put a distance of about one foot between them, in frontal direction. Now, if we close one eye, we can see that the pencil which is farther from us appears much shorter than the one closer to us. We normally are not aware of this because of the amending function of the brain to project an even and unwrinkled picture of actuality.

Observation can be defined as the act through which, one becomes aware of the existence of objects and events. The process sometimes is part of intentional examination of something for the task of collecting facts. Observation is based on the sense organs. They mediate between the human organism and the physical world which we cannot reach without them. It is difficult, probably even impossible, to separate the act of observation from the process of interpretation by means of words and concepts. Language is a tool of communication which functions by means of symbols. It is also an inexact tool. In the light of these considerations, it seems rather justified to propose that observation, including scientific observation, is not an absolutely precise process. Furthermore, it also appears that essentially there is no difference between a scientific or artistic observational judgment. Thus, for example, statements, like "there are five dishes on the table", "that is a friendly dog", or "this is a round tower", are observational judgements regardless of who made them.

Science cannot investigate or describe ultimate reality. It cannot concern itself with the 'Ding an sich', the noumenon of Kant, the thing in itself which is beyond the experience of our senses. Reality is always larger and richer than its concepts. The observations of the scientist are regarded as facts. However, these facts are not the things themselves, but empirically verifiable statements about phenomena. Thus, facts are reflections organized and conceived by the human mind. Through the mind set of the scientist they evolve into conceptual paradigms. The same facts may give rise to different interpretations. The Ptolemaic conceptual paradigm, e.g., was commensurate with the observed fact of the rising sun. The Copernican conceptual scheme replaced it with the paradigm of the earth moving around the sun.

The scientist is looking for uniformities, universal qualities to be found in nature and common to all bodies. His aim is to establish universal laws based on generalizations. Newton's law of universal gravitation, for instance, or his laws of motion represent generalizations. Yet the generalizations of science are tentative and limited in range. Science essentially is based on skepticism. Its faith is doubt, and so it constantly undermines its own foundations. It has been discovered, for example, that the neutrino -- a subatomic particle emitted during raioactive beta decay -- lacks electric charge and rest mass, and thus it defies the law of "universal' gravitation. This law is simply not valid in the realm of quantum mechanics, in the microscopic world of the atom.

Therefore the scope and range of scientific truth is limited. Even the exact sciences, astronomy, physics and chemistry are not infallible in this respect. Furthermore, the idealized model of the scientific method embraces controlled experimentation. However, controlled experimentation in most scientific disciplines is not possible. Paleoantology, oceanography, geology, zoology, botany, climatology, and history proceed through observation, description, analysis and comparison, rather than by means of experiments. The method of these sciences is essentially the clinician's case method. The clinical method historically is much older than controlled experimentation. Its foundations were laid down by the ancient Greek physician Hippocrates in the fifth century B.C.. He is regarded as the father of medicine who proposed the rational study of the human body and its functions by clinical observation.

A properly verifiable statement on the painter's canvas about a landscape or a still life is as much a fact as a reading of a thermometer in the laboratory. Equal quantities of yellow and blue pigments mixed together on the painter's palette always yield green color, an algorithmic feat which is comparable to the arithmetic marvel of $1 + 3 = 4$; although the first, in my opinion, surpasses the latter. Paintings are made of colors and forms. A simple horizontal line drawn on the canvas will divide the pictorial plane into ground and sky.

Constable's paintings are based on observation, precision, objectivity, and generalization. These are scientific qualities. He himself viewed painting as a science, and suggested that pictures were scientific experiments.

Constable's assertions, however, generate several problems. One of them is the problem of experimentation. For, a scientific experiment ought to be repeatable and predictable by independent experimenters. A thermometer reading, for instance, will confirm in different places and at any time that under similar conditions water boils at the same temperature. Another example is provided by a vacuum, an enclosed space empty of matter in which gas pressure is significantly less than atmospheric pressure. In such space no noise, no music can be heard because the vacuum does not transmit sound (and heat) waves. No matter where or when you conduct the experiment, the result is the same.

Now, as we have seen, mixing colors or drawing lines can be seen as formalized, routine operations which, like experiments, always give the same results. Thus, there are algorithmic elements in painting which are repeatable and predictable. However, a painting is not the sum total of formalized, calculated, algorithmic clusters of forms and colors, but the unprecedented combination of routine and heuristic elements. Thus, unlike a scientific experiment, a completed art work is a unique thing. In contrast to science which is general, art is particular. The creative artist's goal is not to copy existing masterpieces but to create original and new ones. Therefore pictures do not fall easily into the category of scientific experiments. A genuine art work always transcends the logical realm of science; it is always particular and unique, never repeatable or predictable.

The German scientist Werner Heisenberg pointed out an intriguing aspect of the difference between art and science. Attending a scientific convention in Washington D.C. during the 1970s, he sat down at the piano and produced an exciting interpretation of Opus 111, the last sonata of Beethoven. Heisenberg remarked: "if I had never lived, someone else would probably have formulated the principle of indeterminacy. If Beethoven had never lived, no one would have written Opus 111." [33]

The controlled experimentation practised in physics and chemistry is not the method of painting. The defining property of painting as a science is the case method based on observation, analysis, comparison and description. But as a descriptive piece of information, unlike a written text, a painting is a visual representation which imparts the image as a spatial whole. Unlike a written text, which has a clearly defined linear structure condensed between its initial and final words, a painting as a tool of communication has no beginning and no end. The time needed for the viewing of a painting is not a chronometrically definable experience. On the other hand reading is a linear experience. Listening to the words of a poem, for instance, is an event of exactly measurable duration.

Constable understood that painting is not only a science, but also poetry. He was aware of the fact that the willingness to represent the truth of nature conflicted with the artist's conditioned aesthetic impulse. Registering the results of precise observations on the canvas was hindered by the painter's emotional screen, his imagination and mind set.

Interestingly enough, Constable maintained that chiaroscuro -- an illusion generating device of the play of light and shade -- was "the soul and medium of art." The technique had been developed during the Renaissance. Through the harmonious rendition of lights and darks, Raphael, Leonardo and others created in their masterpieces the illusion of objects surrounded by space. Chiaroscuro plays a central role in Rembrandt's work as well.

It was C.R. Leslie who pointed out that many artist see chiaroscuro nowhere, "but Constable saw it everywhere, and in all its beauty."[34] Constable despised the "pastorality of the opera house", and the art "which sprang out of the French Revolution."[35] He felt contempt for the works of Jacques Louis David (1748-1825) who presented romanticist themes in neoclassical form. He believed that the imitation of preceding styles with little reference to nature led to the deterioration of art. According to him, "David and his contemporaries exhibited their stern and heartless petrifactions of men and women -- with trees, rocks, tables, and chairs -- all equally bound to the ground by relentless outline and destitute of chiaroscuro, the soul and medium of art."[36]

Light is central to both Newton and Constable. The scientist and the artist alike investigated and experimented with it. Newton summed up his experience concerning the phenomenon of light in the *Opticks*. Constable painted it. His great secret of painting was based on a profound knowledge of the light of nature. The play of light and shadow, reflections on bright, shining objects intrigued and fascinated him. There was only one artist in England of the nineteenth century whose poetic passion for light surpassed that of Constable: Turner. Constable admired Turner's art, his "airy visions tinted with steam." But Constable's investigations were of a more scientific nature.

In 1822 he began a careful study of pure cloud formations. In the resulting works the sky grew into overwhelming proportions and the ground diminished, or even entirely disappeared from the pictorial plane. The landscapes evolved into cloudscapes.

The dominant role of the skies in Constable's painting is related to the publication of Luke Howard's book, *The Climate of London* (1818-20).[37] The artist took great interest in the emerging scientific ideas of his time. He had followed the developments in geology, engineering and anatomy. Howard's book especially drew his attention. It was the author of *The Climate of London* who classified clouds and divided them into major groups. Howard called the formations of ice crystals at high altitudes (above ten thousand meters) cirrus clouds. He gave the names altostratus, altocumulus and nimbostratus to middle clouds which lie between two thousand and six thousand meters above the earth's surface. Their color varies from white to grey. Low clouds close to the surface of the earth have been termed nimbus, stratus and strato-cumulus. Nimbus clouds are dark formations which frequently cannot be seen because of the rain or the snow that falls from them. The fine drops of drizzly rain often originate from the smooth, even sheets of stratus clouds.

Constable adopted the new climatological nomenclature. He used them in his notes which he wrote on the back of his paintings. In his work the lighting of the picture is closely related to the sky studies, to the distribution of the cloud formations as well as to the position of the source of illumination: the sun. It seems that the painter advanced the tenet that it is the sky which generates the mood of the scene as a totality. Besides, the sky features also an important ornamental effect in landscape painting. The play of light and shade in the sky is laced with the contours of the ground in the works that Constable painted throughout the latter part of his life. The painter applied the technique of chiaroscuro as a unifying compositional device with remarkable aesthetic results. Viewing these cloudscapes can be an exceedingly pleasing experience. The sky studies in hindsight seem to possess a rather contemporary quality which comes close to the stage of abstract expressionism. In this respect the English landscape painter mediates between the art of Jacob van Ruisdael, Rembrandt and other Dutch masters on the one hand, and the works of twentieth century American artist, such as: Arshile Gorky, Jackson Pollock, and Willem de Kooning, on the other.

Art as an inward experience is a particular journey of the individual across various levels of spiritual elevation. Confronted with his subject matter and working in the open air of South-East England, Constable was in a state of hypnotic self-awareness, a condition of highly enhanced consciousness. The sky became a metaphor for him. It began to play the same role as alchemy did for Newton: a playground for unrestricted imagination and the consummation of creative aspirations. As a natural painter, Constable tried his best to transcribe the static features of the physical environment into faithfully rendered images. But the skies were not static. The light was frequently changing, and the cloud formations were dynamic. The same sky lit by gleaming sunshine could turn in a moment into an opaque veil of haze, or into a huge dome overcast with the billowing masses of amorphous nimbostrati. The sky was both an artistic challenge and an archetypal symbol. The flying birds were more than metaphors of the eternal quest of man to follow Icarus into the heights, to be reborn and rise from the ashes of the fire with the phoenix. The sky evoked the flight of fancy and imagination. But it was there. It was 'real' and therefore 'scientific'. Thus, Constable was able to carry on with his art without violating the restraints inflicted upon him as a natural painter.

In 1828 Constable inherited a fortune from his father-in-law which put an end to his financial worries. But in the same year his beloved wife, Maria Bicknell, died of consumption. In the wake of this tragedy the artist expressed his immense grief by painting "Hadleigh Castle", a work which is regarded a pivotal landmark of English romanticism. On the whole, however, critics and scholars consider Constable as an artist who on principle escaped the influence of romanticism. But this is a misleading generalization.

The term romanticism meant different things in different countries, and even in one country its use could be confusing. F.L. Lucas in *The Decline and Fall of the Romantic Ideal* (1948) counted more than eleven thousand definitions of romanticism. Jacques Barzun, in *Classic, Romantic and Modern* (1961), suggested to differentiate between romantic behaviour, which is a universal trait of human behavior, and romanticism, which is a historical phenomenon pertaining to the eighteenth and nineteenth centuries. Romanticism, undoubtedly, was a complicated movement, an aesthetic and social polyglot.[38] It arose gradually and exhibited many phases in art, literature, philosophy, religion and politics. Victor Hugo identified it with the liberation of the artist, and with individualism. Indeed, romanticism as a movement started at the close of the eighteenth century in reaction against a mechanistic view of life, against academic formalism. It revolted against the restraint imposed upon the artist by the traditional canons of classicism. Romanticism exalted nature above artifice, the exotic above the common, sensibility above the intellect, and placed the search for the infinite and the absolute at a higher level than the here and now.

The Industrial Revolution in England coincided with the ascent and decline of romanticism. The development of science and technology allowed the rise of machine production, and this in turn altered the economic and social structure of the country. The process of industrialization brought about intensive urban growth. In the cities a new social class, the working proletariat struggled for survival and power. Similar changes occurred on the European Continent, particularly in France and Germany. The dramatic transformations precipitated nostalgia for an idealized historical past as well as utopian visions of the future. The mind was wandering back and forth in time.[39]

An industrial society depends on scientific progress and technological innovations. Revolutionary thought was bound up with the liberation of the mind. Romanticist imagination was a virtue which did not hinder industrial development, but encouraged it. It was associated with science and technology. The romanticist imagination stimulated the human spirit and was affiliated with the progress of science and technology. Goethe wrote extensively on the theory of color, on botany and his theory of organic evolution anticipated Darwinism. Blake invented new engraving techniques. And Constable's insistence to paint in the open air, directly from nature was an innovation which placed him within the category of romanticism. He was a romanticist.

In addition to the Industrial Revolution, another central propelling force drove the world on a course of irreversible changes: the French Revolution. It had a profound impact on the nineteenth century. The buds of nationalism were in the air. Thus, it is not very surprising that the leading philosophers of the era preoccupied themselves with the problem of the relationship of diversity and unity, inertia and transformation. Hegel was particularly concerned with the problem of continuity and change, being and becoming. In his grand philosophical system he delineated the intrinsic mechanism through which transformation occurs. In contrast to Kant, Hegel found a solution to overcome the transcendentalism of the noumenon, the thing in itself. According to him within the framework of history the evolving human spirit represents the coalescent identity of the subject and the object. He described the transformations of the human mind throughout history, from the stage of consciousness as mere sensory experience to the stage of reflective awareness. In this last stage the mind is aware of itself as absolute knowledge. Science, art and religion -- in fact all social and political institutions -- in Hegel's view develop by means of a dialectical triad: The mind comprehends its object and constructs a thesis. This is contradicted by evidence and leads to the emergence of an antithesis. In the third stage the mind arrives at a resolution through synthesis. This is a never ending process which repeats itself again and again. In this manner Hegel outlined the invisible structure and inner mechanism of historical evolution.

It seems that the genesis of romanticism can be found in England of the early eighteenth century. It can be discerned in the explicit shift in feeling and sensibility with regard to nature and the order of things. Feeling and sensibility found their specific expression in poetry and culminated in the lyrics of Wordsworth, Byron, Coleridge, Shelley and Keats. Nature played a central role in the works of these poets. Shelley, for example, wrote an "Ode to the West Wind" (1821), in the same year that Constable painted "The Hay Wain" and began his systematic study of the skies. Similarly to Constable, Wordsworth also was fascinated with the poetic qualities of the countryside: the unadorned beauty of the ordinary, everyday aspects of bucolic life, pastorality and tranquility. Wordsworth drew for inspiration on natural scenes which he described eloquently in pure ordinary tongue. His aim was to express actual personal experience through the words of everyday language "really used by men." In the light of the existing similarities and parallels between Constable and Wordsworth the corollary is quite evident: If these qualities in Wordsworth are romanticist traits, then they must hold true of Constable as well. So, we end up again with the conclusion that, in spite of the claims to the contrary, Constable was a romanticist.

Bertrand Russell attacked the romanticists. According to him they substituted aesthetic norms for utilitarian standards. As an example, he compares the earth worm with the tiger. "The earth-worm is useful, but not beautiful; the tiger is beautiful, but not useful. Darwin (who was not a romantic) praised the earth-worm; Blake praised the tiger."[40] Russell points out that the romanticists liked strange ancient ruins, the melancholy of destroyed families, pirates and ghosts. He regarded Jean Jacques Rousseau (1712-1778) as the author of the romanticist movement. He accused him of extending subjectivity to the domain of politics, of the madness of anarchism, and even of the crimes of Hitler. On the other hand, Russell found in the contribution of the radical philosophers of the French Revolution the profound source that catapulted itself to "Marx and issues in Soviet Russia."[41]

Russell is a great philosopher and a shrewd observer. However, to lay the blame on a person for crimes perpetrated by others about two hundred years later is unfair and absurd. Besides, the non-romanticist Darwin contributed more to Nazi ideology than the romanticist Rousseau did. For, it was the father of the theory of evolution who glorified the eternal struggle for life existing in nature. And it was Darwin who was fascinated by the cruel beauty surrounding the perennial war of nature and the violence involved in the survival of the fittest. The Nazis tried to justify their atrocities through the scientific theories of Darwinism.

Russell is wrong concerning Marx as well. For, Marx was not a scientist, but a romanticist disciple of Hegel, an imaginative prophet and a visionary of messianic zeal. And as to "issues in Soviet Russia": It is difficult to find another place on the earth where the yawning gap between ideology and reality is wider. In the Soviet Union it is hard to differentiate the tiger from the earth worm, or, perhaps, the bear from the leech.

Logicians have little understanding of Rousseau. It was Ernst Cassirer who pointed out that Rousseau knew more about human nature than all the philosophers of the Enlightenment taken together. Rationalist philosophers, such as: Voltaire, Diderot and d'Alembert saw man in scientific terms, within the confines of physical and mathematical laws. Yet Rousseau saw man as a socio-political being dominated by instincts and emotions. He was well aware of the irrational, Dionysian side of man. Rousseau was perhaps the first thinker who questioned the basic power of reason. He realized that science can deal only with a limited range of the human experience. What Russell denounces as the irrationalism of Rousseau is, in effect, the realism of an outstanding sage who fathomed the nature of man, the conflicting tendencies of the human psyche. Rousseau realized that man must solve his problems by himself within the framework of human society as a political and ethical community. He warned that "the fools who endlessly complain about nature" should learn that the real source of their troubles is not nature but they themselves. Thus, the supposedly irrationalist Rousseau was the most resolute advocate of reason.

Constable's aspiration to accurately record the non-urban scenery of England, his rejection of neo-classicism, his method of painting in the open air, his sensibility and admiration for nature are romanticist traits. Constable's mind set was based on visual thinking. It operated through precise observation and common sense. In contrast to him the romanticist painter Henry Fuseli (1741-1825) had a Gothic literary imagination. Fuseli,[42] a Swiss born artist and Professor of Painting at the Royal Academy, was a teacher of Constable and a friend of Blake. His unrestrained imagination and enthusiasm for the grotesque found their expression in idiosyncratic mythological images. In "The Nightmare", for instance, a sleeping woman in a nightgown is portrayed as visited by a luminous pale horse and by a grinning devil.

Fuseli was well known not only for his stylization of form, extravagance of movement, eroticism, and depiction of nightmare, but also for his sarcasms and eccentricities. There were many anecdotes circulating about his strange manners. One of them told the story that once Fuseli entered an exhibition hall and opened his umbrella in front of the paintings. When an astonished friend asked him, why did he open up his umbrella, the artist replied: "Oh, because I am going to have a look at Mr. Constable's painting."[43] Through an eccentric act, or a practical joke, Fuseli in effect complemented Constable for his illusionary accomplishments, for his visual naturalism.

Since romanticism is not a clearly conceived phenomenon, its various aspects can be confusing. The movement was, furthermore, at cross-purposes with its own aspirations. Sometimes romanticism is defined as a movement in which imagination domineers over reason, over the sense of fact and the actual. But if we take this sort of a definition seriously, we can find ourselves in a position in which it is difficult to draw a divining line between science and art. Newton, for instance, dealt with the problem of the absolute and the infinite. The whole Newtonian system of classical physics is built on these imaginary attributes. Besides, for Newton's part science was nothing but part of his effort to understand the divine nature of the universe. It reinforced his religious beliefs. If we add to all this the fact that he was an alchemist as well, than it seems quite reasonable to conclude that in effect Newton was a romantic scientist!

It is true that for some romanticists, among them Fuseli, Blake and Turner, the imagination played a decisive role in the process of aesthetic communication. These artists saw beauty in the dreamy quality of mythological subjects. For them beauty was not identical with the art work proper, but arose from associated ideas which the imagination was encouraged to conjure up. It resulted from the interaction between the object of art and the beholder. Thus, beauty was an aesthetic experience which had to transcend the framework of visual reality.

It is also true that numerous romanticists preoccupied themselves with the occult, with demonology, ghosts, the supernatural, with evil and mysterious forces beyond human control. Unfortunately, however, history has vindicated that demonic, evil forces beyond human control are not the invention of our imagination. They are real, within us, and exert a real impact on history. The bloodsheds, the persecutions, the witch-hunts, the tortures in the chambers of the Inquisition were actual events. The Nazis were real, and so is the uncontrollable danger and fear of a nuclear holocaust. The rationalists concerned themselves with reason. They brushed aside and ignored the existence of evil. It was the romanticists who discovered the reality of the dark side of human nature. They explored the domain of dreams, the world of the unconscious. They understood that dreams are real, because dreams are facts. In this respect they were precursors of Freud, the pioneers of modern psychoanalysis.

The romanticist mind affiliated the vision of nature with the religious experience. Constable's painting and Wordsworth's poetry share the same mystical affinity, the same oceanic feeling that wants to dissolve the soul within the great cosmic womb of the universe. The same pantheistic inclination that characterizes their work can also be discerned in eastern philosophies. It finds its expression in the cosmic spirit of Hinduism and of Tao: the sensibility for the inner truth inherent in things and the feeling of the identity with nature.

Constable saw in nature a reinforcement of the truth of Christianity. He believed that nature was part of the great chain of being and a reflection of a divinely created system. In the mirror of nature man was able to perceive, momentarily at least, through his poetic sensibility and intellectual faculty the transcendental truth of the absolute and the infinite. Forms and colors were manifestations of the divine essence to which the artist responded. Nature was a mirror of man's duality: It was both material and spiritual. The artist reacted to the subtleties of forms and colors that revealed themselves in nature and transposed them on the canvas. Constable thought of nature as a work of art. Its essence could not be reduced to a few generalized formulae. For, as he said:

> the world is wide; no two days are alike, nor even two hours; neither were there ever two leaves of a tree alike since the creation of the world; and the genuine productions of art, like those of nature, are all distinct from each other.

Constable was a quiet person guided by common sense. He was not a revolutionary character. But his art -- his break with the tradition of neo-classicism, his method of painting directly from nature -- represented a revolution. The impressionists owed a great deal to his technique. However, they did not adopt his philosophy. The impressionists separated art from moral considerations. They identified color with light and divorced them from symbolical values. They only were interested in the purely optical aspects of vision devoid of previous knowledge and experience. All that they wanted was to depict the colors of the world as image and appearance. But the Dutch post-impressionist Vincent van Gogh (1853-1890) admired Constable's work.[44] Similarly to the great English landscape painter, van Gogh also was guided by a deep poetic sensibility, and through his pantheistic feeling and the passion of his tormented soul he became entirely absorbed by nature.

Interestingly enough, not only Constable influenced an important group of painters but Newton as well. After the publication of *Opticks*, its author's theory of colors became a dominant source of influence for scientists and painters alike.

Among Constable's contemporaries the scientists T. Young, B.T. Rumford, and the painters B. West, H. Howard and T. Phillips all had adopted a Newtonian approach to the phenomenon of color.[45] These scientists and painters also shared the belief that the simplest pattern of color harmony was formed by the juxtaposition of contrasting complementarities: green and red, violet and yellow, blue and orange. The impressionists were not swayed only by Delacroix, Corot, Turner and Constable, but by Newton as well. For the latter's theory of colors was carried over into the optical research of the French chemist Eugéne Chevreul whose studies of light and color exerted a stimulating influence on the impressionists.[46] Chevreul's *Principles of Harmony and Contrast of Colors and their Application to the Arts_* was published in 1839. The theoretical foundations of Seurat's pointillist technique, to a great extent, were based on this book (and on the work of other scientists such as Helmholtz, Rood, and Henry). By juxtaposing complementary colors on the canvas, yellow and blue dots, for example, Seurat achieved a green of greater purity than by the traditional method of mixing them on the palette.

Religious feeling played a pivotal role in both Constable's and Newton's life. According to the great physicist's biographer, F.E. Manuel, despite the prosaic story of the apple dropping in Newton's garden, "it is impossible to ignore the religious overtones of a theory of the universe called forth by the fruit that at once occasioned man's fall into mortal sin and led to wordly knowledge."[47]

One of the striking parallels between Constable's and Newton's mental processes might be found in their respective self-awareness and spiritual elevation. The painter's hypnotic stage of consciousness in painting the cloud formations of the sky is comparable to the intense concentration of the scientist that often came close to the state of mystic meditation. Newton's scientific breakthroughs were frequently bound up with a sort of secular exaltation.

The secret of Newton's creative powers was tied to his superior faculty to concentrate on scientific problems. "I keep the subject constantly before me", he commented once concerning his method of discoveries, "and wait till the first dawnings open slowly by little and little into the full and clear light."[48] As Newton's Cambridge

University notebook indicated, the scientist was aware of the existing connection between physical conditions and creativity. Dealing with "Imagination and Phantasie and Invention", he differentiated between factors which could enhance or disturb, and confuse the creative function of the mind.

William Whiston, Newton's successor in the Lucasian Chair at Cambridge, said of Sir Isaac that in mathematics he

> could sometimes see almost by intuition, even without demonstration, as was the case in that famous proposition in his *Principia*, that *all parallelograms* circumscribed about the conjugate diameters of an ellipsis are equal; which he told Mr. Cotes he used before it had ever been demonstrated by any one, as it was afterward. And when he did but propose conjectures in natural philosophy, he almost always knew them to be true at the same time.[49]

Manuel has suggested that in a sense Newton's approach to creativity was analogous to that advocated by Maimonides, the great medieval Jewish philosopher, concerning prophecy. According to Maimonides, the imaginative faculty of the true prophet should be restrained by the rational side of his intellect. Newton's scientific enunciations that stemmed from his states of illumination had been viewed by the scientist himself as similar to the symbolic messages revealed in prophecy. Newton operated with the peculiar belief that his consciousness was divinely inspired, but that its insights always had to be subjected to scientific verification.[50]

The period between 1664 and 1666 was a glorious interval in the life of Isaac Newton and in the history of science. It culminated in the so called 'annus mirabilis', the year of wonders, in which the great scientist laid down the foundations of his pivotal discoveries. In this unique episode of his life Newton conducted early prismatic experiments, improved the technique of grinding lenses and completed his theory of colors. It was through these optical experiments that he discovered the infinite transitory grades between red and violet and formulated a theory concerning the substance of primary colors. Besides his studies of colored light, Newton also made observations of comets between 1664 and 1666. It was probably in the annus mirabilis as well that the young scientist intuited and tested the hypothesis of universal attraction, an insight triggered by the meaningful coincidence of the falling apple. However, the successful mathematical proof of the inverse square law of gravitation was worked out only at a later phase of his life.

It has been suggested that a unique combination of events and circumstances brought about the creative powers of Newton's scientific genius. Similarly to Constable, he spent his youth in the countryside, and it was the countryside that shaped the underlying character of the artist and of the scientist alike. Constable's landscapes were inspired by Suffolk County, Newton's mind was stimulated by the rustic environment of Lincolnshire.

It appears that prior to the annus mirabilis Newton suffered a mental crisis, and that later on during his Cambridge years there were rumors that he had gone mad. In Manuel's view, "Newton's melancholy temper reflected the emotional climate of mid-seventeenth-century England"[51], and like other ambivalent neurotics, he had a profound need for certainty. Thus, the scientific genius' conviction that mathematical laws governed the world served him as his palladium.[52]

The plague which brought Newton from Cambridge back to Woolsthorpe in June 1665 was an important event in his intellectual development. In the safety of his isolated manor, the physicist began to regard himself as a surviving elect of the epidemic. Newton's equipoise of mind from his childhood was disturbed by the lack of fatherly love and approval. The deep anxieties which deranged his psyche were relieved during the episode of the plague. He saw his sparing as a sign of divine grace and of heavenly approbation. He was a survivor, and survivors frequently experience waves of an irrepressible need to express their stimulated creative energies.

Chapter Two

MATHEMATICS AS APPLIED SCIENCE
AND AS SUBJECT MATTER
IN THE VISUAL ARTS

Introduction

This chapter deals with an array of selected aspects of the interaction of mathematics and art. My fascination with the subject has been a long-standing affair. However, since I am not a professional mathematician, I would like to approach it with prudent diffidence.

Mathematics as a creative endeavor holds a rather unique position among the arts and sciences. It is both a humanistic study and a science. This dual status results from the facts that the subject matter of mathematics is concerned with mental constructs, reproducible ideas, which often can be brought to corresponding relationships with the external world of actuality.

It is rather an intriguing phenomenon that many artists are attracted to mathematics, and that numerous mathematicians are actively involved in the arts. This is certainly not a coincidence. For despite the fact that a science of mathematical aesthetics does not exist,[1] aesthetic properties are deeply ingrained into the fabric of mathematics, and mathematical traits abound in the arts.

Recently I was immensely delighted to read a brilliant essay written by Professor P.R. Halmos, the Editor of *The American Mathematical Monthly*, in which, among other things, he says:

> Talk to a painter (I did) and talk to a mathematician, and you'll be amazed at how similarly they react. Almost every aspect of the life and the art of a mathematician has its counterpart in painting, and vice versa.[2]

Reviewing Halmos' book, *Selecta: Expository Writing* (1983), R.P. Boas has observed that it is a refreshing event to have such a work explaining advanced mathematics superbly and in a comprehensible way.[3] As Boas points out avant-garde mathematicians talk in esoteric language which even professionals fail to understand, and he draws a parallel with avant-garde music: "Modern mathematics (like modern music) has the reputation of being abtruse, incomprehensible, and remote from reality."[4] I realize with considerable sadness that it takes courage to explain mathematics in a comprehensible way, because as Boas says, Halmos is "unafraid of having people look down on him."[5] It is noteworthy that there have always been eminent mathematicians who possessed the rare faculty of being able to communicate the highly abstract subject matter of mathematics to non-mathematicians. A case

46

in point is the lecture on the foundations of geometry that Bernhard Riemann delivered in Germany at the University of Göttingen. The enormously successful lecture was attended by the whole body of the university's learned men, yet was given without a single equation.[6] Other great mathematicians, such as Bertrand Russell and A.N. Whitehead, also addressed wide audiences in everyday language.

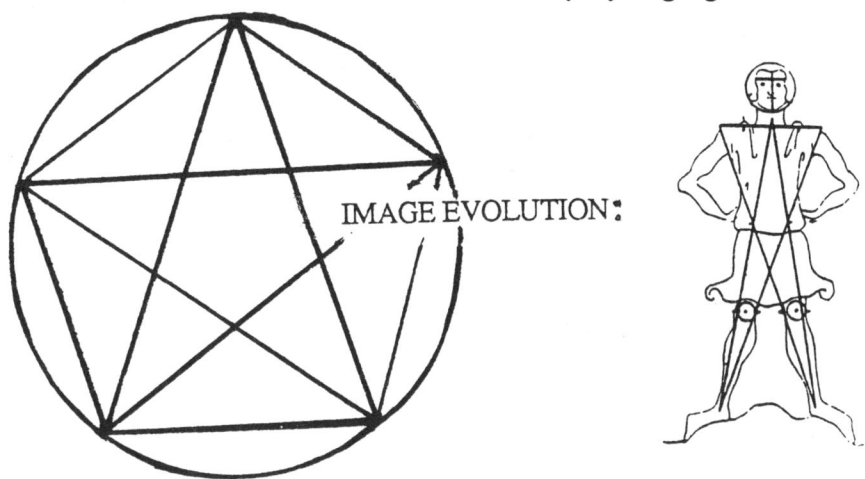

IMAGE EVOLUTION:

combination of planning and coincidence. Above Left: Star shaped figure (pentagram), inscribed within a circle and a pentagon, produces smaller pentagon. The figure has a set of golden section properties. Above Right: Human figure superimposed upon a pentagram by Villard (13th century). Below Left: Kandinsky's "Inner Relation" (1925). Below Right: "Painted Melodies" series by the author.

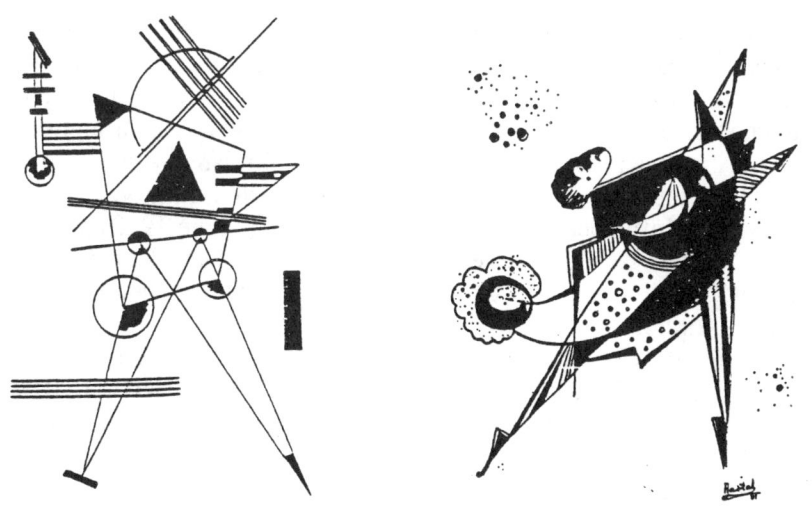

The name of Bertrand Russell is tied to one of the central hypotheses concerning the relationship of art and mathematics, which is an integral part of the infrastructure of my conceptual framework: One of the common denominators of art and mathematics finds its expression in the epistemological observation that they both are invented worlds. Both mathematics and art are semiotic attempts to structure reality by ways of symbols. However, geometrical space, for instance, is no closer to reality than the painted space of the artist. In 1959 Bertrand Russell sadly commented:

> I wanted certainty in the kind of way in which people want religious faith. I thought that certainty is more likely to be found in mathematics than elsewhere . . . But after some twenty years of arduous toil, I came to the conclusion that there was nothing more that I could do in the way of making mathematical knowledge indubitable.[7]

It is noteworthy that science itself is not in a better position: "Einstein's space is no closer to reality than Van Gogh's sky".[8]
The famous mathematician G.H. Hardy said:

> A mathematician like a painter or a poet is a maker of patterns. The mathematician's patterns, like the painter's or the poet's, must be beautiful; ideas like the colors or the words must fit together in a harmonious way. Beauty is the first test: there is no permanent place in the world for ugly mathematics.[9]

On the whole this seems to be a valid statement. It should be noted, however, that in avant-garde painting the concept of beauty became a non-existent entity. For some artists the word beauty is an anathema. I suspect that this is a development that was brought about by the far-reaching influence of logical positivism. Since beauty is neither a tautology nor an empirically verifiable quality, the logical positivists, influenced by Hume and flourishing in the 1920s and 1930s at the Vienna Circle, doubted or denied its existence. Kurt Gödel, the inventor or discoverer of the incompleteness theorem, belonged to the Vienna Circle.

Another reason for the tendency to abolish beauty, or to reduce it to the status of being merely a byproduct of the creative process, appears to be the total break up of the Renaissance tradition. For the

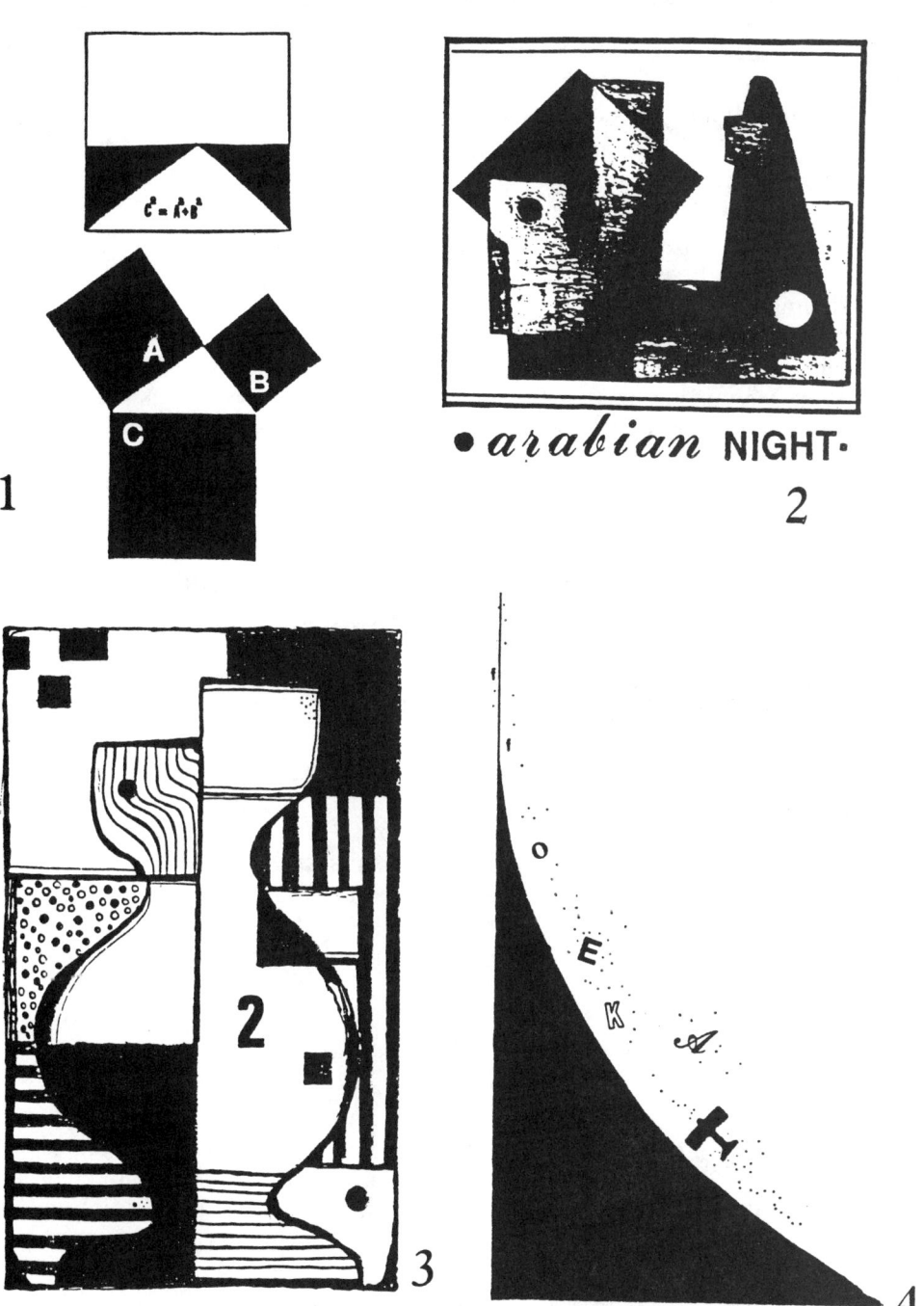

FOUR QUASI-MATHEMATICAL WORKS

which deliberately transcend the realm of geometry: 1. Pythagorean Landscape 2. Arabian Night 3. Two 4. Take off

salient defining property of modern art is the break up of aesthetic form, color, design, composition and content.[10] In the new aesthetics adopted by the painter, art is not a cathartic experience but an expression of the human condition. It is difficult for the artist to create beauty in a world of pollution, alienation and violence; a world of extensive ugliness which lives under the perpetual threat of nuclear self-destruction.

In a sense, man has no nature but history. The ideas of both art and science evolve from the same deep structure of human culture. From the unconscious common pool of culture apparently coincidental patterns emerge which manifest themselves in the parallel processes and in the analogous ideas of art, mathematics and science. Similarly to the mathematician and the scientist, the artist is guided by the restless human will to investigate and to explore the unknown. Like mathematics and science, art is perennial expansion.

A case in point with regard to the existing parallels between mathematics and art can be found in abstraction. For, the increasing importance of applied mathematical abstraction which is gaining momentum in the sciences, corresponds to the development of abstraction in painting and in design. The noncommutative property of Arthur Cayley's matrices provides another example. In my opinion it is analogous to surrealist paintings.

Research into the interaction of mathematics and painting is an underdeveloped field. The investigation of their relationship has the potential of yielding very significant results, meaningful bearings on the development of both pure and applied mathematics. It is my hope that this treatise will stimulate interest in the subject as well as encourage collaboration for joined projects of mathematicians and artists.

Intuition And Aesthetics

The term intuition denotes the human faculty of immediate knowledge without conscious preliminary thinking. This uninferred form of knowledge is a direct insight or apprehension. To what extent it is linked to innate wisdom or to empirical experience is unclear. Leibniz, who simultaneously with Newton developed the theory of calculus in the last quarter of the seventeenth century, distinguished between intuitive truths of reason and intuitive truths of facts. According to his conception humans intuit both what they perceive and the general principles which order their reasoning. Henri Bergson (1859-1941) assumed that intuition is capable of grasping the world in

AAA	ACA	GAA	GCA	CAA	CCA	UAA	UCA
AAG	ACG	GAG	GCG	CAG	CCG	UAG	UCG
AAC	ACC	GAC	GCC	CAC	CCC	UAC	UCC
AAU	ACU	GAU	GCU	CAU	CCU	UAU	UCU
AGA	AUA	GGA	GUA	CGA	CUA	UGA	UUA
AGG	AUG	GGG	GUG	CGG	CUG	UGG	UUG
AGC	AUC	GGC	GUC	CGC	CUC	UGC	UUC
AGU	AUU	GGU	GUU	CGU	CUU	UGU	UUU

64 trinucleotides

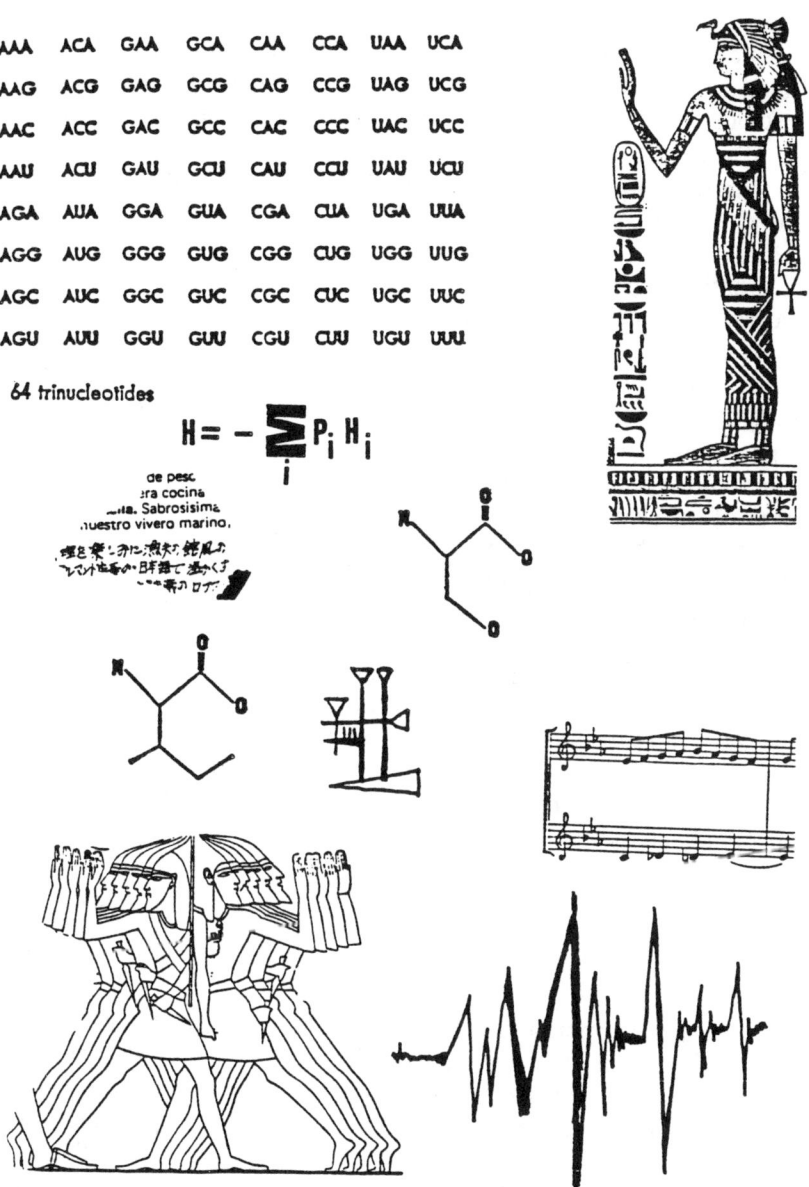

$$H = - \sum_i P_i H_i$$

de pesc
:ra cocina
...la. Sabrosisima
.iuestro vivero marino.

ENCODED INFORMATION

its fluidity, in contract to discursive reason that breaks its flow. He argued to the effect that discursive reason falsifies the experience of existence as an unbroken continuity because, among other things, it spatializes time.[11]

The Italian philosopher Benedetto Croce (1866-1952), assigned a central role to aesthetics in his system. In his view the core of aesthetics is individuality which is bound up with the imagination of the creative person. Imagination is tied to intuition, which, when successfully expressed, is the work of art.

Mathematicians throughout the ages paid attention to the existing relationship between beauty and their subject. Pythagoras assumed that beauty is an inherent quality of numbers, because 'all things have form, all things are form and all forms can be defined by numbers'.[12] The Greek philosopher is credited with the important discovery that it is the length of the string of a musical instrument which determines the pitch of a note. Arthur Koestler suggests that this Pythagorean reduction of quality to quantity represents the first historical step to apply mathematics to the human experience, and therefore it can be regarded as the genesis of science.

Pythagoras viewed mathematics as an integral part of philosophy, which to him was the highest revelation of music. In his system numbers were represented by dots structured as shapes. Six, for instance, was a triangular number (represented by six dots), four was a square number, whereas twelve was an oblong number as shown respectively below:

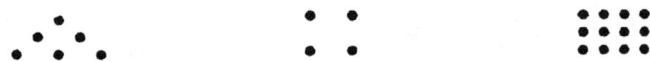

In Cézanne's approach to art, two and half millenia later, a kindred idea had developed into a regulative principle. The painter maintained that nature could be regarded as an ensemble of curved geometrical forms: cylinders, cones and spheres. The Cubists, among them Picasso, Braque and Lipchitz, relied on Cézanne's aesthetic theory in advancing their geometrical style. The conjecture that through metamorphosis the Pythagorean tenet concerning the existence of an intrinsic relationship between nature and mathematical form was catapulted into Cézanne's theory of art needs further investigation.

Aristotle held that "the mathematical sciences particularly exhibit order, symmetry, and limitation, and these are the greatest forms of the beautiful."[13] For his part beauty was an organic unity in which every element had its defined role and contributed to the quality of the whole. In Plato beauty referred to the symmetry and the proportion of form: The teacher of Aristotle believed that beauty was to be found primarily in the abstract ideas out of which the physical world was structured as an echo.

A common denominator of painting and mathematics is to be found in the domain of creativity. Henri Poincaré (1854-1912) assumed that the aesthetic faculty is the dominant trait in mathematical creativity. To logic he assigned only a secondary role. Commenting on Poincaré's theory of discovery, Michael Polanyi says:

> Discovery takes place in two more or less separate stages, an arduous straining of the imagination is followed by a virtually spontaneous appearance of the solution. In his classic study of heuristic, Poincaré has described cases in which these two phases were sharply separated: the effort of the imagination had ceased for several hours, when the bright idea turned up. Poincaré thinks that first a strenuous search loosens possible bits of a solution and that discovery is then achieved by an effortless integration of these bits. He calls this integration an illumination; I shall name it intuition.[14]

The mathematician's judgements as well as his choices of problems are guided by aesthetic factors. Paul Dirac goes even further. In his view, the beauty of an equation is more important than its correspondence to the result of the experiment. Nevertheless, even when the experiment bears out the equation, the theoretician is still in the company of the artist. "We must be clear", said Niels Bohr once in a conversation with Heisenberg, "that, when it comes to atoms, language can be used only as in poetry. The poet, too, is not nearly so concerned with describing facts as with creating images and establishing mental connections."[15]

Werner Heisenberg thought that the fundamental elements of art are similar to the basic components of mathematics. Aesthetics is a notoriously elusive discipline, notwithstanding the German scientist's statement that "equality and inequality, repetition and symmetry, certain group structures play the fundamental role both in art and in mathematics."[16]

It is intriguing to compare these views with the opinions of the most influential artist of the twentieth century: Pablo Picasso. Unlike

Leonardo da Vinci or Paul Klee, the Spanish painter had never produced a coherent body of theoretical writings on art. Nevertheless, Picasso often stimulated his intimate friends in conversations, and established a firm reputation as an unfathomable fountainhead of swift witticisms and brief paradoxes.

Emphasizing the central role of intuition in painting, Picasso said:

> I can hardly understand the importance given to the word research in connection with modern painting. In my opinion to search means nothing in painting. To find, is the thing . . . When I paint, my object is to show what I have found and not what I am looking for. In art intentions are not sufficient and, as we say in Spanish: love must be proved by facts and not by reasons.[17]

But Picasso's thought is characterized by its natural dialectics. The painter knew that truth has many facets comprising polarities and multitudes. In 1956, two decades after that he declared that "search means nothing in painting", he had changed his mind. "I never do a painting as a work of art", he said. "All of them are researches. I search incessantly and there is a logical sequence in all this research. That is why I number them. It is an experiment in time. I number them and date them."[18]

Picasso had an ambivalent love and hate relationship towards beauty. Braque once said to him: "Basically you have always loved classical beauty". His friend agreed. Thus, according to Picasso beauty transcends history. Or as he put it: "They don't invent a type of beauty every year."[19]

However, Picasso contradicted himself again:

> I have a horror of people who speak about the beautiful. What is the beautiful? One must speak of problems in painting! . . . Academic training in beauty is a sham . . . Art is not the application of a canon of beauty but what the instinct and the brain can conceive beyond any canon . . . [20]

Picasso ridiculed academic efforts to define the nature of beauty. To him it was a word without sense because he could not account for the origin of its meaning or where it was leading to. "Beauty", he said, do you know exactly where its opposite is to be found? If someone were to show me that there exists a positive ugliness, that would be something else. . . . The academy devised the formula, not long ago they submitted the senses to the 'official' judgment of what is beautiful and what is ugly. The Renaissance invented the size of noses. Since then reality has gone to the devil.[21]

Different mathematical methods may vary in terms of their aesthetic appeal. What makes one proof of a theorem aesthetically more delightful than another? The answer can lie in such components as efficacy, simplicity and purity of vision.[22] Let us compare this with another statement of Picasso. In 1933, after a visit to the Louvre he said:

With the Greeks there's always an aesthetic element. I prefer the virile realism of Rome, which doesn't embellish. The truthfullness of Roman art -- it's like their buildings, utilitarian but all the more beautiful in their genuine simplicity.[23]

The parallel is quite clear. Moreover, the painter's words elucidate his conception of beauty. Thus, in Picasso's view aesthetics and beauty are not overlapping synonyms but rather irreconcilable entities: Beauty is not decoration.

Birkhoff's Aesthetic Measure

In 1933 appeared George D. Birkhoff's *Aesthetic Measure*, a book in which the author tried to quantify the aesthetic experience. The renowned mathematician postulated that it is the ratio of order and complexity, connected with the aesthetic demand for 'unity in variety' which determine the aesthetic effect. Birkhoff's aim was to provide some rational basis to the establishment of a scientific aesthetics in which intuitive comparisons concerning the artistic value of objects can be made according to a mathematical formula. He assumed that the aesthetic experience consists of three successive phases: 1) attention, 2) the feeling of value and 3) the realization of order.

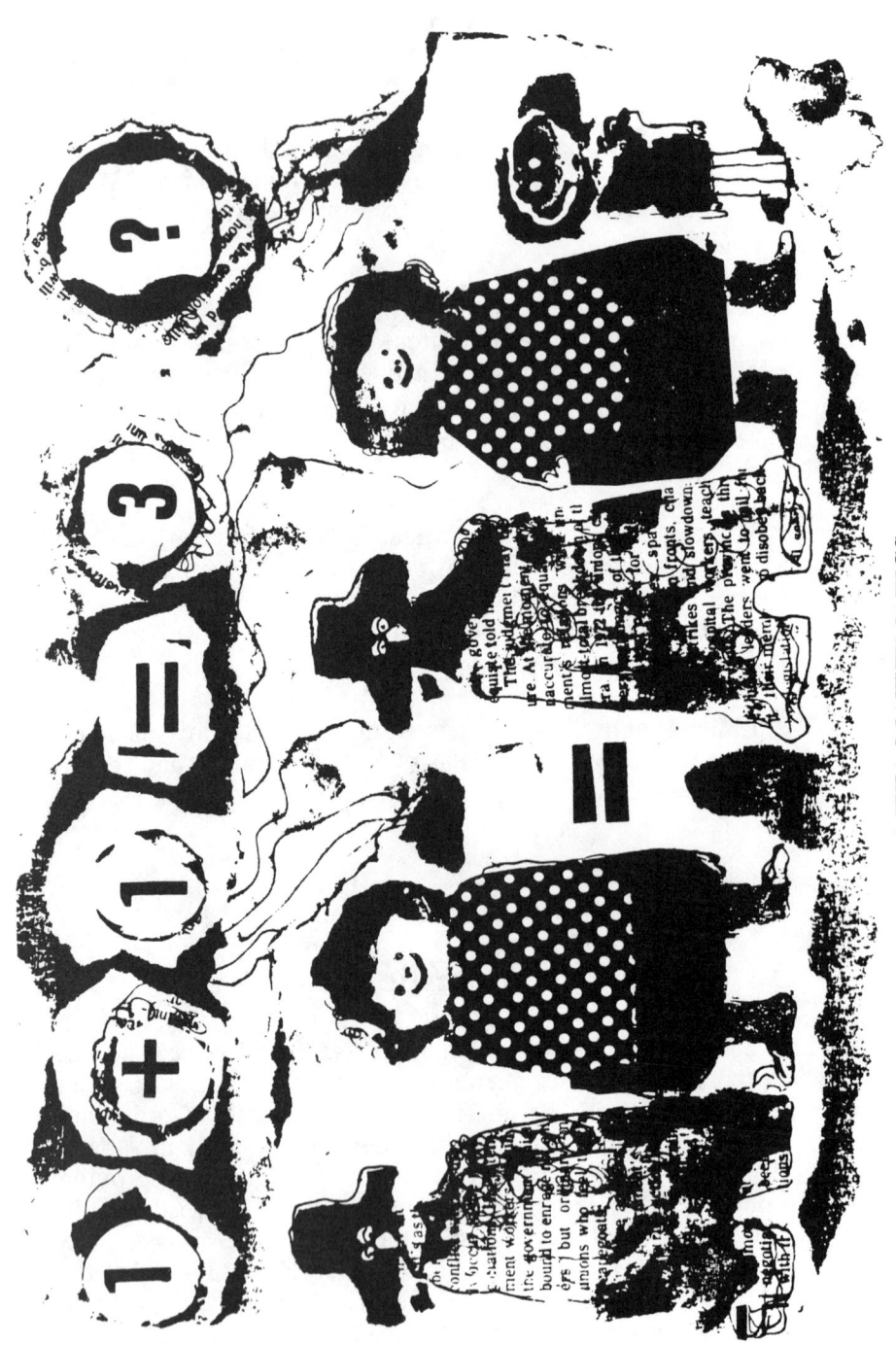

Attention, explains Birkhoff, is necessary for the act of perception, and it increases in proportion to the complexity (C) of the object. It is rewarded by the feeling of value which he calls aesthetic measure (M). The third phase, the realization of order (O) is characterized by a subconscious, more or less concealed apprehension of harmony, symmetry, or constitution.

In his attempt at formulating mathematically the problem, Birkhoff contended that the

> analysis of the aesthetic experience suggests that the aesthetic feelings arise primarily because of an unusual degree of harmonious interrelation within the object. More definitely, if we regard M, O, and C as measurable variables, we are led to write
>
> $$M = \frac{O}{C}$$
>
> and thus to embody in a basic formula the conjecture that the aesthetic measure is determined by the density of order relations in the aesthetic object.[24]

Criticism against Birkhoff's thesis can be levelled on several grounds. My first objection arises in connection with the assumption that a determined relationship exists between the feeling of aesthetic value and the aesthetic object. This assumption implies the belief that intrinsic aesthetic qualities exist independently of the observer. To suppose this is worse than to believe that the taste of an apple, for instance, is in the apple and not in the mouth. Taste is one of the most complex neurological phenomena and the sensation we experience while eating a fruit is the result of inextricable interactions between the sensory system of the organism and the biochemical molecules of the fruit. We all know that certain foods taste good to some people but are not appealing to others. The reasons for this stem from differences in the tasting mechanism of the nervous system, from disparities in upbringing and culture. Notwithstanding that in the Western world raw oysters and clams are acceptable food, Japanese-style raw fish, e.g., is considered by many as less palatable, because of the thought that eating raw fish is distasteful.

The aesthetics of visual perception is even more elusive a domain than the theory of food tasting and gastronomy. In painting the aesthetic effect is the outcome of intricate interaction occurring between the image and the observer. This subject-object interface-dynamics is structured by a long list of variables. A great deal of these variable are determinants which are independent of the aesthetic image but brought into specific relationship with it through the individual viewer, as well as by environmental conditions. Thus the outcome of the aesthetic effect is a particular configuration determined not merely by the art work but also by weather conditions, lighting, physical space, mood of the observer, his or her sharpness of eyesight, health, personal experience, intelligence, cultural and education background. When Impressionism as a new style of painting appeared on the scene, critics and audience alike reacted with contempt and ridicule. Nowadays the same paintings are among the most treasured objects of museums and widely appreciated by the masses.

Another weakness of Birkhoff's approach lies in the fact that he seems to identify the aesthetic effect with beauty as a manifestation of the pleasure principle. Yet as we have seen above, we should not take for granted that the artist's sole aim is to create beauty, or that all successful art works are the results of this aspiration. Artists like Goya, Klee, or Picasso did not paint in order to please the eyes. Daumier was imprisoned in 1832 for representing King Louis Philippe as Gargantua, and his images of scenes in the Courts of Justice, and those of every-day life lack any romantic feeling. Similarly to Daumier, the American realist Ben Shahn viewed art as a vehicle to express ideas, and did not find poverty picturesque at all.

Another objection to Birkhoff's thesis might arise from the consideration that order is a built-in trait of complexity and therefore his formula contains a tautological fallacy.

Besides, an original art work as a unique qualitative piece of creativity transcends quantification; it cannot be reduced to a simple mathematical formula.

A specific problem crops up also when art as idea comes to the fore. For, the picture is just the tip of the iceberg: It must be related to the historical context. Let us take Claude Monet (1840-1926) as an example. It was in 1874 that the French painter exhibited in Paris *An Impression*, the painting that gave the name to the whole impressionist movement. Monet's impressionist *Haystacks* series cannot be properly enjoyed and understood without the spectator's awareness that the artist was exploring the painterly ramifications of the theory that color is light.

In a similar manner, one cannot appreciate adequately Picasso's *Guernica* (1936) -- a salient artistic landmark of this century -- without the historical background of the Spanish Civil War, and without the iconographic idiom of cubism. Picasso said of the mural that it was the only work in which he deliberately created a political allegory. He denied that his work was symbolic. According to him only *Guernica* was symbolic. In it the bull represents brutality, and the horse represents the people. The painter insisted that in other works of his a bull was only an image of a bull, and a horse was only a picture of a horse, without any symbolic meaning.

In the light of these considerations it is possible to come to the conclusion that the art work is an alchemic hybrid of ideas and images which defies quantitative analysis. The aesthetic experience cannot be exhausted by mathematical means. Art as a whole is a gestalt which is more than the sum total of its parts. To illustrate this principle, let us consider a series of four images representing stylized faces made of six variables (x, y, 3, +, 0, 8) and a constant circular container:

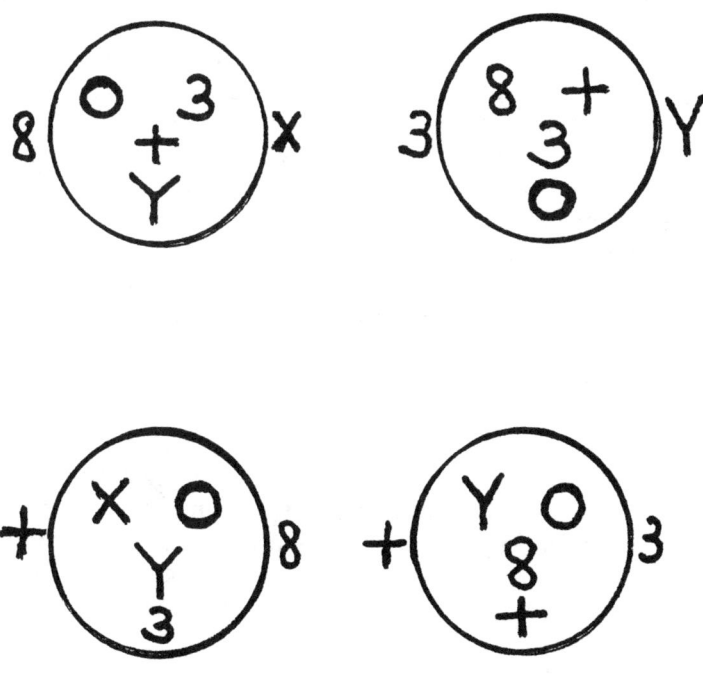

The visual patterns formed in this manner resemble human faces, despite the fact that they are not made of isomorphic elements. The perception of the images is guided by contextual familiarity -- the relative positions of the constituents of facial anatomy (eyes, nose, mouth and ears) -- regardless of the arithmetical values of the mathematical symbols. The latter are entirely irrelevant with regard to the visual interpretation of the message. The variables interlaced with the circular container coalesce as gestalts capable of evoking individual character percepts. These physiognomical clusters result from associative determinants, that is to say, from the psychological background of the observer. The dynamic interaction between the viewer and the series of these elusive images seems to induce visual tension due to perceptual ambiguity.

The Medieval Link

Obviously there exist conspicuous differences between mathematics and the visual arts. After all the first is involved in the systematic study of quantities, in the investigation of algebraic and geometrical relations, whereas the latter is concerned with image making and perception. While mathematics investigates the logical qualities of numerical and spatial proportions, painting explores the psychological relations of poetic qualities through the visualization of consciousness.

Our compartmental age tends to enhance the distinctions. However, from a historical point of view, not merely the differentiation between pure and applied mathematics seems to be a modern phenomenon but even the differentiation between art and science. In the Middle Ages arithmetic, geometry, music and astronomy formed the quadrivium, which together with the trivium of grammar, rhetoric and logic comprised the seven liberal arts.

The Pythagorean number mysticism was carried over into the Middle Ages. The medieval monks rediscovered the Greek philosopher's work and it became again a celebrated doctrine. The Pythagoreans believed that all world phenomena were ordered by numbers, especially by the first four integers: 1, 2, 3, 4; the tetrakis. Accordingly, they structured their mystical view of the world within the four disciplines of mathemata that evolved in the Middle Ages into the quadrivium.

Historical continuity is a rather bumpy and sinuous phenomenon. It never completely prevails neither in science nor in art. In science holism versus atomism, idealism, against materialism, rationalism against empiricism seem to alternate and compete with each other. In

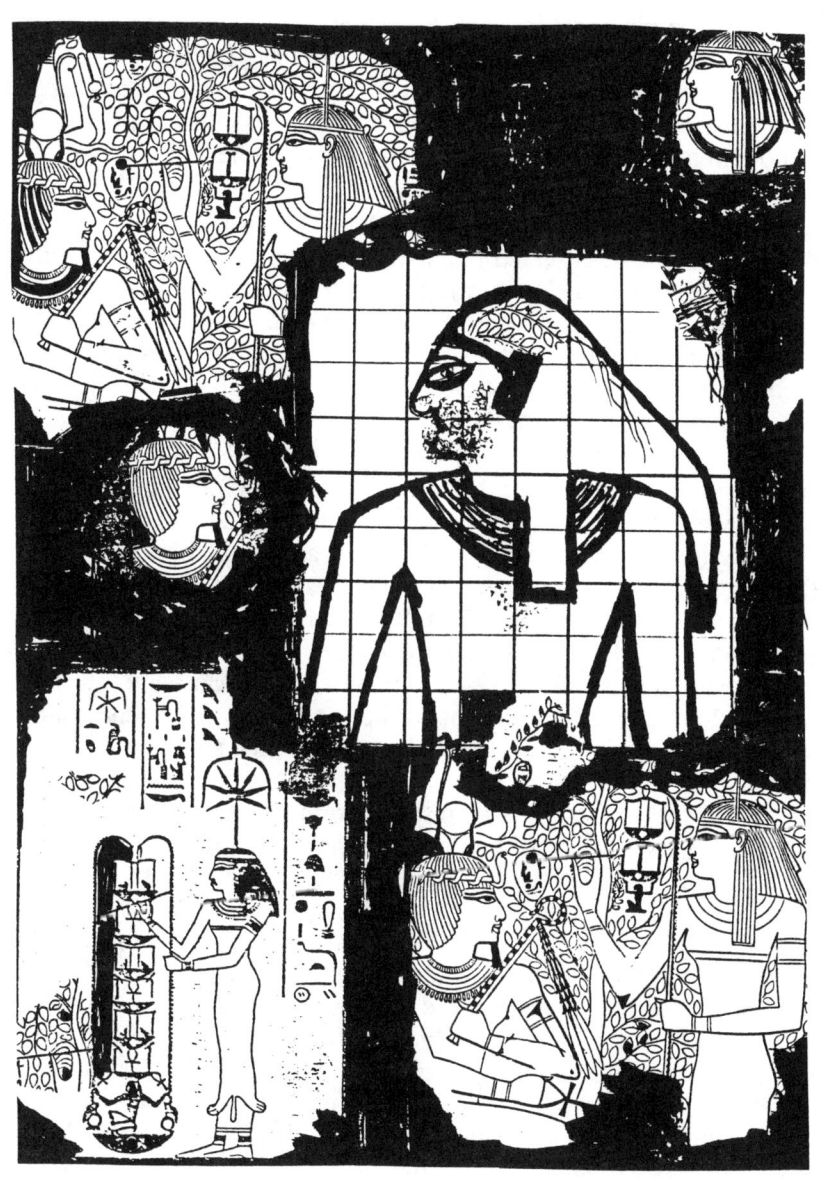

COMPOSITION WITH EGYPTIAN MOTIFS

61

art a similar phenomenon can be discerned. In a sense, art can be viewed as the struggle between expressionism and realism.

At various ages throughout history artists relied more on mathematics in the implementation of their work than in others. An important aspect that brings together art and mathematics concerns the aesthetic theory of human proportions.

It was Erwin Panofsky who pointed out that the theory of human proportions always affected the history of artistic styles.[25] The artists of ancient Egypt were very little bothered by considerations of optical naturalism. Devices of perceptual illusionism, like perspective or foreshortening, were absent from their images. but they operated with a theory of human proportion which was essentially mathematical in character. Egyptian artists constructed their designs by using a geometrical grid of equal squares. They drew their pictures by superimposing the outlines of the figure on this network.[*] Human images were drawn in frontal projection but the head was represented in profile with one eye looking straightforward at the observer, and the legs were twisted by ninety degrees in correspondence with the direction of the head. The strict rules of the Egyptian aesthetic canon were based on a modular system which did not change for thousands of years. The later Egyptian canon divided the length of the human body into twenty one modular units on the equal square network. On this scale the length of the head was represented by three units, similarly to those of the feet.

The Greek artists freed themselves from the modular restrictions of the Egyptians. They did not use atomic building blocks in the construction of their images. Instead, they operated with a theory of human proportions founded on observation and the imitation of natural appearances. The canon of Polyclitus was based on the harmonious relationship of the body as an integral whole.

In the Roman architect and engineer Vitruvius the arithmetic proportions of the human body resurface. The sixteenth century mathematician Geronimo Cardano claimed that the theory of proportions of Vitruvius was founded on music.

It appears that the medieval architect and engineer Villard de Honnecourt was familiar with the writings of Vitruvius. In 1235 he

---

[*] See the central figure in *"Composition with Egyptian Motifs"*, page 61.

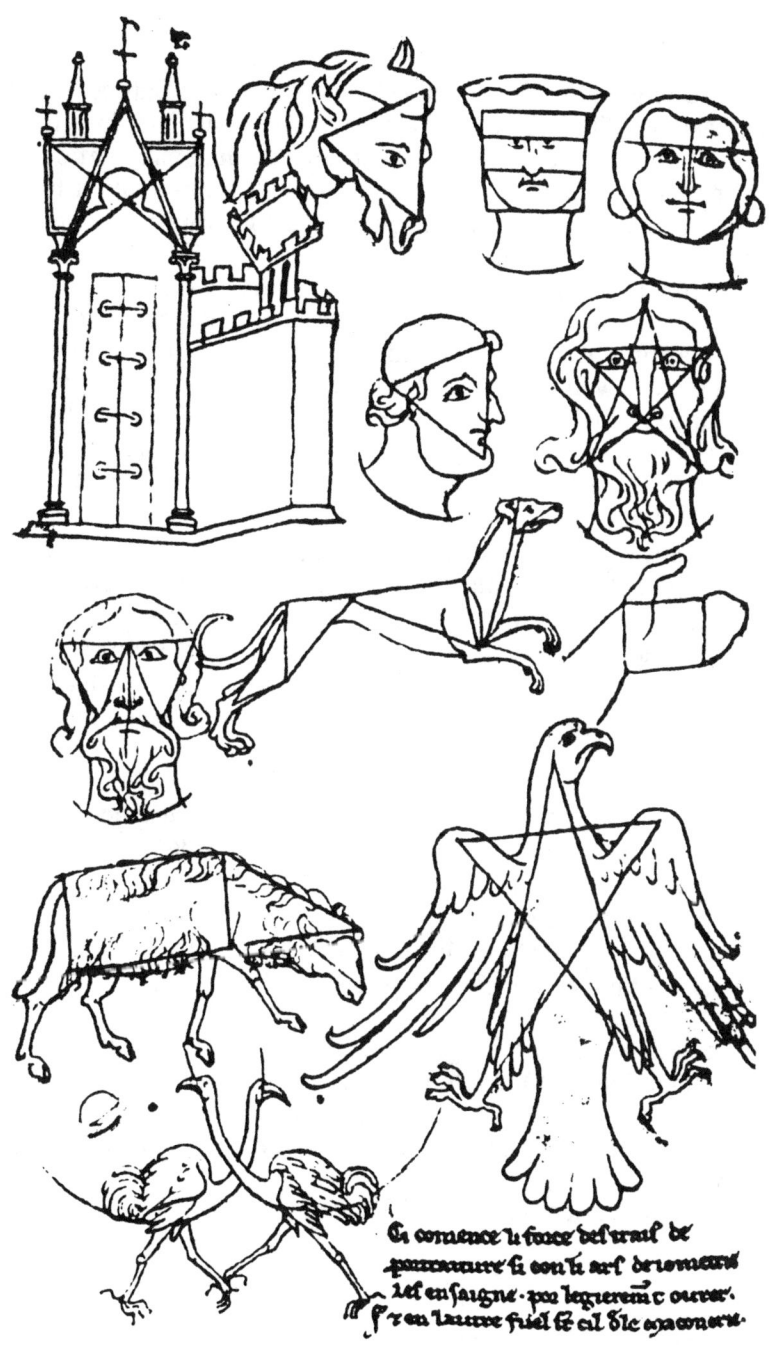

Ci comence li force des trais de
pourtraiture si con li ars de iometne
les ensaigne por legierement ouvrer.
Et en laurre fuel se cil sle maçonerie.

"DIAGRAMMATIC FIGURES"

Villard de Honnecourt, 13th century.

was invited to travel from his native France to central Europe in order to undertake building projects in Hungary. Five years later he returned to France. Villard's drawings of men and animals are particularly interesting. His images are not based on precise observation but on geometrical conceptualization. In some respect he can be regarded as a precursor of modern cubism.

Working in his home Province of Picardy, Villard produced a sketchbook which he filled with hundreds of images representing hoisting machines, water mills, birds, wild animals, horses, insects, a cat and a dog, as well as people. He adhered to a scheme of symmetry and proportion which he may possibly have learnt from the writings of Vitruvius. In one of Villard's planimetrically conceived human figures a male figure is superimposed over a vertically elongated pentagram, with total defiance in respect to the anatomical composition of the human organism.[*] The artist also drew human heads made of squares, rectangles, triangles and pentagrams. Similarly to Egyptian art, Villard applied geometrical design to his images in order to allow their reproduction at a different scale. One of the drawings shows a human face displayed within a square.[**] The division of the face into three small rectangles is in perfect agreement with the Vitruvian canon of proportions:

> If we take the height of the face itself, the distance from the bottom of the chin to the under side of the nostrils is one third of it; the nose from the under side of the nostrils to a line between the eyebrows is the same; from there to the lowest roots of the hair is also a third comprising the forehead.[26]

In accordance with the Pythagorean tenet which attributed such immense importance to the tetrakis (1, 2, 3, 4), Renaissance men held that the most pleasing rectangles to the human eye were those whose sides were made of the plain arithmetic relations of musical harmony (1:2, 1:3, 1:4, . . .).

Leon Battista Alberti (1404-1472) wrote:

---

[*] See "Image Evolution", page 47.

[**] See illustration, page 63.

> . . . I am every day more and more convinced of the truth of the Pythagoras saying, that Nature is sure to act consistently, and with a constant analogy in all her operations: from whence I conclude that the same numbers by means of which the agreement of sounds affects our ears with delight, are the very same which please our eyes and mind.[27]

The peculiar triad of mathematics, painting, and music as an aesthetic configuration materialized itself in various aspects of modern art. Cézanne's work represents a revival of the geometrical aesthetic tradition. The cubist painters found Cézanne's approach to painting meaningful and combined geometrical schemes with primitive art. They were rather concerned with the idea of the object than with its actual physical appearance. In 1912 the technique of collage was introduced by Braque and Picasso, a watershed which marked the end of analytical cubism and the beginning of synthetic cubism.

The cubists liked to collect musical instruments and to decorate their studios with them. The sculptor Jacques Lipchitz said that musical instruments appealed to the cubists because they were simple, neutral and non-academic things which were always interesting, unusual, and could be controlled. Moreover, they liked them because the artists explored abstract relations through musical instruments. Their unusual shapes also "served as the basis for intricate compositions."[28]

The work of the abstract painter and musician Wassily Kandinsky (1866-1944) represents an emphatically explicit meeting point between painting, music, and mathematics. The Russian artist relied on the views of men like Goethe, and Delacroix when he pointed out the existing deep relationship between music and painting. Kandinsky asserted that painting should not concern itself with the reproduction of natural phenomena but rather with the expression of the artist's soul in terms of form and color alone. "And from this", he said, "results that modern desire for rhythm in painting, for mathematical, abstract construction, for repeated notes of color, for setting color in motion."[29]

In Kandinsky's *Point and Line to Plane* (1926) there is a quite intriguing diagram (No 23) entitled, "Inner Relation of a complex of straight lines to a curve from the picture 'Black Triangle' (1925)". It evokes Villard de Honnecourt's human figure in a pentagram but Kandinsky's image is entirely abstract (See, "Image Evolution", page 47).

65

Non-Euclidean Space

It was known already in antiquity that geometrical problems are relevant to the art of painting. The Alexandrian Greek mathematician Euclid in the *Opticks* discussed theories of vision and perspective, although the latter he treated to a rather limited extent.

Sometime during the Renaissance the Costruzione Legittima, the modern mathematical study of perspective was born. It was probably invented by Filippo Brunelleschi in the first quarter of the fifteenth century, and improved by Alberti, Paolo Uccello and Piero della Francesca.

According to Giorgio Vasari (1511-1574), Piero della Francesca once drew a vase

> on a system of squares, showing the mouth and base
> from the front, the back, and from the sides; in this
> amazing piece of work he drew every little detail with
> great subtlety, foreshortening in a very graceful way
> the curves of all the circles.[30]

Thus, in certain respect Piero can be regarded as a forerunner of modern cubism. The Renaissance characters who were most engaged in the study of perspective were not mathematicians in the modern sense of the term but artists, humanists aspiring to become universal men. It is noteworthy that Vasari, himself a painter, was aware of the fact that the artist should use mathematics with caution. Describing the life of the great Florentine painter Paolo Uccello, he warns:

> Artists who devote more attention to perspective than
> to figures develop a dry and angular style because of
> their anxiety to examine things too minutely; and,
> moreover, they usually end up solitary, eccentric,
> melancholy, and poor, as indeed did Paolo Uccello
> himself.[31]

In 1912 the cubist painters Albert Gleizes and Jean Metzinger pointed out that their aim was to investigate pictorial form and the space which it generates. However, the painter's space should not be confused with pure Euclidean visual space. "If we wished to tie the painter's space to a particular geometry, we should have to refer it to the non-Euclidean scientists, we should have to study at some length of Riemann's theorems", they said. For, visual space results from the harmony of the sensations of convergence and accommodation of the eye. For the picture, a flat surface, the accommodation is negative. Therefore the convergence which perspective teaches us to simulate cannot evoke the idea of depth.[32]

The Danish physicist Niels Bohr was fascinated with modern painting. In his personal collection of modern art Metzinger's "Lady with a Horse" occupied a central place. Bohr explained that he liked the cubist painting "because it defied all the laws of mathematics."[33]

Since I was interested to find out what did Bohr mean by saying that Metzinger's work defied all the laws of mathematics, I posed the question to Aage Bohr and V.F. Weisskopf. They both had intimate familiarity with Bohr's thought and with the Metzinger painting. According to Dr. Aage Bohr, his father "appreciated that the painting could create illusions in, for example, giving the impression that planes were intersecting in a manner that is impossible in the real world."[34]

Dr. V.F. Weisskopf expressed a similar view.

Now, the interesting thing is that, writing on "Art and Science", Weisskopf mentions a conversation which took place between Felix Bloch and Werner Heisenberg that contradicts his and Aage Bohr's opinion alike:

Bloch was reporting to Heisenberg some new ideas about the relevance of certain mathematical structures of space when Heisenberg, his mind drifting into other avenues of experience, exclaimed, 'Space is blue and birds are flying in it!'[35]

Heisenberg's reaction is in fact a statement which implies a conceptual flip-flop, a gestalt-like figure-ground shift. The figure below illustrates the flip-flop analogue through the figure-ground change of the pedestal into two faces in profile, and vice versa:

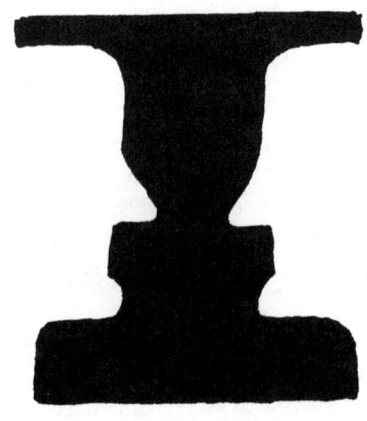

The conceptual flip-flop itself lies in an epistemological fallacy. For, in the Bohr-Weisskopf interpretation of the Metzinger painting, this non-objective work defies the laws of mathematics, because it views mathematics as a discipline which represents the laws of nature. In Heisenberg's exclamation, however, a polar opinion is incorporated to the effect that mathematics is an abstraction which does not conform to reality.

This is in accordance with the notion advocated by Bertrand Russell, A.N. Whitehead and John G. Kemeny that mathematics is not a study of the world and that mathematical propositions are not factual. Instead, these mathematicians view their discipline as an analytical study of relationships, a form of highly developed logic entirely devoid of subject matter whose protagonists are integers.[36]

Contemporary art shares with mathematics a great deal of specific properties. Similarly to mathematics, painting is also a semiotic system, a particular universe of symbols. Modern art has given up the idea of mimesis. It does not imitate reality but renders it. Like pure mathematics, abstract art is also a study of form devoid of subject matter. In pure abstraction form and content unite. Thus, the form of a musical composition or the form of an abstract painting (its shapes, colors, texture and composition) are their contents.

The human mind is both mathematical and poetic. Its dual function can be reduced to one single quality: It is metaphorical. Man is a symbol making being. I think that there are amazing poetic traits in mathematics that find their expression in perplexing dimensions, in the mystery of numbers, in lacy structures, in the dialectics of complexity and simplicity, in the elegance of the mathematical theorem and in the beauty of its proof. The mathematical intuition of infinity is a poetic idea without empirical evidence. Obviously, not even with the help of all the computers in the world we can keep count to reach the edges of unlimited limits.

On the other hand, art is not pure poetry either. It has its own inherent logic. Both the mathematician and the painter are immersed in the study and exploration of analogies. These are similar or isomorphic relations which the painter and the mathematician express in symbols. A mathematical statement which says in symbols that A:Z is the same as the relation B:Y, is comparable with the relationship of a house and a tree depicted on the canvas as a picture of a house and a tree.

But I would like to illustrate the difference between artistic and mathematical logic. Their *plane* of departure can be shown through the analogy of two different airports: mathematics and concrete poetry.

Concrete poetry, of course, is not the antonym of abstract poetry. In any case it is a field of intriguing artistic activity which is based on the ancient pictographic principle of the unity of the idea and the image. My concrete poem entitled "The Plane", attempts to show the break up of the common logical infrastructure of mathematics and art:

$$IO \quad = \quad I+I+I+I+I+I+I+I+I$$

$$I+O \quad = \quad I$$

$$I+O \quad = \quad \text{✈}$$

At the moment of the take off, the plane enters a new universe of symbols. The three equations incorporated in the concrete poem are all valid. The third equation which says: I + O = airplane, is not valid mathematically because it violates the established rules of arithmetic symbols. However, in terms of visual logic the equation is correct.

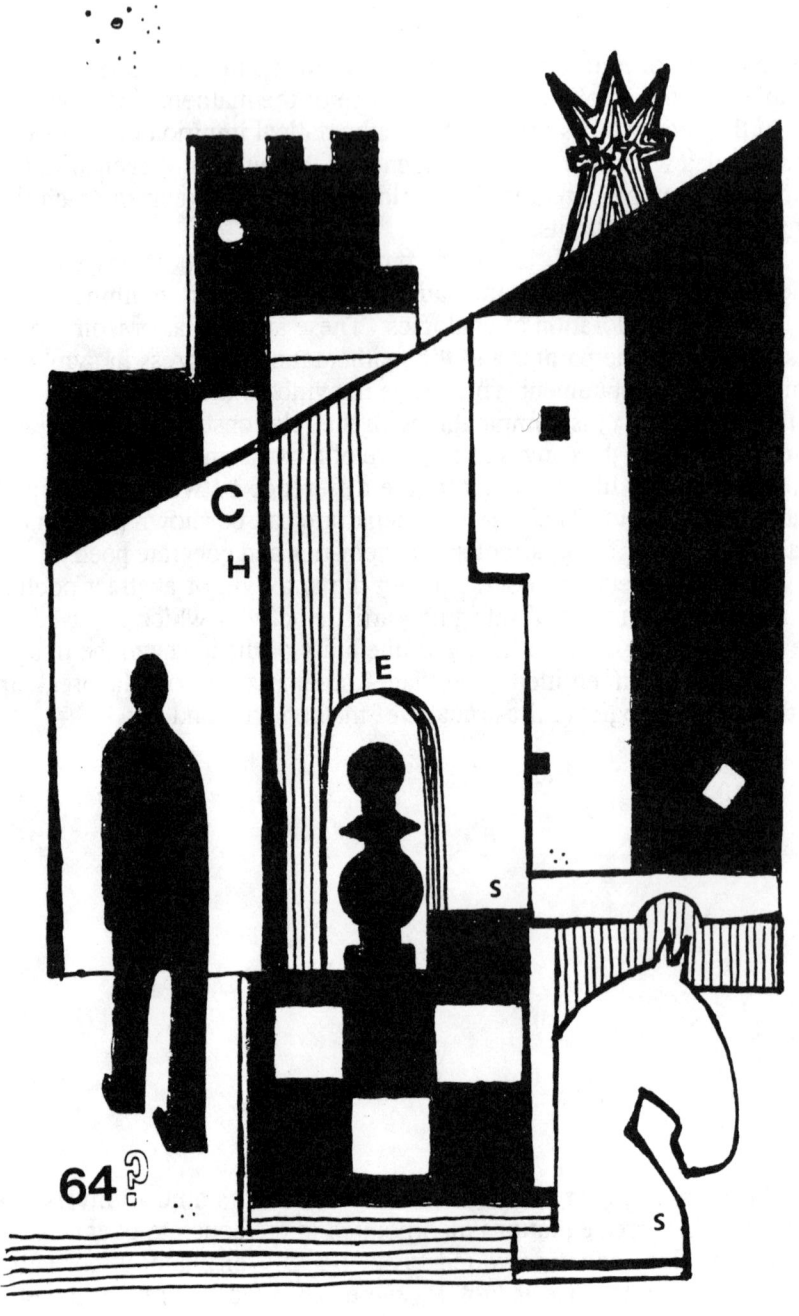

CHESS: 64?

A geometrical composition based on an oil painting of 1977. The array
of personal and collective symbols is structured in non-Euclidean space.

70

A Voyage To Dürer And Back
Along The Fibonaccian Spiral

Artists use mathematics both as a device to aid composition and as a choice of subject matter. This can be seen quite clearly in the work of the great German artist Albrecht Dürer (1471-1528). Beyond his artistic genius and outstanding technical skills he was also an original thinker who contributed to the development of geometry and established a school of anthropomorphic science. He had also authored theoretical treatises on the laws of perspective and on human proportions.

In 1495 Dürer travelled to Italy, absorbed the spirit of the Southern Renaissance and came to the conclusion that geometry was the right foundation of all painting. In his theoretical writings the German artist wrote on polygons, discussed the five regular Platonic solids, the seven Archimedean solids, and invented some of his own. He is also credited with the invention of the limaçon, or the snail curve. His fascinating tiling patterns in the shape of the pentagon aroused Galileo's imagination.

Dürer's work had an impact on Kepler's scientific thought as well. Following the method of the Greek geometer Apollonius, he demonstrated that the plane sections of a circular cone are ellipses, paraboles and hyperbolas. Although the method is theoretically correct, a minor slip of the ruler or the compass can result, e.g., in an egg-shaped ellipse.[37] Indeed, this is probably what happened when the artist constructed the ellipse, and he ended up with an egg-shaped image.[*] In contrast to the egg-shaped ellipse, a true ellipse has two axes of symmetry. The method that Dürer used harbingered the procedure of Cartesian analytical geometry. A century later Johannes Kepler (1571-1630) was in fact quite fascinated by the implications of Dürer's geometrical accomplishment, yet perplexed to a considerable extent by the egg-shaped ellipse. As it turned out, it was Kepler who discovered that the orbits of the planets in the solar system are ellipses.

During the Renaissance many artists shared the belief that the proportions of the human body represented the visual materialization of musical harmony. Renaissance theoreticians built mathematical systems to quantify theproportions of the human anatomy in accordance with geometrical and arithmetical codes. These mathematical systems

---

[*] See page 73.

were specifically bound up with the divine proportion or the golden section to which Plato assigned supernatural importance. It is probably within the bounds of truth to say that the Pythagoreans, who asserted that all phenomena may be reduced to numerical relations, were familiar with the golden section (AB cut at C, so that CB: AC = AC: AB).

At the beginning of his artistic career Dürer approached the anatomical proportions of man with a planimetrical scheme similar to that used by Villard de Honnecourt in the thirteenth century. Under Alberti's and Leonardo da Vinci's influence, however, he abandoned the planimetrical method, and improved further Alberti's modular system in which the smallest unit was 1/600. Yet eventually Dürer came to the conclusion that there is no one ideal canon of beauty. He opposed the impositions of mathematical constraints upon the creative process, including the application of geometrical or arithmetical canons to the representation of the human body. As an ardent and profound learner of aesthetic systems Dürer collected twenty six different systems of anatomical canons and laid down the foundations for the taxonomy of human proportions.

Dürer extended the scope and range of his subject matter to the realm of mathematics. His master print *Melancolia I* [38] is heavily loaded with mathematical symbols. This engraving appears to be an allegory on creativity and the condition of the artist. A winged contemplating muse is seated in the foreground holding a compass. The radiating light in the background illuminates under a rain-bow like arc the word Melencolia (I). An irregular geometrical solid hides part of a ladder leaning on a wall of a section of a building. By the side of a pair of scales, in the company of a bell and an hour-glass, a magic square is displayed:

16	3	2	13
5	10	11	8
9	6	7	12
4	15	14	1

The two middle numbers of the bottom line date the picture: 1514. The sum total of each horizontal and vertical line is 34. The integers 3 and 4, as well as their added sum (7) have been charged with astrological and magical meanings. T. Lynch has suggested that in fact the magic square was the clue to the irregular solid in Dürer's composition, which he found to be an optical illusion. In my opinion, since the visible sides of the solid are pentagonal, it is intrinsically related to the golden

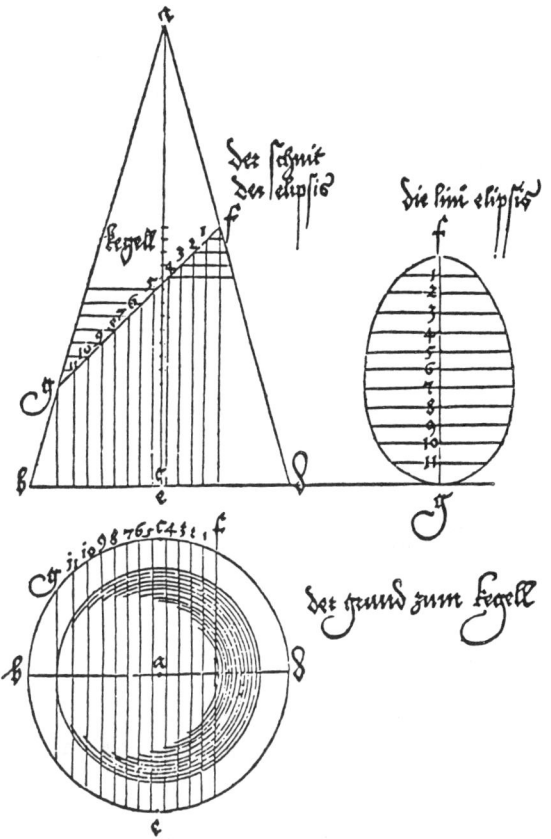

Above: Dürer's egg-shaped ellipse
Below: A method described by Dürer to draw in perspective.
The eye of the artist is fixed by a device, and a frame divided into
squares is placed between him and the model.

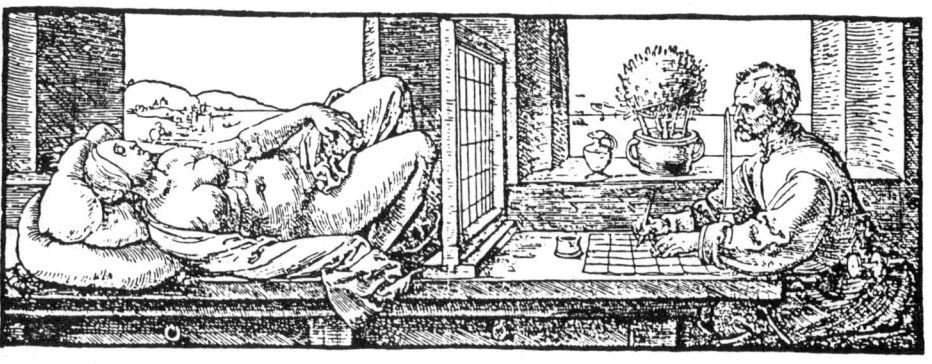

73

section, an extraordinary aesthetic proportion which mediates between art, mathematics and nature. In any case, Lynch is probably right that Dürer's message in *Melencolia I* was, "Put your faith in Heaven for nothing on earth can be trusted to be what it seems." [39] Among the numerous personal metaphors that the artists employed in his enigmatic picture, the Quadrivium (arithmetic, astronomy, geometry, music) is symbolized by the magic square, the hour glass, the compass and the bell.

Another Renaissance artist, Jacopo de Barbari also used mathematics as his subject matter. He was a German-Italian painter whom Dürer met during his sojourn in Venice. In a portrait of the famous Italian mathematician Fra Luca Pacioli which Jacopo painted, a dodecahedron and a display of a semi-regular Archimedean solid appear on the table in the foreground. The image includes a large polyhedron which seems to float in the air.

Both Pacioli and de Barbari were active in Venice. Pacioli was probably a student of the artist and mathematician Pietro Franceschi.[40] He revealed immense interest in painting throughout his life, and Leonardo da Vinci was a friend of him. In 1509 appeared Pacioli's book on the golden section, the *Divina Proportione* in which the drawings are attributed to Leonardo da Vinci.

The golden section is an irrational proportion. It was regarded to possess intrinsic aesthetic qualities, some hidden harmony in tune with the cosmic mathematical infrastructure of the universe. In a rectangle constructed according to the divine proportion the width should be 0.6180 of the length.

Four hundred years after the publication of Pacioli's book on the golden ration, Sir Theodore Andrea Cook argued in *The Curves of Life* (1914) that in fact it is this irrational ratio "what we call Beauty both in a natural object and in a masterpiece of art."[41]

The golden section has cast its spell on modern artists as well. The *Section d'Or* cubists did not choose the title of their magazine by coincidence (whose one and only issue appeared in 1912). The theorists of synthetic cubism, Metzinger and Gleizes; young artists like Frank Kupka, Marcel Duchamp, Jacques Villon and Francis Picabia were all discussing eagerly the Nabis theories of ideal proportions and the exquisite beauty of geometric forms. In their attempt to depict the dynamism and richness of life, the harmonious proportions of the golden ratio played a substantial role.

Artists aided by modern technological devices continue to investigate and explore the inexhaustible aspects of the divine

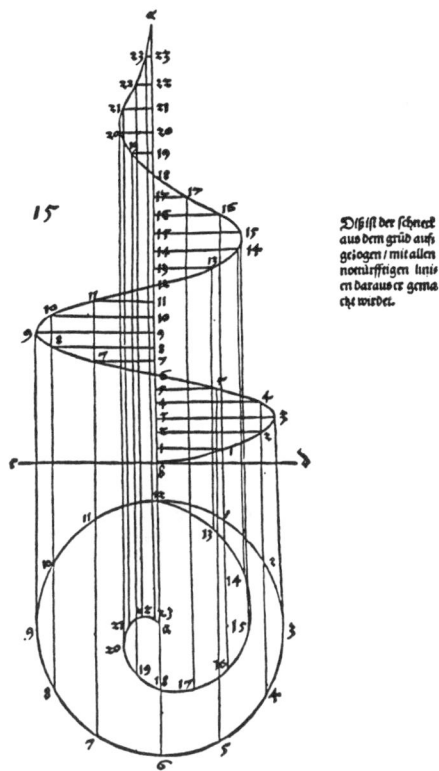

Diß ist der schneck
aus dem grüd auß
gezogen / mit allen
nottürfftigen linis
en daraus er gema
cht wirdet.

Above: Dürer's plan for making a conical helix from a flat spiral.
Below: Dürer's engraving from 1525 illustrates his invention for
drawing in perspective.

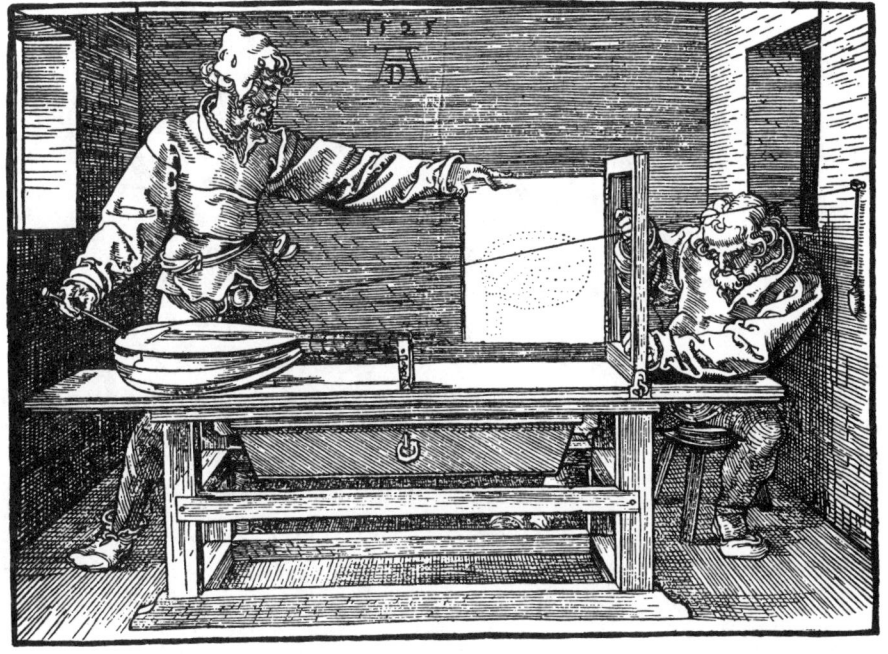

Fibonacci 1202
Mario Merz 1970

esplorazione di uno
spazio biologico

investigation of
biological space

abbandonare il progetto
di catturare coprire
e uccidere lo spazio

Abandon the project
of capturing
and killing space

↑ igloo
Fibonacci

la spirale incontra
la linea di direzione
ai punti indicati
dalla numerazione

the spiral meets
the line of direction
at the enumerated
points

Details from the conceptual work of the Italian artist Mario Merz, with comments in Italian and English explaining his Fibonacci Series project.
From: Ursula Meyer, *Conceptual Art* (New York, 1972).
Reprinted with permission.

proportion. The British artist and mathematician Robert Dixon, for instance, has studied the phyllotaxis -- the spiral leaf arrangements of plants – by computer aided graphics. He approached the study of flower forms as a study of the circle and golden ratio.[42]

The golden section is bound up with the geometrical progression discovered by the greatest medieval mathematician Leonardo Fibonacci. The mathematician of Pisa in the *Liber Abaci* , a book dealing with arithmetic and algebra which he authored in 1202, discussed as an example the imaginary breeding results of a group of rabbits. The sequence which he arrived at consists of these terms: 1, 1, 2, 3, 5, 8, 13, 21, 34, 55, 89, 144, 233, 377, 610, and so on. This implies that the n th term of the sequence can be expressed as $Q_n = Q_{n-1} + Q_{n-2}$; $Q_0 = 0$, $Q_1 = 1$

Thus, adding two neighboring numbers in the series, in the direction of its progress, will yield a subsequent term. An amazing property of the Fibonacci series is its built-in relationship to the golden ratio, to regular and star pentagons, as well as to the Pythagoras theorem and to trigonometry.[43]

The equations

$$Q = 1/2 (1 + \sqrt{5})$$

and

$$Q = 1/2 (\sqrt{5} - 1)$$

correspond to the numerical values of the golden section, which are respectively 1.6180339 and 0.6180339. In comparison, ratios between ensuing terms of the Fibonaccian geometrical progression approximate consecutively these numbers:

Subsequent numbers			
g	h	Ratios $\dfrac{g}{h}$	$\dfrac{h}{g}$
1	1	1.0	1.0
2	1	2.0	0.5
3	2	1.5	0.666666
5	3	1.666666	0.6
8	5	1.6	0.625
13	8	1.625	0.6153846
. . .	. . .	. . .	. . .
377	233	1.618025	0.618037

610	377	1.618037	0.618032
987	610	1.618032	0.618034
1597	987	1.607902	0.618033

and so on

The geometrical progression has exerted its influence on the contemporary art world. Mario Merz, for example is a conceptualist who has adopted the Fibonacci sequence as his aesthetic subject matter. Made of neon and wire, in 1970 the Italian artist presented a work, at the Sonnabend Gallery of New York, entitled "Relationship of Growth Within the Development of a Tree Outlined in an Unbroken Line According to the Fibonacci Series".

Merz operates with a conceptual framework founded on the assumption that numbers are an abstract human invention that constitute an environment. This artificial environment is not physical, although it can be counted. He has applied the Fibonacci series to the balcony of the Guggenheim museum in spiral tension, to the exuberant helical arch of Nuremberg Palace, and to other buildings. According to the artist, he superimposes the Fibonacci series upon architectural elements in order to enhance the visual presence and to generate increased tensions in the existing spatial environment. He believes that by counting numbers are transformed from abstract entities into concrete things.

To the question, "What is the Fibonacci series?", Merz replies:

> It is the proliferation of numbers. Numbers reproduce themselves like men, bees or rabbits. If they did not reproduce they would cease to exist. The numbers 1,2,3,4,5,6,7,8 and 9 are the enumeration of dead elements. Instead, the series is mathematics in expansion, that is to say living mathematics.[44]

It is noteworthy that conceptual art represents a radical break with the ideals of traditional aesthetics. Conceptualism in a sense is a manifestation of the continuity of the Dada spirit, a revival of Marcel Duchamp's readymade style. In conceptual art the idea becomes more

78

important than its effective visual presentation. Art descends from its cathartic height to the level of information sharing.

Aspects Of Infinity:
Leonardo, Cantor, And
The Immaterial Blue Of Yves Klein

The enigmatic idea of the infinite has excited the imagination of artists and poets throughout the ages. Its incomprehensible mystery stimulated mathematicians and scientists. Philosophers did not cease to ponder over its meaning. The Pythagorean philosopher Archytas, a friend of Plato, held that space was infinite. He challenged those who maintained the opposite view by urging them to explain why was it impossible to reach beyond the edge of the finite. The finite history of infinity contains speculations both over infinite series and infinite being.

Aristotle's conception of the infinite included the potential eternality of time and of being. He also said that potential infinity is incorporated within number series as the infinite of the process of addition and the process of divisibility. Centuries later Spinoza concluded that the material and spiritual attributes of existence were different aspects of one and the same reality. According to him the notion of the infinite is bound up with the meaning of the word God, because "by God, I mean a being absolutely infinite -- that is, a substance consisting in infinite attributes, of which each expresses eternal and infinite essentiality."[45]

The mathematical meaning of infinity can be brought into focus and defined as a quantity greater than any finite quantity. It is meaningful to say that the set of integers 1, 2, 3, 4, . . . n, tends to infinity since there is always an (n+1) which is greater than it. Infinity as limit has also definite meaning, like in the eqation $f(x) = 1/x$, in which $f(x)$ tends to infinity as x tends to zero. However, there are mathematical aspects in the theory of infinity which render the discipline into an ambivalent whole. In advanced set theory, for instance, transfinite cardinal numbers may have a plurality of meaning. Plurality of meanings, of course, is not limited in mathematics to the realm of infinity. This can be demonstrated by the fact that it is possible, for instance, to multiply by zero, whereas to divide by zero is a mathematical tabu. This inconsistency is frequently taken for granted, notwithstanding that zero is a number.

Long before Newton and Leibniz invented the calculus, it was already known that the part contains the whole. The invention of holography by D. Gabor in 1948 provided empirical evidence to this amazing conception of reality which obviously contradicts our intuition. Yet the hologram, which reconstructs an observed scene three dimensionally by means of interference patterns between waves illuminated by lasers, is indeed based on the philosophical principle that the part contains the whole.

Leonardo da Vinci (1452-1519), perhaps the most salient creative genius of the Italian Renaissance, represents the prototype of the ideal universal man of the late Middle Ages. For a certain period of his life he was so overwhelmed by the mathematical impulse that he abandoned painting. In his *Notebooks* , Leonardo stipulated not to let anyone who is not a mathematician to read the elements of his work.

However, Leonardo was not a great mathematician. For his part mathematics was a fundamental instrument to provide proof for scientific observation. In the beginning the artist shared with other Florentine painters the Pythagorean idea that harmony could be expressed through numbers. He clung to the almost religious belief that it was absolutely necessary to apply mathematics to science in order to reach certainty. But this absolute faith in mathematics had been shattered in later years.[46]

As a profound observer of appearances, Leonardo gradually came to the cogent conclusion that everything in the world was in a dynamic process of flux. So, to give plastic expression to the continuity of reality the artist also must portray the world in its flux. Leonardo's outstanding artistic achievement had been crystallized into such masterpieces as *The Last Supper* (1497), *The Virgin of the Rocks* (c.1506-8), and *The Mona Lisa* (1503). In these and other paintings the artist aimed to establish the coalescent point of grace and beauty.

Nevertheless, in the latter part of his life, Leonardo concluded that the perennial continuity of existence could not be portrayed by static mathematical means. His series of drawings on the theme of the Deluge (1514) reflects the artist's changed attitude with regard to the mathematical underpinning of the world. In the images, entropy has its upper hand, order disappears and chaos asserts itself in amorphous form.

Leonardo developed an interest in the problem of the infinite as part of his quest for absolute certainty. He approached this mathematical problem too as an aesthetic problem, as a specific issue related to the general theory of perspective. "All the problems of Perspective are made clear by the five terms of mathematics which are the point, the line, the angle, the surface and the solid", he wrote. And a point is not part of a line. The smallest natural point is larger than all mathematical points, and this is proved because the natural point has continuity, and anything that is continuous is infinitely divisible; but the mathematical point is indivisible because it has not size ... If one single point placed in a circle may be the starting point of an infinite number of lines, and the termination of an infinite number of lines, there must be an infinite number of points separate from this point, and these, when reunited, become one again, whence it follows that the part may be equal to the whole.[47]

Thus, Leonardo contradicted Euclid's axiom that the whole is greater than any one of its parts. The artist had asserted that an infinite set of lines can pass through a point simultaneously.

In historical hindsight it is possible to talk about Leonardo's contribution to the modern mathematical theory of the infinite founded by Georg Cantor. Galileo Galilei (1564-1642) is credited with the first clear formulation of the mathematical paradox of infinite sets which Cantor[48] developed into transfinite arithmetics. Leonardo's own important contribution to the mathematical development of Galileo, his crucial role in the rise and evolution of advanced arithmetic thought has been ignored.

Galileo was not only a great pioneer of science but also an accomplished painter and musician. He devoted part of his intellectual energy to the solution of the problem of infinity. He noted that every integer n can be brought into a one to one corresponding relationship with their doubles 2n. Here is a sample of this kind of pairing:

1	2	3	4	5	6	7	8	9	... n
2	4	6	8	10	12	14	16	18	... 2n

The pairing of the regular set of integers with even numbers results in a paradox which contradicts our intuition. There seem to be as many even integers as the whole set of integers, yet at the same time there are obviously more integers than just even integers.

You cannot "hope to reach infinity", wrote Galileo, "by passing from large numbers to other successively larger and larger". For,

all the numerals that have been written up to now by all the calculators in the world, laid end to end, would

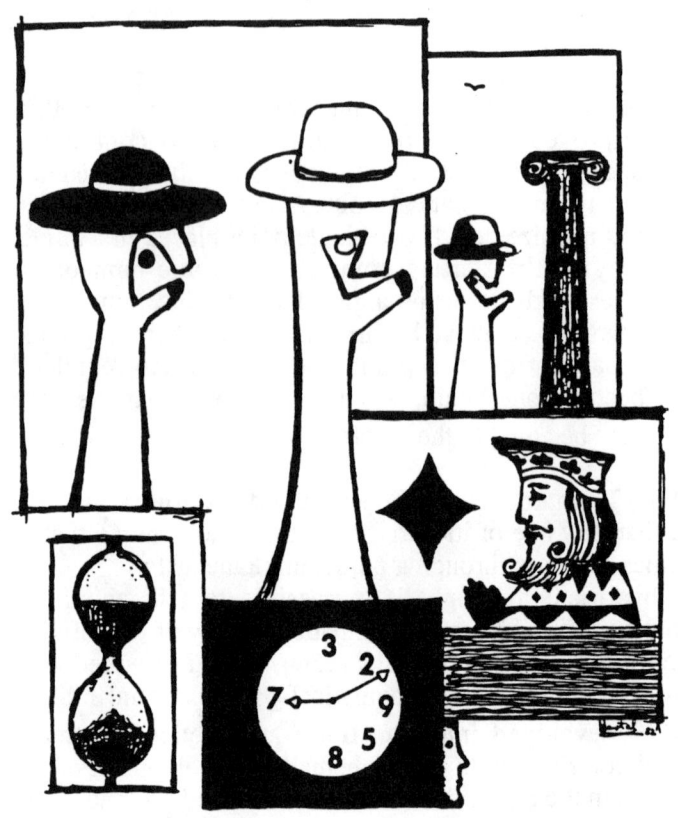

COLUMNS WITH BERGSONIAN CLOCK

ink on paper, 1982.

The confused numbers of the clock symbolize the arbitrary progression of psychological events in the stream of consciousness. Memories, for instance, can surface in an associative manner without any real correspondence to chronological order. An actual clock is an analogical machine which spatializes temporal segments of the fluid cosmic womb of existence.

The three 'columns' with the hats are anthropomorphic figures which can be seen as grotesque faces and also as hands. Perception remains ambiguous, for the mind is undecided with regard to the exact nature of these images. An analogous situation exists in the domain of transfinite sets. The mathematical fact, for example, that there are just as many even numbers as the whole set of integers, is contradicted by our intuition, and the mind cannot finalize and reconcile the ambiguity of the paradox.

yield a number that is no closer to infinity than is 3, or 7, or any other particular number.[49]

It is possible to demonstrate geometrically that the number of points on a line one centimeter long, for instance, is equal to the number of points to be found on a line which is a thousand times longer. It is also possible to prove "that there are in all time as many years as there are days."[50] This, in my opinion, is a poetic conjecture, a mathematical allegory, since there is no way to validate it empirically. Substantiation of the metaphor would necessitate eternal life.

Georg Cantor (1845-1918) himself was born in St. Petersburg into a family of painters and musicians. His mathematical breakthrough in the domain of infinite sets represents a triumphal landmark in intellectual history. It is bound up with the accomplishments of Leonardo and Galileo (as well as of others). However, it was not Galileo who got rid of the intellectual restrictions inherent in Euclid's system but Leonardo. In fact, the founder of modern transfinite arithmetics, Cantor, had returned to Leonardo's non-Euclidean conception of the infinite: The whole as an infinite set is not greater than the part. Although Galileo knew that the part maintains the whole, he could not reconcile his arithmetic findings with Euclid's axiom that the whole is greater than the part.

The theme of infinity as aesthetic subject matter crops up in the works of many contemporary artists. The Dutch M.C. Escher (1898-1972) is well known for his mathematically oriented oeuvre. In order to overcome the natural limitations imposed upon the artist in his impossible quest of representing the infinite -- "no one can draw a line that is not a boundary line; every line splits a singularity into a plurality"[51] --Escher resorted to the visualization of such mathematical concepts as the Limit and the Möbius Strip. In 1963, e.g., the artist produced a woodcut in red, black and gray-green showing a Möbius Strip. On this visual topological image eight red ants crawl along, demonstrating the one-sidedness of the device.

Interestingly enough, Gary Stephen contends that "Escher is reflexively dismissed by artists." According to him the Dutch graphic artist is too aloof, his detached viewpoint of existence is extremely impersonal, "he leaves no poetic ends", and his work is guilty of "systematic disorientation."[52] The trouble with Stephen's criticism, in my opinion, lies in the fact that his poetic counterpoint -- abstract art -- is the product of the same human condition which created Escher's art. Abstract art is a symbol of human alienation, and it is guilty of disorientation as well. Besides, numerous works by Escher can be seen as minimalist and constructivist abstractions with the same potential amount of poetry as similar works might have in this category.

Following World War II, the American color field painter Barnett Newman (1905-1970) embarked for his mystic voyage to the absolute. Aided by the chromatic experience of abstract expressionism, Newman wanted "to wrest truth from the void", and "to dig into metaphysical secrets."[53] His huge, over-sized canvases were meant to signify continuity beyond the field of vision and carried the artist's conscious aspiration to express the idea of infinite space. Space for Newman was the boundless primordial container of chaotic form, the Cabalistic envelope of the eternal mystery of life and death.

On the other side of the Atlantic, Yves Klein was preoccupied with the enigma of the infinite. Despite his short life (he died in 1962 at the age of 34), Klein was an enormously influential self-taught artist. His monochrome canvases represented complex symbols that were intertwined with the immeasurable and the absolute. He wanted to create works made of pure spirit and mind. His uniformly applied blue paintings were metamorphosed in 1958 into a bizarre exhibition held at the Galerie Iris Clert in Paris.

The exhibition consisted of pure empty space: *The Void* ; and was painted in immaterial blue and without any actual pictorial images. "Pictures are merely the 'ashes' of art", Klein explained. "The authentic quality of a picture, its 'being' itself, once created, is found beyond the visible."[54]

The artist's exhibition of the infinite intangible reality was presented as "The Pictorial Material Sensibility in the State of Prime Matter". The bizarre rituals of the show included blue invitations, blue cocktails, and two republican guards in official uniform. The event took place in a small building of about one hundred feet square but was attended by two thousand visitors. Klein sold two immaterial 'works' from the exhibition in exchange of one kilogram gold for each.

The work of the French mathematician Benoit B. Mandelbrot, the inventor of fractal geometry, is concerned with both art and infinity. He claims that by statistical means and by computer graphics he has solved the mathematical problem of imposing geometrical order on the morphology of the amorphous, which centuries ago was a source of despair for Leonardo da Vinci. Fractal geometry concerns the wiggles or fractals of the infinitely small and the infinitely big alike. A coastline for example, unlike on the map -- which is a gross abstraction -- is an infinitely long formation. However, according to Mandelbrot, by his method both the infinite wiggles of coastlines and the turbulances of Leonardo's "Deluge" can be handled. Mandelbrot regards fractal geometry also as a new form of geometric art.[55]

van   ishingpoi   ntvani   shin   gpoin

v   anishingpoi   ntvanish   ingpo   i

vanishingpointv   anishingp   ointva   n

vanishingpoin   tvanishingpo   intvani s

VANISHINGP   OINTVANISHINGP   OINTVA

VANISHIN   GPOINTVANISHINGPOI   NT

VANISHING POINT

A visual experiment in generating the illusion of three dimensional spatial perception on a two dimensional surface by the combination of words and dots.

Illusion And Paradox

A painting referring to visual space is always an illusion and a paradox. Psychologists distinguish between illusions, hallucinations and delusions. Illusions are distorted or mistaken perceptions caused by the falsification of stimulus patterns. In contrast to them, hallucinations are false perceptions, whereas delusions are mistaken beliefs. A painting referring to visual space is always an illusion because its message is communicated by the distortion of perception. At the same time it is also a paradox because the illusion of three dimensional space is represented on a two dimensional surface.

Euclid in the *Optics* already paid some attention to the geometrical aspects of the illusion of perspective. Roman wall paintings, at Pompeii for instance, had created the illusion of reality and depth. However, Roman artists achieved the illusion of realism rather by the manipulation of the techniques of aerial perspective than by the geometrical treatment of spatial recession. The illusion of reality achieved its trompe l'oeil stage only later when Renaissance and Baroque masters developed detailed geometrical systems of linear perspective and of color.

The inherent illusionism of art is a dialectic property which can bring us a step closer to the stage of recognizing truth. I think that the apprehension of this has contributed to the increased interest that mathematicians, computer scientists, investigators of artificial intelligence, psychologists and brain researchers reveal in art, especially in modern art.

Consciousness provides an essential link between mathematics and the visual arts. This can be seen through the analogue that I have found between the paradox of transfinite sets and *Columns with Bergsonian Clock*, an ink on paper drawing which I made in the year of 1982.[*] This planimetrically conceived work is structured in non-Euclidean space. Its cluster of personal symbols includes three strange hat wearing columns. These three anthropomorphic columns can be perceived either as bizarre heads or as hands trying to catch a little ball. Perception of the exact nature of these outlandish creatures is blocked by ambiguity. The brain is confounded in its attempt to interpret the visual message delivered to it by the eye and by the optical nerve. The optical illusion that the image arouses is intellectually stimulating: It is an experience of the voyage of consciousness to the gates of the unknown. At the same time the image can be also disappointing for

---

[*] See page 82.

certain people, because it fails to satisfy the human need for assurance and understanding.

An analogous situation exists in the realm of the arithmetic of infinite sets. Similarly to Newton, who said that he saw further than others because he stood on the shoulders of giants, Georg Cantor relied on the work of predecessors, such as Leonardo and Galileo, in developing the mathematics of infinity. It is an arithmetical fact that since the whole transfinite set of integers can be brought into a one to one pairing relationship with the whole infinite set of even numbers, their respective sums are equal. In other words, the set of even numbers is just as big as the set of integers. Their conceptual paradox transcends the limits of understanding, because the mathematical fact is contradicted by the intuitive determinants of comprehension. The mind is baffled by the apparent contradiction. It cannot dissolve the ambiguity built into the paradox, and fails to satisfy our need for certitude and clarity.

The Italian mathematician Michele Emmer rather recently produced two films on the works of M.C. Escher and Max Bill. They deal with the illusionary images of the Dutch graphic artist as well as with the Swiss sculptor's plastic interpretation of the Möbius band, respectively.

According to the Canadian mathematician H.S.M. Coxeter, Escher's genius anticipated many of the results of a group of Russian scientists who in the 1950s combined the systematic repetition of colors with the systematic repetition of shapes in order to extend the theory of crystallographic groups. According to Emmer, Escher constructed mathematical theories founded on the integration of intuition and the empirical method.[56]

Emmer also discussed the existing connections between geometrical abstraction -- the grid-like patterns of Piet Mondrian -- and mathematics. At a debate conference held under the auspices of the University of Edinburgh in 1981 (where he presented the above mentioned films), Emmer said that some of Escher's prints utilize impossible objects, optical illusions devised by L.S. and R. Penrose in 1958.

One of these lithograph, *Belvedere* features a series of striking optical illusions. A ladder appearing in the picture, for example, is drawn in a spatial position which is thoroughly absurd, nevertheless it looks normal. This ladder touches with its top the outer wall of the upper floor as expected, yet it stands with its base inside the house. Emmer suggests that Escher designed this print in 1958, before he saw the impossible object described by the Penroses in *The British Journal of Psychology*.

However, it is important to remember that optical illusions are not a new phenomenon in art history. Escher was an ardent student of the aesthetic legacy of the past and he had investigated the visual morphology of various cultures in the East and West alike. He also copied the masterpieces of such great masters as Albrecht Dürer and Hieronymus Bosch. There is no particular reason to believe that he was not familiar with the intriguing and popular work of the British satirist and comic artist of genius: William Hogarth (1697-1764). Thus, Hogarth's etching, *Frontispiece to Kerby*, widely reproduced in textbooks on perspective and elsewhere, must have been known to Escher. It is drawn in absolutely baffling perspective, and utilizes the optical illusion of impossible objects in a series of visual paradoxes as part of the composition.

Conclusion

Artists use mathematics as a device to aid pictorial composition and as a choice of subject matter. Research into the interface-dynamics of mathematics and the visual arts allows deeper understanding of their common problems. It also enhances multi-disciplinary crossfertilization and interaction between distinct domains.

The human mind is both mathematical and poetic: Its essential modus operandi is metaphorical. Beyond the division of mathematics into pure and applied fields, and the parallel division of the visual arts into fine art and commercial art, the common goal of the mathematician and the artist is to impose order on the apparent amorphousness of existence. Both mathematics and painting are invented worlds, semiotic attempts to structure reality by way of symbols. The mathematical universe is not closer to actuality than the metaphorical cosmos of the painted canvas.

The mathematician and the painter alike deal with analogies, with isomorphic and palindromic relations, with equations and paradoxes. Mathematics, as far as it is a domain of highly developed logic, resembles abstract art, because the latter is also a study of form devoid of subject matter.

Painting can be viewed as an endeavor concerned with the poetic and logical qualities of visualized consciousness, whereas mathematics is a study concerned with the logical and poetic qualities of quantities. The attribution of poetic traits to mathematics is based on the fact that concepts like infinity, the null-graph, imaginary and surrealist numbers are non-empirical conjectures.

Intuition as the pivotal underpinning of the creative process provides an infrastructural theoretical bridge for the investigation of the common denominators of art and mathematics. The painter and the mathematician alike are concerned with aesthetics. The similarities and the differences between the semiotic sets and the metaphorical tools utilized by the mathematician and the painter form an additional aspect for inter-disciplinary investigation. Obviously there are also enormous level intervals and disparities between mathematics and painting, which in McLuhanian terms boil down to the observation that 'the medium is the message'.

Chapter Three
VISUAL PERCEPTION AND PAINTING

Despite the fact that art offers an extraordinarily rich reservoir of imagery, its scientific investigation is an underdeveloped field. Yet it can easily lend itself to interdisciplinary studies in many areas. The discipline of psychology appears to be unrivalled in this respect. The issues of aesthetics and of psychology are cogently intertwined. Since art is a thing of the mind, its scientific study is always concerned with psychology.[1]

When in the 1950s the art historian E.H. Gombrich visited the gestalt psychologist Wolfgang Köhler at Princeton, the latter reassured him "that the complex questions encountered in the practice of art are still of potential interest to psychological research".[2] In the 1980s the psychology of arts continues to lag behind the psychology of other fields. The reasons for this situation are related to the unfamiliarity of most psychologists with the art world, and to the widespread belief that the arts do not lend themselves to the rigours of empirical investigation.[3]

The cardinal common denominator of art and psychology is located in the domain of perception. Art as a perceptual process is a mystery. The magical transformation of forms and colors into a recognizable image of things beyond themselves is an alchemical marvel. The process of perception, its relationship to reality (that is to say to the external world) always fascinated the artist. The history of art can be written in terms of aesthetic perception. Of course, the artist cannot transcribe what he perceives. Instead, he translates what he sees into the terms of his medium.

From the point of view of the art historian, a pivotal question is why does style change? The problem of style is tied to the problem of perception. What is the explanation to the fact that throughout the ages different nations depicted the world around us in so different ways? The history of art becomes possible as a result of transcendence. The personal vision of the artist is transcended at some point and evolves into a communal expression.

The relationship between seeing and knowing is a central issue in art. Since the paleolithic age artists relied on their knowledge in order to represent the world in their art. The impressionist movement that emerged in France in the nineteenth century was perhaps the first attempt to separate seeing from knowing. The impressionist painters believed that it was possible to record their retinal images on the canvas as pure sensory perceptions devoid of all cognitive content. The subsequent collapse of representation in art is bound up to a considerable extent with the impressionist approach to visual perception.

It is noteworthy that Pliny the Elder in his *Natural History* , a work authored in the first century, already observed that

> the mind is the real instrument of sight and observation, the eyes act as a sort of vessel receiving and transmitting the visible portion of the consciousness.[4]

A similar view was expressed by the Arab philosopher Alhazen in the eleventh century, who asserted that in the process of perception sensation, knowledge and inference are intertwined.[5]

The neo-Kantian philosopher and scientist Hermann von Helmholtz (1821-1894) claimed that the effortless and direct nature of perception was only an illusory feeling. The senses provide to the organism inaccurate and ambiguous data. Thus, perceptions rely on indefinite sources of information, and consequently they must be structured into hypotheses by the mind. The ambiguous input of information is supplemented by the perceiver and evolves into an intuitive, unconscious guesswork.[6]

The German neo-classical sculptor Adolf Hildebrand incorporated Helmholtz's constructivist theory of perception into the body of his writings concerning art. His book, *The Problem of Form in the Figurative Arts* (1893) attacked the epistemological infrastructure of the impressionist aspiration to disentangle seeing from knowing. The most influential English critic of the Victorian period, John Ruskin (1819-1900), defended in *Modern Painters* Turner's controversial style, and postulated that the painter's aim was to return to the unadulterated truth of natural optics. Two decades before Hildebrand's book came out, Ruskin summed up his aesthetic principles in *The Eagle's Nest* (1872). The artist's aim, said Ruskin, ought to first "represent visual appearances only, never memory knowledge."[7] It was this philosophy of art which allied him with the French impressionists, although he was not aware of the link that had been established.

The French sculptor Auguste Rodin (1840-1917) stressed that "the only principle in art is to copy what you see",[8] And the painter Claude Monet (1840-1926) advised that "when you go out to paint, try to forget what object you have before you, a tree, a house, a field, or whatever." According to him all that the painter has to do is to think: "here is a little square of blue, here an oblong of pink, here a streak of yellow, and paint it just as it looks", the exact shape and color, until an impression of the scene emerges.[9]

Sir Herbert Read suggests that painting before Paul Cézanne (1839-1906) was characterized by architectonic composition. Pictorial space was conceived in terms of balance and symmetry. The artist planned the composition as an architect plans and organizes a blueprint. Painters used a priori principles, preconceived patterns such as perspective and elevation, in order to structure their compositions. But these preconceived patterns are not authentic external stimuli of the perceptual process. They are superimposed artificial conceptual schemes. A landscape by Cézanne on the other hand has nothing to do with intellectual preconceptions. A Cézanne is the result of composition based on the direct contact of eye and nature. As a gestalt its "'composition' is determined by what happens 'in the eye' -- the automatic selection of a focal point, limitation of boundaries, subordination of details and colours to the law of the whole."[10]

These representational aesthetic theories run contrary to the constructivist conception of perception. In *The Problem of Form in the Figurative Arts* Hildebrand asserted that the task of the artist is to impose tactile values on his retinal impressions. There is no escape from memories and from prior experience. Since a sphere, for instance, appears on the retina merely as an image of a flat disc, vision must consequently rely on memories of movement and of touch in order to perceive it three dimensionally. The artist cannot eliminate prior knowledge ingrained deeply into the human memory through experience. Without this prior knowledge the perception of the world would be impossible at all. The response of the organism to external stimuli involves processing by autogenic factors.

From a point of view of perceptual psychology it is not clear at all how an attenuated representational image of reality can convey so convincingly its visual message. For images are always attenuated. After all, the artist always abstracts: Objects have less properties in the picture than in actuality. A tree depicted on the canvas does not have all its leaves of its crown, the grass does not contain all the blades that real grass contains and the light of the sun is much brighter than the painter's brightest colors. And these are not the only limitations of the painted image in comparison to actuality. The most paradoxical property of painting is that on a two-dimensional surface it depicts a three-dimensional world. We cannot walk around the objects represented on the canvas. Their colors, texture and scale are also different from reality.

An additional paradoxical trait of pictorial information is concerned with the binocular cue. The binocular cue is a depth signal. The separation of the two human eyes involves disparity in visual angle formation when viewing of a single object takes place. When the eyes are focusing at a farther object they converge at a smaller angle than when they look at an object at a nearer distance. Unlike in the three-dimensional visual world, on the flat surface of a realistic painting the objects of the background and those of the foreground are perched on the same equidistant two-dimensional plane. Nevertheless, the spectator is ready to be taken in by the optical illusion; and despite the fact that the binocular cue is set aside binocular perception is working: The painting is seen as a three-dimensional scene.

Another visual paradox involves the depth cue of motion parallax. The term denotes the apparent movement of unequally distant objects in the field of vision. Motion parallax is the result of eye movements. It easily can be demonstrated while we are looking out of the window of a travelling car or train. As we move, objects located nearer to us are displaced at a faster pace than the more distant ones. A simple experiment can show the direction of apparent object movement resulting from parallax. All we have to do is to hold two simple objects, at different distance, before our eyes. As we move our eyes from side to side, the relative position of the static objects will change too. The object nearer to the eyes will seem to move in the direction opposite to the shift, whereas the farther in the same direction.

However, in front of a painting the situation is different. Even if we move our head, the objects displayed in the equidistant composition are displace at an equal rate. Similarly to the lack of binocular cue, the lack of motion parallax while viewing a realistic painting does not demolish the aesthetic experience. The pictorial cues of linear and aerial perspective are capable of generating the illusion of three-dimensional scenery.

E.H. Gombrich has adopted a constructivist theory of perception as his analytical device, which he applies to the study of art history. He clings to the assumption that perception cannot be separated from inference, and equates seeing with interpreting. His conceptual framework is supported by a wide crossdisciplinary lattice. Thus, Gombrich points out that the problem of perception transcends the realm of psychology and of art history. It is a problem shared by every scientific field. For Karl Popper's assertion concerning "the priority of the scientific hypothesis over the recording of sense data" [11], which he established in *The Logic of Scientific Discovery* (1935), is based on the constructivist theory of perception.

The art historian and the physicist may develop a common Weltanschauung: "It was from Dr. Gottfried Spiegler, an X-ray physicist", says Gombrich, "that I learned to see the interpretation of all images as philosophical problem."[12]

The constructivist theory espouses the assumption that the mechanism of perception is a mental projection based on knowledge, experience and expectation. Gombrich believes that a painting is like an inkblot in a psychological Rorschach test: The observer must have his or her share of interpretation in the process of pictorial perception. The image configuration on the two-dimensional surface of the canvas constitutes arrays of ambiguity. To conjure up a three dimensional world from a two-dimensional picture is an ambiguous process which involves reconstruction by means of projection.

Psychologists and psychiatrists often use projective techniques in their efforts to infer psychodynamics and to interpret behavior in Freudian or other terms. The most commonly used projective tests are the Thematic Apperception Test (TAT) and the Rorschach technique. The TAT was introduced to the scientific community in 1938 when its inventor Henry Murray published his *Exploration in Personality*. [13] Since then the technique became a major landmark in the application and development of the projective approach to the study of personality.

The most widely used projective technique was published by a Jungian analyst, the Swiss psychiatrist Hermann Rorschach, in 1921. It has been the subject of more than three thousand studies since its introduction. The test consists of ten symmetrical inkblots in black and white as well as in color. The client is supposed to examine the inkblot cards and to say what he or she can see in them. Through the associative projections of the client, the analyst tries to interpret the response patterns in terms of sexual conflict, anxiety, style of communication, hostility, brain damage, and so on.[14]

The working of the human mind is essentially metaphorical. It is metaphorical not only in the sense that thought is bound up with language and that all words are symbols. The human mind is metaphorical because it conjures, projects and imagines. It proceeds in poetic images.

Gombrich suggests that Leone Battista Alberti (1404-72) was probably right by saying that the origin of art is in projection.[15] His hypothesis can be supported by circumstantial evidence. For, since days of yore human imagination used to cast various patterns onto the stars of the night sky. These patterns have been arbitrary formations. Different nations call the same stars by different names. The Ursa Major constellation of the northern sky, for instance, is known in England as the Plough, and as the Big Dipper in North America. The same cluster of stars in France is called the Casserole. In China people saw in the Ursa Major the Celestial Bureaucrat and his optimistic petitioners, whereas the imagination of native Americans and of ancient Greeks discerned the tail of the Great Bear in these group of seven stars. In medieval Europe the same constellation was called Charle's Wain, or Wagon.

The latter name still survives in various languages, such as Hebrew (Agala), and Hungarian (Göncölszekér).

Inhabitants of other civilizations in the universe probably project different images into their different starry constellations, says Carl Sagan; "other Rorschach tests for other minds."[16]

Leonardo da Vinci (1452-1519) , the outstanding genius of the Italian Renaissance, was an early constructivist by his aesthetic outlook. His *Notebooks* describe a projective device for study, a new way, according to him, "of developing and arousing the mind to various inventions." It is a rather trivial, but nevertheless an extremely useful method, he explains.

> And this is, when you look at a wall spotted with stains, or with a mixture of stones, if you have to devise some scene, you may discover a resemblance to various landscapes, beautified with mountains, rivers, rocks, trees, plains, wide valleys and hills in varied arrangement; or strange faces and costumes, and an endless variety of objects, which you could reduce to complete and well-drawn forms. And these appear on such walls confusedly, like the sounds of bells in whose jangle you may find any name or word you choose to imagine.

According to Gombrich, the Rorschach test is the rival of the artist's pattern book. It was in 1785 that Alexander Cozens' system of blot drawings were published in England under the title of *A New Method of Assisting the Invention in Drawing Original Compositions.* The idea of the new method came to him from Leonardo. Cozens advised amateur landscape painters interested in a new approach to creativity to apply accidental inkblots as a source of imagery and as a blueprint for pictorial composition. Although he showed considerable psychological insight, and presented a deliberate challenge to academic traditions, his unconventional method encountered vehement objection and ridicule at the time.

The German romanticist poet Justinus Kerner experimented with inkblots in order to stir up his imagination. The bisymmetrical images that he produced on folded paper evoked his spiritualist fantasies and served as source material of his poetic aspirations. Kerner's *Kleksographien* was published in 1857 in Stuttgart. It seems very likely that the poet's projective method was carried over into the world of psychiatry and metamorphosed itself to the diagnostic test developed by Rorschach. Thus Kerner's inkblots may represent the historical link which combines Cozens' blotting system with the Rorschach test.[18]

From a historical point of view Leonardo should be accredited as the originator of the principle on which the psychodiagnostic test is based. His extraordinary genius put into motion an accelerating array of intellectual stimuli that brought about astonishing chain reactions in many fields. Painter, engineer, architect, pioneer of modern anatomy and science, Leonardo da Vinci is remembered not merely for representing the highest achievements of the universal man of the Renaissance, but often for his prophetic mind as well. The scope and range of his work extend from the mechanical to the metaphysical. His rich kaleidoscope of ideas influenced such diverse fields as the mathematics of the infinite, physiology, embryology, comparative anatomy, military science, aircraft and submarine development, perception and perspective.

Filippo Brunelleschi (1377-1446) already in the beginning of the fifteenth century experimented with architectural construction based on the mathematical treatment of perspective. In the 1420s the painter Masaccio abandoned the abstract, decorative and symbolical methods of Gothic art in order to adopt the new, Renaissance style: the mathematical handling of the visual experience. Other artists, among them Donatello, Piero della Francesca, Uccello, and Ghiberti, followed suit in applying Brunelleschi's invention to art. In this manner by Leonardo's time the theory and practice of perspective had achieved a remarkable level of development.

Nevertheless it was Leonardo who gave the first detailed description of the pyramidal theory of perspective:

> Painting is based upon perspective which is nothing else than a thorough knowledge of the function of the eye. And this function simply consists in receiving in a pyramid the forms and colors of all objects placed before it. I say in a pyramid, because there is no object so small that it will not be larger than the spot where these pyramids are received into the eye. Therefore if you extend the lines from the edges of each body as they converge you will bring them to a

single point, and necessarily the said lines must form
a pyramid.[19]

Leonardo distinguished three branches of perspective. According to him, the first deals with the apparent diminution of objects as they recede from the spectator. The second branch concerns changes in colors as a result of their recession from the eye; whereas the third one explains the blurring effect: how objects receding from the eye should appear less distinct in proportion. Thus, in Leonardo's system the three kinds of perspective are linear perspective, color perspective, and the perspective of disappearance.[20]

Some of his observations concerning perspective found their expression in axiomatic form: "Of several bodies of equal size and tone", states Leonardo, for instance, "that which is farthest will appear lightest and smallest." Or here is another example: "Of several bodies, all equally large and equally distant, that which is most brightly illuminated will appear to the eye nearest and largest."[21]

Leonardo was working in Milan as Lodovico Sforza's court painter and engineer, when Albrecht Dürer of Nuremberg made his journey to Venice and Bologna to study more about the new science of perspective. Dürer thoroughly absorbed the spirit of the Italian Renaissance and carried it back with him into his native Germany. Several of his mechanical devices for drawing in perspective, which he invented and described in his theoretical treatises of the 1520s, were based on Leonardo's method.

It is noteworthy that Leonardo himself relied on Euclid's *Optics*, an ancient attempt to establish a geometrical relationship between visible objects and visual images. His pyramidal theory grew out of the Greek mathematician's observation that since objects are perceived by straight rays of light which converge in the eye, the visual system can be considered as a pyramid: The base of the pyramid is the object, its vertex is the eye.

Dürer's mechanical devices for drawing in perspective took advantage of Leonardo's advise: "Place a sheet of not too transparent paper between the object and the light and you can draw it very well."[22] An engraving by Dürer from the year of 1525 shows a drawing instrument in which the eye of the observer is replaced by a string. Since one end of the string is fixed, the other one allows the artist to use it as a pointer. He applied it to indicate various parts of his subject matter in order to record them on the glass plate in correct perspective. Other engravings by Dürer depict similar scenes, but the artist's eye is fixed by an optical instrument, and between it and the subject a grid made of black thread or a glass plate is interposed.

These images recall the words of Leonardo:

> Perspective is nothing else than the seeing a place behind a sheet of glass, smooth and quite transparent, on the surface of which all the things may be marked that are behind this glass. The things approach the point of the eye in pyramids, and these pyramids are intersected on the glass plane.[23]

According to Leonardo, the painted image has such an enormous power over the observer, that it can fool humans and animals alike. He had seen paintings, he says, that deceived dogs to the extent that they tried to bite dogs painted on the canvas, and a monkey that behaved in an incredibly foolish manner in front of the painted image of another monkey. Even birds can be taken in by the illusionist effects of art. Leonardo claims that he had seen, for example, swallows that tried to come to rest on painted iron bars before the windows of buildings.

He also noticed the mysterious impact of painting on lovers. For, by means of painting, says Leonardo, lovers are impelled towards the images of the beloved, and speak to the portraits of the beloved.

Theodore Andrea Cook contended that it was the genius of Leonardo which founded the experimental method, before Bacon or any other philosopher established it. He also claimed that Leonardo should be credited with the honor of having announced, before Copernicus, that 'the sun did not move', and discovered the circulation of the blood before Harvey.[24]

In any case, Leonardo da Vinci was an empiricist. He broke with the scholastic tradition of the middle age, and based his train of reasoning on observation and experiment. This can be seen, e.g., from his discussion concerning the blueness of the atmosphere. Why is the sky blue? Leonardo gave extensive thought to the question and came to the conclusion that the blue color of the atmosphere is caused by the darkness beyond it. First he supports this conclusion by observation:

> I say that the blueness we see in the atmosphere is not intrinsic color, but is caused by warm vapor evaporated in minute insensible atoms on which the solar rays fall, rendering them luminous against the infinite darkness of the fiery sphere which lies beyond and includes it. And this may be seen, as I saw it, by

anyone going up Monboso, a peak of the Alps which divide France from Italy.[25]

The description based on observation evolves into explanation founded on the authority of experimental evidence:

> Experience shows us that the air must have darkness beyond it and hence appears blue. If you produce a small quantity of smoke from dry wood and the rays of the sun fall on this smoke, and if you then place behind the smoke a piece of black velvet on which the sun does not shine, you will see that all the smoke which is between the eye and the black stuff will appear of a beautiful blue color. And if instead of the velvet you place a white cloth smoke, that is too thick smoke, hinders, and too thin smoke does not produce, the perfection of this blue color. Hence a moderate amount of smoke produces the finest blue . . . This I mention in order to show that the blueness of the atmosphere is caused by the darkness beyond it . . . for those who cannot confirm my experience on Monboso.[26]

Notwithstanding the long historical tradition of the constructivist approach to perception and its wide-spread influence, there are other psychological schools as well. Following World War II, for instance, James J. Gibson advanced his conception of the perceptual process which became known as a direct registration theory.[27] If Leonardo can be regarded as precursor of perceptual constructivism, then the origins of the registrationist doctrine can be traced back to the thought of the English philosopher John Locke (1632-1704). The mind in Locke's view is a tabula rasa on which experience writes. According to him, it is from the inscriptions caused by experience that our reliable inferences emerge with regard to the nature of the world: The initial human condition is a blank slate, a dark closet which must be furnished from without, because innate ideas do not exist.

It is noteworthy that the image theory of perception developed in the fifth century B.C. by the Greek philosophers Leucippus and Democritus anticipated Locke's ideas concerning perception. They believed that the perceptual process was the outcome of images of things which entered through the sense organs.

100

Unlike the constructivist theory of perception, the direct registration theory views perception as a process built upon the clearly defined flux of unambiguous data. It delineates the perceptual process in terms of correspondence: As the nervous system processes the input of information, advanced by the light of the environment through the eyes, the emerging images represented in our consciousness preserve the relational structure of the world. The result is veridical perception in which the appearance of objects in the mind, including their textures, edges, hues, and contrasts correspond to actuality. This conception of perception regards the input-output procession of information as a direct, effortless endeavor devoid of guesswork and interpretation.

In 1954 Gibson put forth the theory that an image can deceive the observer and look realistic, because the light rays emitted from the picture are identical in wave length and intensity to the light rays of the represented actual scene.[28] He tried to support his thesis of point to point correspondence between object and picture with various laboratory experiments. In these experiments subjects were indeed deceived and could not distinguish two dimensional realistic images from three dimensional objects. However, Gibson allowed to use only one eye in these experiments. Moreover, observers were not allowed to move their heads. The experiments were so devised that the binocular and parallax cues were excluded from the perceptual process.

In any case, the facts do not bear out Gibson's thesis that pictures and actual three dimensional objects give off the same light rays to the eye. The thesis is untenable, because black and white pictures have different light frequencies from ordinary color frequencies to be found in the regular environment. But there are additional fallacies built into the edifice of the direct registration theory. It cannot explain the phenomenon of distortion. For, if a point to point correspondence exists in the perceptual process which leads to the recognition of accurate pictorial images and their objects, then how do we recognize deformed, semi-abstract figures, and caricatures?

In the face of criticism levelled against his theory, Gibson revised it. In a paper published in the journal *Leonardo* (1971) he stressed that the central feature of the direct registration theory is based on the assumption that in the perceptual process the subject-object relationship is preserved. Thus, the point to point correspondence between picture and actual scene should not be taken literally, but as a principle of 'higher order correspondence'.[29]

It was between the two world wars that the German psychologists Kurt Koffka and Wolfgang Köhler collaborated with the Prague born Max Wertheimer in the development of gestalt psychology. The

German word, gestalt, denotes form and configuration. It stands for the principle that the whole is more than the sum total of its parts. It considers the perceptual process as a series of totalities, rather than an array of isolated, atomistic elements.

According to gestalt theory, the perceptual process is guided by universal, innate organizing principles. It is determined by built-in hereditary factors. This conception is contrary to the constructivist theory which asserts that perception is a process guided by acquired knowledge.

In fact, it is possible to view gestalt theory as a synthesis of the direct registration theory and the constructivist approach to perception. Similarly to the direct registration theory, gestalt psychology maintains that perception is direct, effortless, and involves no inferences or guesswork. However, unlike the direct registration theory, it assumes that the perceiver does process the information flowing through the sense organs. Accordingly, the input of sense data is transformed by the so called 'simplicity principle', and not by knowledge. This implies that light patterns of objects arriving at the retina are structured in the cerebrum as 'brain fields'. The gestalt psychologists claim that the brain fields assert themselves as the simplest and the most economic patters of mental organization. The simplicity principle programmed by the brain determines how the world is perceived.

Simplicity is not a quantitative concept. A pattern that consists of seven dots, e.g., can be simpler than a configuration of five dots:

The dot is the simplest visual unit. Lines can be regarded as made of dots. A set of a few dots and lines easily lends itself to be perceived three dimensionally. In accordance with the simplicity principle, the perceptual process is propelled from the abstract level to the concrete, gravitating from the elementary two dimensional pattern to the complex world of three dimensional images. Thus, two juxtaposed dots and a curved line placed within a circle arouse the image of a friendly smiling face; and two rectangles and a triangle can generate a landscape crossed by a road:

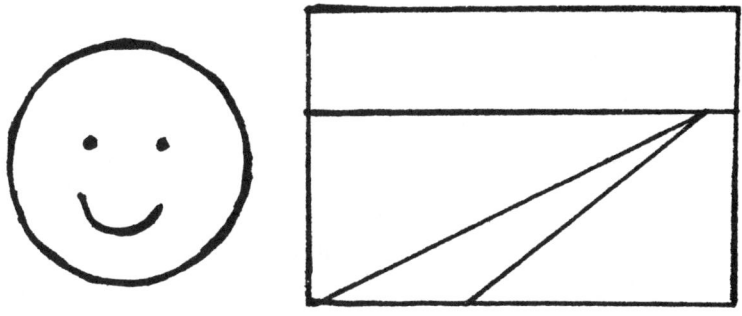

THE SIMPLICITY PRINCIPLE PROPELLS THE PERCEPTUAL
PROCESS FROM ABSTRACT TO CONCRETE.

Gestalt psychology views the perceptual process also in terms of the tendency for order, symmetry, balance, and regularity. Most people prefer a balanced, well organized composition over a chaotic one. Meaning is an additional important trait: Pure abstract art did not become as popular a movement as impressionism, because it is much harder to understand the first than the latter. Or at least this seems to be the case.

The law of perceptual inertia can be mentioned here as well. A triangle, for example, which is broken, that is to say a part of it is missing, will probably stimulate its beholder to complete it mentally:

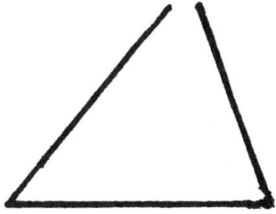

A wide array of visual phenomena can be explained by both the gestalt theory and the constructivist theory of perception. The images do not falsify the theories. The existence of optical illusions reveals, however, the weakness of the direct registration theory. It cannot account for the phenomenon of visual illusions. In fact, their existence contradicts the theory, and proves that the subject-object relationship as perceptual process can be an ambiguous and misleading experience.

103

The shortcomings of the simplicity principle of gestalt theory can be shown as well. The simplicity principle does not always work in a consistent manner. In the context of a painting, a daub of paint next to a group of horses, for instance, might be interpreted by the spectator as another horse, whereas next to a group of trees it might be perceived, perhaps, as another tree.

Photographic textbooks often warn the beginner not to take pictures when the background to the photographed person interferes undiserably with the aims and the clarity of the pictorial composition. Otherwise, a person standing before a tree, for instance, easily can end up with a picture in which branches are growing out of his or her head. In terms of the simplicity principle of the gestalt theory, it would be consistent to accept this sort of intuitive interpretation of the pictorial message. According to the gestalt theory the perceptual process is spontaneous, devoid of any conscious inference or guesswork. However, in order to interpret the photograph correctly, that is to say, to separate the branches of the tree from the head, one must apply acquired knowledge of conscious inference. Thus, appropriate reading of the photograph involves a perceptual process which is explained best by the constructivist theory.

Berlin born Rudolf Arnheim, professor of psychology at Harvard (1968-74), applied gestalt theory to the study of art. Along with Henry Schaefer-Simmern, he is convinced that every man is a potential artist, that the human approach to the world is essentially artistic: inventive, imaginative, symbolical and holistic. Therefore, the study of art is not an ivory tower, 'but an indispensable part of the study of man.'[30]

In *Art and Visual Perception* (1956) Arnheim discussed the pictorial properties of form, balance, space, light color, growth, and movement from a point of view of gestalt psychology. In this book he traced back the origins of gestalt psychology to Christian von Ehrenfels' essay of 1890. It was von Ehrenfels who pointed out that the appearance of things depends on their relative position and function in the configuration as a totality: If each person in a group of twelve auditors listened to one of the twelve tones of a melody, the sum total of their experience would be different from the perception of an individual who listened to the same melody as a whole.

According to Arnheim, the visual process is not a mechanical recording of individual perceptual atoms but the grasping of meaningful configurations. He approaches the problem of perception as an interplay between the world and the perceiver: "The mind always functions as a whole. All perceiving is also thinking, all reasoning is also intuition, all observation is also invention."[31]

In Arnheim's opinion the scientist can learn from the artist. After all, the scientist's analytical method pigeonholes the world by breaking its fundamental unity into conceptual compartments. In contrast to the piece by piece analysis of the scientist, the artist's method is guided by the realization that a whole cannot be created by adding up isolated parts. The great scientific achievements have resulted in spite of the fact that the scientist's reasoning functions at a relatively simple level, because it excludes the complexities of context and interaction. With art it is different. A work of art cannot be made or understood without the faculty of perceiving the integrated structure of a whole.

In *Visual Thinking* (1969) Arnheim advanced the thesis that all forms of thinking are essentially perceptual in nature, and that the process of vision involves reasoning. Thus, the ancient dichotomy between perception and thinking is a misleading fallacy. Psychological tradition used to exclude the senses from cognition, says Arnheim. He includes all mental operations involved in the receiving, storing and processing of information in the term cognition: sensory perception, memory, thinking, as well as learning. Cognitive operations, such as : exploration, abstraction, analysis and synthesis, selection, grasping of essentials, completion, correction, comparison, putting in context, and problem solving in general, are essential thinking processes. Arnheim contends that these "cognitive operations called thinking are not the privilege of mental processes above and beyond perception but the essential ingredients of perception itself."[32]

Arnheim supports his arguments with empirical evidence which frequently relies on various visual masterpieces selected from the history of art. But, in my opinion, some of his findings are misconstrued. As he discusses the nature of pictures, symbols, and signs, for example, he explains the failure of Courbet's intention to give visual expression to a symbolic message by means of a pictorial realism. Courbet's *L'Atelier* (1855) tried to show the conflict between practical life on the one hand, and feeling and thought on the other. The artist did not succeed in expressing his allegoric theme, because, as Arnheim suggests, "the more lifelike a piece of sculpture or painting, the more difficult may the artist find it to make his point symbolically."[33]

He levels a similar argument against René Magritte's *Ceci n'est pas une pipe*. This painting by the surrealist master shows a realistically painted tobacco pipe with the inscription contradicting the picture. In Arnheim's view, Magritte is a pedestrian surrealist who failed to express fantasy and deeper meaning.

What Arnheim fails to see, however, is the fact that art cannot be separated from its cultural context. Language represents the pivotal metaphysical foundations of culture, and words are its basic building blocks. Art works are curious hybrids, alchemical amalgams of images and words. This point can be illustrated by various ways. If words could be ignored, art critics would not exist; and catalogs of exhibitions, for instance, would not attach a name to every work on display. Even when the artist tries to avoid naming, he says: this work is untitled. However, the word 'untitled', is also a word. So, this is still naming. The word still denotes and connotes; it still guides and directs. There is no escape from words.

Since gestalt psychology views perception as a process in which inference is guided by the simplicity principle, and not by the complex levels of acquired knowledge, it is unable to cope with the intricate ramification stemming from the lattice of quibbling and of visual ambiguity. Accordingly, Arnheim comments on Magritte's *Ceci n'est pas une pipe* with the words: "Unfortunately a pipe is all it is."[34]

In order to understand the Belgian artist's fascinating and perplexing series of pipe paintings, it is necessary to keep in mind that he was very conscious of the symbol-object mystery. The philosophically inclined painter was less interested in the exploration of the hinterland of dreams and emotions, than in the investigation of the nature of reality. As a magic realist, Magritte manipulated the objects of the physical world by depicting them on the canvas in altered scale, and juxtaposing them in unexpected combinations. He succeeded in creating a disturbing world of peculiar illusions and visual metaphors in order to explore the ontological infrastructure of a greater whole. It is noteworthy that Magritte exerted considerable influence on artist such as, George Segal, Jim Dine, Claes Oldenburg, and even Salvador Dali came under his sway.

Magritte's pipe paintings are concerned with the relationship of words and images. They provide empirical evidence for the hypothesis that objects can be more than one thing. A painting, for instance, exists at different ontological levels: It is a visual metaphor, an image, a cluster of forms and colors, a configuration of pigments and textures, and integral part of reality, as well as an idea, and a word.

In 1966 Magritte painted *The Two Mysteries* in which a huge pipe seems to float in the air. A smaller pipe also appears on the canvas in the form of a painting within a painting, a painterly analogue of films which deal with filmmaking, or books which tell the story of authors writing books. This smaller pipe echoes the bigger one, its painted framework rhymes with the actual painting. The spatial relationship of the two pipes is characterized by its depth ambiguity. But there is an additional feature in the painting, which is of utmost importance: The painting within the painting carries the following inscription: "This is not a pipe." At the first glance, the bigger floating pipe asserts itself as a real object, that shows the difference between a genuine pipe and its smaller painted image incorporated into the same composition. The observer tends to get the impression that a real pipe differs from a symbol. However, the apprehension is swiftly to come that there is no real pipe in the painting, and that the bigger pipe on the canvas is just as much a symbol as the smaller one.

It is interesting that *The Two Mysteries* drew the attention of Douglas R. Hofstadter, a computer scientist involved in the development of artificial intelligence. According to him, the writing "Ceci n'est pas une pipe" in Magritte's painting is a central feature by means of which the artist presents his comment on the symbol-object mystery. In order not to confuse image with reality he suggests to come so close to the painting until the whole canvas turns into a surface of colored smudges. But ironically at that very moment everything turns into smudges, including the writing, "This is note a pipe." So, meaning is lost, and "the verbal message of the painting self-destructs in a most Gödelian way."[35]

In 1962 appeared Arnheim's book, *The Genesis of a Painting: Picasso's Guernica.* In it the author tried to reconstruct the metamorphoses, as well as the continuity and logic underlying the development of one of the most important cultural landmarks of the twentieth century.[36]

Arnheim explained Picasso's creative process in terms of the artist's conscious aesthetic goals, his plastic view as a vivid and powerful statement about the human condition. In his interpretation *Guernica* evolved as a painting in order to allow the artist to express his conscious vision. Thus, Arnheim's analysis of Picasso's creative process is contrary to Freud's approach to Leonardo da Vinci's work. Freud did not relate Leonardo's art to its socio-historical context, did not see it as the result of conscious motivation. Instead, he talked of the artist's unconscious psyche, his psycho-sexual motives, which he analyzed in terms of Leonardo's personality and childhood experiences.

Arnheim is wrong in assuming that Picasso's way of creating *Guernica* can be turned into a universal model of artistic creativity. The incubative period of the first glimmering idea which finally is crystallized in the painting is hardly susceptible to empirical study. Every artist is different, each individual idea is unique. The creative process is not based on a universal formula. Its cardinal constituents --

intuition and conscious planning -- in each specific artwork form an idiosyncratic blend. Besides, a painting is not an expression of an idea in the form of an image on the canvas. The artist can never realize his idea because the transition from the imaginary to the real is impossible. In every ontological stage the medium is the message. The painter does not realize or objectify his vision but constructs a material analogue of it.[37] In contrast to the mental image of the artist, which is lax and dim and amorphous, the finished painting is a physical object existing in visible space; the result of brushstrokes -- a cluster of forms, colors, and textures. It is a synergic alloy of the mental and the physical; a peculiar amalgam in which the interaction of feeling, thought, energy and matter is frozen into metamorphic substance.

All aspects of seeing concern the psychologist and the artist alike. Therefore it is small wonder that the psychologist can turn to the study of art for the investigation of perceptual phenomena. Art offers an inexhaustible visual repository. The artist on the other hand can find in psychology an indispensable tool to broaden his or her intellectual eyeshot and creative horizon.

Adelbert Ames, Jr., was an American artist who turned to the study of psychology in order to understand better the painter's primary field of concern: vision.

The son of a governor of Mississippi and a U.S. senator, Ames was born in Lowell, Massachusetts, on August 19, 1880. He was educated at Harvard and became a successful lawyer. However, he felt no abiding interest for pursuing the inescapable entanglements which an established career in law involve, and between 1910 and 1914 he undertook the study of painting in order to become an artist. It seems that Ames' principal art teachers were his mother and his sister, Blanche.[38]

Although he had no formal training, he excelled in art as well. In 1910 he entered the competition of designing a trademark for the Shawmut Bank of Boston. Ames won the prize with his Indian head, an original sculpture which became the world-famous symbol of the Shawmut Association Banks.[39]

However, Ames was not satisfied with his career as an artist. He was a perfectionist searching for absolute aesthetic congruity. He was especially disturbed by the yawning gap that he discovered to exist between the pictorial representation of the object and the object itself. The willingness to improve his artistic skills prompted another significant twist in his professional development. Ames wanted to learn more about the anatomy and physiology of perception in order to become a better artist. It was this decision of learning more about how we see things that took him to Clark University, and into his work on physiological optics and the psychology of perception.[40]

From 1914 to 1917 Ames was a research fellow at Clark University. His work was interrupted by World War I. On his return from military service in 1919 he resumed his research. After the war Ames was affiliated with Dartmouth College in Hanover of New Hampshire where he held the post of research professor in physiological optics between 1920 and 1946.

Ames began his experiments with colors, lenses, cameras and eyeglasses already at Clark University. In 1919 he contacted Charles A. Proctor, professor of physics at Dartmouth college, and collaborated with him in the investigation of the optical characteristics of the eye as a camera. Ames constructed an artificial eye made of glass, and undertook the examination of hundreds of human eyes in order to study the problem of ocular anomalies. In the process he discovered a previously unknown abnormality which he named aniseikonia (1926). It denotes an ocular abnormality: The images formed by the two eyes differ in shape and in size. Together with Gordon H. Gliddon, Ames developed a series of patented optical instruments for the correction of eye defects. Following the discovery of aniseikonia, hundreds of patients from all over the world came to Dartmouth seeking help for treatment of their abnormal vision. It was in the light of their needs that Ames initiated the establishment of the Dartmouth Eye Institute and the clinics affiliated with it. There he continued his research as director, and guided the work of more than thirty scientists.

In the last phase of his life, Ames arrived at the conclusion that physiological optics alone is unable to provide satisfying answers to the questions posed by the investigator of the perceptual process. Thus, in the period which extends from the end of World War II to the year of his death in 1955, he increasingly moved toward the direction of psychological research. During 1949-1955 he was director of the Hanover Institute for Associated Research, where he concerned himself specifically with the broader philosophical aspects of perception in its relationship to both normal and pathological human behavior. He believed that the perceptual process represents an important key to the understanding of human behavior.

Alfred North Whitehead regarded Ames as 'an authentic genius', and John Dewey described his contribution to the research of perception as "by far the most important work done in the psychological-philosophical field during this century."[41] The versatility of Ames as a lawyer, artist, physicist, optical physiologist, medical researcher, psychologist, and philosopher, prompted Horace Kallen to compare his genius with that of Leonardo da Vinci.

Ames combined the creative approach of the artist with the working method of the scientist. As an artist concerned with the investigation of perceptual phenomena, he invented a series of ingenious demonstrations which transposed the painter's two dimensional world of illusions to three dimensional illusion generating environments. Yet, Ames' working method was based on the classic scientific model. Thus, he was concerned both with the experimental demonstration of observable phenomena and with their theoretical interpretation.

Ames was well aware of the wealth of perceptual information carried over to us through the historical continuity of the artistic heritage. He used the inexhaustible visual repository of art history, as well as the theoretical knowledge accumulated throughout the centuries, in the scientific study of perceptual phenomena. After the Dartmouth Eye Institute was closed in 1949, the perceptual demonstrations that he developed were continued at the Psychology Research Center of Princeton University in New Jersey. The demonstrations were subsequently also adopted by numerous research centers throughout the world.

Leonardo had noted that "of several bodies, all equally large and equally distant, that which is most brightly illuminated will appear to the eye nearest and largest."[42] Ames applied this centuries-old observation to test its validity through the 'Star Point Demonstration'.

A star point is a minute source of light which represents the simplest possible visual experience. The apparatus, which Ames devised for the demonstration, consists of a light-tight box with three small holes and built in lights. The star points are viewed in a dark room. The experiment occurs under conditions of monocular vision. If the experimenter turns on the switch that lights two star points and manipulates the rheostat so that one light is brighter than the other, the observer will perceive the brighter star point as nearer than the dimmer one.

In another experiment, the experimenter turns on the central star point of the box which is located between the two outer star points. The result is that the observer feels that the distance increases between the two outer star points.

A third experiment also involves apparent movement of lights. If the experimenter turns the rheostat back and forth, so that the relative brightness and dimness of the two outer star points of the apparatus are changing, the observer will experience the relative movement of these lights, forward and back to each other.

Ames drew from the Star Point Demonstration the following inferences: 1) The perceptual awareness of the observed phenomena concerning distance differences or movement of star points does not correspond to actual events. 2) The perceptual interpretation of the observed phenomena results from the observer's own contribution. 3) the observed phenomena concerning the apparent movement and distance difference of the star points result from personal assumptions: The observer assumes somehow that the star points possess equal brightness; and that the brighter of similar objects is closer than the dimmer one. 4) If these assumptions are not aided by innate ideas, they can only stem from the observer's own past experience.

Another intriguing experiment that Ames conceived is known as the Rotating Trapezoid Demonstration.[43] It consists in a trapezoidal window, slowly rotating around a vertical axis, while a small cube is attached to its top corner, and a round tube protrudes through its middle section.

Although the window is rotating about its axis, the observer perceives its movement as if it were oscillating, instead of rotating. Moreover, he or she sees the small cube departing from the window and encircling it. In addition to this, most observers also see a series of transformations occurring in the tube: It appears to bend, to change its length, or break through the window.

If the trapezoidal window is replaced with a rectangular one, the observer will perceive none of the events described above; even if all other conditions of the experiment remain the same. Similarly to the findings based on the Star Point Demonstration, Ames inferred that the perceptual events related to the Rotating Trapezoid Demonstration are the result of the assumptive behavior of the perceiver. The strange perceptual events are generated by the observer's own belief that a window is a rectangular object. The use of the trapezoidal window in the experiment brings about unfamiliar spatial configurations. It breaks up the observer's gestalt of expectations which, along with other factors, determines the content of perception.

Ames also demonstrated that the substance of a familiar object cannot be established simply from a knowledge of the physical appearance of the object: Different physical objects can cause similar perceptions. A case in point is the Chair Demonstration. Its apparatus consists of three sets of strings in different arrangements, which are placed into a large wooden box with three peepholes. Viewed from the peepholes, the observer is made to believe that what is seen inside the box is not three different arrangements of strings, but three chairs.

The best known apparatus that Ames devised are probably his monocular and binocular distorted rooms. All of them appear to be normal rectangular rooms. However, the walls of the binocular rooms are not ordinary panels but curved surfaces, whereas in the monocular rooms floors slope down to the side, and one edge of the back wall is protruding more than the other. Thus, the floor plan forms a trapezium in which one back wall corner can be twice as far from the viewing point as the other. Objects placed within these rooms give rise to distorted perceptions, yet the rooms retain their ordinary appearance. For example, two individuals of equal height in such a distorted room might look to an observer as a giant and a dwarf.

On the basis of his demonstrations, Ames inferred that perception is a creative act. The eyes and the brain, which constitute the visual system, do not receive images passively. It is possible to discern two distinct stages in the perceptual process. In the first stage, as the eyes translate patterns of light into nerve impulses and send them to the brain, the instant of perception eventuates in an intuitive hypothesis about the nature of the percept. In other words, the observer makes a guess. The second stage is characterized by validation or correction. When the viewer encounters an environmental situation that gives rise to distorted perception, the guess must be modified. It is through these two stages of automatic guessing and of inferential correction that perception proceeds. Thus, if the observer of the distorted room, e.g., realizes that the two individuals seen as a giant and a dwarf are, in fact, two persons of equal height, then the next most logical conclusion should be that something is wrong with the room. Seeing is a process which involves trials, errors, and corrections.

In 1922 appeared "Vision and the Technique of Art", a paper which grew out from Ames' collaboration with his sister, the painter Blanche Ames, and with the physicist C.A. Proctor.[44] The authors asserted that the technique of art depends on the laws of vision, and therefore "a picture in its general form should be similar to our retinal impressions."[45] This view of painting, however, poses the problem of how to overcome the difficulty of analyzing the nature of images of objects upon which the eye was not focused. Adelbert Ames, Jr., hoped to determine scientifically the characteristics of these unfocused images of objects. As the eye focuses on an object, the foveal field of vision produces a clear image, but the peripheral area of vision is blurred. This runs contrary to the nature of painting. For, in order to make the picture pleasing and to produce the illusion of depth, the artist must reproduce the characteristic qualities of the images of objects upon which the eye is not focused. Thus, pictorial realism is in fact a lie because it unaturally renders every part of the depicted scenery in simultaneous foci.

According to the authors, every object is projected on the retina in terms of form, color, accentuation of line and chromatic edges. The artist should not aim at the reproduction of reality: "A pictorial representation of nature to be technically satisfactory from an artistic point of view should be similar to our subjective impression."[46] A striking example of this principle can be found in the so called barrel distortion. The barrel distortion effect is caused by the spherical form of the eye. It makes straight lines that do not pass through the axis of vision to appear curved. It also causes objects away from the axis to shrink as images. The distortion affects all visible objects. Its existence can be easily demonstrated by staring at the middle of a rectilinearly bounded field of vision, such as a book or a room, where the curvature of the boundary lines can be noted. The writers suggest that either consciously or unconsciously great painters like, Leonardo da Vinci, Rembrandt, Israels, Millet, Turner and others, took advantage of the barrel distortion and incorporated its effect into their painted images. In about 1912 and in the following years, Adelbert Ames and Blanche Ames experimented with the barrel distortion by producing a series of paintings. They found that the pictures painted by the latter "in which the detail of the distorted features approximated in its characteristics the way it is imaged upon the retina the distortion ceases to be noticeable and gives a pleasing and natural effect."[47]

In spite of his scientific posture, Ames was critical of science. "Scientists are the super-superstitionists", he said. "By their identifying value in inanimate objects, they become the magician (soothsayer) of the modern age. Superstition is irrational thought proceeding from ignorance."[48] Ames aimed his verbal arrows at the naive epistemological conception of reality with which the majority of scientists seem to approach actuality.

Ames' own way of thinking was determined by the synergic integration of art and science. He was very aware of how the scientist's reasoning differed from that of the artist. Once, delivering a lecture, he remarked: "Ask a scientist and a poet to describe a woman's gown, and the scientist will tell you the wave length of light rays from the colors of the gown. The poet will give you a different vision."

Ames attacked the unscientific belief of scientists that it is possible to know the inherent nature of objects. For his part, the separation of the objects of the external world from human sensations and percepts was a severe fallacy which he termed as the superstition of objectification.

From a philosophical point of view, Ames was a pragmatist clinging to a mediating position between idealist solipsism and mechanistic materialism.

More than two hundred years elapsed since Dr. Samuel Johnson kicked a stone to contradict the solipsist Bishop Berkeley's argument that a stone is only an idea in the mind, created by the perceiver's thought of it. Although he did not deny the existence of an external world, Berkeley maintained that even the physical world existed only as idea, a pure thought in the mind of God.

But as the Ames demonstrations show, the world is neither pure subject nor pure object. According to Ames the objects of the external world are real: It is the lack of correspondence between our sensations and percepts on the one hand, and the objects of the world, on the other, which gives rise to illusions. However, illusions are not outside of reality. For, "it would be equally logical to assume that the illusions" and similar "autisms are real and that the external objects and qualities are illusions."[49] After all, argues Ames, objects and qualities do not exist in their own right in nature. Nature is in constant flux. The whole dilemma concerning the correspondence of the external world to its perception is primarily due to our insistence to separate the perceptual process from reality. It is this insistence which leads to the superstition of objectification.

Ames held that what we know can never exactly correspond to the immediate situation. It is possible to speak of similarity or analogy, but not of precise correspondence. Our senses, sensations and ideas do not exactly describe the external world and its objects. What they give us, at most, is a prognosis of their significance. Perceptions depend on the experience of the past. In certain respect, explains Ames, "past experience is more truly the source of the visual impression than the object."[50] It is difficult to overestimate the significance of the past experience in the perceptual process. The immediate situation acts as a catalytic agent which in the perceptual process produces the significance of past experience as the source of sense impressions. "That is, the organism brings to an immediate situation a potentiality for sensually experiencing the significances of all past experience . . . "[51]

As Ames pointed out, the demonstrations devised by him seem to prove that perceptions are illusory because in concrete situations the perceiver makes erroneous assumptions. However, it should be born in mind, he said, that an illusory perception in itself is not an error. It turns into a mistake only when the falsity is accepted as trustworthy perception upon which reliable directives and purposeful actions are based.

According to Ames, illusory perceptions are extremely important psychological mechanisms. In fact, they are an indispensable human faculty which allows the organism to behave effectively: "It is only through illusory experience that the significance of situations, heretofore undifferentiated from other situations, are disclosed to us." The process of evolution is bound up, in a sense, with the adjusting and altering of perceptual patterns which guide the organism to carry out its purposes.

For Ames the world was an unknowable place, and the belief in a material world that exists in its own right just another illusion. But it is not always easy to apprehend illusions. Everyone knows that liking or disliking an object, for instance, is a subjective aspect of our consciousness. The case of science is much more intriguing. "In science they have different arbitrarily chosen standards: one in astronomy and another in atomic physics, neither of which makes experiential sense to us", he wrote into his notebook on January 22, 1946. And he added:

> If all human standards are eliminated as is done by science, what is left? Accumulations of atoms. That's what the table is . . . A mass of billions and billions of atoms, with distances between them relative to astronomical distances and continually changing, never the same, unpredictable and disintegrating. That's what's there we are looking at. But there is not the lightest resemblance between what we know is there when we eliminate all human standards and what is in our consciousness in terms of perception. This seems to make it easier to understand why what we sense in perception is not inherently in the object we are looking at but in the significance of what we are looking at to us as human beings.[53]

Ames brought art to science and science to art. This can be seen in his painting method, in his theoretical writings and comments. Even his demonstrations can be seen as works of science and works of art. Placed within the context of a museum or art gallery, today they would be called conceptualist investigations, or environmental installations.

115

Throughout the centuries there were always artists to be found at the crossroads where art and science converge. Georges Seurat was one of them. His work is relevant to the problem of perception because of his investigations concerning the application of scientific theories of color to painting.

The son of a French bailiff and property owner, originally from Champagne, Seurat was born in Paris on December 2, 1859. His teachers included the sculptor Justin Lequien, and the painter Henri Lehmann. The latter was a disciple of Ingres, and Seurat came under his sway in entering the Ecole des Beaux-Arts in 1878.

Seurat was endowed with an exceptionally rational mind, and wanted to base art on scientific principles. In the school library he found Humbert de Superville's *Essai sur les signes inconditionnels de l'art*, a book published in 1827, which became a permanent source of inspiration for the rest of his brief life. He also read the work of David Sutton, who combined musicology and mathematics in his *Phenomena of Vision* (1880). The symbolist literature and painting of the age, including the monumental images of Puvis de Chavannes, affected his artistic development too. These influences were coupled by Seurat's obsession with the scientific theories of color and aesthetic harmony. When he met Michel-Eugéne Chevreul, the famous chemist already reached the ripe age of one hundred years. His reputation was based on *De la loi du contraste simultané*, a treatise which dealt with the creation of color harmony through contrast and analogy, as well as the interaction of juxtaposed complementaries. The book was published back in 1839, and it was regarded more as a manual for artists than an original contribution to science. In spite of the fact that it was antiquated, the community of artists continued to use the book even during the 1880s.

Seurat also studied diligently Charles Blanc's theories concerning optical mixture and gradation which were based on the work of Chevreul, of Delacroix and of oriental artists. It seems that the principles of scientific color mixture by the additive method had been anticipated to some extent by artists prior to Seurat. Corot and the impressionists juxtaposed colors to be combined by the perceiving eye as an empirical method of painting. Their accomplishments, however, did not satisfy Seurat's quest for the discovery of scientifically based formulas to systematize the method of optical painting.

The impressionists tried to base their technique on the assumption that the reconstruction of the optical qualities of natural light was possible through the method of painting. Since sunlight contains all the colors of the spectrum, they argued, and these colors are broken through a prism, it is also possible to converse the process by recombining the broken colors in painting. The impressionist painters wanted to duplicate the images of nature by painting in the open air with pure prismatic colors. They believed that the perceiver's eye functioned similarly to the prism, and in the viewing process it reconstructed the broken colors of the canvas into the analogous experience of natural light.

As a neo-impressionist, Seurat created a new style during the years of 1884-1886. During this chromo-luminarist period he perfected the technique of pointillism, a method of painting with tiny, detached strokes of pure color. Both Seurat and his enthusiastic disciple, Paul Signac (1863-1935), disliked the term pointillism. Instead, they used the term divisionism.

A treatise written by an American scientist played a pivotal role in Seurat's emergence as the leading exponent of neo-impressionism. It was N.O. Rood's *The Theory of Colors*, which the artist read in French. In contrast to Chevreul and Blanc, Rood supported his description of color behavior with laboratory experiments and rigorous measurements. His practical instructions equipped the artist with workable knowledge about the specific purpose of procuring enhanced luminosity in painting.[54] From this source Seurat also became aware of the important difference existing between the subtractive and the additive principle of color blending.

The technique of optical blending as a method of painting evolved empirically throughout the centuries. The great Flemish painter of the baroque, Peter Paul Rubens, never used, for instance, black for shadows. In this respect he was certainly at one with the impressionists. Through observations, Delacroix, and later the impressionists, discovered that the complementary color of every primary hue is found in its shadow. Thus, a yellow object, for example, casts a violet shadow, and the shadows of red and blue objects are made of greenish and orange colored reflections, respectively.

By placing pure colors in juxtaposition on the canvas, the impressionists often intended to generate effects of optical mixture. If they put, for instance, pure red and blue side by side on the canvas, the colors were supposed to combine within the spectator's eye into a vibrant violet. In the traditional subtractive method of painting pigments have been mixed on the artist's palette. Mixing colored pigments is subtractive because each pigment absorbs or subtracts from the white light its characteristic portion. In this manner only the hues reflected in common by all the component paints reach the observer's eye. In the subtractive method a mixture of the three primary colors, red, yellow, and blue, will yield black.

117

In contrast to the subtractive technique, in the optical mixing of colors the three primary colors of light are red, blue, and green. In the additive method these primary beams of light, if they are projected on the same spot, will produce white light by being added to each other. The impressionists and Seurat alike believed that the optical blending of colors produces enhanced luminosity on the canvas. In comparison to it, the subtractive technique of mixing colors on the palette yields duller effects.

A closely packed mosaic of red and green dots, for example, can generate a thrilling optical experience of yellow. The additive method of optical blending is widely used in modern technology. It represents the basis of color television, and of certain branches in the printing trade.

However, as early as 1824 Chevreul warned artists to avoid placing complementary colors next to each other, because the optical interaction of these colors dimmed their original brightness. It was this empirical observation which prompted painters throughout the history of art to outline intuitively areas of color in black, or separate them by a white line. Although theoretically optical mixture in painting is possible, the impressionist aspiration to reconstruct the qualities of natural light through the spectator's eye involves a series of fallacies. These conceptual errors are related to the fact that the medium is the message. It is impossible, for instance, to duplicate the incredible brightness of the sun by the painter's faint pigments. Another confusion arises from the mistaken assumption that the primary colors of the artist's palette and the physicist's primaries for mixtures of light are the same colors. They are not. For the artist, green, e.g., is a secondary color derived from the blending of yellow and blue. Yet, for the physicist green is a primary, and just as pure a color as red and blue.[55]

Moreover, the eye does not duplicate the work of the prism. The eye is an integral part of the human organism, and without the function of the brain vision cannot take place. Unlike the mechanical function of the prism, the function of the eye is part of an intelligent process. It is also noteworthy that the colored lights reflected from pigments are never as brilliant and pure as those emanating from a prism. Finally, scientific facts are not always applicable to painting. The retinal fusion of blue and yellow dots into a luminous green, for instance, is a perception which easily can be repeated under laboratory conditions. However, it frequently will not work in the framework of a painting, due to the interaction of the various colors present in the composition.

In the *Les Nourritures terrestres*, André Gide replaced the sententious precept of Descartes, "I think, therefore I am", with another apothegm: "I feel, therefore I am." The impressionists could take Gide's adage as the motto of their own movement. For impressionism strove for becoming a purely visual and instinctive form of art. The painters of this movement wanted to record with their prismatic colors the fleeting moments of life, the ephemeral segments of the world as retinal experience. So, they painted out of doors the breeze rippling the surface of the water, stirring the foliage; and the reflections of light seen in an urban setting, or in a grassy meadow.

Although Seurat was influenced and affiliated with the impressionists, he gradually departed from them: He rejected Monet's dictum, that the artist paints just as birds sing. As he increasingly became obsessed with the scientific principles of color organization, he decided to substitute the detailed optical analysis of light effects and colors for the spontaneous creative method of impressionism. He believed that by studying the scientific laws governing the behavior of color, and by accurately observing the world, he could paint pictures that duplicated the images of nature and enhanced the color experience too. He was determined to surpass the impressionists by improving their methods with well-founded theories.

Seurat's *Bathers, Asniéres* (1883-4) was the artist's first huge painting shown in public. Unlike the impressionists, he worked from a number of detailed studies executed on the spot and completed later in the studio. In order to paint it, Seurat utilized Rood's color disc showing the complementary of every color. His chromoluminarist method relied on Rood's color wheel whieh allowed him to juxtapose complementary colors with the end in view to achieve greater luminosity. Perhaps under the influence of radical political ideas which appealed to the painter, the subject matter of the composition included working class bathers portrayed in an industrial landscape.

Seurat painted his most known canvas–*Sunday Afternoon on the Island of La Grande Jatte*–during the period of 1884-6, and it was displayed at the eighth and last impressionist exhibition (1886). Nowadays this huge canvas of 205 x 281.7 cm is in the collection of the Art Institute of Chicago. This painting is a bizarre conglomeration of divisionist and impressionist techniques, elements of fashion design, mixed perspectives, architectural composition and classicism. The scene depicts the Seine with its sail boats and steamers, and the people strolling on the island or stretched out on the colorful grass under the trees and a blazing summer sky. Seurat shared Piero della Francesca's fascination with mathematics, as well as Cézanne's passion to make impressionism solid and durable: to 're-do Poussin from nature'. Indeed, the figures of *La Grande Jatte* are frozen to postures of timeless stability like those to be found in Piero della Francesca's paintings.

Seurat was so preoccupied with this painting that he apparently forgot not merely his duties and friends, but even his meals. His overwhelming involvement with art undermined his health.

It was during this period that Pissarro came under the sway of Seurat. As a result he adopted the divisionist method of painting, along with his son Lucien, and a group of other artists.[56]

The buds of several modern art movements seem to be built into Seurat's work. The composition of *La Grande Jatte* was made from several viewing points, and the resulting broken perspective represents an anticipation of cubism. The stylized architectural organization of the painting points toward the direction that later asserted itself in geometric abstraction. Besides, the entire impressionist movement can be conceived as the precursor of abstract art, because its central concerns were light and color, which are abstract qualities.

According to the neo-impressionist theory, the dots of a devisionist painting produce more luminous effects than those obtainable from pigments on the palette. When viewed from a distance big enough to look at the entire work, the separate marks of the pointillist colors are supposed to merge in the spectator's eye into a brilliant harmonious whole. The facts, however, do not bear out the theory. For, in actuality, the blending of colors in the eye is incomplete and inconsistent. The dots do not disappear at once, but from different viewing distances, because their sizes are different. The continuity of the process of retinal fusion is interrupted by the dynamic interaction of the spectator's eye movements and the shifting arrays of color configurations. The directions of eye movements are unpredictable, and they can give rise to diverse color combinations.

The process of retinal fusion is interrupted also by the physiological phenomenon of afterimages. The afterimage is the continuation of a sensory experience after the cessation of the stimulus. For example, an individual staring at a given color for a while, will perceive its complementary color as an afterimage.[57]

It is possible also to add that the artist's harmony is not necessarily the spectator's harmony. After all color harmony, despite the efforts of the scientists and artists to establish its well-founded laws, has a status which is similar to that of beauty: It is in the eye of the beholder.[58]

Notwithstanding the fact that the actual visual effects of divisionism did not correspond to its theoretical predictions, the shimmering neo-impressionist mosaics with their unexpected perceptual results have become the engaging source of much aesthetic joy and satisfaction for both artists and their audiences. And regardless of the scientific validity of the neo-impressionist theory, pointillism emerged as one of the most important art movements of the nineteenth century. It also steered a new course to the development of modern art.

It would be wrong to assume that, science, unlike art, is based on absolutely correct theories. With respect to Seurat's scientific sources it is illuminating to take notice that Rood's system of color harmony, for instance, was grounded not only on the accomplishments of modern physics, but also on arbitrary judgments deriving from a wide array of traditional artistic sources. Contrary to the popular belief, even in science, the most rational and precise human endeavor, "it is not all important to be Right (it may even be that there is no way of ever determining what is Right); it is merely necessary to be right enough for the times."[59]

In the last four years of his life Seurat got acquainted with the theories of Charles Henry. The scientist stimulated the painter's interest in the expressive possibilities of color and line. Relying on Rod and Helmholtz concerning the physical laws of color and light, Henry also used the mathematics of Gauss and the golden section in his grand synthesis to achieve aesthetic harmony in visual compositions. Henry claimed that different sensations produce measurable physiological effects in the organism.

Seurat believed that harmony is the analogy between opposites and between similar elements expressed in combinations of tone, of color, and of line on the canvas. Cheerfulness, according to him, should assert itself in a pictorial composition in terms of tonal value as a luminous or lighter tonality against a darker one; "in terms of color, a warm dominant color; in terms of line, lines above the horizontal." On the other hand, sadness can be expressed in terms of tonal value as "a dominant dark tonality; in terms of color, a cold dominant color; and in terms of line, downward directions."[60]

In paintings, such as *The Circus* and *Le Chahut*, Seurat tried to implement these aesthetic principles. In these works he was less concerned with the correspondence of the image to nature than with the pictorial representation of emotions, rhythm and harmony. As against the descent of the "A" motif, the ascending "V" is lavishly applied, symbolizing the gleeful atmosphere depicted in both paintings. In *The Circus*, this motif evolves on the right side of the picture into an abstract expression of laughter, which is symbolized by the yellow, angular wave.

Seurat never finished *The Circus*, although he showed the uncompleted work at the eighth Salon des Indépendants. As an organizer of the exhibition, he exhausted himself and became ill. A common cold that he caught developed into a severe complication, and killed him. Seurat died of infectious angina on March 29, 1891.

Already during his lifetime, he was accused of creating an impersonal, mechanical, and hence, a nonartistic style. Critics said of Seurat that since he relied on scientific formulae, he was not really an artist. Renoir disavowed the neo-impressionist doctrine, and contended that the constituents of art cannot be reduced to a petrified theory. Pissarro was also critical, notwithstanding the fact that up to a point he too practised devisionism.

But the critic Félix Fénéon was sympathetic. He explained that the neo-impressionists' aspiration was by no means to subordinate art to science. Instead, they wanted to take advantage of scientific facts capable of directing their eye and of enhancing the exactness of their vision. Science could guide, perfect, and control the optical sensibilities of the painter. Scientific formulae, however, could not replace artistic talent. An individual without the genius of a Seurat can read for ever the treatises of Professor Rood, yet he will never paint *La Grande Jatte*. According to Fénéon, the neo-impressionist method demands an exceptionally delicate eye and artistic integrity. It is a style which is accessible only to painters.[61]

Henry himself who contributed a significant portion to the scientific theories that shaped Seurat's artistic vision and guided his intuition, argued along similar lines: "It is not to be asserted that I wish to substitute the mechanism of an instrument for the creation of the artist. Genius is inimitable."[62]

The rise of pointillism represents an important historical phase in art, and in the psychological understanding of space as an optical experience related to color. For the artists of the Renaissance, from Giotto to Raphael, reality was space, which contained color. They added color to the various objects depicted in the painting in a rather arbitrary fashion, just in order to animate the composition. The art of Seurat represents a radical transformation of this conception of color. In Seurat, like in Cézanne, color is the reality which gives birth to space.

However, Seurat did not exhaust his creative energies in the development of pointillism. The new art of well-founded harmony was not merely a problem of color but the quest for the distillation of a timeless essence from the chaotic conglomerate of themes and possibilities. Had Seurat concerned himself with the problem of color alone, or subordinated art to science, he would not exert such decisive influence on Delaunay, Braque, Gris, Picasso, and others.[63] The new art styles that have sprung from Seurat's work lend support to the conjecture that the individualist images he so eloquently articulated expressed a new collective sense of consciousness as well.

Seurat was a witness of fast industrial development and of dilapidated urban growth. He saw the poverty of the Parisian masses. It seems that the traumatic experience of accelerating transformation, the permanent feeling of existential uncertainty characterizing modern life filled him with immense yearning for solidity, order, and harmony. But he could not change the world. So he found what he longed for in the abiding, systematic organization of a new kind of pictorial order. Thus, neo-impressionism was born out of the mundane lattice of the industrial revolution, and it was based on the synergic interaction of art and science. Seurat tried to revolutionize the cognitive status of art, and the weighty repercussions of his attempt still reverberate in the fabric of contemporary culture.

The rise of Op Art is tied to Seurat's name. The British artist Bridget Riley originally painted in an impressionist style, but in 1959 she switched to pointillism. Soon she began to investigate the visual effects of juxtaposed lines and dots, and evolved the findings to repetative, black and white, abstract compositions. In 1967 she began to apply color as well. Riley's work is based on the idiosyncratic balance of artistic intuition and carefully controlled experimentation. For her part a painting is a field of visual energy which tends to accumulate in shimmering optical effects and tensions. Riley's painted images, such as *Fall*, *Current*, and *Drift*, with their movement generating, undulating stripes, found their way not only to art galleries, but also into books of science. The psychologist D. W. Massaro discusses her work in *Experimental Psychology and Information Processing* (1975). She points out that the vibrating effects generated by Riley's paintings are caused by the fine lines to be found in them. Their modus operandi is similar to the effects created by the fine lines of Wolfgang Ludwig's *Cinematic Painting*.[64]

The fine lines of Riley's *Fall* or *Current*, however, are sinuous entities, in contrast to Ludwig's converging straight spokes. It seems that in the works of both artists the static patterns generate perceptual vibrations because too many details are concentrated in a relatively small visual field. The density of visual information, the closeness of the fine lines, leads to optical difficulty in perceptual adaptation. The neuropsychologist R.L. Gregory suggests that Riley's paintings, as well as other examples of op art, produce visual vibrations because the closely spaced lines eventuate in extreme contrast which overload primarily retinal, or visual circuits.[65]

Similar patterns to Ludwig's *Cinematic Painting*, consisting of sharp and soft radial edges, were used for the study of depth effects in the 1920s, and described by A. Ames, Jr., C.A. Proctor, and B. Ames.[66]

Looking at certain visual patterns can be a highly disturbing experience. These patterns can be extremely simple, such as repeated parallel lines, or wheels containing finely lined rays. According to D.M. MacKay, these visual patterns upset the perceptual system due to their redundancy. The trouble with this hypothesis is, says Gregory, that certain repetitive, redundant structures disturb the visual apparatus, whereas some do not.[67]

It is also possible that the disturbing optical effects result from after images generated by the actual visual patterns. These after images interfere with the original layout as the source of the optical stimulus. The interplay between veridical stimulus and the perception of after images can produce moiré patterns. The flickering circular shapes which can be seen on a pattern of straight lines converging into a center are projected moiré effects. Normally, moiré patterns are engaging image structures made of overlapping geometrical forms of repetitive elements. When two grid patterns, for instance, are superimposed visual moiré structures emerge.

To the scientist the visual arts offer tangible proof that there is a difference between the reality of the world and the reality presented to us through perception. Although the phenomenological experience presents the shapes and colors of objects in such a compelling and familiar manner that the identity of the world and its image is taken for granted, the scientific investigation of visual phenomena through art obviously contradicts this popular assumption.

Abstract art particularly is an excellent tool for analyzing visual phenomena because it represents a system of controlled demonstration. By controlling and manipulating a limited number of stimulus variables in the painting, the artist explores their perceptual effects.

The visual mechanisms of the perceptual process include involuntary eye movements. The fast oscillation of the eyeballs consisting of between thirty to one hundred cycles per second is one of these eye movements. This rapid movement of the eyeballs of which we are not aware is described in the psychological literature under the term of nystagmus. D. W. Massaro rejects the hypothesis that nystagmus plays a role in the production of the vibrating effects perceived in Riley's or Ludwig's paintings.[68] The rapid oscillations of the eye, a process in which the eyeballs move only a very limited distance, add nothing to the visual stimulus. Nystagmus is an insignificant event as far as visual information processing is concerned. It can be compared to the meaningless background noise which does not interfere with the significant content of auditory information processing either.

The fast tremors of the eye in nystagmus involve slight but permanent interruptions of the perceptual process. Thus, the stable image that our visual system presents to us about the world is merely an illusion. In actuality the image of a scene projected on the retina is constantly jerking.

The little understood mechanisms of the perceptual system has another kind of eye movements as well: the saccades. These are larger jumps of the eye than the movements of nystagmus. They are also slower: The oscillation frequency of the saccadic eye movement is up to five times per second. Similarly to nystagmus, saccades occur also as an unconscious process during which perception is suppressed. However, the visual apparatus curbs the intermissions to rise into the level of consciousness. Instead, it produces an illusion in which scenes from successive fixations are combined into a continuous view. So, despite the mincing effect of the saccadic eye movements, we see the world in terms of continuous pictures, and not as a set of oscillating chunks.

It is possible to explore the relationship between saccadic eye movements and after images through the arrangement of a set of black discs as shown below:

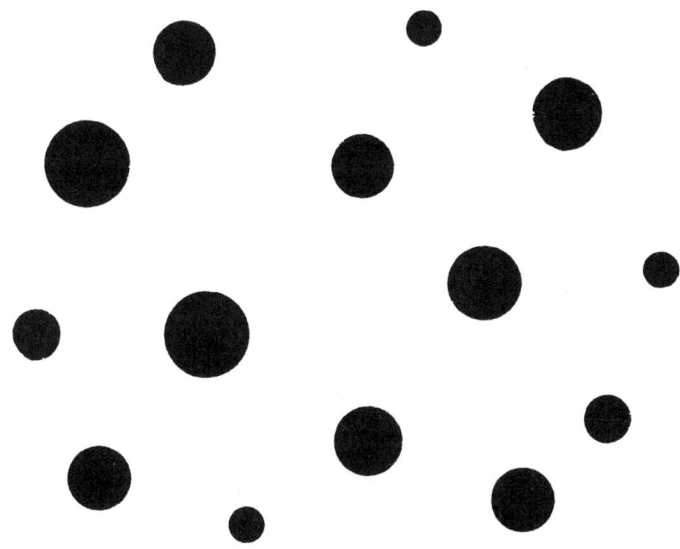

As the eye moves across the array of black discs, after a while white discs begin to appear beside them. These white discs appear literally out of nowhere. The illusion is the result of saccades combined with the temporary excitation of the light receptors in the retina, the rods and cones. As the eye moves from one black disc to another, the contrasting white field which separates them prevents the continuity of fixation. Therefore, the visual scene is segmented. In other words this means that the image of one disc is not integrated entirely with the next one. Due to the sharp contrast of tonal value existing between black and white, the light receptors of the retina fail to adapt themselves to the changing scenario. The receptors receiving light from the white surface become overwhelmingly light adapted in comparison to those which obtain light from the black discs. Each saccadic eye movement changes the scene on the retina as well. As the eye moves from the black discs and fixates on the white surface after images emerge. The appearance of white discs on a white surface as after images is due to the greater sensitivity of those receptors to light that were fixated on the black discs than those which became light adapted in staring at the white background. Those retinal receptors which previously were fixated on the black discs became dark-adapted, and therefore they react with increased light sensitivity to the stimulus of the white surface.

The term op art was coined in America. The first time it appeared in print was in 1964 when the October issue of *Time* magazine came out. But like in many other instances, the phenomenon preceded the name. Op art is as old as art itself. From prehistoric times artist explored and exploited the optical fallibility of the eye.

The stone age artists in the caves of Lascaux, Altamira, or Pech-Merle, painted superposed animals which by their partial overlapping create the illusion of depth.[69] Even more than these paleolithic images, the abstract patterns of prehistoric pottery and of textiles represent plastic expressions congenial to op art.

Illusionistic effects used by the ancients can be seen in the *Battle of Issus* , a Pompeian mosaic depicting the victory of Alexander the Great over the Persian King Darius. The striking depth illusions achieved in this mural stem from the superimposed parts of the bodies of fighting soldiers and their horses. The Romans liked to paint illusionistic landscapes showing wide vistas rendered on their windowless walls.

It was the Sienese painter Simone Martini who in the fourteenth century relinquished the medieval tradition of representing the protagonists as the largest figures in the painting. Though he was not aware of the perceptual phenomenon which was described about three centuries later in Descartes' *Dioptrics* (1637) as size constancy, Simone Martini painted according to what he knew: All people in the background as well as in the foreground, regardless of their distance from the observer, were represented in the painting equal in size. He knew that people remain of the same size, regardless where they are, and simply ignored the perceptual fact that as people or things recede from the spectator, they seem to decrease in size.

But Giotto di Bondone (1267-1337), a contemporary artist of Simone Martini, already distinguished between retinal image and knowledge based on conceptual experience. He broke with the size constancy habit and took a further step toward representational realism. His art was characterized by more striking depth illusion than Simone Martini's paintings. Notwithstanding the occasional awkwardness of his depth illusions, from Giotto, through Brunelleschi, Piero della Francesca, Masaccio, Uccello, and Leonardo, the road was open to the perfection of illusory depth representation. The giants of the Italian Renaissance evolved the theory and practice of high realism through the quasi-mathematical laws of perspective.

Artists outside of Italy adopted quite similar techniques. The Dutch masters of the seventeenth century, Rembrandt and Ruisdael, although departed from the ideals of classicism, clung to the method of perspective, and pursued the quest for illusionism. Rather than depicting clearly defined forms, Rembrandt expressed emotions. In his works the interplay of light and shadow evoked moods. The pictorial effects that he accomplished through the technique of chiaroscuro make him a forerunner of both op art and expressionism. In contrast to Rembrandt who expressed the inner landscapes of the human psyche, Ruisdael painted the physical world in a style in which the illusion of depth seems to be stretched to infinity. He exerted a profound influence on the painterly development of the great English landscape painter of the nineteenth century, John Constable. In the latter's work illusionism acquired its trompe l'oeil level of perfection.

The nineteenth century represents the great watershed in the history of modern art. The tradition of academic painting lagged behind the aesthetic needs of the new world created by the French Revolution as well as by the Industrial Revolution. The invention of photography prompted innovative artists to search for new ways of plastic expression. The reciprocal influence of art and photography produced a complex, new stylistic organism, a form of aesthetic symbiosis.

The reappraisal of the aesthetic heritage led the impressionists to adopt scientific theories of the age, which they applied to their art. However, the invention of photography gave rise to ambivalent reactions within the artistic community. The camera meant both unfair competition and new possibilities for the artist.

Delacroix welcomed the discovery of the camera, and Courbet's paintings of the Chateau of Chillon (1874) were based on a photograph taken in 1867 by Adolphe Braun.[70] Seurat too was interested in the new art of photography. He was convinced that the dynamism of movement can be investigated through photography. In *Le Chahut* Seurat integrated compositional elements which are most similar to the chronophotographs of Étienne-Jules Marey. The painter also became acquainted with the photographic studies of E. Muybridge. The English photographer experimented with instantaneous photography. His pictures of animal locomotion demonstrated that, notwithstanding the common view to the contrary, it was possible indeed during the gallop of the horse that the animal lifted all four legs off the ground at once. However, Muybridge's photographic series of animal locomotion also contradicted traditional artistic representations. Seurat noticed that the posture of the horse depicted in his *Le Cirque* was not in line with Muybridge's discoveries. When Puvis de Chavannes came to see the Indépendants' exhibition in March 1891, Seurat said to Signac: "He will notice the mistake I have made in the horse."[71] Puvis de Chavannes, the decorator of many official buildings in France, including the Hôtel de Ville and the Pantheon of Paris, was also known as an ardent student of Muybridge's photographs.

The development of photography played an important role in the breaking up of the Renaissance tradition, because it prompted visionary painters to strive for the radical transformation of the cognitive status of art. Seurat, Cézanne, and van Gogh established new styles which abolished the traditional laws of perspective from painting. The cubists introduced non-Euclidean space into the pictorial plane. And they differentiated between seeing and knowing as well.

When Picasso saw an eye, wrote Gertrude Stein,

> the other one did not exist for him and only the one he saw did exist for him and as a painter, and particularly as a Spanish painter, he was right, one sees what one sees, the rest is a reconstruction from memory and painters have nothing to do with reconstructions, nothing to do with memory, they concern themselves only with visible things and so the cubism of Picasso was an effort to make a picture of these visible things and the result was disconcerting for him and for the others . . . even for

his most intimate friends, even for Guillaume Apollinaire.[72]

Thus, Picasso's approach to the problem of visual perception rested on the assumption that the painter should express the results of his analyzed vision as he saw them, and not as appearance associated with knowledge. His aim was to express the reality of the visual world in terms of idea and essence: A reality decomposed in the creative process and reassambled by the painter as analogues of the whole.

In contrast to the artists of the Renaissance who were moved by a passion for depicting the appearances of the world through the illusionism of painting, the cubists abandoned the use of illusory effects from their art. They had grown bored with painting as the imitations of objects.

At certain point of its development cubism began to invent forms rather than deriving them from the analysis of visible things. With the debut of the collage in 1912, Braque and Picasso left behind the analytical phase of cubism and introduced synthetic cubism. The collage as a pasted up assemblage of actual playing cards, strings, corrugated cardboards, newspapers, and other similar objects, represented a new form of synthetic reality. It changed the ontological status of painting by decreasing the distance between art and actuality. For through the incorporation of cards, strings, and pieces of paper, not illusory imitations but segments of the real world became inlaid and charged with a new role as art.

However, it was not the affiliation of cubism with abstraction itself which eliminated the use of illusionistic devices from it. Abstraction was merely a by-product of cubism. Artists like Braque and Picasso deliberately stopped short of reaching the stage of total abstraction.[73]

Interestingly enough, it was the subsequent development of abstract art which revived the pursuit of illusionism in painting. The most conspicuous examples in this respect can be found in op art, a branch of abstract painting. Through the dynamic properties of their works, op artists, like Victor Vasarely, Josef Albers, and Yaacov Agam, generate illusory images and sensations in the visual system of the spectator.

Born in the Hungarian City of Pécs, on April 9, 1908, Vasarely first attended medical school in Budapest, and only later decided to pursue an artistic career. In 1928 he joined Alexander Bortnyik's school of graphic arts, the "Mühely", which was founded on the model of the famous Bauhaus art school in Weimar. Here he became acquainted with the visual poetry of Chagall, the purist machine forms of Le Corbusier, the white square on a white ground suprematism of Malevich, and with the aesthetics of Kandinsky. The latter viewed abstract art as a visual analogue of music and mathematics.

In 1930 Vasarely arrived in Paris. In the years that followed he crystallized the aesthetic principles which constitute the foundations of his plastic output. Vasarely saw the future of art in the abolition of traditional easel painting and figuration. Instead, he wanted to see the intelligent adaptation of art to our mechanical age, an age characterized by rapid urbanization, dynamism, and the conquests of science. Especially under the impact of gestalt theory, he was deliberately and passionately searching for an artistic idiom capable of generating perceptual shocks. The optical ingredients of this abstract idiom were geometrical forms, rhythm, balance, simplicity, movement, colored and luminous stimulants.

Vasarely approached art in terms of communal needs and integration. His aesthetic vision was bound up with architecture, monumentalism, and the application of new materials. Similarly to the work of the Israeli artist Yaacov Agam, Vasarely's paintings can be described as cinetic art. In contrast to kinetic art which is a function of mechanical movement, cineticism is bound up with optical ambiguity, and multi-dimensional illusions. [74] In Agam's polymorphic images three dimensional surfaces are transformed into various visual compositions. The metamorphoses occur as a result of the changing viewing positions of the observer.

In the 1950s and 1960s Vasarely exhibited his work in New York, Oslo, Milan, London, Brussels, Cologne, Buenos Aires, Boston and Helsinki. Through these exhibitions the artist strengthened his international position.

At an early stage of his career, Vasarely devoted his creative energy to the passionate search for pure composition and for plastic essence. His attempt to combine form and color into an intertwined whole should be seen in the light of this search. He implemented the idea of the plastic union of form and color through complicated research. The process led to the invention of a peculiar visual language. It is based on the interplay of color permutations and geometrical forms which lend themselves to unlimited visual combinations. In Vasarely's system form is defined by color. His alphabet of colors consists of red, gray, cobalt violet, ultramarine, chrome yellow, and emerald green. All of these six fundamental hues are used in tonal variations from light to dark, and can yield an infinite number of both colored and formal algorithms.[75]

Numerous works of Vasarely are based on the repetitive use of the square motif. Among his favorite optical illusions the so called Hermann grid maintains a central position (*Eridan III*, 1956, *Supernovae*, 1959-61).

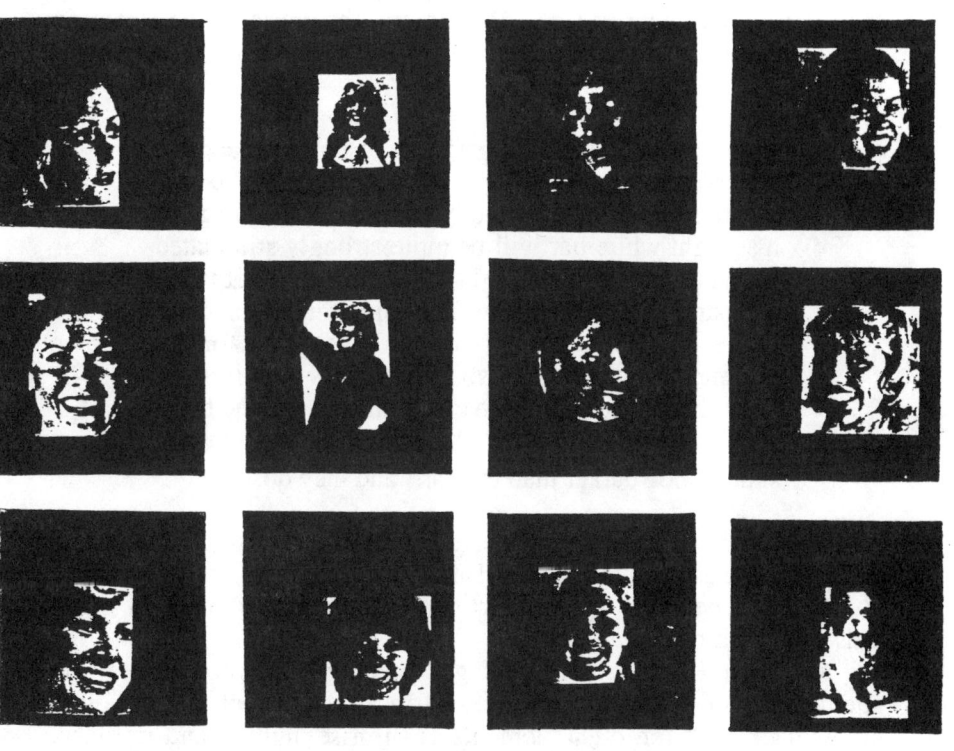

COLLAGE WITH HERMANN GRID

Unlike in Vasarely's pure geometrical abstractions, the collage shown above consists of a series of images superimposed on twelve black squares. At the intersections of the white lines separating the squares small grey dots seem to appear out of nowhere. As my collage demonstrates, the perceptual effect occurring here -- known as the Hermann grid phenomenon -- is not eliminited by the interference of the pictorial content of the inlaid photographs.

The bulk of visual information is processed in the visual cortex of the brain. According to Colin Blakemore, the cause of the Hermann grid phenomenon does not originite in the visual cortex, but in the retina:

> Imagine the image of a grid falling on the receptive fields of retinal ganglion cells. A cell with its on-centre receptive field directly underneath the image of a straight white bar will be quite strongly stimulated because rather little light falls on its inhibitory surround. But a receptive field lying directly under a white cross will have twice as much light on its inhibitory surround and so the neuron's activity will be much reduced. If these ganglion cells tell the brain about the brightness of the stimulus, the crosses should look darker than the bars, and they do.[76]

The course of art history is steered by trials and errors. Change and continuity are established by the visual dialogue. In this respect art is a conversation between artists. Artists respond to the works of other artists by creating new ones.

My own Herman grid collage oversteps the bounds of the attenuated subject matter inherent in op art. Through animation it brings back such forgotten elements as surprise, humor, and mystery. The result is a composite, multi-functional image based on the old and the new.

Op art has excluded both figuration and symbolism from its visual repository. As a visual comment on this predicament, another collage of mine -- *Cinematism Transcended* -- came into existence. It consists of a series of radial designs rendered in six squarely units. These patterns evolved as part of trial and error procedures, the results of heuristic analysis. I had a dual aim in this experiment. On the one hand I wanted to explore the perceptual properties of a physically static yet optically oscillating wheel, and on the other hand to transcend the prescribed confines of op art. The resulting collage seems to support the hypothesis that the perceptual vibrations are caused by the overloading of the visual apparatus. In the first upper left wheel, perceptual tension increases as the eye moves from the rim of the wheel along the thinning bars towards the hub. The density of the visual information around the centre of the wheel strains optical information processing, and generates moiré effects. Superimposition of a smaller circle around the hub of the right upper wheel decreases the gamut of oscillation, due to the introduction of a structuring, eye fixating constituent. By the reduction of the number of spokes in the right middle wheel visual information density decreases as well, and the vibrations disappear.

The domain of op art is transcended through the right bottom unit of the collage. The hub of the wheel is enlarged, and the spokes radiating from it form a rather irregular pattern. Transcendence occurs as the pattern is transformed, through image mutation, into a symbol of the rising sun. This pictorial transformation has nothing to do with op art. The rising sun is an archetypal symbol. Painted red, it is also used as a flag of the Japanese navy.

The investigation of color is a central field of involvement for many artists. The scientist might unweave the rainbow, to paraphrase Keats, but the artist enhances the color experience. However, not all artists are colorists. Picasso and Braque, for instance, were not concerned with color but with form. In contrast to them, the works of Delaunay, Picabia, Léger, and Chagall represent a triumphal celebration of brilliant color.

The American artist Ben Shahn was once struck by the enormous difference existing between the old pictures hung on the walls of the Pennsylvania Academy and the paintings of contemporary artists. "I remember experiencing a certain thrill of pride as I noted the contrast", he wrote in *The Shape of Content:*

> The new pictures constituted a very river of color . . .
> they glowed richly. And in comparison, the older
> paintings, certainly constituting some of the very
> finest in pre-impressionist art, seemed almost a gray-
> to-tan monotone. I felt proud of my contemporaries,
> and of painting. The forms of the new works stood
> out bold and clear and the colors were infinite.[77]

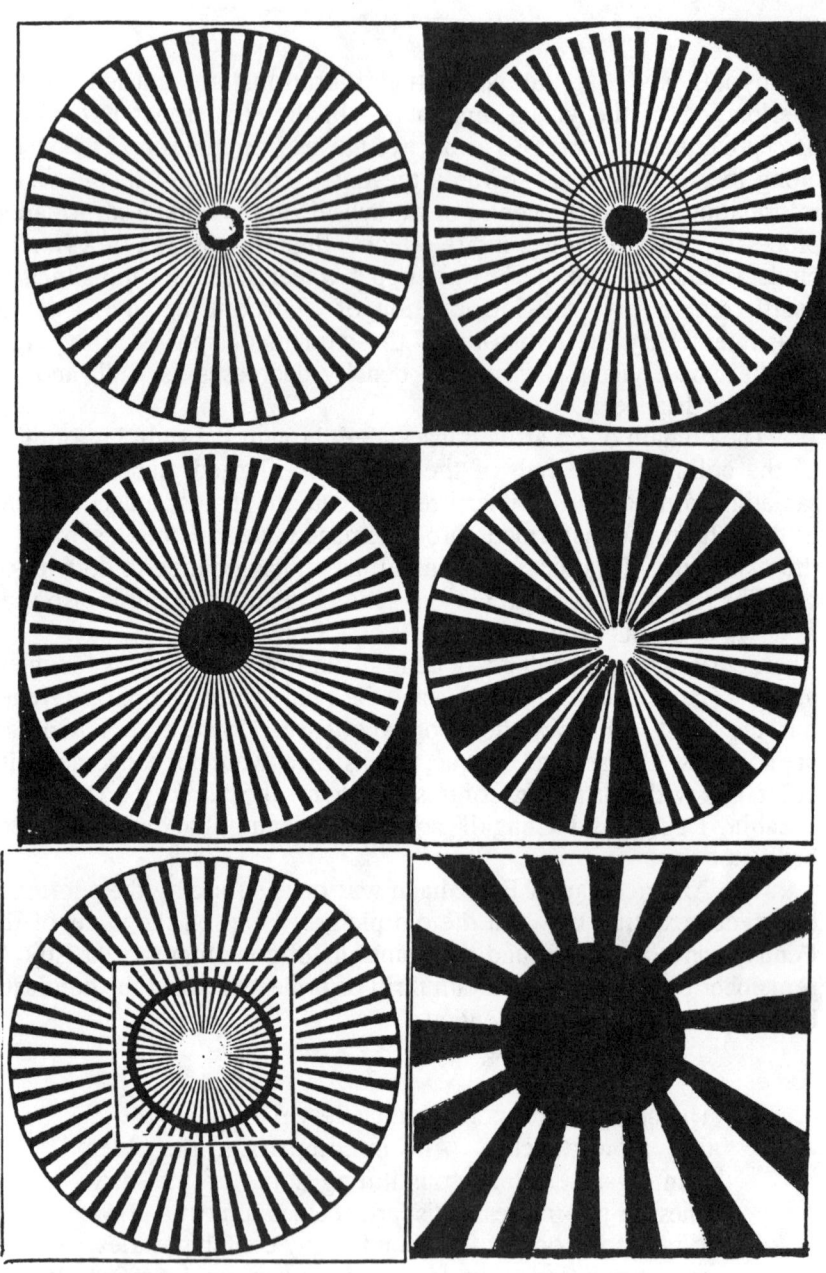

CINEMATISM TRANSCENDED   collage, 1985

The static patterns generate optical vibrations, due to the overloading of the visual apparatus. At the right bottom the pattern is transformed through image mutation into an archetypal symbol of the rising sun.

For the scientist color is the gamut of wavelengths, or frequencies of light, discernible to the eye. However, color is not an objective phenomenon, but a sensation. It is not a specific , intrinsic property of light rays and objects. Color is a   visual   content of consciousness. It evolves as an interaction between the light entering the eye and the brain. It is the latter which interprets the wavelength distribution of the light rays. The process is analogous to the sensation of taste. The taste of an apple, for instance, is not an intrinsic property of the fruit, but an interaction between the apple and the person eating it. As a sensory modality, taste is determined by the chemical receptors of the nose and the tongue.

The subjective nature of color as a sensation is demonstrated through the phenomenon of color blindness. This congenital visual defect is characterized by partial or complete inability to see colors. The totally color blind person sees only shades of gray. This does not mean, of course, that the world perceived by the color blind is less real than the world seen by others. There are no absolute or monopolistic models of reality.

Nevertheless, color plays a central role in visual perception. The optical data with which the eye is constantly flooded consist of intertwined shapes and colors. According to color scientist Harald Kueppers, about forty percent "of all of the information that an individual normally receives consists of information about color."[78]

The artist can and should be interested in the physical study of light and color, in the physiological properties of the perceptual system. For the artist, however, color is not a physical or psycho-physiological problem. For the artist color is both a visual metaphor and a poetic reality. It is a source of joy, a celebration of life and a manifestation of the beauty of existence. The world is colorful. Its palette analogues are manipulated environments which in the image making process the artist transcribes onto the surface of the canvas.

Josef Albers was one of the most conspicuous colorists of the twentieth century, whose passion of logic and logic of passion turned art into science and science to art. Born in Germany, in 1888, Albers began to paint in an abstract style in 1913, and became a teacher at the Bauhaus. When the school was closed down by the Nazis in 1933, he emigrated, and in 1939 he became a naturalized American. Albers taught in the United States at Black Mountain College in North Carolina, and at Yale. He died in 1976.

Albers was influenced by the constructivists. His geometrical abstractions evolved as the materialization of his strife for the simple and the absolute. It was at Yale University, serving as chairman of the department of architecture and design, that he began to develop his renowned series of lithographs and paintings under the title of *Homage to the Square*. These clear-cut, hard-edge, rectangular images parallel the obsession of Mondrian with the horizontal and the vertical. Albers was both a minimalist and an op artist. In his book, *Interaction of Colors* (1963), he demonstrated numerous fascinating optical illusions related to the behavior of color. He showed, for instance, that due to the impact of the background hues, one and the same color can look as two different colors, whereas two different colors can be made looking identical. He also took advantage of the perceptual fact that chromatically close colors can generate the illusion of a third color. His optical investigations had been extended to the realm of reversed after images, and to the Bezold effect. The latter is related to the discovery of Wilhelm von Bezold (1837-1907) "that certain strong colors, when evenly distributed, changed entirely the effect of his rug designs." His discovery, explains Albers, was similary to that of the French Impressionists, who "aimed at an optical mixture effect. Instead of mixing their colors on their palettes, they applied them in small dabs on the canvas so that the colors were mixed, at a distance, in our eyes."[79]

I admired Albers's contribution to the study and understanding of visual perception; his scientific method of color investigation, and his application of mathematical precision to the domain of art. Yet I was also amazed at the consistency of his self imposed confines. After all, for a considerable period of his life Albers painted nothing but squares. It was in the wake of these thoughts that I made the concrete poem, "Tribute to Josef Albers, Homage to the Ellipse". The ellipse is a neglected aesthetic form. In contrast to the square, which is a rarely found shape in nature, the ellipse abounds in the world around us. Biological organisms, including the human body, contain infinite numbers of ellipses. Our earth itself is an ellipsoid which, together with other planets, moves around the sun on elliptic orbits.

An optical illusion, which was known already in antiquity, concerns the apparent orbit of the full moon moving from the horizon to the zenith. The image of the horizontal disc of the moon looks larger than its zenithal counterpart. Artists frequently paint the moon as a device to enhance the sense of space, to balance the composition, or in order to express symbolic as well as poetic content.

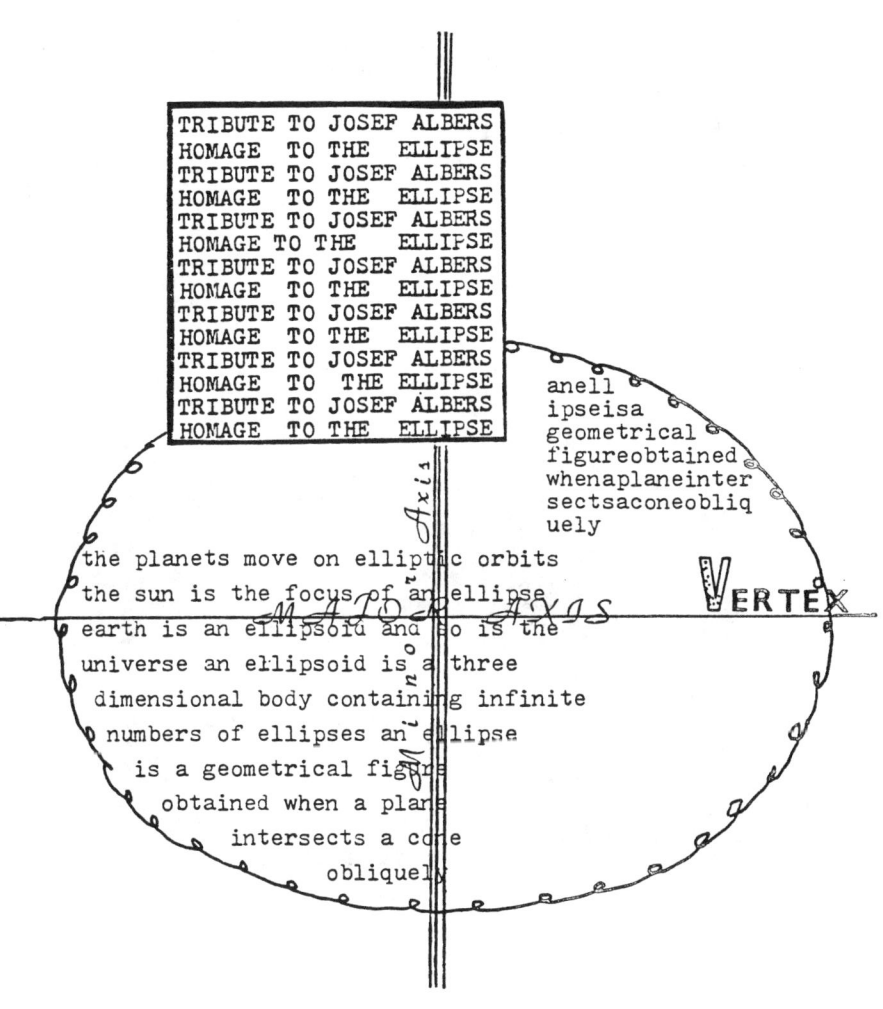

TRIBUTE TO JOSEF ALBERS
HOMAGE TO THE ELLIPSE
TRIBUTE TO JOSEF ALBERS
HOMAGE TO THE ELLIPSE
TRIBUTE TO JOSEF ALBERS
HOMAGE TO THE ELLIPSE
TRIBUTE TO JOSEF ALBERS
HOMAGE TO THE ELLIPSE
TRIBUTE TO JOSEF ALBERS
HOMAGE TO THE ELLIPSE
TRIBUTE TO JOSEF ALBERS
HOMAGE TO THE ELLIPSE
TRIBUTE TO JOSEF ALBERS
HOMAGE TO THE ELLIPSE

anell
ipseisa
geometrical
figureobtained
whenaplaneinter
sectsaconeobliq
uely

the planets move on elliptic orbits
the sun is the focus of an ellipse
earth is an ellipsoid and so is the
universe an ellipsoid is a three
dimensional body containing infinite
numbers of ellipses an ellipse
is a geometrical figure
obtained when a plane
intersects a cone
obliquely

VERTEX

Axis

MAJOR AXIS

TRIBUTE TO JOSEPH ALBERS, HOMAGE TO THE ELLIPSE.

137

The Alexandrian astronomer and mathematician Ptolemy in the second century suggested that the moon illusion is linked to the size constancy phenomenon: The moon appearing on the horizon looks larger than in the zenith due to the discrepancy of distance perception. For, objects at the horizon tend to recede; they look farther away from the observer than those at the zenith.

Notwithstanding the arguments of E.G. Boring and of his colleagues at Harvard, psychologists I. Rock and L. Kaufman in the 1960s postulated that Ptolemy was right with regard to the nature of the moon illusion.[80]

The moon illusion can be related also to the Ebbinghaus illusion which is shown below:

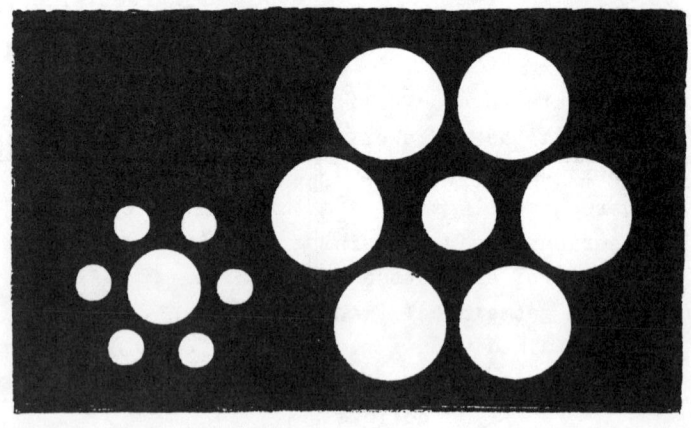

THE EBBINGHAUS ILLUSION

In this illusion the two central circles appear to be unequal, despite the fact that they are equal This geometrical illusion lends itself to theoretical explanation through the holistic approach of gestalt psychology. Particular details of a pattern cannot be judged independently, because each individual part of the image is dependent on the whole. It is the context which determines the nature of perception.

Figure and background act upon one another, depend on each other. The whole is greater than the sum total of its parts.

In the perceptual process the size of a thing is judged in comparison to other elements in the visual field. By applying the gestalt theory to the moon illusion, we find that the moon at the horizon appears larger than usual, because its image interacts with other objects. Near the horizon there is little space, or none at all, between the moon and the contours of the terrain. But in contrast to the horizontal moon, the zenithal moon appears to be much smaller because it is surrounded by large empty space.[81]

The ancient architects were aware of the importance of optical illusions. The builders of the Parthenon, Ictinus and Callicrates, in the fifth century B.C. built the wonderful temple on the Acropolis made of marble in which they utilized various sorts of optical deceptions. In order to make the façade of the temple appear straight, they altered the proportions of the building to compensate for perceptual curvature distortions. They were aware of the irradiation illusion as well: They knew that a bright object appears to be bigger than a dark one. To offset this illusion Ictinus and Callicrates built the Parthenon so that the columns viewed against the dark walls of the temple are thinner than the angle columns which are usually seen against the luminous sky.

The Roman architect Vitruvius discussed various aspects of perceptual illusions relevant to his vocation. Thus, in *The Ten Books on Architecture* he said, for instance, that the builder must take into consideration the appropriate proportions of architectural elements: "For the eye is always in search of beauty, and if we do not gratify its desire for pleasure" by measured adjustments, "and thus make compensation for ocular deception, a clumsy and awkward appearance will be presented to the beholder."[82]

A specific category of optical illusions is concerned with the phenomenon of depth reversing figures. One of these was investigated by the Swiss crystallographer, L.A. Necker in the first half of the nineteenth century. The perceptual device, known as Necker's cube, is a plane projection of a cube viewed from a distance. Its characteristic optical effect finds its expression in the spontaneous process of alternating perspectives.

The perceptual depth reverse is an optical flip-flop in which the observer sees the cube as if from above at one time, and at another time as if from below. The triggering impulse of the depth reverse seems to be generated by the brain, and not by retinal information.

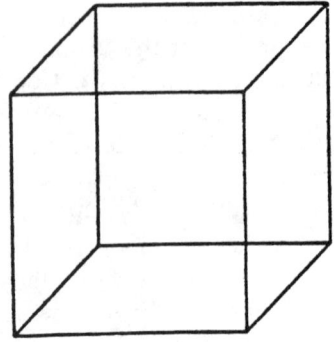

THE NECKER CUBE (1832)

Another depth re-versing structure lends itself to different perceptual interpretations. It can be imagined as an open box, or a roof seen from above. It may be the visual representation of an elongated pamphlet, or of a restaurant menu as well.

FLIP-FLOP PATTERN

As an ambiguous flip-flop pattern it is seen either from the inside or from the outside. A similar pattern, when it is turned by ninety degree, is called Mach's figure; after the Austrian physicist Ernst Mach (1838-1916) who described it.

140

Both in the Necker cube and in the Flip-Flop Pattern shown on page 140, the perceptual somersault of the switching perspective is spontaneous. The brain in fact never makes up its mind how to finalize the depth interpretation, and it remains undecided with regard to which side is indeed in or out.

The scientific investigation of optical illusions in the nineteenth century began to gather momentum. Since the 1850s more than a thousand scientific papers dealing with the subject were published. Despite the considerable amount of this published research, psychologists consider the accumulated knowledge about the precise mechanism of illusion formation as far from being satisfactory. The process through which optical stimuli are transformed into images is still a complete mystery.

An airplane accident which occurred in 1965 underlines the importance of the understanding of the perceptual process in general, and of the nature of optical illusions in particular. On December 4th of that year, an Eastern Airlines Lockheed 1049 C and TWA Boeing 707 collided at approximately 11,000 feet in the sky, in the vicinity of New York. Four people died and forty nine others were injured in the accident. According to the U.S. Civil Aeronautics Board, the tragedy resulted from an optical deception. Due to a perceptual illusion created by the sloping contours of cloud formations, the Lockheed crew misjudged the altitude separation and collided with the Boeing.

The optical effect which caused the accident is known as the Poggendorff illusion. The Lockheed airliner was forced to make an emergency landing. It crashed on an open field and was consumed by flames. The accident is reported in *Seeing is Deceiving: The Psychology of Visual Illusions* (1978), by Stanley Coren and Joan Stern Girgus. "Perhaps the idea that visual illusions are interesting but relatively unimportant oddities of perception is itself merely another illusion", the authors conclude.[83]

The Poggendorff illusion was discovered in the nineteenth century. It was in the year of 1860 that the astronomer F. Zöllner, of the City of Leipzig, described in a scientific paper an illusion of direction and an illusion of location. In these types of illusions the direction of a figure is distorted in perception, or the location of spatial constituents appears to be shifted. Similarly to all other kinds of visual illusions, deceptions of direction and location too result from the existing discordance between actual physical conditions and their percepts.

In Zöllner's illusion the vertical lines, intersected by the fishbone like short diagonals, seem to diverge, but they are in fact parallel. Further scrutiny of the figure shows, that not only the direction of the

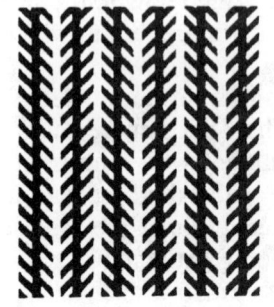

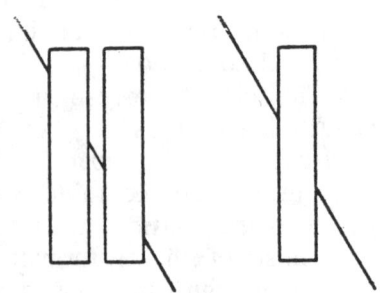

ZÖLLNER'S FIGURE   POGGENDORFF'S FIGURE

parallel lines seems to be distorted, but the intersecting diagonals appear to be displaced as well.

Zöllner submitted his treatise for publication in the *Annalen der Physik,* and it was the journal's editor who noticed the twofold illusionary properties of the pattern. In the revised version of the paper, Zöllner paid tribute to his editor and named the newly discovered optical phenomenon Poggendorff illusion.

The Poggendorff figure is a geometrical pattern which involves location distortion: As a straight oblique line passes through a rectangle it appears to be jagged. The same apparent discontinuity occurs when the line crosses a set of parallel rectangles.

Optical phenomena have no universal explanation, because they are so different. The physiological mechanisms of after images, for instance, differ from those responsible for the Zöllner and Poggendorff illusions. On the other hand, it is noteworthy that the entire phenomenon of perception is based on falsity. For, perception does not present to our consciousness a carbon copy of actuality. Instead of the unbroken wholeness of the world as a totality, we perceive symbolized abstractions. In any case, we become aware of misperceptions only when the incongruous nature nature of the sensation surfaces through comparison. When more information becomes available, which provides clues and reliable controls, then the realization and the correction of visual illusions become possible as well.

As experiments demonstrate, the perceptual process never yields an absolute revelation of actuality. What we see is always a personal construction of reality, never a sure thing. Percepts heavily rely on past experience. We are able to carry out taken for granted simple actions, such as opening a door, descending the stairs, or crossing the street, because our past experience taught us how to succeed in them. Successful action depends on correct prediction which is a combination of past experience and inferred probability. Our acts are determined to a considerable extent by what we perceive, they lead to new perceptions, and also generate new acts.

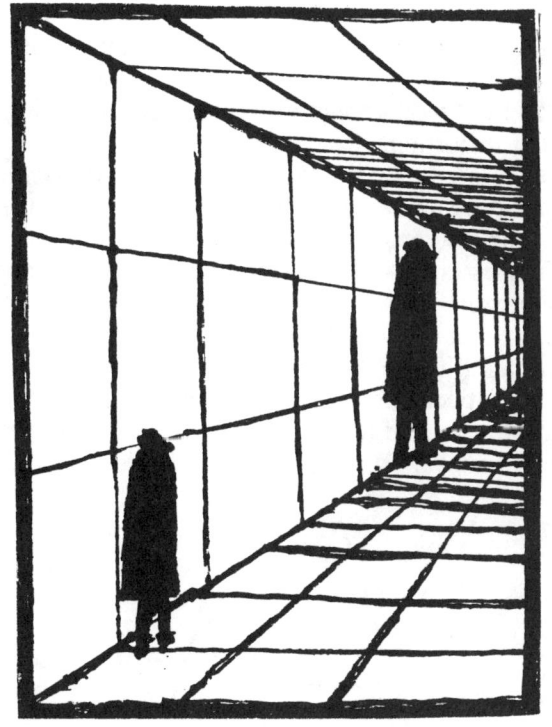

THE CORRIDOR ILLUSION

Visual illusions are quite common in everyday life. Radar operators for example, must be aware of the fact that flight paths often appear on the screen as normally distanced whereas in reality the aircrafts are on collision orbit. The misperception is caused by a variation of the Poggendorff illusion. In a different context, the interplay of various architectural elements can give rise to unwanted optical effects asserting themselves as discontinuous lines, misplaced columns, and windows. Modern high rise buildings frequently upset the delicate optical balance of older streets and squares. They can destroy thoroughly the human scale, and dwarf the sublime spires of ancient cathedrals. Finally, and again in a different context, various optical illusions are to be blamed for many car accidents. Moiré patterns, after images, distortions of perspective, location and direction, cause drivers to misperceive distances as well as pavement and traffic conditions.

One of the most well known visual illusions involving perspective is the corridor distortion. The two lonely human figures seen in the picture above appear to be of different height. The one that is farther away from the spectator seems to be taller. But in fact they are of the same height. The discrepancy between the actual size and the apparent size of the figures is the result of their relative location in a visual system of converging lines.

Another salient perspective illusion is the so called Ponzo distortion. In this illusion the lower line of the horizontal pair seems shorter than the upper one, although their length is the same. The optical distortion is related to the corridor illusion in the sense that it is again a system of converging lines which generates the deception.

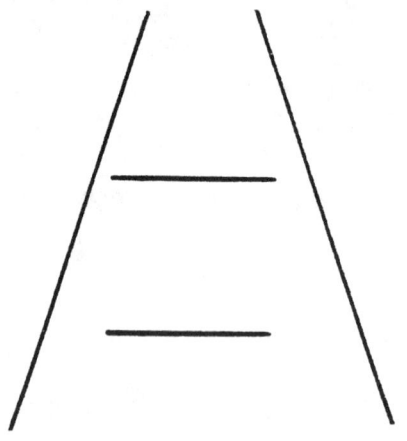

THE PONZO ILLUSION

144

An additional optical illusion produced by converging lines is the Müller-Lyer illusion. It was first introduced in 1889 by the German psychologist Franz Müller-Lyer. It consists of a pair of parallel lines enclosed in four arrowheads. Despite the fact that the two lines are the same length, the one with the outgoing fins looks longer than the line with the ingoing arrowheads.

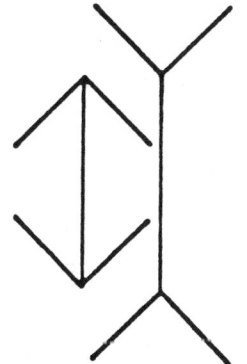 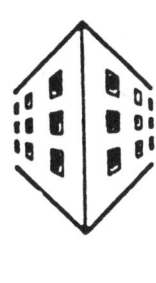 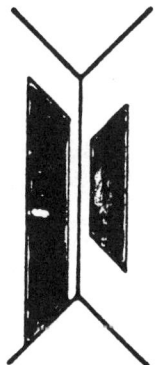

THE MÜLLER-LYER ILLUSION
AND ITS THREE DIMENSIONAL INTERPRETATION.

145

R.L. Gregory has suggested the application of the perspective theory of perception to the Müller-Lyer illusion. According to him, the arrow with the ingoing fins could be perceived as an external corner of an architectural complex, whereas the arrow with the outgoing fins could be seen as the inside corner of a room.[84]

This is of course a perceptual possibility. Indeed, the line with the wings directed inward is endowed with perspective cues which are capable of turning the two dimensional figure into a three dimensional projection. Thus, the central axis of the figure is seen as an outside corner of a building. On the other hand, the arrowheads turning their wings outwards give rise to a projection of an interior scene. Here the central axis represents the vertical edge of the corner of a room, whereas the angles of the arrows pointing outwards represent the intersections of the walls with the floor and with the ceiling.

The perception of depth involves apparent changes in the size of the observed object. In the context of the converging lines of the corridor illusion and of the Ponzo illusion visual constituents of equal length appear to be larger the farther away they are from the observer. In the Müller-Lyer illusion, however, the situation is different. For, how are we supposed to interpret the relative spatial positions of its two main parts? After all, both can be imagined moving back and forth in space, together or separately.

Gregory has tried to apply a general perspective theory to the Müller-Lyer illusion. This means that "those parts of illusion figures which would represent distant features are enlarged, and those parts corresponding to near features are shrunk."[85] He suggests that the ingoing arrows representing the inside corner recede in depth, and that the out-going arrows representing the outside corner move toward the observer. In terms of the perspective theory this of course implies that the size of the out-going arrows increases.

However, the application of the perspective theory to the Müller-Lyer illusion is an inconsistent one. As I mentioned above, the two major elements of this illusion are basically independent units that can be imagined moving back and forth in space, together or separately. Consequently, it is possible to imagine that the arrow set representing the interior corner is moving away from the observer. But in this case, why should the receding corner of a room increase its apparent size? Assuming that it does is contrary to the mechanism of constancy scaling. It upsets the tendency to perceive objects as the same size, regardless of the position of the viewer. It is also contrary to the perspective view of spatial recession, whereby the apparent size of objects decreases as they move away from the observer. Interestingly enough, the bare architectural complex depicted in Max Ernst's painting, *The Virgin Punishing the Infant Jesus* (1928), features a pair of receding and approaching corners in which the arrowheads turning their wings outwards are farther away from the observer than those with wings directed inward.

At the end of the nineteenth century researchers from Cambridge University conducted studies with the Müller-Lyer illusion among the tribes living on the Pacific Islands. They found that the islanders in the region of their investigation, between New Guinea and Australia, were much less susceptible to the optical distortion than subjects of Western countries.[86]

In the 1960s a more systematic study of optical illusions was implemented across cultures. The Müller-Lyer illusion played a central role in this cross cultural research. M.H. Segall, D.T. Campbell, and M.J. Herskovitz tested the susceptibility distribution of about two thousand subjects from fourteen non-European sites and from the United States. They hypothesized that if the perceptual process is determined by environmental factors, then various groups of people must react differently to the same optical illusions. Segall and his associates assumed particularly that the straight lines, rectangular shapes, which abound in 'carpentered' Western countries ought to generate different visual responses from the percepts of people living in non-geometrical environments. Their findings indicate that, indeed, Americans are more susceptible to the Müller-Lyer illusion than people who live in the third world.[87]

The Zulus of South Africa live in a visual environment which is very different from Western surroundings. Their villages consist of beehive shaped huts. The perspective features of distance here seem to be different from those to be found in geometrical environments. The Zulu world is characterized by round forms. They plough their land in curves, instead of straight furrows. Their susceptibility to the Müller-Lyer illusion is smaller than of Westerners.

However, certain extent of susceptibility to optical illusions does exist in non-Western cultures as well. The perceptual response to them is in fact universal.

In my opinion, the Müller-Lyer illusion can be interpreted in terms of visual ambiguity. The same symbol can stand for a variety of things. The perspective theory extended to the case of the Müller-Lyer illusion demonstrates that the figure can be seen three dimensionally. But it does not provide a convincing explanation for the apparent difference in the length of the two sets of arrows.

My first ambiguity inspired conjecture is a simple anthropomorphic hypothesis. We tend to project on the external world the human attributes of our own ontological condition. Personification is a fundamental aspect of the human mind's metaphoric function.

As an anthropomorphic configuration, the Müller-Lyer set of arrows are capable of generating the abstract, stylized contours of two human figures, as shown below:

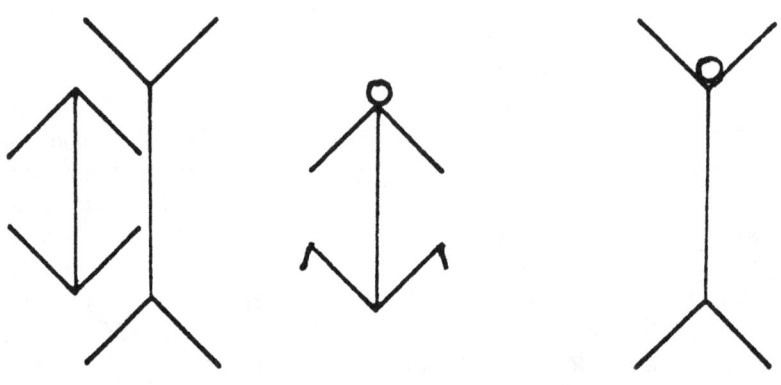

THE MÜLLER-LYER ILLUSION AND ITS ANTHROPOMORPHIC
INTERPRETATION.

Thus, the axis with the in-going arrows represent a kneeling figure, whereas the line with the out-going arrows represent another one, standing with the feet apart, and with hands extended upwards. The kneeling figure suggests a shorter image of the body than the standing one. The outstretched body of the latter produces an elongated percept. Since an optical illusion is a misconstrued visual hypothesis, further scrutiny is needed to discover the error. This can be accomplished when the observer decides to measure the actual length of the two central segments of the Müller-Lyer illusion, and finds that they are in fact equal.

My second ambiguity guided assumption is an ideo-emphatic proposition. It treats the Müller-Lyer illusion as a pictographic symbol.

Central to the ideo-empathic conception of the Müller-Lyer figure is the assertion that the observer intuitively is inclined to grasp it as a

148

visual symbol of the subject-object differentiation. In other words, the set of arrowheads asserts itself as an unconscious pictorial expression of inwardness and outwardness. The arrow with the in-going fins and the arrow with the out-going fins act upon one another. They form a gestalt relationship in which the whole is more than the sum total of its parts. The out-going arrowheads suggest spatial expansion, and lead to perceptual inertia. On the other hand, the effect of the in-going arrowheads of the figure is the opposite. They suggest withdrawal and contraction.

Thus, the observer unconsciously associates the in-going arrowheads with inwardness, and the out-going arrowheads with outwardness. The automatic process of reasoning gives rise to the projective inference that what is inside is ought to be smaller than what is outside. The inner parts of the body are smaller than the skin which envelops it, the table is bigger than the drawer, the house is smaller than the city, and so forth.

The Müller-Lyer figure is a powerful abstract symbol, a dynamic pictogram which is capable of expressing the dialectical tensions of opposites. The fact that the illusion affects more people of Western origin than others, is probably related to the rise of scientific reasoning in Western societies. The abstract separation of the internal world of the human psyche from the external material world is less common in the third world than in industrial civilizations.

The separation of the psyche from matter is frequently attributed to stem from the work of the French mathematician and rationalist philosopher René Descartes (1596-1650). He based his conception of nature on the essential division between the immaterial thought of the mind and the material world which manifests itself in extension. Descartes isolated the human ego from its material environment and confined it to the inner part of the body. The Cartesian split eventuated in the modern scientific view of mechanical materialism which regards mind and matter as two substantially different things. Descartes' analytic method of reasoning has allowed scientists to accomplish the technological triumphs of the space age. But the same celebrated method also led to scientific reductionism, the mistaken assumption that it is possible to understand the ultimate nature of reality as a whole by the isolated investigation of its constituent parts. Due to the Cartesian split physicians tend to ignore the psychological aspects of illness, and, on the other hand, psychotherapists often ignore the existence of their patients' bodies, for instance.

In a Cartesian context the Müller-Lyer illusion can be regarded as a two dimensional abstract symbol which enhances visual ambiguity and disorientation. In a sense we see what we know. The geometrical pictogram as a visual representation of inwardness and outwardness seems to trigger dualistic analytical inferences. The Western mind tends to take it for granted that what is expanding is bigger than what is shrinking in every respect. Thus, due to perceptual inertia and the operational effect of precipitated knowledge, the observer constructs a false hypothesis concerning the actual length of the two central axes of the Müller-Lyer figure.

Illusions and ambiguous patterns are not the same. All visual illusions are ambiguous figures, but not all ambiguous figures, involve visual illusions. A visual illusion is the result of false assumptions that produce discrepancy between optical perception and veridical reality. Genuine visual ambiguity, on the other hand, is an alternative perceptual experience, in which more than one coherent interpretation can be constructed to the same image. Let us take, for instance, the following figure:

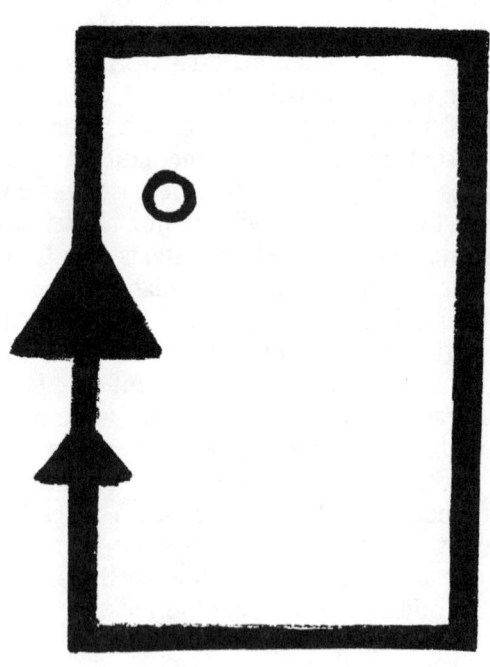

It can be seen as a set consisting of a rectangle, a circle, and as a two dimensional representation of an aircraft. Due to the anthropomorphic tendency of visual perception, the image, however, can be interpreted as a stylized human face as well. Both mental constructions are consistent and meaningful readings. The image is not a visual illusion, since it does not involve false perceptual hypotheses. Its various formal elements do not produce visual distortions. Instead, they lend themselves to individually valid but alternating decipherments.

Ambiguity is one of the defining properties of art itself. Expressive machinations capable of more than one meaning are among the very roots of painting, poetry, and drama. The ambiguity coefficient increases with the enhancement of the level of abstraction. The more abstract is the work, the more ambiguity it evokes.

The most abstract media are dance and music. These are also the most ambiguous art forms. For Schopenhauer music is the most prominent among the arts, because it 'speaks its own language',[88] and does not reproduce ideas in another medium like literature, for instance, which uses words to describe things.

Perhaps all the arts aspire to achieve the status of music in which form and content unite. Thus, it is not an accident that Wassily Kandinsky, one of the salient pioneers of modern abstract art, was not only a painter but a musician too.

The crux of the conceptual framework of modern art is bound up with the distilled assumption that the artist does not imitate reality but renders it. The defining property of contemporary art is the break up of its various aspects. The rise of such artistic trends as cubism, dada, expressionism, and surrealism, abolished the objectivity of visual semblance and actuality. This, in turn, has inevitably entailed the surfacing of emotional strata, the distortion of rational anatomy, and the introduction of ambiguous perspective, spatial depth, and form. Art in the twentieth century features "shattered surfaces, broken color, segmented compositions, dissolved forms and shredded images."[89]

In every historical period art provides access to the deep structure of society and culture. The great schism of modern art manifesting itself in the dichotomic existence of realism and non-objective art, reflects the schizophrenic character of our century. We live in an age which has raised great hopes of economic progress and scientific achievements, but is unable to solve the problems of poverty, famine, unemployment, and violence; an age in which people live under the threatening shadow of nuclear self-destruction.

The existential anxiety of contemporary man living in an alienated technological society, the sense of Kafkaesque nightmare, the 'ontological insecurity'[90] and despair, have found their artistic expression in dada, surrealism, and abstract expressionism.

Art is ambiguous because reality is ambiguous. Art is complicated, multifarious, just as reality itself. The part contains the whole, and the whole contains the part, in a similar manner to the Leibnizian monads, or to the laser beam generated three dimensional holographic images.

The problem of ambiguity is linked to the problem of existential uncertainty. Through art we can search for the meaning of existence. The competing, multiple meanings manifesting themselves in painting, or sculpture, underline and illuminate more fully the complexities of reality.

According to Harold Rosenberg, "much of the best art of this century belongs to a visual debate about what art is."[91] An art work, such as a collage by Kurt Schwitters, or Georges Braque, is an ambiguous object characterized by existential insecurity. It is at the same time a masterpiece, and a piece of junk.

Man is a symbol making being, and symbols are loaded with ambiguities. Symbols are gateways to the unknown. They arise from the unconscious layers of the psyche, and create allegories, parables, imagery, and metaphors. Equivocalness is an intrinsic property of all figurative language, of all art. The great poets and artists of all ages—among them Dante, Dürer, Blake, and Picasso—always conveyed their visions metaphorically.

The problem of perceptual ambiguity has bearings on the development of artificial intelligence as well. Researchers of artificial intelligence try, for instance, to mimic mechanically the human faculty of interpreting two dimensional line drawings as three dimensional images. David A. Huffman and Max B. Clowes demonstrated "that a line drawing can be interpreted as a three dimensional scene only of all its vertexes can be labeled consistently from a set of 16 allowable kinds of vertex."[92]

However, not all line drawings can be labeled consistently. An impossible monument, like the one shown above, is an undecidable figure which by means of the labeling system is ruled out in the computer program as a possible representation of a three dimensional object. But some drawings lend themselves to consistent labeling and nevertheless they cannot represent real objects.[93]

The impossible monument figure has two upper pillars which are transformed into three bottom columns. It is a visual paradox related to

152

the so called two pronged trident, known also as the devil's fork. It is a disturbing image which throws the observer into a stage of cognitive

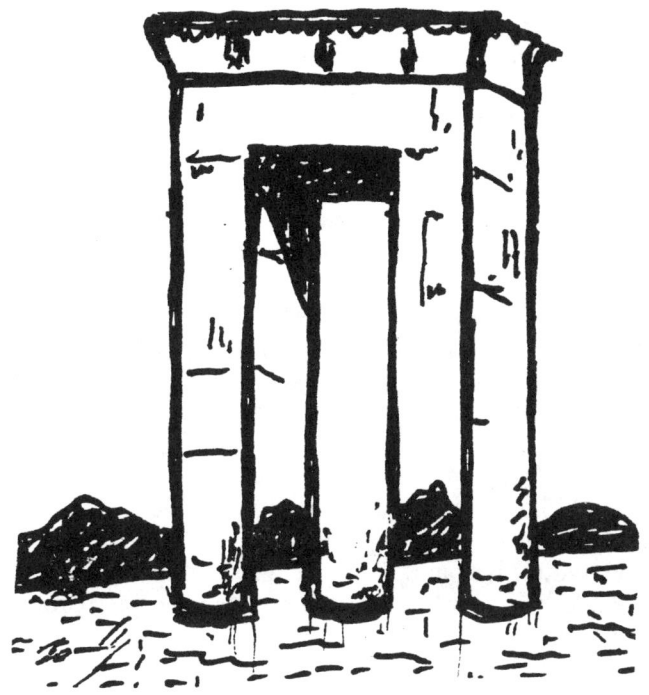

IMPOSSIBLE MONUMENT

confusion. The brain is unable to make sense of it because it fails to provide a meaningful interpretation with regard to the exact nature of the representation. It cannot form a consistent perceptual hypothesis. The input data processed by the visual apparatus yield befuddled output.

In fact, the visual paradox is created by the middle column: It appears to be in two places at the same time, evolving out of the empty space that separates the two angular upper pillars of the monument.

The case of minimal art provides some intriguing insights concerning the nature of perceptual ambiguity. In the 1960s the minimalists advanced simple geometrical and monumental forms, rigid spatial structures, 'hard edge', and huge scale, maintaining that these features represented clarity and content. Artists such as Morris Louis, Ellsworth Kelly, and Frank Stella painted nonrepresentational images which were often of monumental size. Aiming at the reduction of painting to its lowest common denominator, the picture plane and color, the minimalists claimed that their art allowed 'no room for confusion or misrepresentation', and eliminated ambiguity.[94]

However, the interaction of hard edge geometrical shapes with negative space, the phenomenon of figure-ground effect and other machinations, are capable of generating much visual indefiniteness. Therefore, minimalism cannot be an ambiguity-free art.

The metaphysical meaning attributed to the art work enhances its vagueness. A cogent case in point is the empty canvas, the aesthetic analogue of the mathematician's null set. The empty canvas is the paradoxical epitome of the alleged clarity of minimalism.

Various artists attached different meanings to the basically same empty canvas. Back in 1918, Kasimir Malevich painted his *White on White* in order to illustrate that the art object itself is meaningless, and that the sensation of color and space as reality is the essence of art. Yet, in contrast to him, Yves Klein between 1957 and 1962 made a series of empty canvases painted with monochrome blue which to him represented chromatic delight, presence, international non-verbal communication, infinity and the search for immaterial truth.

Robert Rauschenberg, a student of Josef Albers, approached the whole problem from a different point of view. For his part, the white canvas series which he painted in the 1950s represented the visual metaphors of silence, where shadows were welcome and participated in the plastic message.

At about the same time, Ad Reinhardt saw his own unitary red, blue and black paintings as attempts of isolating art from perception, and from the problems of mankind. He tried to concentrate on art's unique nature and crystallize 'Art as Art' by means of reducing painting to its bare essentials.

For the abstract expressionist Barnett Newman, a New York painter of metaphysical qualities, monochrome color field painting represented concerns of faith and values. It also stood for Jewish mysticism, for the tragedy of life and death, the enigma of genesis, and the attempt to escape from the chaos of shape. Newman's *Ornament I* (1948) was made of dark red color divided into two halves by a vertical stripe of impasto in the same color. In his later work, the painter aimed to enhance the visionary character of his work. He created a peculiar visual rhythm through the interplay of occasional vertical and huge color fields.

The big color field paintings of Jules Olitski belong to the same category. His atmospheric, vibrating color field paintings from the 1960s and 1970s were essentially empty canvases. They represented the artist's preoccupation with aspects of flatness, shape of support, and pigment, as the unique features, and the defining properties of the art of painting.

It is noteworthy that the phenomenon of attributing abstract or metaphysical meanings to symbolic objects does not exist in the domain of art alone. Flags, for instance, are symbolic objects which can stand for the land, the ideals, and the governments of entire nations. A country's flag encourages its people to unite. It also can stir them to joy and to sacrifice.

Money is another example. It is a symbol too, and an ambiguous object. For, after all, its value is not intrinsic, but an attached one which is accepted by the public by common agreement. Without this common public agreement money is absolutely worthless. Therefore, it is quite true to say that seeing is believing; but the opposite is also true: believing is seeing.

In the summer 1983 issue of *Leonardo*, Professor Judith Farr Tormey of Temple University, Philadelphia, and Professor Alan Tormey of the University of Maryland, Baltimore County, discussed the relationship of art and ambiguity. Narrowing down the range and scope of their subject matter, the authors differentiated 'disjunctive ambiguity' from other kindred forms of perceptual phenomena. Thus, they excluded, for instance, paradoxicality, anamorphism, and indeterminacy from their taxonomy. Instead, the Tormeys' system of classification implies three disjunctive forms of ambiguity: 1) Depth ambiguity; 2) Object ambiguity; and 3) Figure-ground ambiguity.[95]

Art works, however, seldom, if ever, consist of isolated categories of perceptual equivocalness. Instead, they usually contain a variety of interwoven visual elements which are susceptible of more than one meaning. The Tormeys use, for instance, Salvador Dali's *Slave Market with the Disappearing Bust of Voltaire* (1940) as an example of object ambiguity.[96] But even if we confine ourselves to their reductionist model, the bust of Voltaire is more than a compositional nucleus featuring object ambiguity. In fact, this central part of Dali's painting is a threesome combination of depth, of figure-ground, and of object ambiguity.

Although the Tormeys' model can be a useful analytical tool in the investigation of perceptual phenomena, it is necessary to transcend it in order to accommodate additional aspects of the relationship of art to ambiguity.

Take, for instance, the impact of culture. Cross cultural anthropological research has shown the importance of the influence of environmental and cultural differences with regard to perception. A newborn infant certainly cannot recognize his or her own image on a photograph. But there are observations from South Africa, Nigeria, and elsewhere that indigenous people frequently fail to recognize the objects with which they are familiar when these are presented on photographs. According to reports, Ghurka recruits reveal considerable difficulties in image identification, and there is a case of a bush Negress who was unable to recognize her own son in a photograph.[97]

A line drawing representing a group of people is susceptible of very different interpretations when it is shown to observers from heterogeneous cultures. It can be perceived, for example, as J. B. Deregowski pointed out, as a family in an outdoor scene by East-African subjects, and as an indoor scene by Westerners. What Westerners see in the same drawing as a rectangular window, is regarded by the East-African observers as a petrol can held on the head of a young black woman.[98] These differences in the interpretation of the same picture stem from dissimilarities of cultural backgrounds, and the variabilities of perceptual associations with environmental familiarities.

Once I made a picture showing the fallen body of a soldier lying on the ground beneath an old machine gun. The machine gun seemed to stand still, and behind it sat a helmeted warrior. I gave the title "Good Old Days" to the picture. When I showed it to a friend of mine, he reacted with the words: "You are a cynic".

I was surprised to hear it, because when I made that picture my intention was not a cynical one at all. On the contrary, what I tried to express was the sad fact that human nature did not change throughout history. Thus, men were killing each other even when there was less air pollution, and the bread was still home made.

It appears then that the addition of the title to a work does not necessarily abolish the crystal ball of ambiguity. For, a visual image advanced as art is a dyadic entity, a curious alchemic hybrid made of words and pictures. Therefore it is a serious error to separate the artist's philosophical ideas from the completed image.

Yet words and pictures are two different symbolic systems. They can merely complement each other. They can never be the same, because the medium is the message. The great artists throughout history understood this, and consequently they felt compelled to express their ideas not only in paintings or sculptures but in words as well. Examples to this effect are many; from the writings of Leonardo to the letters of Van Gogh, or the books of Kandinsky and of Chagall.

Since we tend to see what we know, what we have learned to see, we easily are trapped by conservatism. Therefore people, including the experts, usually prefer conventional, stereotyped art that reinforces their individual taste, normative values and concepts. Thus, people restrain themselves from new tendencies.

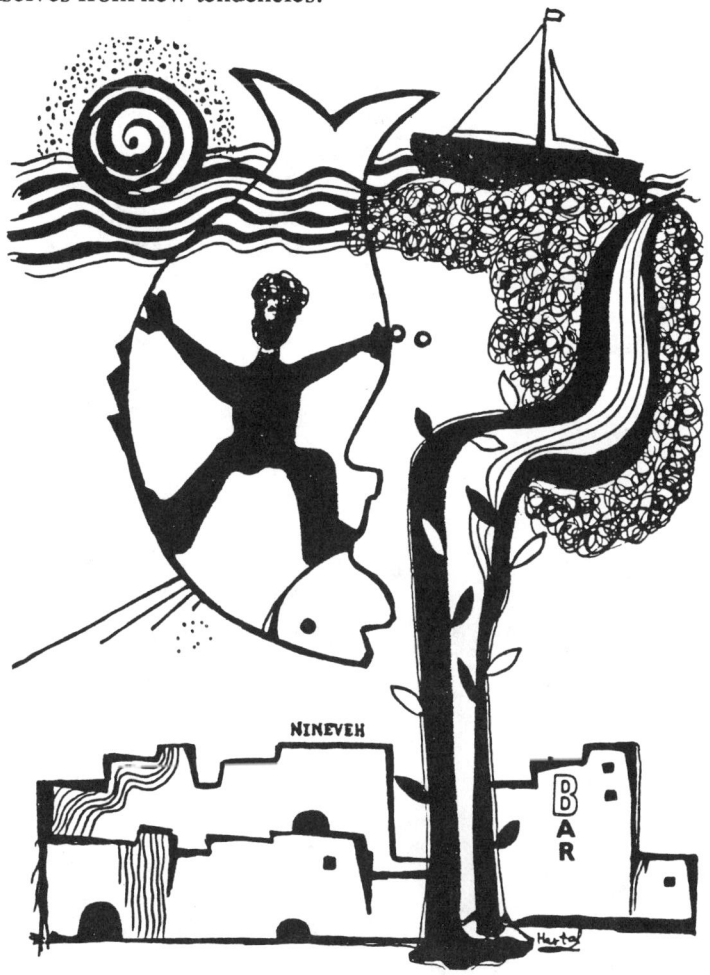

HIS NAME WAS JONAH

A visual composition featuring multiform perceptual ambiguity. The pen and ink drawing is a version of the author's painting on the Biblical story of Jonah (acrylic, 18" x 24", 1976). A figure-ground ambiguity is to be found along the common meeting line which forms the bottom part of the perpendicularly diving whale and the anxious profile of the prophet. The non-Euclidean space of the composition involves depth ambiguity. Part of the sea functions also as Jonah's hair, and therefore it is an object-ambiguous constituent of the image.

157

In the light of these considerations it is important to bear in mind that the splitting apart of substance and form leads to a distorted view of the creative process. It also results in the misperception of the visual message.

Consequently, the perceptual equivocalness of an image, such as *Good Old Days*, does not seem to stem from the intrinsic visual properties of the composition. Rather, it is the result of sub-cultural projections. In this manner, the image can be viewed as an array of perceptual stimuli capable of generating attitude ambiguities.

In painting the problem of form is bound up with the problem of content. This holds particularly true of abstract art. In abstract painting form and content unite. Therefore, the subject matter of an abstract image is determined by its way of implementation.

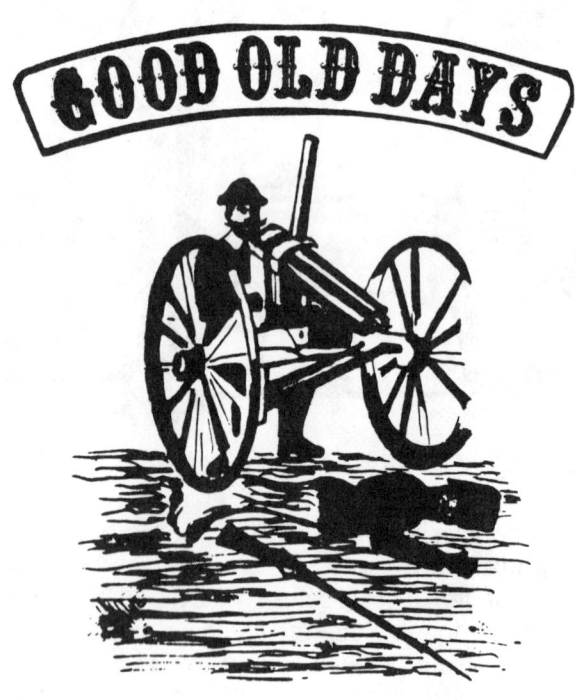

But man is a symbol making being, and he often attributes metaphysical significance to abstract objects. Abstract art is not an exception. Kandinsky, for instance, wanted artists to express the inner spirit of the beautiful through abstract paintings. His vision was to arrive at a stage where painting would turn into a conscious creation of harmony uttered in mathematical form: A new plastic idiom shaped as the equivalent of music.

Piet Mondrian's work can be seen as an attempt to materialize Kandinsky's goals. He developed a rigid vocabulary of flat geometrical patterns based on the grid system, and applied the primary colors of red, yellow, and blue, as well as black, white and grey, to his paintings. He tried to eliminate all associations with emotions and with perceptible reality. Instead, he aimed at turning the flat picture surface into a subtle array of equilibriums, visual counterpoints analogous to musical rhythms. The artist considered his paintings as specific devices of contemplation mediating between subject and object, the individual and the universal; expressions of the mystical unity between man and cosmos.

Music encounters painting, science and mathematics in John Cage's 4'33'. It is a conceptual composition influenced by Robert Rauschenberg's all white paintings.

When Cage presented 4'33, he instructed the pianist to sit frozen and maintain silence for four minutes and thirty-three seconds without striking one single note. The noises coming from the audience, coughing, clapping and complaining, became in this manner the sound for the passive musical piece. The duration of the work is 273 seconds. That corresponds to -273 degree on the Celsius scale, or absolute zero temperature, at which music cannot be heard, because all molecular motion quietly comes to an end.

As I have pointed out above, even figurative or realistic pictures involve a variety of perceptual ambiguities. And it seems that as the degree of abstraction increases, the degree of ambiguity increases as well.

Take, for example, my *Opus 60.*[*] Its thematic ambiguity is evident. But what does it represent? This question is sort of an anathema in abstract art. It should not be asked. For, abstract art represents nothing, except its own presence. In Kantian terms it is the thing-in-itself, a Ding-an-sich. In other words, an abstract image is an external source of experience. It is an unknowable noumenon which is inaccessible to speculative reason.

---

[*] See page 160.

However, this kind of reasoning is based on pure fiction. For, to contend that an abstract painting is a Ding-an-sich is an interpretation in itself. A picture is inevitably a phenomenon, a perceived object of thought inseparable from our consciousness. All art is conceptual. A painting is a magical amalgam of forms, colors, and ideas.

Now, let me return to *Opus 60*. What does it represent? In the light of the arguments presented above, this question now seems to have acquired a license of being posed.

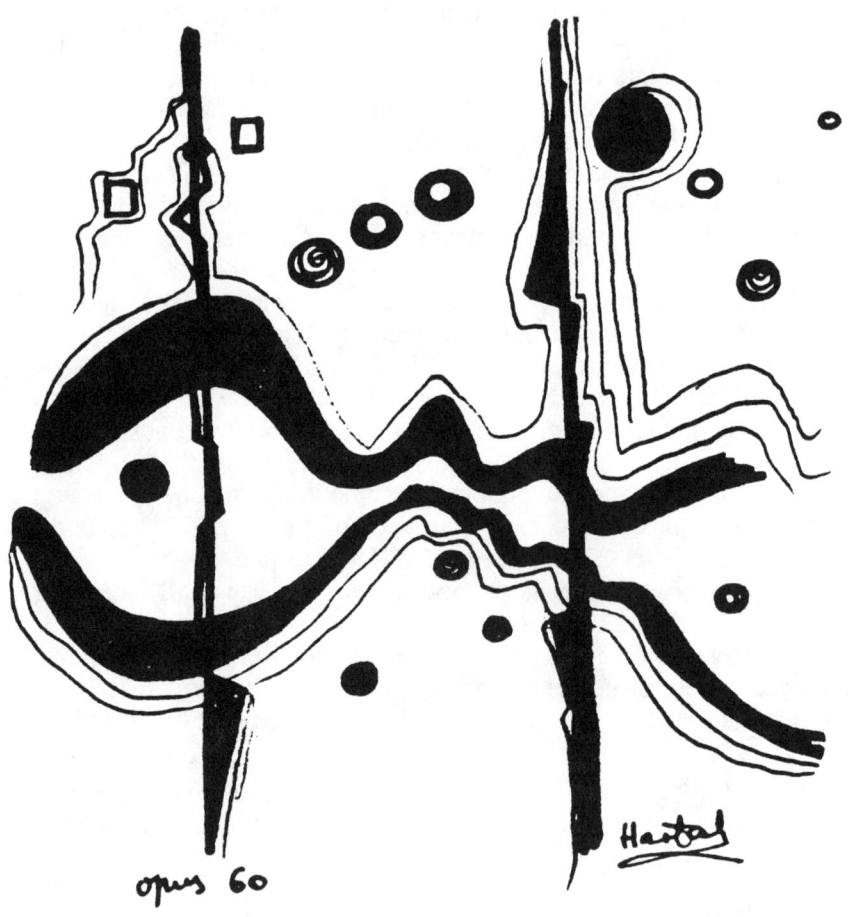

OPUS 60

Opus 60 is a study that belongs to a series of drawings and paintings which I did in the early 1980s as part of my Painted Melodies project. It concerns the relationship of painting and music.

Both painting and music can mesmerize the audience and induce altered states of consciousness. But to what extent is the medium the message? And is it possible to transform one medium into another? Can we visualize music?

The task of transforming one medium into another seems to be like that of squaring the circle. For, painting is a spatial art, expressed in color and in form, which communicates through the visual system of the human organism. Music, on the other hand, is a temporal medium, the art of sound, which we enjoy through our auditory organs.

Notwithstanding all this, there must be some sort of allotropy, synesthesia or cross-modality in existence as the hidden fabric of an underlying order common to all the arts. Art is not disassociated from nature, nothing can be independent of it. The sinuous, rippling properties of the universe must be reflected somehow in the common infrastructure of the arts.

And, indeed, despite their variety, complexity, and wealth, all art forms reveal the same basic laws. Even the most revolutionary artists articulated their work by the same pivotal concepts: symmetry and change, tension and relaxation, repetition and contrast, variation and unity. Furthermore, such aesthetic elements as form, line, rhythm, texture, color or timbre, harmony, focus, style, climax, and composition, can be applied to all the arts.

Artists always knew this. Beethoven's ambition was to be a tone-poet. Picasso saw in the colors of his palette sleeping words; and Chagall stressed the fundamental unity of painting and poetry.

In contrast to artists such as Kandinsky and Mondrian, who approached the painting-music relationship in terms of the color-tone analogue, I approached it in terms of form. It is possible to visualize music because it is the result of wave motion.

Form is a potential physical materialization of the invisible cosmic order. Painting and music are specific languages. They assert themselves as entirely different physical entities, but their intrinsic similarities are structured according to a universal and dialectical paradigm. "A gramaphone record, the musical idea, the written notes, and the sound waves", says Wittgenstein, "all stand to one another in the same internal relation of depicting that holds between language and the world. They are all constructed according to a common logical pattern."[99]

161

Opus 60 is one of the abstract images which have constituted the series of "Painted Melodies". Other pictures of the series had been painted in a figurative style. The two visual idioms correspond to the parallel stratification of music. For, the thesis that music is completely abstract is wrong. In actuality there are two types of music: programmatic and absolute. Programme music results from the attempts of the musician to reproduce or suggest literary ideas, and to evoke mental pictures. Music is also capable of imitating natural sounds. Thus, it is absolute music which corresponds to abstraction in painting.

The exploration of the relationship of painting and music led to the completion of a series of experiments in which I applied musical notes isomorphically to the canvas. Since the notes taken, e.g., from the works of Mozart, Beethoven, and Mussorgsky correspond structurally to the actual sounds of music, the resulting images provide empirical proof to the hypothesis that musical form can be transformed into painting.

In the focus of *Painted Melodies* stood Mussorgsky's "Pictures at an Exhibition", orchestrated by Ravel. The project refracted the musical piece of the Russian composer, originally written as a piano suite, and metamorphosed it into visual images, in a similar manner to the transformation of time into geometrical space. Neither music nor time are objects. Yet through the playing of the musical instrument, music evolves into a meaningful experience, whereas the experience of time is converted into the rotation of the hour hand. Through the machine of the clock duration asserts itself as an object.

Painting is both an art and a science; and so is music. In the undertaking and implementation of the "Painted Melodies" project my primary aim, however, was not quantification, measurement and mapping. Consequently, the resulting images are not accurate isomorphic translations, but unique visual metaphors of the exploratory idea to transform music into painting.[100]

I would like to end this discussion on visual perception with a remark concerning the existing ties between incongruous semantic coding and ambiguity. Let us look at the rectangular design suggesting the message: Black and White. It contains two semi-circles and the words 'black and'. The word black is written into the white semi-circle. The other semi-circle, which is plain black, invites the viewer to complete the missing word from the three word sentence. As a result, the black semi-circle becomes a perceptual stimulus which triggers a verbal 'white' response.

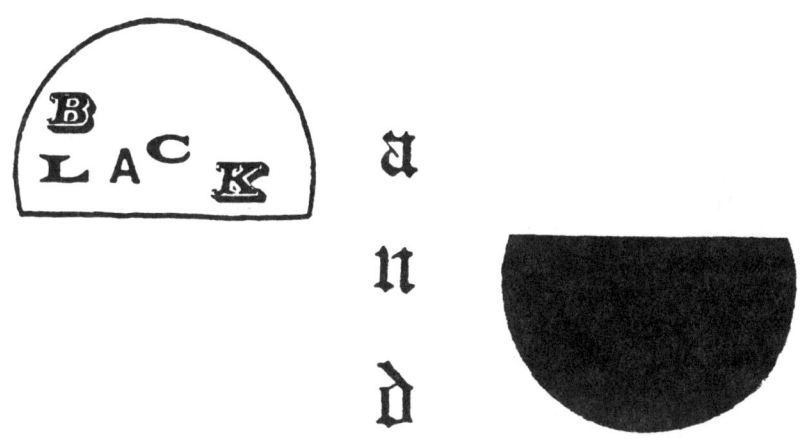

BLACK AND WHITE

The ambiguity implied in *Black and White* arises due to the incongruous rendition of the design, which features an intertwined typographical and plastic message. The resulting peculiar quibble can be termed as code ambiguity.

Black and White belongs to the specific category of visual designs in which non-linguistic material may replace words and take up semantic functions. The visual images in this category of design are concerned with the relationship of language to visual form and content. They are also bound up with the problem of abstraction.

The earliest known example of this type of work can be traced back to the ancient Greek poet Simmias, who among other things, composed a poem which was shaped as an egg. Since the work was written about eggs, the poet's arrangement of the letters helped to present the theme.

In 1920 Piet Mondrian, Theo van Doesburg, and Anthony Kok called for the abolition of the duality of form and content. They stressed the impotency of the word whose meaning has been killed by psychoanalysis, and clumsy rhetoric. Later, certain types of artistic creativity aiming at the unification of form and content became known as 'concrete poetry'.[101]

Concrete poetry offers a reduced, attenuated language. However, it seems to be in tune with the development of contemporary society. The scientific-technological outlook of this century cannot allocate much time for the reading of long poems. Although concrete poems are obviously inferior in comparison to the poetic masterpieces of past centuries, their relative importance lies outside of the realm of traditional poetry. The considerable significance of concrete poetry is due to its aesthetic experimentations, the new avenues of narration it explores, and its contribution to the development of rapid methods of communication.

Chapter Four

BEYOND TECHNOLOGY:
THE AESTHETICS OF THE SUBWAY

Introduction

This chapter is concerned with a neglected realm of urban history: public art. Urban historians dealing with the increasing complexity of city life recognize that the study of the physical environment is inevitable if we want to have a better understanding of the process of urbanization and the evolution of individual cities. The physical environment is the matrix of urbanization, the interacting container that affects social structures and processes, as well as is effected by them. Public art is an integral part of the physical environment. However, it is much more than that. For, art is both visual history and cultural utility. It was Benedetto Croce who stressed that the survival of art through the passage of centuries implies the phenomenon of eternal present. And Friedrich Schiller, following Plato and Kant, suggested in the end of the eighteenth century that the aesthetic function of art advances humanity from a sensuous to a rational stage of existence. The two basic drives in man, the sensuous and the rational, are synthesized and elevated to a higher plane which is manifested in the play impulse. It is this play impulse that assumes form in art, allows man to free himself from his sensuous nature and provides him with his social character. Among modern thinkers who support Schiller's play theory are Herbert Marcuse, Johan Huizinga and Sir Herbert Read.

Since art as specialization tends to be linked with city life, public art is predominantly an urban phenomenon. The contemporary variants of urban art are stratified, and they assert themselves as a foremost factor in the physical appearance of cities. The commercial messages predominate. Similarly to the airwaves and the printed media, it is the big corporate advertisers who control most city walls and billboards for their commercial messages. After sunset the glaring and colorful advertisements flickering and lighting up the night, along with the traffic lights, dominate the urban landscape, more than its concrete and brick skeleton do.

Art is information and through public art the city turns into a huge-scale environmental information system. To a certain extent street art is the epidermis of the city. Accordingly, it changes frequently, the city peels off the outer layer of its skeleton, whereas the buildings themselves are less subject to drastic transformations. The stimulating information conveyed through public art is an important ingredient of the magic which is inherent in urban life. At the same time urban art also reveals the basic character of this magic: the illusion of reality and the reality of illusion—self deception.

This chapter deals with non-commercial forms of public art executed by professional artists. Most of these art works were created for the Metro of Montreal between the years 1966-1976.

Those processes that shaped and determined the syntax and semantics of public art forms in the Metro began well before the works were actually implemented. Therefore, this thesis provides information in a nutshell about certain historical aspects that are necessary for the comprehension of Metro art. It is also an attempt to approach the subject in an interdisciplinary way, to place it into the quality of urban life, to anatomize and interpret its historical meaning.

The origin of art is in magic. Contemporary urban art shares with primitive art the presumably unconscious strife for unus mundus, that is to say, it mediates between man and his environment. Yet at the same time art mediates between man and man as well. For, as a great artist of this century put it:

> The public function of art has always been one of creating community. That is not necessarily its intention, but it is its result . . . The incidental items of reality remain without value or common recognition until they are symbolized, re-created, and imbued with value. The potato field or the auto repair shop remain without quality or awareness, or the sense of community until they are turned into literature by a Faulkner or a Steinbeck or a Thomas Wolfe, or into art by a Van Gogh.[1]

Art is a universal impulse and present in all societies of mankind. The relation of the artist to society embraces the expression he gives to the more ultimate standards and values of his community. Thus, with religion and philosophy, art makes known the collective character of a people, and so integrates, unites and guides it by establishing its nature and its ideals.

The emergence of different communities and life styles entails changes in the social roles of the artist as well. In hunting and gathering societies the primary role of the artist was to influence and control the cosmic forces of nature by means of magic. The agricultural revolution brought forward significant changes. More food could be produced in less area and the farmer could feed more than his own family. This was enormously important because it was the food surplus that enabled the rise of the city. For, a fraction of the population first had to be free from cultivation of the land in order to

167

form cities. Another indispensable condition was the development of a transportation system making food supply and communication with the hinterland possible. The accelerating process of urbanization has dramatically changed the social stratification of mankind. The industrial revolution led to a reversed situation: for the first time in history the majority of the population in western type societies became city dwellers. The city is much more than a concentration of the population. It is a place of specialization, a diversity and enhancement of the human condition. It is a conglomeration of the means upon which thought operates. It offers schools, universities, libraries, museums, planetariums, theatres, arenas, zoos and botanic gardens. It provides information processing, as well as services of health, fire and police protection. Cities are the fountainhead of new methods and materials, the hotbed of ideas.

But the city is also a place of cultural, political and social tensions. The physical and aesthetical deterioration of environment is also most apparent in the city. The existentialist anxiety, the process of alienation, the dehumanizing effects of urban life lead to crime and riots. For crime and riots are symptoms of psychological maladjustment. They suggest that our cities have come far from being an optimal place for human life. The break-down of traditional cultural patterns alone can lead to mental disturbances. Correlation can be found also between population density, crime rates and increased mental illness when unemployment, poverty and poor physical environment add negative factors to the gestalt of existence. The rise of the impersonal metropolis and environmental deterioration impose more active roles for the artist. For the physical environment without art is very oppressive and demeaning to the human spirit.

Public art is an important vehicle to bridge the gulf between our social and technological condition. Since the industrial revolution this gulf is widening. It results in the separation of object from subject, the divorce between producer and product, in alienation. The process has affected the artist by turning him into an eccentric, creating commodities of luxury, objects of blue-chip investments for well-to-do connoisseurs. Art became unrelated to the problems of the people and isolated from the masses. Art has been created in ivory towers, in olympic solitude, but usually also through great sufferings and poverty. And the place where art is stored and displayed--the museum--is as well the embodiment of the idea that art is an isolated enclave of culture. So, it enhances the separation between art and the people.

In the 1960's a revival of public art occurred in the U.S. and spread into Canada. The artists' goal has been the democratization of art, to place art into direct contact with the community instead of hiding it behind museum walls. The most common form of public art has been the mural. Interestingly enough not all the murals are the works of professional artists. Naive and folk art is created by non-professionals who paint social statements, metaphors, and decorate the streets where their life is. In this manner the community tries to reclaim its territory and identity which are endangered by the revelations of overwhelming commercialism.

The ethnic stratification of Montreal turns her into a unique city. Public art is a revealing dimension of the process of urbanization and of city life. The conflicts, tensions and contradictions of the vivid encounter between the tendencies of cultural diffusion and inertia assert themselves in public art as well. The art forms in the Metro of Montreal reflect local values: The pride and ethnic consciousness of the French Canadian, the history of the city from an English viewpoint, as well as the aesthetic schism between contemporary art and the traditional school.

The Metro Is More Than Technology: The Problem Of Aesthetics And The Quality Of Life

On the second of November, 1966 a small article in the Montreal English newspaper *The Gazette* announced that the Metro of the city is an indicator of existing cultural differences between French and Anglo-Saxon Canada. The proclamation was based on Dr. O.M. Solandt's speech to the national pollution conference. He pointed out that in the past, even those who were profoundly aware of the differences between French and English Canada could not describe them, nor could they give tangible illustrations of their existence. The Metro shows the difference. Though they have paid a little extra, as compared to the expenses of the Toronto Subway, the Montrealers are delighted with their choice, because they have obtained architectural elegance and decoration.

In contrast to the New York, or the Toronto subway, the planners of the Montreal Metro have developed a different approach. It was based on the assumption that the construction of an efficient underground transportation system is not merely a technological problem, but aesthetical as well. The importance of the aesthetical aspect drew its strength from paying attention to the existing linkage between the quality of life and that of physical environment. For, free time is not the exclusive criterion of the quality of life. The quality of life is rather determined by the availability, and accessibility of services, working conditions and the nature of the physical environment--both natural and cultural--such as climate, the degree of pollution, topography, architecture and urban pattern.

In the pre-industrial city walking time limited the distance between home and working place. Cities in the past were small. But the industrial revolution has changed everything. It divorced the two major parts of man's life--his work and his home. This became possible through the rise and development of public transport systems. Movement became the lifeblood of the city. Consequently, there is a continuous and vast traffic circulation in the conurbation network, stemming mainly from the two-way daily movement of the commuters between center and suburb.

The duration of the commuter's access to work is not free time. It must be viewed as forced time. The use of public transportation, such as the subway, is a filtering activity. The commuter, or anyone who uses the public transportation, is disposed to the superimposing physical features of the system. During the compulsory time of the access, filtration takes place. The nature of filtration depends on the integrated technological and aesthetical qualities of the system, which assert behaviour moulding influence. Hence, the aesthetical design is extremely important. Art is capable of evolving catharsis; it can elevate and purify.

The users of the Metro of Montreal approach their destinations through various stations designed by different architects.[2] Each station has its specific features and identity. Ten of the twenty-six stations of the original network which were in operation in 1967 were planned by the department of architecture of the municipality, while the sixteen others were entrusted to private architects. This led to the invention of new urban forms. Each station has its specific features and identity. Each of them possesses, diversely, the ability to highlight mundane events, to inspire and uplift the soul and the mind.

The Montreal Transportation Commission And Urban Renewal

Montreal's population stood at one hundred thousand in 1861, the year when the first public transportation system of the city made its debute. The initial network comprised six miles in which horse-drawn streetcars were used. During the winter the rail carriages were replaced with sleds. In 1889 more than eight million passengers were transported over the thirty miles long network of streets by the company's more than three hundred vehicles and a thousand horses.

Following the electrification of the urban transportation systems in the U.S.A., Montreal electrified between 1892 and 1896 its public transportation service as well. Thus, at the turn of the century it was possible to go by tramway from Montreal to Lachine, St. Laurent, Cartierville, and Bout-de-L'Ille. The electric tramway united various suburban districts, and from the year of 1911 began an epoch of annexations by the City of Montreal.

Montreal was an innovating city before its modern subway appeared on the scene. The first pay-as-you-enter streetcars in the world were introduced here in 1905, and became a great success also in U.S. cities. The streetcars were produced at the Hochelaga factories and were safer and faster than the previously built carriages.

Buses made in Montreal their first appearance in 1914. The public transportation system of the city reached its maximum extension twenty years later to cover some 320 miles. At the out-break of the Second World War the system owned 224 buses, 929 trams, 7 trolley buses, and the number of people transported annually by it reached two hundred million.[3]

The City of Montreal transferred public transport into its own hands and in 1951 it established the Montreal Transportation Commission. This was the beginning of serious planning for developing a rapid transit system. Two years later the blueprint of the Montreal subway was submitted to the city. However, realization took more than a decade. Construction began only in 1962, after that Jean Drapeau made the Metro one of the issues of the 1960 mayoralty campaign.[4] In 1966, the first trains of the underground system were in operation. Its trains were the first in the Western Hemisphere rolling on rubber tires. The rubber tired wheels enable quiet ride, and contribute significantly to the environmental quality of the system by eliminating a major source of noise pollution. This can be more important than it might seem at the first glance.[5] There is evidence that noise in the 90-decibel range--that is, between the noise level of operating food blender and that of heavy automobile traffic--may cause severe damage and irreversible changes in the nervous system. Long exposures to amplified rock music has caused permanent hearing loss. Yet, at the same time the rubber tires also increase the chance of mishap and accident.

In 1967, on the occasion of Expo '67, the World Exhibition that took place in Montreal, the first part of the Metro was completed. It extended for 22 km and comprised three lines. In 1972 the Metro had 369 carriages. In the same year the number of buses in M.T.C. service was 1852. An eastward extension of line one of the Metro added in 1976 nine stations along 4.5 miles of track.[6]

Montreal was not quick in developing its subway. The first subway in the world was built in London during the 1860s, and the motive power of its trains already in 1890 was provided by electricity. But in the 1980s Montreal joined Berlin, Boston, Hamburg, London, Mexico City, Moscow, New York, Osaka, Paris, Tokyo and Toronto in operating electrical underground passenger trains with running tracks more than 40 km in length. The three longest systems of these belonged to New York (1,152 km), London (435 km) and Paris (253 km). In 1987 the Montreal Metro had 693 carriages serving sixty stations along the fifty seven route kilometres of its four lines.

Yet, despite the efforts of developing the city's public transportation system, traffic volumes show a declining tendency. In the decade between 1950 and 1960 a decline of about 25% occurred, that is to say, the passenger traffic using the M.T.C. services decreased from 370 million to 280 million. Influenced by the opening of the Metro and Expo '67, the volume reached 308 million in 1968, but since then a downward trend occurred again. Fortunately, for the Metro, monthly variations of traffic volumes are much smaller than in surface transport. Thus, it seems that the Metro retains its popularity and in terms of traffic volume it carries more than 125 million people a year. This is due to the fact that the number of visitors to Man and His World during the summer months compensates for those who are away on vacation and that only few students use the Metro during the school year. According to a survey conducted in 1970-71 by the Montreal Urban Community Transport Commission on a 4% sample of the metropolitan population, the private car is the most important vehicle of transportation, whereas public transport accounts for 28.6% of travel to work, and for 22.6% of all travel.[7]

The construction of the Metro has played a pivotal role in the renewal of downtown Montreal. It was bound up with extensive demolition along the axis of de Maisonneuve Boulevard and other areas of the city core. The stations have led to modified urban landscapes. The Atwater terminus has attracted high-rise buildings such as Alexis Nihon and Westmount Square, whereas large parking areas have been set up at Henri Bourassa and Longueuil. Metro planners have given consideration to the problem of integrated public transportation facilities. And, indeed, the subway is linked to other forms of surface transport: to the Central and Windsor railway terminus (Place Bonaventure) and the Voyageur bus terminal (Berri-de-Montigny).

The construction of the Metro has given rise also to the appearance of an underground city containing elegant shopping malls, such as the Place Bonaventure, Place Ville Marie, Place du Canada, Eaton's, The Bay, the Sheraton-Mount Royal Hotel promenade and others.

According to Vincent Ponte, the city planner responsible for most of the developing center of downtown Montreal, the elegance and sophistication of the multi-level central business district, its pedestrian system, have become for Montreal an emblem of a new self-image. It is both beautiful and practical.

> Montreal always surprises people who imagine Canadian cities in general to be, somehow, in a state of continual hibernation. With its Gallic sociability, its fine restaurants, its uninhibited night life Montreal is to the contrary about as lively a city as can be found anywhere in the Northern hemisphere. And its now famous pedestrian system, which currently bonds together about a third of the 185 acres constituting the core of the downtown business district, has provided a channel through which this immense social vitality can flow, a physical manifestation that serves to heighten its intensity. Almost three continuous miles of sheltered galleries and shopping malls penetrate through block after heavily built-up block, over- or underpassing streets and offering a continually shifting kaleidoscope of vistas, now broad, now confined, with glimpses into shops and boutiques and out into sunken courtyards open to the sky where tables are gaily set out under greenery in summertime.[8]

In his poetically inspired style Ponte does not miss to point out that the roots of this new urban core are implied in the visions of such persons as Leonardo da Vinci and Antonio Sant'Elia. A five hundred years old sketch in Leonardo's sketch book, for instance, shows a Renaissance town plan in which pedestrian walkways are placed above the level of the street. The other Italian genius, Antonio Sant'Elia, a futurist architect, created plans showing a multi-level city comprising streets, elevated walkways and subways. Sant'Elia created these blueprints after returning from a visit to New York in 1912. They included sky bridges and people movers in order to allow uninterrupted circulation from one end of town to the other, just as Leonardo himself suggested it five centuries ago.

However, it was not until 1930 that the first multi-level city was constructed. This was New York's Rockefeller Center, the first pedestrian mall. Since then other cities experimented with multi-level systems as well. But, according to Ponte,

> Montreal's multilevel system remains unique because of its size and complexity. From its original 1962 starting point in Place Ville Marie, it has spread two blocks south into Place Bonaventure, an $85 million trade center offering over three million square feet . . . By 1985, the promenade system is expected to link up 100 of downtown's 185 acres with more than six miles of promenades and shopping malls. It will then be capable of accommodating half-a-million people at a time, where they can shop and go about their business in a pleasant, climate-controlled environment free from rain, cold and heat, and removed from the sound and smell and hazards of traffic.[9]

As it turned out, reality surpassed the planners' forecasts. By 1986 the multilevel system of promenades and shopping malls in downtown Montreal extended to eight miles in length.

The Artists Protest

The Metro is a vital element of this multi-level system, its spinal column. "From the time of its inception, planners felt that Montreal's Metro should offer comfort and a pleasurable environment as well as functionality. And the city's administration pushed the idea that art should follow the public underground."[10] The municipal authorities believed that private corporations would sponsor the beautification of the subway, and turn it into the underground gallery of Montreal. And, indeed, the Metro has its murals, stained glass windows, enameled steel frescoes, ceramics and sculptures.

Yet, artists, architects, museum curators and critics all expressed their objection to the policy and aesthetics concerning the decorations for Montreal's Metro. According to Dusty Vineberg the protest was made "with mounting intensity and unanimity rare in the art world".[11] One art critic envisaged the results of the planned art for the Metro and described it, "an underground museum of horrors".[12] The sixty member strong Society of Professional Artists of Quebec (Société des Artistes Professionels du Québec - SAPQ) made its protest public after a letter, dated December 11, 1967, sent to Mayor Jean Drapeau remained unanswered. The letter was signed by Mario Merola, president of the Society, and members of the executive, Guido Molinari, Marcelle Ferron, Rita Briansky, Claude Goulet, Real Arsenault, and Jordi Bonnet.[13]

The discontent of the artists stemmed from two different issues. One was procedural, the other aesthetic. The artists objected to the fact that caricaturist Robert Lapalme was made sole judge in the selection of participating artists. He held his mandate from Mayor Drapeau while commissioning of artists for the project of art in the Metro. In their open letter the artists pointed out that Lapalme maintained an unusual and very undemocratic position: being both judge and contestant--a one man jury who was also to create the works for the Beaubien and the Place d'Armes stations. Instead of such a rather absurd commission, the SAPQ called for the formation of a mixed committee composed of experts such as artists, designers, and architects who would reconsider art proposals for the huge Metro project.

Further objection to the Drapeau-Lapalme conception of this project came on grounds of apparent near-insistence on representational art. The Society of Professional Artists of Quebec, in their open letter, stressed that what Mr. Lapalme is commissioning is, in fact, "an outmoded series of picture-stories, ridiculously unsuitable to the context of a subway that is said to be the most modern in the world". According to the letter writers, the pictorial and representational approach in art is an aberration.

The first art project for the Metro was completed in December 1967, and sponsored by Steinberg's Limited. It has been a 45 foot long mural of painted glass depicting the history of music in Montreal by Frederic Back. This was in accordance with the hopes of the municipal authorities that the art works for the subway "would be sponsored by private corporations and that, theoretically they would visually depict the history of Montreal".[14] Though a news release issued by the City Hall of Montreal in October 1977 calls the Metro an "Underground Art Gallery"[15], a decade earlier Robert Lapalme was reported to say that he understands his mandate from Mayor Drapeau not to create an art gallery, but to emphasize the history of Montreal: "We are not taking art and putting history into it; history comes first".[16]

To this, art critic Yves Robillard responded that history is a subject to be taught at school, not in the Metro; whereas a museum curator added: "It's a good idea but today you should not do things like that".[17]

The letter published by the Society of Professional Artists of Quebec claims that the idea of decorating Metro walls with anecdotal, narrative and descriptive picture stories is more than aesthetic aberration, it is an antisocial act as well. Since Metro users have only a short time for perception the art should be "for spectators on the go or, in fact, even on the run".[18] The Metro user has

> neither time nor desire to decode some prosaic messages meant to edify or educate him through petty events of history. Any art that would require the spectator to stop in order to perceive it would then provoke traffic jams and hence become antifunctional and antisocial.[19]

Furthermore, the artists suggest that since the general effect of the Metro is an audio-visual performance with a high frequency quality-- after all, the subway is filled with busy people--what is really needed is a contemporary plastic language integrated with architecture. This plastic language should maintain a high degree of visual intensity, must be simple and direct, and radiate living sensations of colour, shape, texture, rhythm and design. This type of art is perceived and assimilated at a glance. It is educational due to its aesthetic qualities, because it is good art, and not because it is good history.

In this manner the Society of Professional Artists of Quebec gave expression to its non-figurative, abstractist commitment.

The president of the Society, Mario Merola, is a non-figurative artist. The son of an Italian father and French-Canadian mother, he was born in Montreal in 1931, and studied here and in Paris. In 1958 he won the first prize in a motional competition for a mural in the Canadian pavilion at the Brussels World's Fair.[20] An admirer of the Quebec artist-craftsmen of the 18th century and the church altars produced by them, Merola regards their work as exemplary coordinated effort of individuals to create a united whole. This 18th century art is a valid influence on his work. Merola is aware of the fact that art grows out of other art. His non-objective sculptures exhibited in 1972 at the Galerie de Montreal did not startle in their novelty. In contemporary terms they revealed the artist's link with op art and minimal art. Merola wants to integrate his work with architecture and an earlier exhibition (1968) was sponsored by the Montreal Society of Architects.[21] In fact, he views his works as pieces of architecture. Accordingly, he accepts willingly the limitations dictated by economy, he strives for integration between aesthetics and social function, and respects the nature and unity of material. His design and technique are based on the dialectical unity of moody, lyrical and cerebral scales. He wants his work to be seen by many people. Therefore, he goes and speaks with architects. "The older artists worked in an environment that did not limit them to isolated efforts . . . Today we have to give more thought to the environment that a work of art fits into, just as they did in the 18th century."[22] And, indeed, most of Merola's work is executed in conjunction with modern architecture. His murals decorate the walls of the Montreal Windsor Hotel (1958), Arena Maurice Richard (Montreal, 1960), City Hall, Greenfield Park, Quebec (1961), and many other buildings.

Merola's strife for integration has its conscious and unconscious historical roots. But it is also supported by contemporary conceptions. For, environmental artists object to plastic isolation: the separation of the art work from an appropriate spatial setting. Modern environmentalism has its historical roots in Medieval and Renaissance commissions involving the collaboration of architect, sculptor and painter. Modern environments are art works which function in a three dimensional space of human scale. American sculptor George Segal (born 1924), for instance, places his plaster figures in carefully reconstructed surroundings (*Cinema*, 1963; *Girl in Doorway*, 1965). His white plaster *Subway Rider* sits in a realistic underground carriage. In 1956 Eduardo Paolozzi created a complex environment in the *This is Tomorrow* exhibition which is regarded as the genesis of pop art. Pop artists like Robert Rauschenberg, Claes Oldenburg, Jim Dine and Louise Nevelson build complex environments including real objects, smells, sounds, and even tastes. Edward Kienholz's *Portable War Memorial* (1968) incorporates a working Coca Cola machine. Ramifications of the movement led to the appearance of *Happenings*, public performances and demonstrations combining poetry, dancing, music, painting, acting and cinema. It seems that the originator of happenings was Allan Kaprow, who launched the movement in 1958 in New York. Happenings usually depend on their shock capacity as they tend to explore the boundaries of acceptable norms. The environmentalist trend has affected also the development of minimal, and conceptual art. The latter frequently involves either the modification of the natural environment, or strives to control the way the spectator reacts to it.

While Robert Lapalme was in charge of the art for the Metro project, he commissioned Mario Merola for the Jarry street station. The work for this station was to be devoted to both French and English kings that were linked to the history of Canada. He, and other important artists, refused to accept the offer, on grounds of aesthetic imposition. For, Merola is a non-figurative artist, and he never worked in representational manner. Therefore, he regarded the suggestion to work in a figurative way as an attempt to dictate style to the artist, and found it being in complete dissonance with the spirit of his accomplished work.[23]

Later, Merola executed for the Sherbrooke station a twelve foot diameter decoration. The work is a porphyl circle in a textured orange colour that animates the area. It is located at the east exit, on the mezzanine of the station. He installed an additional work on a much larger scale (28 m^2 X 36 m^2) at Charlevoix, a station on the 1978 extension line to the Angrignon terminus, West Montreal. Merola's work here consists of two hand blown, stained glass windows in different colours. The colour tones of the design generate a feeling of vertical movement. The windows are in the center of the stairwell beginning at entrance level and reaching out to the mezzanine.[24]

Abstract Art As Political Statement: Marcelle Ferron And The Champ De Mars Station

As aforementioned, Marcelle Ferron also signed her name on the protesting artists' letter to Mayor Drapeau. Twenty years earlier she signed another interesting document: the *Refus Global*. The *Refus Global*, in Dennis Reid's opinion, is not only the most important aesthetic statement a Canadian has ever made, but "perhaps the single most important social document in Quebec history".[25] It was a hand assembled mimeographed book, simply illustrated with a few half tones and wrapped around with Jean-Paul Riopelle's drawing. The first four hundred copies appeared on August 9, 1948. Its key-essay was written by the French-Canadian artist Paul-Emile Borduas (1905-60). He called for a permanent break with the customs of society, for personal liberation, and departure from the outmoded conservatism of the Catholic Church. Critics tried to argue that the *Refus Global* has nothing to do with the realm of aesthetics. But Borduas and his followers knew from experience that well-grounded creativity is possible only in a liberated atmosphere, and thus politics is an essential concern of the artist. Although in his early carrier Borduas was a religious church painter, he underwent a process of mutations, became a pioneer of Canadian abstract painting, and a cultural hero with a symbolic, as well as mythic significance for radical Quebec intellectuals.

After the Second World War Borduas and his followers became involved in an intensive effort of launching a Canadian painting that would be in accordance, for the first time, with the deepest needs of Quebec society. They looked for inspiration to European surrealism and developed its specific Canadian version--*Automatisme*. Yet, Quebec responded with anger. Gérard Pelletier, a liberal Catholic intellectual, rejected Borduas' surrealist ideas in an editorial of the newspaper *Le Devoir* (November 13, 1948). Catholics cannot accept the rule of instinct because they believe in sin, argued Pelletier. In the *Refus Global* Borduas closed the door on Christianity.

Politicians and clergy alike reacted with passionate rage. Two months before *Le Devoir* had published its attack, Borduas received a letter advising him that Paul Sauvé, the minister of social welfare and youth of Quebec, had ordered the immediate dismissal from his teaching post at the Ecole du Meuble, because of the writings and manifestoes he had published. It is noteworthy that as early as 1946, René Bergeron, in his book *Art et Bolchevisme*, described the modern art trends in Quebec as anathema to good Catholics. According to Bergeron, the surrealists were violently anti-Christian demons, followers of Marx and Freud.

Marcelle Ferron was a member of *Les Automatistes*.[26] She was born in Louisville, Quebec, in 1924, became interested in art at age 15 at the convent she attended, and later worked with Borduas.[27] In 1950 she exhibited together with another *Automatiste*, Jean-Paul Mousseau. Two young students of the Jesuit Collége Saint-Marie, who attended the vernissage, were expelled from their alma mater for being present at the opening of the show. In the later fifties Ferron lived in France. There she was questioned by the police for Algerian sympathies.[28] To her astonishment the French police held a personal file about her activities. The dossier was assembled by the RCMP in 1948; after that Ferron signed the *Refus Global*.

She made the art work for the Champ de Mars Metro station. It consists of a play of colour and movement on the stained glass walls of the above-ground upper structure of the station. Ferron's design was carried out by the craftsmen of Superseal Company of St. Hyacinthe,

Quebec. The stained glass windows extend over a combined area of 2000 square feet. The artist's free-form shapes flow and break from one wall section to another. Natural light streaming through the fluid colours of the stained glass animates the interior of the station.

Marcelle Ferron was the only artist invited to contribute from her talent to the Metro without a specific theme. Unlike the other artists, she was free to decide about the nature of the design, because the art work was the gift of the provincial government of Quebec. Ferron herself was not paid for the design. Quebec premier Daniel Johnson made it clear, for the Drapeau administration, that Ferron is the aesthetic master of the project. He stipulated that there should be no pressure for changes, no interference whatever concerning the design.[29]

Now, we have arrived at a position that the aforesaid enables us to make some important observations. As we saw, Marcelle Ferron was the only non-figurative artist commissioned while Robert Lapalme was in charge of the Metro decoration project. Though abstract art is conspicuous by its absence of definite themes, it is not, and cannot be deprived or divorced from history. Therefore, in the light of French-Canadian history, in the context of Quebec, Marcelle Ferron's abstract design for the Champ de Mars Metro station is a political statement, even if it lacks any explicit assertion. For, *Les Automatistes* were a rebellious group of artists, who declared war against the alliance between clergy and politicians, against the traditional values of Quebec establishment. The Catholic Church of Quebec represented not only backwardness in cultural and socio-economical terms, but also political inertia and cooperation within the framework of the Canadian Federation. Mayor Jean Drapeau has been the exemplary French-Canadian federalist, an urbanite dominated by the cosmopolitan atmosphere of Montreal. The themes that he suggested for the art in the Metro project--the French and English kings connected with the history of Canada--reflect the dual world of the federalist. In contrast to him, premier Daniel Johnson (1966-68), the leader of the Union National party, represents the radical Quebec politician. It was Johnson who insisted that only a new constitution based on the principle of two nations would prevent Quebec seceding from the rest of Canada. And it was he who gave the abstract designs of Marcelle Ferron as a gift to the Champ de Mars Metro station, a rather cosmopolitan symbol of not so cosmopolitan aspirations.

The Identity Of The Plasticiens' Conception And The Aesthetic Strategy Of The Protesting Artists

Another executive member of the Society of Professional Artists of Quebec, who signed his name on the letter of protest sent to Mayor Drapeau, was Guido Molinari, who later became professor of fine arts at the Sir George Williams Campus of Concordia University. Molinari is an important Canadian painter who, from the age of twelve, wanted to be an artist. The son of a noted musical director, Joseph Charles, and Marie Mathilda Evelyn Dini-Molinari, Guido was born in 1933 in Montreal. His family circle included students of Paul-Emile Borduas and followers of *Les Automatistes*. Molinari became conscious of the international non-figurative art movement in 1949 when he saw the *Automatiste* exhibition. Two years after the appearance of Borduas' tradition shattering *Refus Global*, at age seventeen (1950) he made a personal research testing the validity of the *Automatiste* belief that painting can be done intuitively, out of the realm of the subconscious. Blindfolded, he painted in the dark in order to explore fully the concept of gestural, spontaneous painting which Borduas and his circle fostered. The results of these experiments were that the young painter rejected the *Automatiste* technique. In the same eight months period of experimentation he also tried the action painting technique developed by Jackson Pollock. Similarly to Canadian *Automatisme* and French *Tachism*, American abstract expressionism (or action painting) as practiced by Pollock, Willem de Kooning, Robert Motherwell, and others, was the ramification of surrealism. Though Molinari was fascinated by experimenting with these techniques, he decided to take a stand in opposition to them, and in 1954 he refused to participate in an *Automatiste* exhibition. The same year has marked the appearance of a new, both international and vernacular movement: *Les Plasticiens*.

In 1954, eight years after the first abstract exhibition in Canada, Borduas freed himself of a long concern with the problem of the representation of infinite surrealist space on the canvas, as the last stage of his painterly development. Though some of the watercolours he made in 1954 still structured shallow space, eventually he absorbed the American abstract expressionist action painting technique. In this manner he learned how to create an image that does not represent anything but itself; a work that closes the gap between making and being, a work in which subject and object are identical.

The year of 1954 marks also the appearance of a new non-figurative ideology represented by the group of *Les Plasticiens*. This new trend was the aesthetic phoenix that rose from the ashes of the *Automatiste* decline. the founders of the group, Louis Belzile (1929), Rodolphe de Repentigny-Juaran (1926-59), Jean-Paul Jerome (1925-), and Fernard Toupin (1930-), were painters who revolted against the irrational, intuitive methods practiced by the *Automatistes*, and were eager to give rise to a more intellectual form of art. Their aims were quite similar to those put forward between the two world wars by the Russian constructivists or by the Dutch *De Stijl* group led by Piet Mondrian and Theo Van Doesburg. The *Plasticiens* wanted to create vehicles of pure and simple aesthetic pleasure devoid of any conscious associative meaning. By means of coloured geometric forms they strove for the presentation of basic plastic facts. Their aim was to display these plastic facts in terms of form, line, tone and texture, to show their ultimate unity in the framework of the painting, and to explore the existing relationships between its purified elements.

Despite the fact that Guido Molinari was not ever a formal member of *Les Plasticiens*, he is closely associated with them. Since 1954 he is a painter of geometric abstraction[30], a hard-edge minimalist aiming at an art divorced from narrative or emotional associations, an art which is based on its formal values. He and the *Plasticiens* preceded American hard-edge painting, because in 1954 abstract expressionism was still the prevailing artistic fad in the U.S.A. Molinari's work involves the exploration of visual perception. His *Angle noir*[31] (1956), is based on the so-called figure-ground effect: foreground and background, black and white straightedged elements of the composition reciprocate. At first the black assumes form and the white serves as background, but it can work also vice versa, until eventually an equilibrium may emerge, a pattern in which form and space are dissolved in visual uncertainty. In 1959 the forerunners of Molinari's stripe paintings began to appear. Following Mondrian in these vertical stripe paintings, he tried to create an effect of anti-gravity. By eliminating horizontal lines and planes from the canvas, Molinari frees the painting from non-vertical pressures and interferences. The vertical stripes, arranged like rhythmic optical mutations, enable the artist to concentrate on the problem of the interaction between various colour fields. They imply the possibility of musical analogy as well, and the colour stripes can be read also as optical equivalents of tonal arrangements. Thus, these works are in accordance with the tenet that all forms of art eventually aspire to achieve the status of music, the most abstract art of all.

Basically, Molinari's approach is analytical. By comparison, the cubists' analytical approach was different. They were preoccupied especially with form, whereas Molinari's views rely on the assumption that the essence of painting is colour. In an interview held in Toronto in 1969 he expressed his *unus mundus* philosophy with the following words:

> My only purpose as an artist is to obliterate the distinction between figure and ground. Why? Well, to me the figure-ground relationship represents a duality. This duality is symbolic of the anthropomorphic view of man that sees him at the centre of the universe and opposed to his environment. I hold that there is a unity between man and his surroundings.[32]

Along with the belief that painting is colour, Molinari also holds that its representational function evolved incidentally. This theory is very doubtful, of course, especially in the light of the magical origins and functions of art.

If we examine and compare the ideas put forth in the *Plasticiens'* manifesto with the proposed aesthetic language described in the letter of protest sent by the Society of Professional Artists of Quebec to Jean Drapeau with regard to the Metro, we find that in fact they are identical. The letter suggests the application of the aesthetic philosophy of the *Plasticiens* as the paramount strategy for the integration of art into the architecture of the Metro.

From Addition To Integration

Not all the artists, however, are adherents of non-figurative art in the Society of Professional Artists of Quebec. Rita Briansky, member of the executive, signed her name on the letter of protest sent to Mayor Drapeau. She was born in Poland in 1925, and came to Canada in 1929.[33] She participated in many one-artist shows and group exhibitions, and is also well-known as a book illustrator. Though basically she is a tender, poetic figurative artist, she refuses to be labelled so "because all art is abstract".[34] But, she has personally not advocated the *Plasticiens'* aesthetics inherent in the letter sent to Mayor Drapeau. As a member of the executive she supported only the central point of the letter, namely that there should be a mixed committee of five experts (architect, engineer, planner, designer, and artist) for every different station, and not only one man: Robert Lapalme. She did not agree with other executive members' claim that the depiction of historical themes would cause traffic jams in the Metro. Eventually she put her signature on the letter, she explains, "because one cannot sign only certain parts of a collective letter. You sign your name on the whole thing."[35]

According to Briansky, the protest of the artists did not change anything. Jean Drapeau refused to negotiate the demand for mixed committees, composed of experts, that would include artists. He said: "We do not need any mixed committees. I am the committee."[36] Briansky did not follow the development of the Metro, and does not know whether the protest, in the long run, had its impacts or not. In any case, she does not rule out the possibility that things have changed since then, because of the artists' protest. Yet, she points out, by no means was there any immediate change.

It seems, however, that the protest of the artist was the stone which had been dropped into the stagnant water of a conservative administration and then the ripples began travelling outward in larger and larger circles. Marcelle Ferron was working recently on a new project for the Metro, and is well aware of the difference between the days of Robert Lapalme and today (1979). She recalls a meeting with Mayor Drapeau at the time of the artists' protest. Out of the three or four artists who were there she remembers only the name of Claude Goulet, a member of the executive and cosignatory of the letter of protest. During the meeting Drapeau was very polite and complimented the artists. But he also said that the art that he has in mind must be for the people. The people do not want modern art, they want something they can understand.[37] "And what about the artists? They are not part of the people?" Ferron objected.[38] And a journalist remarked: The public is much more open and ready to welcome new and daring forms of expression, than the city administration imagines. The success of Expo furnishes evidence to this.[39]

In any case, since that meeting, things have changed completely. Marcelle Ferron does not know exactly how the changes took place. She points out that from the time that Jean Dumontier is in charge of architecture for the Montreal Urban Community's *Bureau de Transport Métropolitain*, there is complete harmony between artist and architect. Artists and architects work in an excellent atmosphere, with mutual respect, and as equal partners.[40]

Since the time of its inception, Montreal's Metro planners advocated the idea of gracing the subway with art. Already in 1966, when the first stage of the system went into operation, there were great differences among its stations. From the beginning different architects were assigned for each station in order to assure the creation of a viable and diverse system. In some stations areas were left for artistic decorations to be added later. Yet, Mario Merola and his colleagues called for the integration of art instead of the addition of decorations. And, indeed, the principle of integration gradually superseded the theory and practice of addition. The actual operation of the subway reinforced the planners' basic assumptions and demonstrated that interesting design and clear lighting are popular with Metro riders. Therefore, the planners not only continued to cling to the idea of varied architecture but decided to increase its importance. And what is more, they opened the door for collaboration with the artists and the aesthetic philosophies they represent. So the idea of integration, rather than addition, became the basic strategy, and according to Jean Dumontier, "the artist must be present along with the architect at the time of conception of the station".[41]

The concept of integration now is universally applied in the Metro. It has been introduced into the subway system of Montreal at the Peel station, on line number one. Interestingly enough the rise of the concept of integration of art into Metro architecture is bound up with non-figurative plastic trends. For, the art works installed in the Metro reveal a tendency toward the abstract. The art at the Berri de Montigny station, the work of Pierre Gaboriau, depicts the founders of Montreal, Jerome Le Royer de La Dauversiére, Paul de Chomedey de Maisonneuve, and Jeanne Mance. At the McGill station one finds historically oriented art as well: Nicolas Sollogoub's back-lighted stained glass window depicting Montreal during the period of 1800-1870. Five large panels illustrate various aspects of city life in Montreal during the nineteenth century. The central panel is dominated by the portraits of Jacques Viger, Montreal's first mayor, and by his successor, Peter McGill. But on the whole, in the stations built later, artistic integration reveals itself in the de-thematization, in the disappearance of concrete subject matter from the art work, and the dissolution of content into form. Syntax and semantics, subject and object have become one identical entity.

As Henry-Russell Hitchcock pointed out, abstract art has been a major source of influence on modern architecture.[42] Architecture, the frozen music, as Johann Wolfgang von Goethe defined it some two centuries ago, has always been an abstract art. But abstract painting, whose object is nonobjectivity–the identity of content and form–is a new development of the twentieth century. In earlier epochs, though painting very often collaborated with architecture, it was always in a subordinate role. The glass painters of the Middle Ages, or the fresco painters of the Renaissance, served the architects by completing and enhancing the beauty of the buildings. However, the modern compartmentalization of disciplines did not exist in the past like nowadays. Frequently, like Leonardo da Vinci, or Michelangelo, the architect was also painter and sculptor. Therefore, it is important to realize that in the framework of contemporary life only real collaboration between architects, painters and sculptors can enhance and further architectural integrity.

The establishment of the famous German Bauhaus in 1919 by Walter Gropius was the first modern step to stress the importance of collaboration between crafts, pure art and architecture. Gradually modern painting and sculpture became the dominant influence in the development of architecture.[43] The world of the abstract painter and sculptor represents, for the architect, the most intelligible visual language. New architectural forms have been invented through the catalytic contacts with the experiments of pioneering artists. Through these experiments the artists have carried out long series of plastic research that can hardly be undertaken at full architectural scale. Cubists like Georges Braque and Pablo Picasso, in the period of the First World War, played a great part in forming the tastes of the first generation of modern architects. Le Corbusier, one of the greatest architects of the twentieth century and a founder of the abstract movement of Purism, assumed that the study of modern painting leads somehow to the formation of a relevant modern taste in all the arts. Surrealist artists, such as Jean Arp or Joan Miro, supplied an alarming jolt to those who conceived the attempts for an immanent artistic synthesis in mechanical and behavioristic terms. The sinuous forms of abstract surrealists suggest biomorphological structures of natural oganisms in contrast to the geometric curves of the Purists, Constructivists and *De Stijl*. Architects like Alvar Aalto and Oscar Niemeyer learned the lessons from the abstract surrealists, and reacted by loosening the rigidity of modern architecture in the 1930's.

Yet, it is also possible to speak in terms of mutual cross-fertilization between painting and architecture. The abstract qualities of architecture crop up as subject matter in the works of many artists, Charles Sheeler (*On a Theme of Farm Buildings*, 1947) and Piet Mondrian (*Broadway Boogie Woogie*, 1942) among them. However, architects like Frank Lloyd Wright and Moshe Safdie expressed the belief in the autonomous character of their profession, that architecture is capable of functioning and fulfilling its mission on its own without the synergistic help of contemporary painting and sculpture.[44]

Nevertheless, interesting edifications may be found even in apparently futile endeavors as to architecture such as the Dada experience. Dada artists, like Marcel Duchamp, Marcel Janco, and Francis Picabia, to name a few, out of plenary despair and humiliated dignity, reacted to the terrible shock of the First World War with tasteless mockery and aimed at shattering all traditional cultural values. Dada oriented artist Kurt Schwitters(1887-1948) was one of those who experimented with ready-made objects. His *Merz* (a meaningless word) constructions were made of commonplace industrial products which he promoted to the status of fine art. Yet, quite surprisingly, the negative intent ended up with rather positive results. The most unlikely fragments, such as torn bus tickets, photograph segments, wine labels, scraps of fabric, wood, chicken wire, and other strange things were able to give birth, of course with the help of the artist, to interesting abstractions featuring almost a lyrical beauty.[45] The message for architects from the Dada experience is that skillful use of commonplace printed matter, such as commercial advertisements, need not necessarily vulgarize the architectural composition. If appropriately related to one another, all sorts of materials–old and new, natural or synthetic–can be utilized in contemporary design, and in line with the grace and dignity of architecture.[46]

Jean-Paul Mousseau And The Peel Station

Now it is time to introduce Jean-Paul Mousseau, an artist who has contributed designs to several Metro stations. Mousseau was born in Montreal in 1927, and studied painting under Paul-Emile Borduas (1946-51).[47] Together with Borduas, he participated in the first abstract exhibition held in Montreal (1946). The other participating artists were Fernard Leduc, Roger Fauteux, Marcel Barbeau, Pierre Gaubreau, and Jean-Paul Riopelle. In 1947 these seven artists became known as the *Automatistes.* In the following year Mousseau signed the manifesto *Refus Global.* In 1953 he was still an exhibitor at the Montreal Place des Arts *Les Automatistes* show, but by May 1955 he joined the group of *Plasticiens* at Guido Molinari's L'Actuelle Gallery which opened in Montreal at that time. In the ensuing years Mousseau extended his activities into the fields of poster work, stage decor, illuminated sculpture and murals. Applying polyester and other synthetic materials, he has lunged into bold aesthetic experimentation. In some of his fiberglass murals he succeeded in generating stained glass window effects. His entry for the 1961 Hydro-Quebec mural composition won the first prize. His huge mural measures 15 by 71 feet and is luminated with the use of 4200 feet of multicoloured neon tubes. Calculations have shown that the same light combinations in the luminated composition will not occur in the next two centuries. His commissions include five murals for Dorval Airport (1959), two stained plastic windows for the Rockland Shopping Center in Town of Mount Royal, Quebec (1959), and a mural for the Montreal Star Building (1961). In 1967 a retrospective exhibition of Mousseau's work was held at the Musée d'art contemporain, Cité du Havre, Montreal. A review on the exhibition stressed that

> it is full of amusing invention, of remembered fun, and of great achievements. It makes us suddenly aware of how much a part of our daily lives this artist's work is. Mousseau has insisted, from the beginning of his life as an artist, on invading all the aspects of visual life, although his disregard for signatures has often resulted in our not knowing it . . . The beginning of the large tiled discs which vibrate their color patterns in the Metro stations are here.[48]

The origins of the tiled discs vibrating at the Peel subway station are in Mousseau's circular paintings which the artist developed after joining the trend of *Les Plasticiens*. The Peel station was the first in which the concept of collaboration between architect and artist, aesthetic integration instead of addition, was brought into full development and successful realization. It opened in 1966, and since then has attracted experts from many countries by reason of its achievement and excellence. Situated on the line number one, the axis that crosses Montreal from east to west, the Peel station is located at an important intersection of downtown Montreal and receives a great number of subway riders. Since the subway rider uses the interior space of the Metro as if it were outdoors, the architectural complexities made up of train tracks, platforms, mezzanines, stairways, escalators and corridors, must be planned very carefully so as to allow for rapid understanding of the system and orientation. The architects, Louis-J. Papineau, Guy Gérin-Lajoie and Michel Le Blanc, have revealed great mastery in combining the various building materials and in the organizing of the architectural masses. Openings and movements of volumes are cleared up by means of directional lights which enable rapid orientation. Advertising posters are integrated artistically on colourful luminous panels located on the platforms. The designers succeeded, after considerable struggle, to avoid the use of commercial posters on corridor walls. They fought to keep out advertising from the corridors in order not to damage the integrity of the station as an architectural whole.

Jean-Paul Mousseau's ceramic tile decorations are inlaid into the station walls and floor. These are sixty-two brightly coloured circular designs spread throughout the station. Six of them are twelve feet, the other fifty-six are six feet in diameter. Their function is to serve as animation for the plain interior and to ease off orientation. The spacing of ceramic tile discs is in line with the rhythm of normal walking pace, resulting in a coloured metaphor, or even the perception of movement. Mousseau's circular patterns are made of rectangular tiles. Their location is the outcome of careful research: the artist took into account the directions of the subway rider's movements, his progress toward the station center, or to the street level exits. The translation of hard edge geometrical abstraction from painting to interior design, from canvas to ceramic tiles, from isolated ivory towers to open urban spaces, leads to message transformations. Mousseau's ceramic motifs, carried out in accurate shapes, colours and texture, break with the gloomy monotony of the passage backgrounds and impose an architectural metamorphosis on the corridors. This includes an optical expansion of the claustrophobic dimensions of corridors, and their integration into the architectural whole.

According to Mousseau the central role of the contemporary artist is the reconciliation of man with his environment. He believes that

> a large interior unity is necessary to those who have the task of building our everyday environment. We must come out of this block-house architecture and re-invent our collective areas. The artist must have the right to speak in situations where form, colour and light are involved. After all, it is his special field . . . Many architects still build for flies and for mice. Their buildings are like their souls, dried out or desolate. It is true that it is not easy to build today. The craft influenced by technique, economy, law, allows a narrower place for aesthetic considerations. Still, architecture, good or bad, communicates. It betrays the degree of social preoccupation of an architect. Calm or aggressive spaces will act upon the man who must inhabit them. Nowadays, the sight of cities is only nothingness or visual pollution. The humanization of public places

remains a vain objective if the builder takes upon himself from the beginning the right to all departures from conscience to fulfil his order.[49]

Mousseau's message concerns not only the field of contemporary planning. For the conflict between the functional school of architecture on the one hand and the aesthetic school on the other is an old one in Canada and elsewhere. Following the Chicago World's Fair of 1893 there was an enhanced interest in the problem of the beautification of cities among Canadian architects.[50] Advocates of the city beautiful movement believed that an ugly environment affects the psychological hygiene of man and that, therefore, the cause of urban beauty was an issue of social interest. The problem of integration as opposed to addition is not new either, as Percy Nobbs' writings attest. Nobbs, Professor of Architecture at McGill University, pointed out in 1904 that architects should understand that one does not add the quality of beauty to a city, but that this quality is a part or is not of its structure. If every building, every street would be made beautiful and "cohere with the general plan; then we will have a beautiful city and not otherwise . . .".[51]

The concept of city beautiful[52] may have declined between the two world wars, but it did not die out. It seems, in fact, that after the Second World War it has undergone metamorphoses and revival. Through a new architecture the reconquest of space will lead to harmony between man and his environment. H. Sivadon reminds us that "mental health can find no surer ground and no better material support than the structure of its architectural environment"[53], and G. Mesmin observes that "the humanization of our civilization developes through the relationship between child, architecture and space".[54] According to Michel Régnier, the major problem of our civilization is city life and urbanization. Possession of space is a part of happiness. But what kind of happiness and meaning can modern cities offer?[55] The daily life of the urbanite occurs in a place characterized by acute social conflicts, alienation, pollution, slums, and run-down areas.

The Subway provides evidence that art not necessarily must be divorced from life and restricted to the artist's studio. The Metro demonstrates that abstract art can be relevant to everyday life and become a normal manifestation of its structure and rhythm. And more than that. For, as Georges Adamczyk put it, the Metro "has made us foresee what the city of the twentieth century can be".[56]

190

Public Art And The Foundation Of SAPQ

Artists are a maverick breed. But, maybe they were not always like that. For the social isolation of the artist seems to be a development bound up with the industrial revolution and the rise of capitalism. The artist is a part of the intellectual solitude, withdrawn in his ivory tower from the practical issues of everyday life. The tendency of much art to appear as a luxury which is irrelevant to the masses of the people is not that of an accidental phenomenon. It is rooted in the advancement of capitalism, the growing separation between subject and object, reality and aspiration. This increasing gap between what exists and what should exist is an intense source of collective discontent, anxiety and frustration. It is a constant ingredient of the human condition in the industrial era and the breeding ground of raging violence.

The rise of capitalist society has produced growing separation between the worker and his product. The artist cannot escape this fate either. The process of alienation affects him as well. He is not free to create. His work is either the result of commercial commission, or fine art commodity hammered through the convulsive interaction of influential styles.

Artists in growing numbers are aware of their isolation. They are eager to enhance communication with the masses and regain integrity. The problem of communication embraces more than the spread of aesthetic information through exhibitions and the media. It involves the issue of breaking down of the distinction between art and life in terms of subject and object, the choice of themes and implementation. The medium becomes the message. For this purpose, the Dada artists developed the technique of collage, using commonplace material (such as newspaper pieces, fabric, metal fragments), and Allan Kaprow introduced the Happenings (1959). Exploring the nature of art and aiming at bringing life closer to it, both Dada artist Marcel Duchamp (1887-1968) and Allan Kaprow brought industrial products into the museum. Later a contrary trend emerged: bringing the museum into the street. Thus, in spite of the fact that public art has a very long history, artists in the 1960's rediscovered mural painting.

The origins of murals, just like that of art in general, can be traced back to prehistoric times. There is surviving evidence that art already existed in the late Pleistocene. In the upper Palaeolithic period early man created painted cave walls in Europe, Asia and Africa. The greatest concentrations of these early cave walls have been discovered in France and Spain. In Altamira, northeast Spain, polychrome animals, which include bison, deer, and wild boar, were painted on the walls. The cave wall paintings in Lascaux, southwest France, depict animals as well. The purpose and meaning of cave art is obscure, because art may have many roles, and in different societies it has different functions. However, it seems that the fundamental drive to produce cave art lies in sympathetic or hunting magic, and belief that the act of animal depiction will help to make the hunt successful. Another school interprets the origin and substance of art in totemistic terms. However, totemism is also related to magic. The carved and painted tree trunk set in front of the house–the totem pole–refers to a wide variety of relationships, including the reverential and the genealogical. The totem is the symbol of the tribe, it reflects the belief in the kinship and mystical relationship between man, trees, animals, and nature. The totem betrays the mediating function of art between man and cosmos; to protect man from evil. It seems that the totems of the North-American Pacific Coast are not so old: they were made in the Nineteenth Century. Their rendering suggests the severe identity crisis that the native tribes experienced through the overwhelming cultural shock that resulted from the stirring contact with the white man.

The ancient Egyptians decorated with art their tombs and temples. Different techniques of mural painting, such as encaustic, tempera, ceramics and fresco date back at least to the Greco-Roman period. Mural painting is different from other pictorial art forms in that it is organically bound up with architecture. The mural partakes of a given space and modifies it. Through colour and thematic treatment the mural is capable of altering significantly the sensation of spatial proportions of the building. Byzantine artists had developed great respect concerning the integration of mosaic decoration into the architectural volume. Yet, the artists of the Renaissance, and even more those of the Baroque period, aimed at the modification of architecture by inventing the representation of illusionistic feeling for space through foreshortening and perspective. Due to their efforts, the walls and ceilings of certain Baroque buildings seem to dissolve almost entirely. The forerunners of easel paintings, murals that could be painted in the artist's studio, appeared in the Sixteenth Century. These were painted with oil on canvas, transported to the site and attached to the wall. But oil pigments are quickly affected by hostile atmospheric conditions and the supporting canvas itself is subject to fast deterioration.

Realizing the broad public significance of murals, the Mexican revolutionary government commissioned, in the 1920s, José Clemente Orozco, Diego Rivera and David Alfaro Siqueiros to decorate the walls of public buildings. The three Communist artists painted with great success in a dramatic, monumental style heroic images commemorating the struggles of life of Mexican peasants and workers.[57] During the depression and Franklin D. Roosevelt's New Deal, thousands of artists were employed in the United States by the government. In the decade between 1933 and 1943 the Federal Arts Project commissioned artists to implement mural paintings in many public buildings. Artists, like Thomas Hart Benton, John Stewart Curry, and Grant Wood, produced murals in a representational manner, characterized by their monumentalism and the heroic interpretation of American life. The Federal Art Project contributed to the strengthening of American unity and cohesiveness.[58]

In Canada public art was a rarity during the years of Depression. Only a few hotels, among them the Chateau Laurier in Ottawa, and, occasionally, universities commissioned artists for mural renderings.[59] The breakthrough came after a long period of stagnation; with the construction of the Metro, and the appearance of environmentalist street art.

The inauguration of the Montreal Metro in 1966 coincided with the foundation of an important artist organization in the summer of that year: The Society of Professional Artists of Quebec (SAPQ). The objectives of this organization were to group together those professionals who practice the plastic arts in Quebec, to protect and advance their economic, social and professional interests, as well as safeguard their professional status throughout the Province.[60] It ties together professionals from different disciplines: painters, sculptors, photographers, designers, graphic, audio-visual, video, multimedia, and tapestry artists. For its members SAPQ provides expositions, contracts, and consignments with dealers, legal aid, gallery space, and information on technical matters. The unifying feature of the Society is not any particular artistic tendency or style, but its commitment to the professional concerns of artists. Since its formation in 1966, SAPQ aimed at enhancing "the role of the visual artists in the cultural life of Quebec, and in so doing to enrich Quebec society itself, and to effect the direction of its evolution".[61] But "despite this particular commitment to cultural development in Quebec, the artistic concerns of members of the SAPQ are international in scope".[62] For the artists who form the Society

> have widely varying backgrounds: from Grand'Mére, Quebec, to Hong Kong, by way of Britain, France, Italy, Poland, and the USSR and other countries; from the Ecole des Beaux-Arts of Montreal to that of

Paris, via the Slade School, the University of Naples and the academies of Fine Arts in Enschede and Vienna.[63]

Operation Balayage

From the beginning of its formation SAPQ was in search of finding ways to socio-political integration and activity. The beginnings of this aspiration date back to Paul-Emile Borduas' *Refus Global*, and the Asbestos strike of 1949, Quebec, during the Maurice Duplessis era. The Duplessis government tried to crush the strike, and it became a political issue which, combined with the scandal stirred up by the *Refus Global* manifesto, seemed

> to shake Quebec society to its very foundations: Asbestos in the relations between capital, labor, church, and power, and Borduas in the area of values, Catholicism and the traditional elite. Borduas demanded for the new artist and for living art a place and a mission which would take the place of those assigned by sterile academicians.[64]

The *Automatiste* will to resolve the tensions and contradictions of Quebec has led to political ramifications and haunting artistic dilemmas. For the artists of Quebec "still waver between painting the revolution and revolutionizing painting, between revolutionizing speech and allowing the revolution to talk".[65]

Representatives from SAPQ met with union leaders and discussed ways of collaboration. In 1966 Quebec artists contributed to an exhibition held in support of the Vietnamese people. Serge Lemoyne exhibited his work, *Monument to U.S. Imperialism*, composed entirely of bandages and blood stains. Various artists made desperate attempts at overcoming the boundaries separating them from the masses by introducing popular subject matters (e.g., hockey game) into their paintings and prints.

The year of 1966, in which SAPQ was founded, marks also the end of the Quiet Revolution. René Levesque, then cabinet minister in the Liberal provincial government of premier Jean Lesage, and one of the generation affected by Borduas' *Refus Global*, advised a Toronto audience that unless there was a new status for Quebec, the province would secede from Confederation within five years or so. In 1970 Robert Bourassa's Liberal Party took over the government in Quebec, but in October the separatist FLQ (Front de Libération du Québec) kidnapped the British diplomat James Cross and murdered Quebec Labor minister Pierre Laporte. A declining standard of living, rising rates of unemployment, led to the General Strike of 1972. But SAPQ already, in 1970, resorted to a militant action. It organized manifestation *Balayage* (House Cleaning) in front of the Musée d'Art Contemporain of Montreal. In the light of the unstable political and economic situation the bourgeoisie lost its confidence that in better days enabled long-term investments in commodities such as art. As a result, many Montreal galleries closed or curtailed activities. The museums offered little help. The Musée du Québec, the Musée d'Art Contemporain, both provincially supported, could afford only very small amounts for purchases. The Montreal Museum of Fine Arts, originally an Anglophone establishment, was run by an American director, David Carter. The artists demanded that it be taken over and run by and for the Québécois. The shrinking market and the growing number of artists increased the gap between what was needed and what has actually been available. The almost complete absence of art patrons in Quebec led to widespread reliance of the artists on provincial and especially federal government support through the grants system. Furthermore, Quebec, including Montreal, has a very low level of visual literacy. Therefore, only the most astute dealers are ready to risk exposing anything but trivia and blue-chip investments. Therefore, with its prospective huge budgets, the art for the Metro project brought new hopes, expectations and enthusiasm to the local artist community. But, it also generated discordance, conflicts and protest, as the Robert Lapalme case has demonstrated.

Quebec artists were active in demonstrations, collaborated with unions and working class community groups, and supported their struggles also by designing posters and publications.

In 1971 the Quebec Government's Ministry of Culture responded positively to the demands made by the artists. In fact, the response was so solicitous that Claude Charron, a member of the National Assembly for the Parti Québécois, warned against the dangers inherent in the new policy. He told the approximately 150 artists present at a conference in Vaudreuil that a government subsidized culture in Quebec can turn into a new Church whose priests will be the artists of today making oppression bearable. His speech shares similarities with the ideas of the philosopher Herbert Marcuse.[66]

Public Art And Tobacco:
The Benson & Hedges Project

While trade union representative André Leclerc asked the artists whether they wanted to go on producing luxury commodities for the bourgeoisie, or to put their art at the service of the Quebec revolution, a Canadian company made a step to steal their thunder. Following American examples, Benson & Hedges, the cigarette company, came forward in order to take the wind out of the artists' sails. In the years of 1971 and 1972 it sponsored the painting of art walls in the cities of Montreal, Quebec City, Ottawa and Winnipeg.[67] Besides their cool out function, these outdoor murals brought a great deal of publicity for the company, and at a relatively low cost, compared to the high expenses of ordinary commercial advertising.

Mayor Jean Drapeau approved the program initiated by Benson & Hedges. On behalf of the city of Montreal, he hailed the project, saying it was in the spirit of the city's commission of murals in the Metro stations. And, he added:

> Art must not be the privilege of the few but must be democratized. This undertaking not only underlies the presence of art in the world of business but should serve to stimulate the desire of Montrealers to visit their museums and galleries.[68]

The large-scale cityscape paintings decorating the walls of buildings spread throughout Montreal, and in the summer of 1976 there were eighty outdoor murals in existence.[69] Many of these murals have been painted in the vicinity of Metro stations, as if they were announcing the presence of the subway's tentacles. These tentacles–the corridors of the Metro–link the cityscapes to the underground art works of the subway, and turn both categories into an integrated whole.

According to the Montreal *Gazette*, the project initiated by Benson & Hedges "seems to be moving art in the right direction–out in the streets for everyone to see and enjoy".[70] For,

> in the last few months the artists have had much to complain about the state of art and the policy of the cultural affairs department. One of their complaints was that artists lack opportunities; and that art should be exposed to more people.[71]

One of the artists commissioned to paint a mural was Francois Déry whose cityscape decorates the walls of the Caisse Populaire Notre-Dame du Trés St. Sacrament at 482 Mount Royal Avenue, near the Metro station, at the corner of Berri Street. Déry is a conceptualist who approaches the artist and his work in terms of energy:

> Consider the creative artist as a center of energy. There are surrounding rings of his immediate creative contacts, other artists, creative schools, live energy environments. As the original creative force is projected into wider circles, its effect becomes less powerful. The creative force is very thin at the periphery of the field where you find workers buying framed chromos. The field has much less force there but it is easier to enter.[72]

Déry's work has contributed to the creation of a new artistic milieu in Montreal. For cityscapes are projects based on the premise that mural paintings are art works which transform the environment. Through the added presence of colour, line, form, texture, light, composition and order, the murals change the gestalt of the city's architecture.

Francois Déry was born and raised in the east-end of Montreal. "I was sent to school with the sisters and then to the fathers", he says. "You know, the strap, the whole bit. The system is designed to break your ego so that you can be indoctrinated."[73] He appreciates the liberated atmosphere, the non-authoritarian methods that surrounded him at the museum school where he studied art under Hugh Leroy's direction. Gradually he became involved in the emerging new art of the 1960's which deals with the problems of milieu and context. This environmental art has rejected the symbolic interpretation of the human experience for the actual experience generated by situations taking place in the milieu. The idea and the process of its implementation are more important than the resulting object. This is conceptual art. It does not sell and it cannot be collected, because it offers none of the tangible security inherent in a carefully produced artistic commodity that lasts. In fact, it has been invented for this purpose. To create an art which is the exploited, humiliated artist's answer to a materialistically oriented society. If there were no art objects, there would be no art dealers and art collectors either. Then art would belong to the artists and to the people. For, the businessmen who dominate the art world are not really interested in art and aesthetics. They do not care a tinker's damn about the artist and his problems. Their concern is profit and nothing else. Thus, the non-establishment artist experiments with happenings, scenes, light-shows, sound explorations, computer art, temporal processes and environmental alterations. Déry's mural at the Mount Royal Metro station is not an art object but an environmental work. It cannot be collected or sold.

Déry objects to Quebec nationalism. He thinks that Montreal has less to offer than the open west. Vancouver has the landscape and a more spacious society.

> In Quebec the energy that should be creative is all mixed up with nationalism. That is not where my head is at. It has got to be a whole earth thing. I want the openness of the west. Things are too blocked here. Did you hear Charlebois described the underground when they asked him for a definition of it. He said, "I don't know what you mean by the underground but if it means anything at all, it means a way of dealing with the establishment without getting involved in all that garbage. You just detour around it."[74]

Francois Déry's mural relates thematically to its environment. The artist used the stylized outlines of trees for the central colour fields of the cityscape. The subject matter echoes the little park facing the art wall. In line with the lessons learnt from colour field painting, he backgrounded outlines with a dark blue semi-circle arranged against a lighter blue. This let the light effects inherent in colour field systems succeed in asserting themselves. Thus, the mural not only has brightened the area but also produced an illusion of more spacious milieu.

Colour field painting is rooted in the *oeuvre* of many abstract painters, among them Joseph Albers, Piet Mondrian, Clyfford Still, Barnett Newman, Mark Rothko, Kenneth Noland, and Frank Stella. Colour field painting is often associated with the use of large-scale canvas, and therefore its handling, transportation, or gallery installation evoke considerable difficulties. The solution for these difficulties may be found in environmental art. A statement made by Charles F. Lombard, president of Benson & Hedges, includes reference to this problem as well:

198

> We are confident that paintings on the walls in the city will enhance Montreal's urban environment. It is our hope that these walls will demonstrate that large-scale art need no longer be confined to museum space but can also be environmental, surrounding all our people, expanding our vision and enriching our lives.[75]

Another artist commissioned in the cityscapes project sponsored by Benson & Hedges was Gary Coward. The street wall of the Sir George Williams Student Union building on Maisonneuve Boulevard has been chosen as its location. Coward, who at the time of the mural's execution was also a lecturer at SGW University, implemented the cityscape in an abstract idiom. Through the usage of pure spectral colours, he painted six vertical sequences rising from glistening waves. The top of the composition is cut off. Thus, the vertical sequences seem to lead the spectator's eye to infinity. In this manner the artist's work is not only suggesting a sense of monumentality but also is appropriately related to the city skyline.

The third chosen artist for the cityscapes project sponsored by the tobacco company was Guy Montpetit, at that time president of SAPQ. He also designed decorations for the subway's L'Assomption station which opened in 1976 as part of the extension of line number one to the east terminus of Honoré-Beaugrand.

Guy Montpetit was born in Montreal in 1938. He studied at the Ecole des Beaux-Arts of Montreal with Albert Dumouchel, and later with S. W. Hayter in Paris. He is a unique holdout of the ideas of the *Plasticiens*, the Montreal movement of painters noted for their pure colour statements, well-defined hard-edge shapes, rhythmical repetitions of forms—all geared to clarity and away from expressionist introvertism. But, in contrast to the lack of sentimentality and impersonality which characterized the *Plasticiens*, Montpetit has aimed at combatting alienation through his art. The iconography of his work is based on clearly defined sinuous lines, hard-edge biomorphic shapes. The morphology is based both on the children's world (toys) and on erotica (*Sex Machine* is the title for a group of his paintings).[76] It is related to the human experience through the artist's will. Thus, Montpetit rejects total abstraction but at the same time he also builds on it. According to Leo Rosshandler of the Montreal Museum of Fine Arts, Montpetit revitalizes abstract purity by injecting into it an anthropomorphic concept, images of humane proportions.[77]

199

In the mid 1960's a small group of environmentalist artists in New York began to produce outdoor murals. Using the techniques of billboard painters, these murals became known also as supergraphics. The goals of the artists were to democratize their art, and through abstract colour field painting to brighten and enliven the city as well. Following the New York example, Guy Montpetit and other members of SAPQ began to make preparations for the creation of supergraphics in Montreal. They searched for appropriate walls, photographed them, created sketches and models and requested sponsorship from the provincial government. But the Quebec government left them, without response, and the idea was put aside. Then the tobacco company, Benson & Hedges, came up with the suggestion of sponsoring art walls in Montreal. When Montpetit learnt about the proposal he commented with surprise and enthusiasm: "The coincidence seems too good to be true. This is a fundamental move for art."[78]

Benson & Hedges submitted the problem of selecting the artists for the project to the Montreal Museum of Fine Arts. Director David Carter, his deputy Leo Rosshandler, and assistant curator Germain Lefebre drew up a list of ten Montreal artist candidates. The artists were asked to present their proposals through maquettes. The winning three that the museum committee selected were Guy Montpetit, Francois Déry and Gary Coward.

The adaptations to the walls were carried out by a New York based company, Environmental Design Associates, headed by Jim O'Haverty, a one-time housepainter who became a supergraphics specialist. The total cost of the project was 20,000 dollars which included priming and sealing, painting, as well as adaptation of plans to the walls chosen for the murals.[79]

The actual painting of the first project was completed in six weeks, by July 1971. The artist was Guy Montpetit. His twin-walled mural situated in the St. Henry district has been cut by Notre Dame Street. The biomorphic composition is made of sinuous lines set into bands and semi-circles. Its morphology evokes sensation of space through the establishment of a figure-ground relationship. The eye-catching, overwhelming burst of colour and the hard-edge forms emerge in sharp contrast to the grey chaos of the environment.

The Paradox Of The Democratization Of Abstract Art

As the late American critic Harold Rosenberg remarked, "it is a hardship of the times that before an artist can fashion an icon he must compose the theology that his icon will reinforce".[80] For, contemporary art is an alchemistic amalgam of words and materials. Art, as the combination of craft and inspiration, belongs to the preindustrial era. The artist of our times stands on the crossroads between the poet and the engineer. His work today is as specialized and esoteric as the sciences.

> Art has become the study and practice of culture in its active day-to-day life. Begin by explaining a single contemporary painting (and the more apparently empty of content it is better), and if you continue describing it you will find yourself touching on more subjects to investigate–philosophical, social, political, historical, scientific, psychological–than are needed for an academic degree.[81]

The language of abstract art, as that of most contemporary art, is ambiguous. If the artist entitles the work he may provide a hint or a solution as to its meaning or his artistic intentions. Interestingly enough Guy Montpetit's double-walled mural in the St. Henri district (4777 and 4780 Notre Dame Street West) is untitled. Another interesting meaningful coincidence is that when Benson & Hedges made its cityscapes project proposal, it stipulated that "the themes be neither political nor erotic".[82] But, Montpetit's mural is very much in line with the work he produced in the same period and it can easily be related to the series of his *Sex Machine* paintings displayed at the Montreal Museum of Fine Arts during the summer of 1970.

Esther Charbit, an active muralist and art teacher, refers explicitly to the twin outdoor wall paintings, without mentioning Montpetit's name, as "The Sex Machine".[83] She claims that aesthetic concerns should not be isolated from the cultural setting, and that what is needed is a meaningful public art and not large scale wall decorations. Murals should be executed with the participation of the people of the neighborhood. Thus, art walls would turn into a kind of forum, into large scale metaphors expressing the feelings and aspirations of the people who live in the neighborhood, like the murals painted in Chicago in the late 1960's and early 1970's.

In the present situation

> art is no longer part and expression of life, but a special domain of the artist, a domain which should be worshipped and supported by his public, but not

participated in. The artist still addresses–or thinks he
addresses–the public, but there is no dialogue.[84]

Various philosophers, among them John Dewey and Ernest Van
Der Haag, suggested that art should become an integral part of life. In
concert with this conception American muralists have experimented
with art wall painting as a process of community development. In
order to realize this, neighborhood residents were brought together and
invited to participate in the creation of murals. They discussed
problems and ideas relevant to their life. They also learned how to
communicate their feelings and give them visual expression. Through
the creation of meaningful murals to them, the neighborhood residents
not only transformed their physical environment, but in the process
they developed also community identity, and a sense of enhanced self-
respect as well.[85]

According to Esther Charbit, public art is in great need nowadays
because of the declining standard of living, the rapidly growing multi-
ethnic population, and the fast-paced deterioration of the physical
environment of North American cities. Referring to Montpetit's mural,
Charbit stresses that though it is a well executed, aesthetically pleasing
decoration, its setting does not meet the requirements of adequate
environmental integration:

> The painting is on two walls with a busy city street
> dividing them. The neighbourhood is run down and
> consists of low income residences and small
> businesses. Both walls of the painting face onto a
> school playground. The subject of the mural:
> undulating and interconnecting sausage shapes in
> muted complementary colors. Title: *The Sex
> Machine.*[86]

The icon and theology of abstract art assert an esoteric language for
the layman. The syntax and semantics of this language are obscure for
him or her and meaningless. Abstract art itself as a vehicle of the
search of man for meaning cannot convey its message except through
visual literacy. Claude Guite, a Montreal environmental muralist and
the leader of a group of seven young people who call themselves *Les
P'tits Soleils*, has complained about difficulties of communication with
neighborhood residents. The group executed murals in the east end of
the city. But the people there "do not like abstracts", said Guite.
"They like to see murals that they can understand at a glance."[87]

202

Guite's remark implies a paradox. For, the aim of the environmental muralists has been the democratization of art through large scale abstract paintings executed on city walls. They have brought art to the street in order to address the public, yet they merely widened the invisible walls of the ivory tower and their speech is autistic.

This paradox is even amplified in the light of the abstract artist's conception regarding the nature of non-representational art. For, as we saw it above, the letter of protest sent by the executive and the members of SAPQ to Mayor Jean Drapeau in December 1967 included the contention that abstract art is more social, more democratic than figurative art. According to the artists, this is so due to the unassuming features of abstract art which lends itself easily to architectural integration, whereas the aberration of figurative art can lead to the formation of human traffic jams in the busy stations.

Avant-Garde Art As Indicator Of The Nature Of Political Regimes

An additional paradox, stemming from the ambiguity inherent in non-objective art, concerns its relationship to politics. We have already seen above that Paul-Emile Borduas' *Refus Global* advocated surrealism and abstraction as the carriers of the will of free expression. Due to the reactionary nature of the ruling establishment in Quebec, abstract art became an anathema for clergy and conservative politicians alike. They associated the avant-garde trends with Freud and Marx.

Since it is my fundamental assumption that nothing can escape the fulcrum of history, art cannot be divorced from the political context. Therefore, the same specific art trend implies different meanings in different historical situations.

The absorption-pace of the abstract trend into the matrix of Canadian culture in general, and that of Quebec in particular, was different from the advancement orbit of non-objective art in the U.S.A. The Armory Show that took place in New York introduced to America as early as 1913 styles such as cubism, fauvism, expressionism, and futurism. Between the two world wars important abstract artists, harassed by the Nazis, left Europe and emigrated to U.S. shores. Among them were Joseph Albers, Lászlo Moholy-Nagy, Amédée Ozenfant, Fernand Léger, William S. Hayter, and Piet Mondrian. The timing and encounter between the new and the old took place in a different atmosphere in the U.S. than in Canada. The appearance of abstract art in Canada and its relationship to the conservative political context and cultural inertia involved a much more shocking experience in Quebec than in the liberal atmosphere of New York. In 1946, when the first abstract exhibition was held in Montreal, non-figurative art was already nothing new in New York. However, in Montreal, as late as 1976, an avant-garde exhibition of local artists organized in honour of the Olympic Games that took place in the city in the summer of that year was demolished by order of Mayor Jean Drapeau. The exhibition–Corridart–functioned on two levels. The first printed commentary and photographic murals, whereas the second level dealt with the experience of art works woven into the living fabric of the street. Thus, Corridart turned Sherbrooke Street into a work of art, an artifact. It restored to the street its collective character, the sense of continuity and communality. "Corridart reidentified the street as the one absolute unit of non-economic investment, the one part of the city that is owned by all."[88]

In the introduction to the street map of Corridart, Melvin Charney stressed that Sherbrooke Street was, in the history of Montreal, a dividing line between the poor and the rich who had traditionally lived below and above it. Corridart included practical jokes, such as the replica of Montreal's lighted cross from Mount Royal placed near to the sidewalk and lying on its side. But most of all, the exhibition pointed to a contradiction between what the street has come to mean and what it should mean in human terms. After a few days of display, the City of Montreal ordered the demolition of Corridart (July 13, 1976).

Interestingly enough, the development and status of avant-garde art in the Soviet Union provide empirical evidence for the existing relationship between the abstract trends and anti-liberal political inertia. In the first phases of the Russian Revolution abstract art was not only officially accepted but, in fact, artists put their work into the service of the Bolsheviks. They designed revolutionary posters, banners, models, and decorations. Casimir Malevich, who launched the Suprematist movement in Russia in 1913, and published its manifesto in collaboration with Bolshevik poet Vladimir Mayakovsky in 1915, exhibited his famous "white and white" paintings in Moscow in 1919, two years after the October Revolution. Other avant-garde Russian trends, such as Rayonism and Constructivism, still flourished in this period. However, in 1921 Lenin denounced Constructivism and after his death the relatively liberal policy toward the arts had come to an end. As a result of the aboutface, experimental art was forced to give way for Social Realism based on the relationship of political propaganda and figurative academic painting.

And there is, of course, the even more obvious example of the fate of non-objective avant-garde art in Nazi-Germany. The National-Socialists could not tolerate it at all. But the relationship of the establishment to avant-garde art is a revealing experience even in the non-totalitarian context. Thus, abstract art is an indicator, sort of a litmus paper that betokens both the acidic or alkaline nature of political regimes. The western style liberal systems tolerate and promote it. At the same time, however, they also try to refine and isolate the aesthetic realm from the variants of political implications that may be attached to art. This tendency is a part of the process of alienation, the widening of the gap between subject and object, and it is in accordance as well with the aspiration of the establishment to safeguard equilibrium.

The tobacco company Benson & Hedges sponsored the cityscapes project but stipulated, among other things, that no political themes would be featured. The aspiration to create a tamed environment devoid of problems and turmoil is well illustrated in David Carter's message, which was written in 1976 while he was still director of the Montreal Museum of Fine Arts:

> Montreal is at the confluence of a cultural crossroads unique in North America. As a bridge among different elements of the community, whether social, ethnic or generation, the Museum's role is vital and one may hope that with increasingly larger government participation that the inevitable temptation of "politization" [sic] does not occur. There is every hope for a healthy dialogue as the Museum grows.[89]

Guy Montpetit Mediates Between Man And The Machine: L'Assomption Station

Artists are only rarely trained politicians, of course. Their statements, however, are not less contradictory than those made by the professional politicians themselves. This does not intend to be criticism. For, existence itself is so complicated and contradictory that its incongruities seem to be a dialectical part of its nature. In other words, there is no escape from contradictions.

Let us return now to Guy Montpetit. According to him:

> Quebec artists are valuable enough to challenge the artists of Canada but the means of communication are

205

not yet there. That is partly their own fault and partly the fault of governmental decision makers. So many of us are scared to involve ourselves with the rest of Canada. I do not believe that faith in nationalism as a French-Canadian means no contact with the rest of the world. Artists in Canada desire very strongly to get together, I have found. And they are interested in our originality as an ethnic group. I think the role of the artists right now, is not to have an option in politics, but to have faith in man. The rest will come along.[90]

As president of SAPQ, Montpetit became involved with the problem of the formation of a multi-disciplinary, multi-purpose national commission for the visual arts. Along with the Quebec Sculptors' Association, and the societies of Quebec Etchers and Engravers, SAPQ proposed, in 1972, to the Secretary of State's Office, the department responsible for cultural affairs in the Federal Government, the establishment of a so-called Plastic Art Umbrella. This commission was regarded as non-political. Its role would be to unite the artists of Canada, defend their rights, make national communication possible, influence and suggest cultural policies (like exhibitions abroad), and provide information.

Through his toy and erotic morphology, Montpetit fights against alienation. At L'Assomption Metro station his mural occupies both sides of a corridor. The laminated plastic wall paintings are executed on a yellow background. Hard-edge cylinders, ovals and circles in unmodulated blue, green, red, and orange combine into a half biomorphic and half geometrical composition. Thus, Montpetit's mural mediates between machine and man. The longer mural measures circa nineteen meters by two, the shorter nine by two. Their bright colours and smooth texture are in sharp contrast to the grey brutality of the concrete tunnel which surrounds them. In addition to these two murals facing one another on both sides of the corridor, there are a series of three smaller triangular panels animating the entrance to the station (3.35m x 0.61m x 2.89m). Through their mediating function the Metro rider is signalized and attuned to encounter the subway experience.

Conclusion

The concentration of the variants of the urban art experience in the Montreal Metro is a vivid contribution to the improvement of the physical environment. It affects the quality of life, and is an emphatic enhancement of the urban condition. At the same time, however, the question can be raised whether the social role of the artist has indeed been a positive contribution to the interest of the public. For, the Metro has been a pivotal project of Montreal's development; but it has also been darkened with euphemistic gloom.

People followed with enthusiasm the erection of skyscrapers along Dorchester street, the development of expressways, shopping plazas, and the construction of the Metro. But only a few called attention to the fact that economic development is not identical with social, cultural, and psychological needs. So, the critics warned that attractive slogans such as urban renewal, progress and development are, in fact, deceptive words, used by those who control huge monetary resources, in order to hide the rip-off. To demonstrate this contention it should be mentioned that about twenty thousand homes of low income residents were destroyed for downtown developments, and their residents were forced to move to more expensive areas. Thus it is not an exaggerated statement that the development of Montreal's city core was accomplished on the backs of the poor.[91] And in this manner the question with regard to the role of the artist is legitimate: What is it?–Beautification, mediation, or protest and criticism?

It is society that expects the artist of devoting his talent to the worship of Apollo and Venus: It demands that art be beautiful, and create a refuge for the mind by transforming the chaos of actuality into the orderliness of art. Thus art turns to be an instrument of stabilization which sustains equilibrium. It operates to reconcile man to his condition, instead of rousing him to change it. In this respect the art of the Montreal Metro is the servant of the downtown development project, it anaesthetizes, and beautifies the rip-off.

The special status of Montreal as the most unique North-American metropolis, the center of exclusive encounter between two great cultures–French and English–is a significant factor of the search for Canadian identity. In the light of this search one can more easily understand Dr. O. M. Solandt who suggests that the Montreal Metro has turned to be the vivid manifestation of the difference between French and English Canada. This seems to imply that Gallic sociability, talkativeness, and the yearning of the Latin soul for visual beauty were channelled into public art and brought forward in the Metro of Montreal, as against the Nordic spirit, the introvert environmental puritanism that characterize the subway of Anglo-Saxon Toronto.

The ethnic division of Montreal gives rise to public art forms which reflect specific political issues and tensions. Gabriel Bastien's work at the Sherbrooke Metro station, for instance, is a two-dimensional monument erected to the memory of the St. Jean Baptiste Society, the French Canadian nationalist group. This mosaic of Venetian marble is enriched by enamels (7.32 m. x 7.32 m.). It depicts the founding banquet of the society, and highlights of its activities. The mosaic is dominated by the image of Ludger Duvernay, the founder of the association. The work has been donated by the French Canadian companies Société nationale de fiducie, Economie mutuelle d'assurance-vie and Société nationalle d'assurances. Another work in this category is to be found at the Papineau station. Artist Jean Cartier portrays in jostled colours and shapes Louis-Joseph Papineau, the Quebec nationalist statesman who led the 1837-38 rebellion against the British domination of Lower Canada. Two additional panels suspended from tunnel roof facing each side of the subway station bridge depict historical scenes of the revolt. The murals are implemented in baked enamel, and were donated by the Société des Artisans, a life insurance company. It is noteworthy that Papineau's revolt was the result of despair. In 1822 a proposal was made by the Chateau Clique and the Tories of Upper Canada to the British Parliament to pass an Act of uniting the two provinces. This would turn French majority in the Lower Canada body of representatives into a minority in the united Canadian Assembly. The proposal, and the fact that the extreme Tories "had branded the French Canadians as an inferior race", [92] were the most important reasons which convinced Papineau that the only expedient was resorting to violence. The rebellion, however, was hopeless from the beginning, since the majority of French Canadians did not take part, and the Catholic clergy denounced it.

As against the Quebecois murals of the Metro, charged with the spirit of nationalist aspirations, stand the works of Nicolas Sollogoub, Maurice Savoie, and Frederic Back, which convey the message of Canadian Confederation, or are devoted to neutral themes, and supported by English, Jewish or other ethnic groups. Thus, Nicolas Sollogoub's five back-lighted stained glass windows (6.10 m. x 1.83 m. each) depicting Montreal in the nineteenth century, with mayors Jacques Viger and Peter McGill on the central panel, at the McGill station, were donated by David M. Steward, president of MacDonald Tobacco Company. Maurice Savoie's wall size terracotta mural in earth tones at the same station was commissioned and owned by Eaton's department store. The mural decorates the main subway entrance to Eaton's. Its theme is inspired by nature: branches, leaves, and flowers. At the Place des Arts station Frederic Back's back lighted stained glass mural inlaid in the east wall of the mezzanine is devoted to music (2.74 m. x 13.72 m.). The stylized images of Calixa Lavallée, Guillaume Couture, Alexis Contant, and Emma Lajeunesse honour Montreal musicians, while the abstract designs on the right of the mural represent the dynamism of contemporary Canadian music. The work was donated by Steinberg's Company.

The art of the Metro also reflects the great schism between the traditional figurative and avant-garde abstract schools. In December 1967 the Société des Artistes Professionnels du Québec sent a letter to Mayor Jean Drapeau protesting against the undemocratic handling of the huge art project commissions for the Metro. The society also demanded collaboration between artists, architects and other experts responsible for the construction of the subway, as well as the integration of abstract art into its architecture. The Montreal Metro planners from the beginning took a stand in favour of the assumption that the subway is more than a technological problem, and realized the behavior moulding influence of aesthetic environment. Jean-Paul Mousseau's abstract ceramic tile circles inlaid into the Peel station walls and floor are an early example of successful integration. However, it was only after the artists' protest that the strategy of adding art works to existing stations has been abandoned, and the principle of integration was fully accepted.

In the specific historical context of Quebec avant-Garde art has been viewed by the conservative establishment as a Marxist-Freudist phenomenon. Paul-Emile Borduas' *Refus Global* called for political liberation as a prerequisite for artistic freedom. Marcelle Ferron's free-form shapes of stained glass, flowing and breaking from one wall section to another, at the Champ de Mars Metro station is an *Automatiste* creation. In the political context of Quebec it implies a revolutionary message, because art cannot be separated from the historical whole, and because Marcelle Ferron signed the *Refus Global* manifesto. Her work at the Metro is a visual manifestation of the creative process used by the *Automatistes*. For, through the nature of its morphology, every art work reveals the applied creative process of its rendering. So, in contrast to geometrical abstraction–to a great extent the result of conscious aesthetic planning–the free-flowing sinuous morphology stemming from the *Automatiste* creative process has primarily been based on the intuitive resources of the unconscious, an anathema for Quebecois Catholics.

In 1966 the Quiet Revolution of Quebec has come to its end. The same year saw the foundation of the Society of Professional Artists of the province (SAPQ). In the ensuing years the Government of Quebec responded positively to many demands made by the artists, and in 1971 Mayor Drapeau called for the democratization of art. His call was in accordance with the concepts of environmental and conceptual artists, and has also been financially supported by private companies, such as Benson & Hedges. However, the attempts made at democratizing art reveal the paradox inherent in contemporary art as a tool of communication: The artists are isolated from the masses, the layman does not understand their language. Art became a specialization.

The entrance to many Montreal Metro stations is signalled by outdoor environmentalist murals that carry the message of aesthetic democratization by means of establishing encounter between the art work and the people. The outdoor muralists also aim at bringing light and colour to the street, to transform the architectural environment, and bridge the gulf between the social and technological condition of man through the mediating function of art. The resulting outdoor frescoes are superscale painted walls that can be as well a quick and economic means of urban renewal of deteriorated areas.

About 1910 Robert Delaunay and Fernand Léger began to explore the relationship between pure colour and architectural space. Léger stressed the importance of collaboration between architecture, painting, and sculpture. According to him:

> The external volume in architecture, the sensations of weight and distance, can be reduced or augmented through the use of colour. A bridge can become invisible and weightless through colour orchestration. Why not undertake a multi-coloured organization of a street–of a whole city?[93]

Léger recalls his meetings with Leon Trotzky during the First World War:

> I used to spend my furloughs in Montparnasse where I happened to meet Trotzky, and we often talked about the thrilling problem of a coloured city. He wanted me to go to Moscow; the idea of a blue street, a yellow street aroused his enthusiasm. I think it is in the housing projects, where the workers live, that the need of colour is strongest for the creation of artificial space. Nothing has so far been attempted. The poor man's family could feel the freedom of space, even

210

with a fine art-work on the wall. They are first of all interested in colour and light. These are the necessities of life. It is free colour that is essential to urban centers.[94]

Other artists, such as Theo van Doesburg, Sophie Tauber-Arp, Le Corbusier, and the Constructivists were engaged in experimenting with the use of colour for architectural spaces, and advocated the idea of using abstract designs in the urban environment. The first articulation of the environmentalist non-objective murals appeared in New York in 1967: Allan D'Arcangelo's supergraphic. Similar art-walls were introduced into Montreal in 1971 with the Cityscapes project.

The street of the huge metropolis means nothing to people as a place. To make people care about the streets they have to develop through time personal relationship with the place. This is possible only when the street does not change its face so fast; neither physically nor socially. Since the meaning of the urban environment is bound up with yearning for symbolism, charm, and aesthetic appeal, their lack signals the meaninglessness of city life.

Supergraphics can be used for the remedial improvement and revitalization of the physical environment. They are a fast and economic visual strategy representing a widening of the range of architecture, a breaking away from the traditional conception of colours as an entity beyond the pale of the science and art of building. For, the articulation of supergraphics implies that colours in themselves are architectural element capable of transforming the gestalt of environment. Yet, at the same time, supergraphics are not the solution for urban renewal, because they merely offer visual relief. Paint is not a panacea. It is just a pill to ease the pain temporarily. Supergraphics may calm down the symptoms, but they do not cure the disease. Their use in run down areas can be effective only as a short term strategy to cheer up the gloomy environment.

But the central issue arising out of the Metro as urban art experience, is the aesthetic necessity, and enhancement of the physical environment; the constructive interaction between art and the people. The aesthetization of the physical environment is not a marginal problem but a fundamental indispensability in order to reconstitute man's lost integrity and dignity. Plato in *The Republic*, long ago, postulated that economy debased culture and morality, and therefore they should be separated. Unfortunately, the Industrial Revolution and the resulting intensive urbanization, though have enormously deepened the scale of civilization in technological terms, only widened the gap between theory and practice, utopia and reality. Nevertheless, art still can fulfill its mission. Its various forms allow us to ascend to the height of our own entirety. For, art shutters the dullness of life, evokes awareness, and functions as the collective memory of mankind. Painting, sculpture, music, literature, and other arts, at their best, provide relief to the soul. Through their cathartic action man is capable to solve emotional problems. With its accumulated insights, subject themes, and paradoxes, art offers us the most important means for active individual development. Thus, in our overrationalized society, programmed mass behavior and mass education, the greatness of art is bound up with its function to prevent us from turning into twisted and computerized automations.

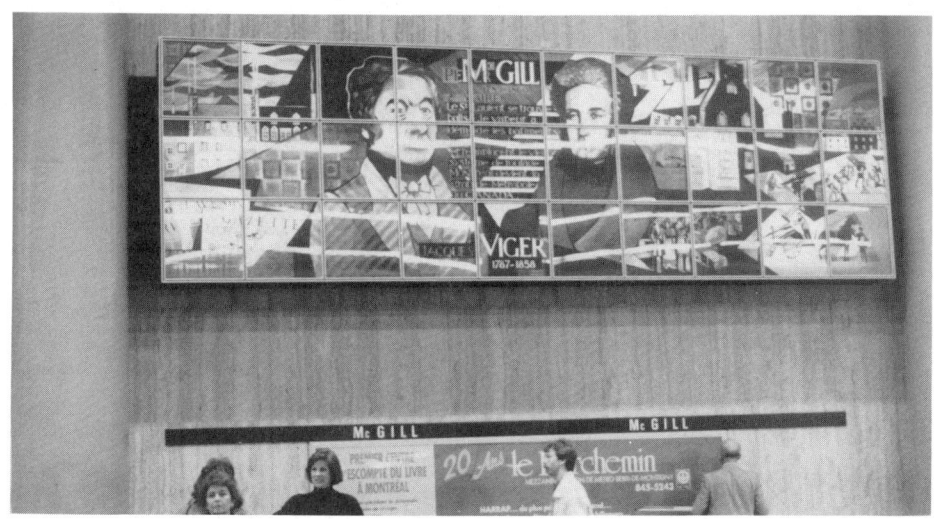

Above: Nicholas Sollogoub: *Jacques Viger and Peter McGill*, the first mayors of Montreal; McGill Metro Station. The central panel of five back-lighted stained glass windows. Donated by MacDonald Tobacco Co., the works reflect the spirit of Canadian Confederation. Environmentally, this type of art represents addition to existing architecture.

Below: A general view of Nicholas Sollogoub's back lighted stained glass windows at the McGill Metro Station, Montreal.

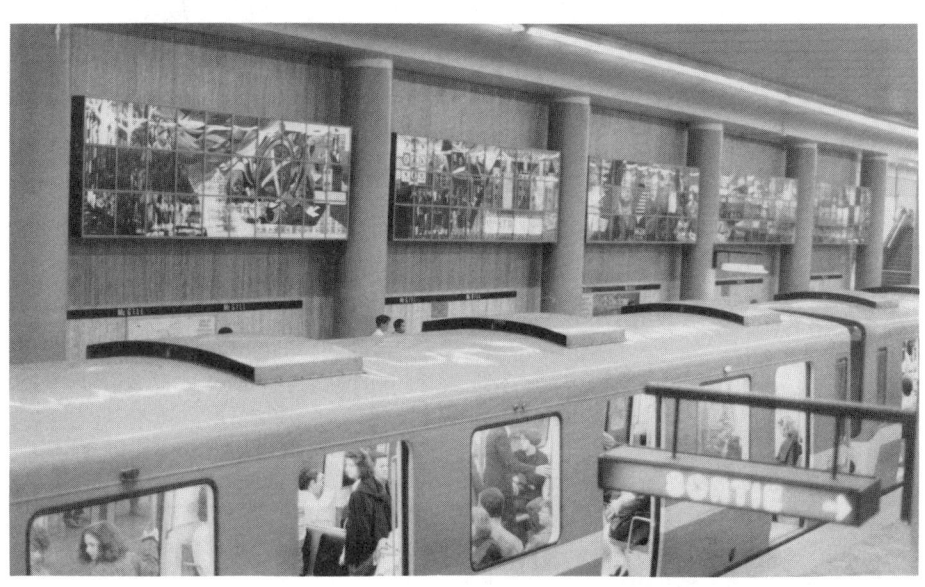

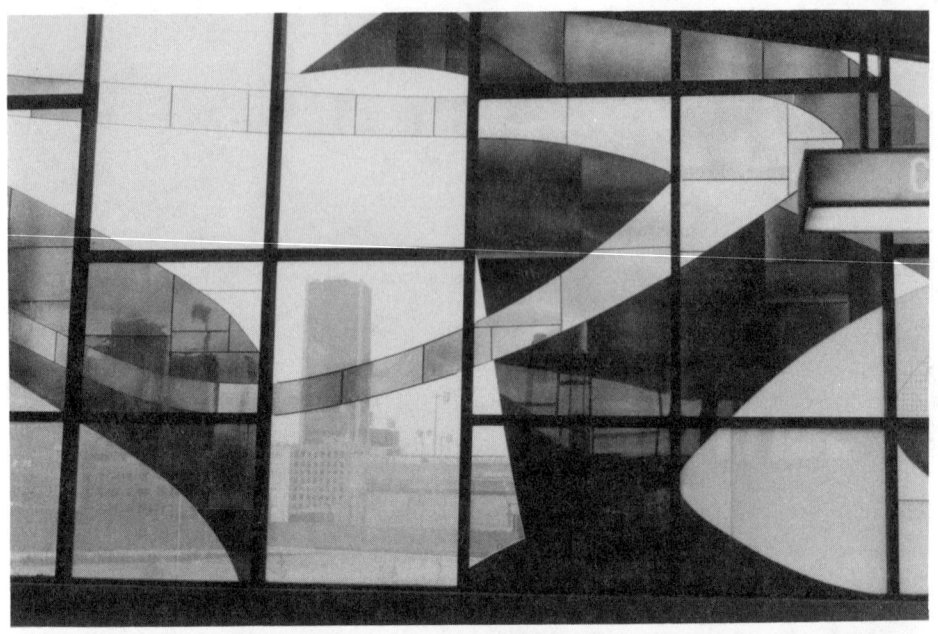

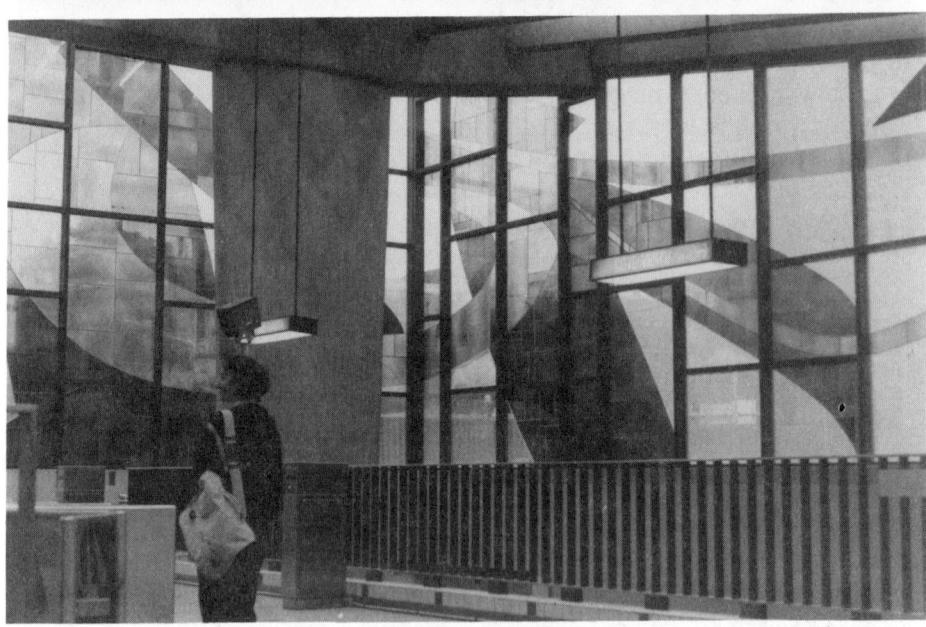

Champ de Mars Station: Marcelle Ferron's sinuous abstractions in colorful stainglass stream natural light and animate the interior. The artist was a member of Les Automatistes, and a cosignatory of Paul-Emile Borduas' *Refus Global*. The art work here is a gift of the Quebec Government. Although abstract art is generally viewed as an expression of cosmopolitanism, in the specific context of French Canada abstract art became a symbol bound up with nationalistic aspirations.

214

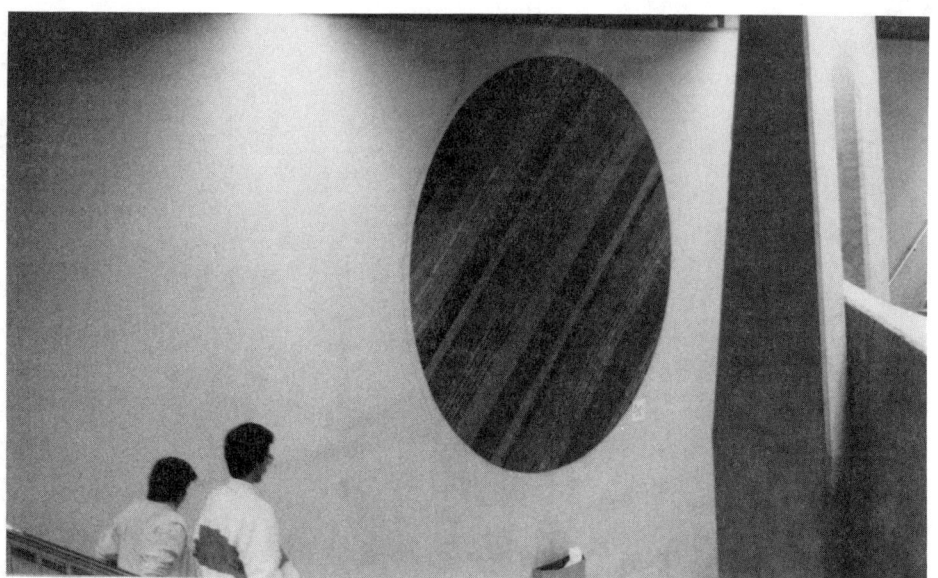

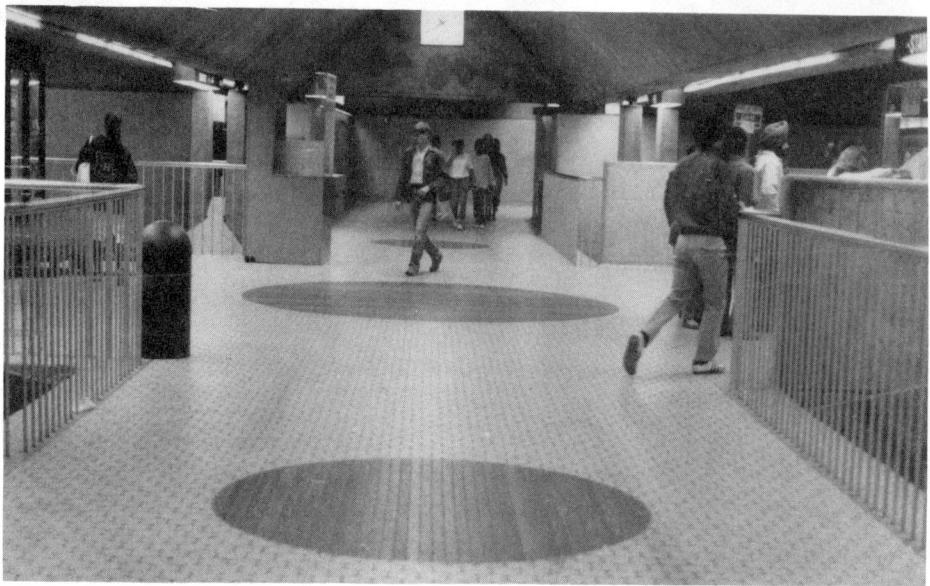

Two Views of Jean-Paul Mousseau's Work at Peel Metro Station: Ceramic Tile Circles inlaid into the walls and the floor. They are well integrated into the station's architecture. The spacing of the circles suggests rolling movement, and the colors animate the otherwise dull environment. The ceramic tile circles also function as a means of orientation: They ease off finding directions.

215

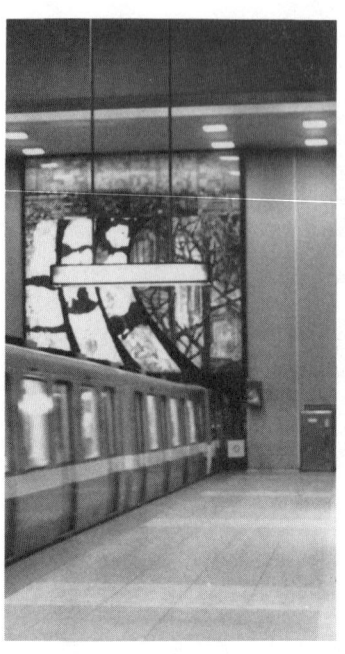
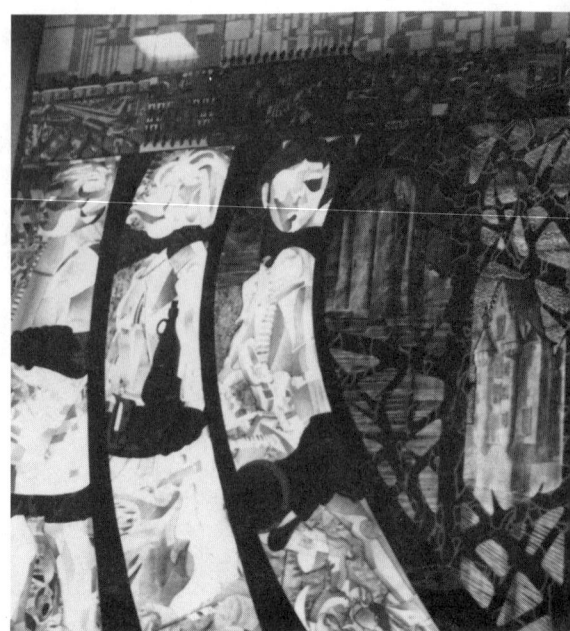

Above: Pierre Gaboriau, Stained Glass at the Berri de Montigny Metro Station, Montreal. It depicts the founding fathers of the city.
Below: Place des Arts Station. Frederick Back's backlighted stained glass mural is devoted to the story of music in Montreal.

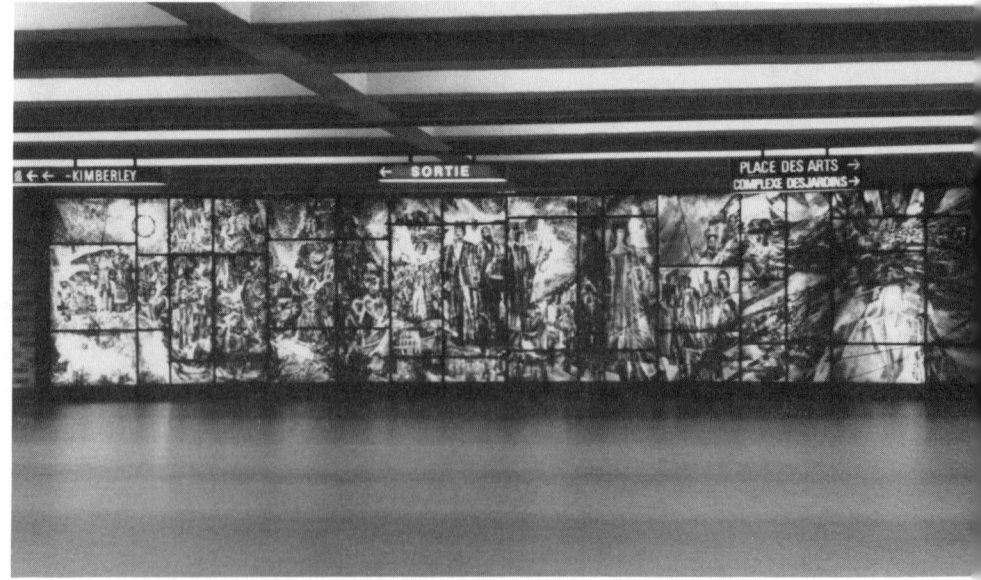

CHAPTER FIVE

ARTIFICIAL INTELLIGENCE AND COGNITIVE MACHINES, CONSCIOUSNESS AND COMPUTER ART

Ancient mythology offers early examples of the human aspiration to produce self-locomoting contrivances and androids. It was Hephaestus, the son of the Greek divine couple of Hera and Zeus, who made Pandora and Talos. The latter was Zeus' gift to Europa. Talos was an android made of bronze. His customary duty consisted of patrolling the beaches of Crete and protecting the island from invaders. Pandora was also commissioned by Zeus. But not as a gift. Zeus sent her to punish the human race for accepting the present of fire, the treasure of the Gods that Prometheus stole from heaven. Pandora could not resist her excessive curiosity. When she opened her ill-natured casket, contrary to instructions, she released all the evils of the world.

A different story belongs to the Swiss physician and alchemist Theophrastus Bombastus von Hohenheim, who is better known as Paracelsus (1493-1541). Although his work was colored with the fantastic beliefs of the times, he rejected Galen's humoral theory of disease, and noted the relationship of paralysis to head injuries, the hereditary pattern of syphilis as well as the association of endemic goiter with cretinism. He also introduced a variety of chemicals such as sulfur, mercury, iron, arsenic and laudanum, in the treatment of specific diseases. Consequently, so it seems, he also became one of the most original contributors to iatrogenesis. For, as critics of modern medicine have pointed out, physicians of our times can pose a paradoxical threat to health. Chemical treatments, e.g., cause considerable damage to the human organism in the process of curing sickness.[1]

However, what makes the life work of Paracelsus especially pertinent to the subject of artificial intelligence is his claim that humankind has the ability to imitate God's greatest miracle, the creation of man. He contended being the possessor of a miraculous recipe for making humans. Moreover, he boasted of creating a little man. This homunculus was brought to life in a hermetically sealed glass. It developed from human sperm buried in horse manure for about forty days, magnetized, and artificially fed with the arcanum of human blood.[2]

In Jewish folklore there are recurring allusions to the creation of artificial human beings. The medieval Eleazar of Worms, a German Jew who was born in the second half of the twelfth century and died seventy years later, produced a golem, an artificial man endowed with life. According to the legend the clay figure automaton was created supernaturally by combining the four letters of the Tetragrammaton which constitute the Holy Name of God. Another similar legend tells the story of the Maharal, Judah Loew, a historical figure who in 1573 became the Chief Rabbi of the city of Prague. He enjoyed the friendship of the astronomers Johannes Kepler and Tycho Brahe. In order to protect the Jewish community against the occasional pogroms that flared up, the Maharal created out of the clay of the banks of the Moldau a humanlike figure. Joseph Golem assumed life in a secret ceremony in which the Holy Name was implanted on his forehead through incantations and prayers. But eventually the Maharal lost control over the android. When the golem attacked its creator, the rabbi removed the Tetragrammaton implanted on his forehead, and the creature died.

Interestingly enough, several important pioneers of computer development regard themselves as the descendants of the Maharal of Prague. They include Norbert Wiener, the father of cybernetics, Marvin Minsky of M.I.T., one of the founders of the domain of artificial intelligence, and John von Neumann, a mathematical genius and a theoretician of modern digital computers.[3]

The field of artificial intelligence is inextricably bound up with the development of the computer. Counting machines have a long history. The Chinese are believed to be the inventors of abacus. This mechanical counting device existed already around 1000 B.C. . It was also known to the Egyptians, to the Greeks, and to the Romans.

The French mathematician and philosopher Blaise Pascal around 1640 invented an adding machine which can be considered as the forerunner of modern high-speed electric calculators. Its most innovative property consisted in the automatic advancement of digit positions. Modern automobile odometers still operate along the same principles. The dashboard instrument in the car shows the length of the traveled distance. As the automobile's transmission revolves, it turns a system of gears marked with digits that indicate the number of miles traveled.

At the end of the seventeenth century the German mathematician and philosopher Gottfried von Leibniz invented an improved version of Pascal's machine. Pascal's calculator could only add and subtract, whereas Leibniz's machine could multiply and divide as well.

However, the solid foundations for the rise of the modern computer were laid down in the nineteenth century. In 1854 the English mathematician George Boole saw the publication of his *Laws of Thought*, a book dealing with the mathematical formalization of the human intellect. Its author aimed to substitute unambiguous mathematical symbols for the ordinary words of formal logic. Boole assumed that all logical statements could be reduced to a series of yes-or-no elements. He also held that these yes-or-no elements could be structured in binary terms. Consequently, the Boolean algebra of thought came to existence, whose protagonists are the numbers 0 and 1. The software of artificial intelligence is based on Boolean algebra. Most computers are digital, and use the binary code. Analog computers, that accept and process analog signals without conversion to numeric values, are employed only to a limited extent. An automobile's speedometer, e.g., is a simple analog computer. It operates by simulating the relations and response of an actual physical system by measuring its quantity in terms of continuity and correspondence.

Modern computer hardware was also born in the nineteenth century. It was the brainchild of Charles Babbage, an English mathematician and polymath. Three decades before the birth of Boolean algebra, Babbage decided to mechanize the process of mathematical computations. In 1821 he advised the Royal Astronomical Society with regard to his plans of constructing an automatic arithmetical machine. Two years later he began to build his 'Difference Engine'. He succeeded in building a small working model, but it was seldom brought into operation. The project proved to be exceedingly costly, and Babbage lost his personal fortune.

Notwithstanding his great financial losses he continued his efforts to construct a working automatic calculator. He designed a second arithmetic machine which he called 'Analytical Engine'. It came quite close to the idea of the contemporary digital computer.

Babbage took advantage of the punched card as a controlling principle. He borrowed it from the textile industry. In 1725 the Frenchman Basile Bouchon designed a coded controlling device for the automatic operation of looms. Patterns of holes punched in a roll of paper programmed the process of wěaving figured silks. This significant invention was further improved during the eighteenth century. In 1801 Joseph Marie Jacquard evolved in France an automatic loom for weaving complex patterns. This machine also operated with a punched card code, and it has remained basically the same to this day. A famous portrait of the inventor was produced by using 24,000 punched cards.

The invention of the automatic loom for weaving complex designs was a pivotal contribution to the development of the modern computer. The originators of the punched card as a controlling device for automatic operation of the machine invented in fact a most effective means of cybernetic communication. Through the punched card transmitting information to the machine became possible. The language was limited to just two instructions: Hole, and No Hole. Through the edifice of Boolean algebra, the same binary system was crystallized into the universal language of today's digital computers.

Babbage adopted the punched card principle from Jacquard's loom, and applied it to the Analytical Engine. He was assisted by Lady Ada Lovelace, Lord Byron's daughter, a brilliant mathematician, and probably the first computer programmer in history.[4]

The Analytical Engine contained all the fundamental aspects of the modern digital computer. It was equipped with a 'mill' or arithmetic unit, and with a 'store' allotted to memory. Additional cybernetic features included sequential program control, and punched card input and output. It was capable of providing automatic printout as well. The Analytical Engine could add and subtract in one second; multiply and divide in one minute. Compared to the vast number crunching abilities of today's advanced computers, this is extremely slow. The supercomputers of the 1980s are capable of carrying out millions of calculations per second.

Nevertheless, the concept of the Analytical Engine was nothing short of a scientific turning point. The trouble was that Babbage was born a century ahead of time. The technology of the Victorian era could not produce the precision required for this sort of machine. The engineers of the nineteenth century were unable to come up with the necessary solutions and Babbage could not put his ideas into effect.

At the end of the nineteenth century Dr. Herman Hollerith, an American statistician, developed a modern punched card technique, and designed a machine to conduct the census of 1890. In 1896 he founded the Tabulating Machine Company which later merged with other establishments, and emerged as the International Business Machines Corporation (IBM).

Forty years later the Harvard mathematician Howard Aiken set out to construct an automatic calculating machine. He tried to combine Babbage ideas with those of Hollerith. The result was an electromechanical device, the first large scale digital computer: Mark I. It weighed thirty five tons, and was completed in 1944.

Back in the late 1930s Professor John Vincent Atanasoff of Iowa State College teamed up with Clifford Berry in order to construct the first electronic computer, the ABC. In the early years of World War II, Atanasoff and Berry brought their work to the attention of John W. Mauchly of the Moore School of Electrical Engineering, a branch of the University of Pennsylvania.

The osmotic diffusion of cybernetic ideas eventuated in the completion of ENIAC, a first generation electronic general purpose computer that operated with about 18,000 vacuum tubes. It was developed by Mauchly, J. Presper Eckert, Jr., and others. Funds for the building of this model came from the U.S. Army. The ENIAC was

221

constructed at the Moore School as a secret war time project. The Army was interested in the development of rapid methods to prepare artillery trajectory tables. The ENIAC was used by the Army until 1955. It could carry out 300 multiplications, and 5,000 additions in one second.

The great mathematician John von Neumann joined the Moore School team working on the development of ENIAC and its improved version, the EDVAC, as a consultant. During the summer of 1945 he sent a 101 page long paper to the University of Philadelphia, entitled "First Draft of a Report to the EDVAC". It became a controversial document. For, it "was credited to John von Neumann", but it "contained a brilliant and complete exposition of all the thinking that had been done at the Moore School on the new computer."[5]

Von Neumann's research report recommended the application of the binary number system to computer design. He pointed out that employing only the digits 0 and 1 is in thorough accord with the two possible conditions of electronic components: On or off, magnetized or not magnetized. Therefore, these two conditions can be used to represent the two binary digits.

The report also proposed that data should be stored within the architecture of the computer itself. It also gave specific instructions concerning the problem of controlling the arithmetic machine. The first computer that was built in accordance with these ideas came into existence at Cambridge University. In 1949 the Cambridge team completed the Electronic Delay Storage Automatic Calculator. The EDSAC employed the binary number system, and it received instructions that were stored internally. It was the first stored program electronic computer in history.

The Electronic Discrete Variable Automatic Computer also utilized the binary number system, and its instructions were given by internally stored programs. EDVAC was completed by the Eckert-Mauchly team in 1952 at the Moore School. It was smaller, more flexible, and more versatile than ENIAC. With its circa 5,900 vacuum tubes it could perform an addition in 864 microseconds and multiplication in 2.9 milliseconds. A microsecond is one-millionth of a second, whereas a millisecond is one-thousandth of a second.

In 1947 three American physicists–John Bardeen, Walter H. Brattain, and William Shockley–invented a tiny semiconductor device capable of controlling the flow of electric current in electronic equipment. The new invention became known as the transistor. It revolutionized the computer industry. In the late 1950s the second generation computers were born in which small light silicon or germanium transistors replaced the bulky and unreliable vacuum tubes. The transistor has several advantages over the vacuum tube. It is more compact, more durable, requires no heater current, and it operates at low voltages with relatively high efficiency. It is also less expensive.

The transistors implanted into the architectural framework of the second generation computers allowed them to perform arithmetic operations ten times faster than those done with the first generation hardware.

The first commercially available transistored automatic computer was the RECOMP II which appeared on the market in December 1957. It had been developed in the U.S.A. by North American Aviation.[6] In the RECOMP II transistors replaced the vacuum tubes as switch elements.

The invention of the circuit chip intensified the computer revolution. The computers of the third generation which came out in the mid 1960s were already quite compact. Their metallic silicon transistors had been reduced to about a half millimetre in size. The development of the silicon chip or integrated circuit in the 1970s gave rise to the computers of the fourth generation. The circuit chip is a large number of crosswired electrical conductors, transistors, and other electronic components, densely and microscopically placed on a semiconductor substance. The semiconductor substance is usually silicon.

According to Dr. Robert Jastrow, an astrophysicist affiliated with NASA, microscopic silicon circuit chips are so densely built that they can both think and remember. They represent a new form of non-biological evolution, "an important step toward the construction of electronic brains resembling the human brain."[7] He points out that the computer industry is engaged today in the development of the machines of the fifth generation. At this transitional phase from the fourth to the fifth generation of computers, "electronic components equivalent to a quarter of a million vacuum tubes fit into an area of a few hundredths of a square inch."[8] In his view, in the 1990s, "the compactness of the neurons and circuits in the human brain should be achieved in computers, and portable artificial intelligence of quasi-human power should be commonplace."[9]

Not all the experts of the field, however, share Jastrow's opinion. Artificial intelligence (AI) is a controversial domain. Dr. Roger C. Schank, head of the AI laboratory at Yale University, observes that

> Computers intimidate us because we imagine they are
> smarter than we are. But a computer really can't do

anything unless you, with your human intelligence, tell it exactly what you want it to do, down to the last detail. Anyone who thinks today's computers are intelligent in the full sense of the word has no appreciation of the extraordinary power of the human mind, much less of the real possibility of developing programs that approach human levels of intelligence. If the computers of the future gain any semblance of intelligence it will be because we have begun to unravel some of the mysteries of human intelligence and model them on the computer.[10]

Schank admits that intelligent machines are possible, but he contends that "they are not here yet, nor will they be here in the very near future."[11]

But the advance of the computer occurs at an incredibly fast pace. At some phase technological changes such as miniaturization, increase of operational speed, and the introduction of interconnected, associative bubble memory, can lead to qualitative quantum leaps.

John von Neumann approached the computer as an analog of the human brain. He observed that the functioning of the nervous system was essentially digital. Its basic component, the nerve cell, the neuron, generates and propagates nerve impulses. Despite the fact that the impulse is a complex electrical, chemical, and mechanical process, it seems to be a well defined operation: "It represents an essentially reproducible, unitary response to a rather wide variety of stimuli", which is "nearly the same under all conditions."[12]

Von Neumann distinguished between two types of communications within the nervous system proper: Communications of logical orders, and communications of numbers. The resulting encoded messages correspond to language and mathematics. He regarded both of them as historical accidents. "Just as languages like Greek or Sanskrit are historical facts and not absolute logical necessities, it is only reasonable to assume that logics and mathematics are similarly historical, accidental forms of expression."[13]

During the first week of March, 1953, Dr. von Neumann delivered the Vanuxem Lectures at Princeton University. His series of four talks was entitled "Machines and Organisms".[14]

Influenced by the mathematical model of the human nervous system of W.S. McCulloch and of W. Pitts, as well as by Alan Turing's conception of the universal automaton, von Neumann concluded that in a sense man can be viewed as a machine. This implied the idea that machines that reach a certain level of organizational complexity are living organisms. His conjecture was that complex automata in the long run can reproduce themselves, and even construct higher hierarchical entities.

The mathematician and computer scientist Dr. John G. Kemeny of Dartmouth College adopted von Neumann's views concerning the self-organizational possibilities inherent in computer technology development.[15] To an article published in 1955 in *Scientific American* he gave the title "Man Viewed as a Machine." In *A Philosopher Looks at Science* (1959), Kemeny stressed that it is misleading to refer to computers as mere calculators. Electronic brains are thinking machines. They can carry out a considerable quantity of cognitive tasks, including to play advanced chess, to learn how to prove mathematical theorems, and to manipulate complex logical arguments. Machines are capable of learning by memorization, and they excel in the cognitive method of trial and error. The possibility exists that, given enough time for the evolution of machine intelligence, electronic brains will reach the technological stage of outdistancing human reasoning in every aspect.[16]

Kemeny envisages the future relationship between man and the cognitive machine as a symbiotic union of two living species. The computer represents a new form of life dedicated to pure intelligence. It processes information, extends our memory and reasoning faculty, caters to our economic and social needs. In return it receives electricity and spare parts.

On February 4, 1984, I wrote a letter to Dr. Kemeny:

> According to my understanding, the reasoning ability of computers is based on logic, on the application of the dyadic Boolean operations; i.e. 1 and 0 corresponding to 'yes' or 'no'. Now, you are of course well aware of the fact: logic is only a narrow realm of human cognition and reasoning. It leaves out the whole area of non-mathematical variables, paradoxes, dialectics, humor, aesthetics, and so on. It seems that the breakthrough in the development of artificial intelligence is tied to the problem of emotions. When the computer will be able to laugh and to cry, it will be capable of outdistancing its developer as well, in every respect. But will it be then our slave or our master?

In the same letter, I also pointed out that Kemeny's description of mathematics can be applied in certain respect to abstract art as well. In *A Philosopher Looks at Science* he approaches mathematics as a study of forms devoid of subject matter. Since the same attributes apply to abstract art and to music, too, I have proposed an interdisciplinary investigation of mathematics and abstract art. In my opinion a project of this kind can be a significant contribution to aesthetics and to scientific research. It might advance the understanding of the crosswires between logic and aesthetics; between common sense and paradox, humor and complementary cognition, intuition, emotion and creativity.

Professor Kemeny's response arrived about two weeks later:

> I am glad that you enjoyed reading *A Philosopher Looks at Science*. On the subject of computer intelligence I have not changed my mind since I wrote that book. I agree with you that human beings have many talents that computers do not have. And I am skeptical that we will see a major change in this area in the near future. The project you propose is a fascinating one.[17]

It was Dr. Arthur L. Samuel who provided the first empirical proof for the cybernetic hypothesis that the thinking machine would someday be able to match and exceed the faculties of human intelligence. For several years he taught an IBM Model 7094 computer to play checkers. In the summer of 1962 the electronic machine won a game against Robert W. Nealey, a former checkers champion of Connecticut.

Samuel refuted the assumption that a machine is only as smart as its programmer. He demonstrated that the machine can learn to play from experience, observation; and it is capable of improving its own performance by recognizing mistakes and by avoiding their recurrence.

Computers excel not merely in crunching vast numbers but also in manipulating logical symbols. The pursuit of well-defined goals led researchers in the field of artificial intelligence to develop heuristic principles. These are trial and error rules of thumb incorporated into the program so that they enable the machine to select the most promising actions. The planning of a sequence of steps is arranged in a branching structure of a search tree. The tree is generally presented in an inverted form, with the branches at the bottom and the root at the top. The root represents the condition existing at the moment of action, whereas the branches stand for the possible procedures, and the ends of the branches show the possible outcomes. Since the search tree is frequently too large, the less promising branches are eliminated from the trunk. Throughout the heuristic search only the most likely circumstances, and the most practical or effective elements are given full scale consideration. Heuristic programs represent significant shortcuts in goal-directed searches. Without these reasonable shortcuts the computer could not carry out its task due to the practically infinite scale of possible branching structures.

Programs based on heuristically directed search are often used to play strategic board games such as backgammon, checkers, and chess. They dispel the myth of the stupid computer. They show that the cybernetic rule of GIGO (garbage in, garbage out) should not be taken without reservations. For, the processing of the input data in the thinking machine does not yield mechanically treated output. The software and the hardware interact in a synergic manner. The cybernetic process is more than the sum total of its parts.

A computer is able to do more than it is programmed to do. The intelligence of the machine is not limited by the program. Chess programs, for instance, frequently perform better than the people who produce them. In fact, as computer scientist David L. Waltz points out, "in many cases the programmer does not know what his program can do until it is run on a computer."[18]

The appearance of the computer constitutes an implicit assault on Cartesian dualism. The arbitrary and mechanistic separation of the mind from the body cannot explain computer behavior. Cartesian dualism is under empirical attack. It cannot account for the fact that the apparently lifeless machine is capable of outwitting its programmer.

It cannot explain strange machine behavior either. D.S. Halacy, Jr., reports, for example, the bizarre story of the pioneer General Electric computer that could not function properly in the dark. During the day it functioned efficiently, "but problems left with it overnight came out horribly botched for no reason that engineers could discover. At last it was found that a light had to be left burning with the scary machine." The subtle electronic balance of the computer had been disturbed by the changes of light and darkness.[19]

Due to the materialistic tradition of science, the engineers of artificial intelligence cannot liberate themselves from the bonds of Cartesian dualism. Yet a better conceptual framework is probably available. It is to be found within the monistic models of reality. The monists assume the existence of unus mundus: Psyche and matter are the same substance; the first is experienced from inside, the latter from outside. Interestingly enough, the conjecture of a mind-matter continuum is along the lines of the theoretical work of such pioneers of quantum mechanics as Niels Bohr and Werner Heisenberg.

As against the behaviorist view that all mental phenomena can be reduced to stimulus and response patterns, a new conceptual scheme arises in which consciousness plays a central role. Does the cognitive machine have consciousness?

In order to make an attempt of answering this intriguing question, first it is necessary to deal with the problem of consciousness proper. Consciousness is a very elusive term. Defining it as the awareness of awareness is not very helpful. The word consciousness is imbued with many connotations. A sleeping person is not aware of the environment. In this respect the term consciousness refers to a state of mental alertness. But when we say, for instance, that an adult is more conscious of social needs than an infant, we are talking in fact about something which is bound up with mental capacity. Another example is when someone wants to raise consciousness towards certain political activity. In the latter context, consciousness denotes forms of cognitive and emotional attitudes.

Robert Ornstein in *The Psychology of Consciousness* approached the problem of consciousness in interdisciplinary terms. For, as Roger Bacon pointed out seven centuries ago, "there are two modes of knowing, those of argument and experience." In his synthetic model consciousness evolves as a multidimensional substance and function of perception and cognition, of time and body energies; the complementary intuitive and rational modes of mental activity expressed through the two hemispheres of the brain.[20]

According to the Swiss psychologist Jean Piaget the early stages of childhood are characterized by a lack of self-consciousness: The infant projects the whole content of consciousness into people and into things, and as a result "a complete absence of the consciousness of the self" precipitates.[21]

This is in total contrast to the conception of art as the exploration of the self through the enhanced consciousness of the adult psyche. One of the defining traits of consciousness is its discontinuity. The kaleidoscopic nature of its flow gave rise to a great deal of artistic experimentation. When André Breton published the *First Manifesto* of surrealism in 1924, he called for a pure psychic way of artistic expression. The surrealists advanced oneirism and automatism by excluding aesthetic or moral preoccupations from the creative process. Writers such as James Joyce, Marcel Proust, and Virginia Woolf chose as the subject matter of their novels the uneven, uninterrupted flow of the stream of consciousness. The exploration of consciousness as an

228

interior monologue became a literary technique as a means to depict the diversity of thoughts and feelings which pass through the mind. It is a technique which is firmly related to the whole cognitive edifice of modern art: The artist does not imitate reality but renders it. The act of rendition occurs through consciousness. This is, of course, a statement which applies to the scientist as well. The scientist reflects on the nature of reality and structures it through consciousness.

As J.Z. Young has pointed out in *Programs of the Brain* (1978), consciousness, as the state of the organism in which the activating programs of the brain make thinking and experiencing possible, is related to the use of language. He rejects the view that humankind acquired consciousness or minds separable from the body.

What distinguishes human beings from animals is the fact that people can refer to themselves through the symbolic representation of language. Being conscious means to experience the self and the world:

> An insight to this question comes from children who are born blind. They only begin to refer to themselves as "I" or "me" after they have learned to play with dolls. 'The acquisition of personal pronouns is closely united with the capacity for symbolic representation of the self, and vision normally plays a central facilitating role in each of these achievements.' Perhaps some of the problems that worry us about such concepts as mind and body and consciousness may resolve themselves if we examine how we have to come to use them, both during individual development and in evolution. If we know more about the origins of language we might be able to work out how the categories of mind and of consciousness developed gradually.[22]

Prior to World War II scientists were in search of the seat of consciousness. The neurologist Wilder Penfield of the Montreal Neurological Institute in the 1930s believed that "the indispensible subtratum of consciousness lies outside the cerebral cortex, probably in the diencephalon (the higher brain-stem)."[23] He only later realized that "to suppose that consciousness or the mind has localization is a failure to understand neurophysiology."[24] In fact the quest for consciousness is a complex and curious version of the frantic spin of the cat that tries to catch its own tail. For what the scientist is searching for is that which is conducting the search.

Cognitive science is a self referential endeavor. It is concerned with knowledge about knowledge. Apperception is meta-knowledge; the mind's perception of itself. But since a foot cannot step on itself, or an eye cannot see itself, how can the mind understand itself?

René Descartes assumed that the seat of consciousness was to be found in the pineal gland. Although he turned to be wrong, "the amusing aspect is that he came so close to that part of the brain in which the essential circuits of the highest brain-mechanism must be active to make consciousness possible."[25]

The American neuropsychologist Karl S. Lashley for three decades was preoccupied with the search for the localized centre of memory. His extensive research brought up evidence supporting the theory that in various forms of learning the cerebral cortex of the brain functions as a unified whole. He also found that certain realms of the brain can take on the functions of damaged cerebral areas. But he ended up with empty hands concerning the old quest for the engram, the hypothetical trace left in the brain as a result of memory and learning.

Karl Pribram, a Stanford brain surgeon and neuropsychologist, is perhaps closer to the solution for the enigma of the brain. He collaborated with Lashley in the attempt to account for the puzzle of memory and learning. Lashley systematically destroyed portions of the brains of trained animals in the experiments he conducted in the laboratory in order to find the engram. No locus of memory was found. Despite the fact that various portions of their brains were devastated, the animals remembered what they learned.

During the 1960s Pribram read in *Scientific American* about the invention of an ingenious method to make three dimensional pictures.[26] It was based on Leibnizian calculus. Pribram adopted the holographic principle of the new lenseless technique of three dimensional photography as a theoretical model which can explain the enigma of memory.

Holography was invented in 1947 by the Hungarian engineer Dennis Gabor. It lends empirical support to the ancient cabalistic idea that the whole is contained in the part. The same idea crops up in the windowless monads of Leibniz whose differential and integral calculus aided Gabor in the invention of the technique of three dimensional photography.

The hologram is a three dimensional image made from a photographic film that has recorded the interference patterns of light waves reflected from an object or a scene. When the film is illuminated with a laser beam, or other source of highly coherent light, a three dimensional picture appears. The hologram demonstrates the validity of the principle that the whole is contained in the part. If an ordinary two dimensional photograph is cut into parts, it is impossible to redevelop the entire image from a given piece of the picture. With the hologram it is different. Since every part contains the whole, any part taken from a hologram is reconstructable, and can be turned into a complete picture. If we cut out a window of a house shown on a hologram, e.g., and redevelop it, the whole house will reappear, not merely the window as on a regular photograph. However, a small piece of a hologram when redeveloped yields a fainter image than the original. This property of the hologram corresponds to the weakened memory of brain damaged individuals. And in a similar manner to the laser generated three dimensional photograph in which each part contains the whole image, memory is not localized in any fixed centre of the brain but distributed throughout.

The English physicist David Bohm assumes that the organization of the universe may be holographic.[27] Holographic theory incorporates a conception of consciousness as a field, which may explain the interaction between mind and matter. From the theory of holography it also follows that every human thought is connected to every other point in the universe. It is a possibility that on a cosmic scale the universe has not dimensionality at all. The fabric of physical reality can be analogous to the non-dimensionality of the dream world. In a cosmic matter-mind continuum there is no division between reality and consciousness, just as in the dream there is no separation of object from subject. The dream cannot be separated from the dreamer.

In the holographic view of consciousness all thoughts are cross referenced with all other thoughts. The idea of the existence of a non-causal, holographic order in nature did not originate in modern physics. The astrologists and alchemists centuries ago had conjectured the existence of non-causal relations.

It is possible to conceive consciousness as a peculiar telescope directed around the vast ocean of the mind, and observing mental facts. However, consciousness is not merely self knowledge resulting from the mind's capacity to reflect upon itself through introspection. For, in a broader sense, consciousness designates not only awareness of our mental states, but these states themselves. If a person thinks of something, that is a state of consciousness, even though she or he is not aware of that. If the person is aware of her or his thinking that is another modification of consciousness. In this respect consciousness seems to be the present state of the mind.

Consciousness is both an agent and a quality of the mind. As an agent it allows the rise of self-awareness, and the perception of the world. As a quality of animate states it is bound up with such bodily and mental events as love, anger, sensation, thinking, knowing, believing, imagining, and willing. These events are not susceptible of quantification. It is impossible to quantify the intensity of joy or that of sorrow. It is meaningless to say, for instance, that the feelings of one person are fifty per cent stronger in comparison with the feelings of another.

The events of consciousness are qualities which cannot be touched, and cannot be localized in space. They have no size, texture, form, or color. The Newtonian co-ordinates of space and time represent a different world. The spatio-temporal attributes of consciousness are personal. The subject matter or content of awareness does not involve energy conservation principles: Matter is neither destroyed nor created. Entropy is not an inevitable and irreversible process. Mental thrusts are capable of enhancing order. Consequently, the Second Law of Thermodynamics is not applicable to the contents of consciousness.

Consciousness is a dimension of the mind. Sigmund Freud, the founder of psychoanalysis, regarded the unconscious strata of the mind as the repository of repressed memories. His former collaborator, Karl Jung went farther. He distinguished between the personal and the collective unconscious. In his view the latter contains archetypes which pervade all human experience. He believed that the unconscious realm of the psyche manifests itself in symbolic form. The symbols can crop up in thoughts and feelings, situations and acts, and particularly in dreams.

Through the collective unconscious which is inherited and common to all humans, "processes of 'psychological osmosis' are going on all the time, both with other human beings and with the general psychic environment."[28]

Jung, together with the physicist Wolfgang Pauli, proposed a non-causal connecting principle which combines apparently isolated events into meaningful coincidences. Such events of synchronicity are well beyond the expectations of chance. Nevertheless, properly documented instances of extraordinary coincidences are by no means a rarity. Jung explains that often inanimate objects seem to harmonize with the unconscious in the organization of symbolic patterns:

> There are numerous well-authenticated stories of clocks stopping at the moment of their owner's death; one was the pendulum clock in the palace of Frederick the Great at Sans Souci, which stopped when the king died. Other common examples are those of a

mirror that breaks, or a picture that falls, when a death occurs . . . Even if skeptics refuse to credit such reports, stories of this kind are always cropping up, and this alone should serve as ample proof of their psychological importance.[29]

In Jung's opinion the 'self' is the protagonist of the process of individuation, and it involves the totality of the psyche. The self is the centre, as well as "the whole circumference which embraces both conscious and unconscious; it is the centre of this totality, just as the ego is the centre of consciousness."[30]

There are solid links between man and the physical environment. Man is not independent of nature, but its product. Through the metabolic process the food we eat is transformed into the living material of our bodies. The viscous, translucent, and colorless protoplasm which is built up in metabolism is the main life sustaining substance of organic cells. The basis of life in both plants and animals is tied to the protoplasm.

Nature is not a lifeless matrix, and life always involves intelligence. There is no unorganized matter in the universe. From the smallest quarks of the atoms to the huge solar system, from the tiny symmetrical molecules of crystals to the vastness of giant galaxies, the so called inanimate matter manifests intelligence.

Human intelligence is the product of the intelligence built into the cosmic fabric of the universe. The same system that governs the various processes of nature, including biological evolution and ecological patterns, is a mental system that governs the human psyche as well.

The British astronomer Arthur Stanley Eddington said in his book *The Nature of the Physical World* (1928) that "the stuff of the world is mind stuff." His arguments in favor of an idealistic Weltanschauung were based on scientific and epistemological considerations. He assumed that the refutation of the mechanical theories of the ether and of the causal behavior of subatomic particles by relativity and quantum theory justified a non-materialistic outlook. He also asserted that since our consciousness mirrors the structure of the objective world, the latter must be made of mind-stuff too.

A half century later Fritjof Capra wrote *The Thao of Physics*. Dr. Capra is a well-known scientist who specializes in theoretical high-energy physics, and divides his time between conducting research and lecturing at American and European universities. Quantum physicists are aware of the problem of consciousness with regard to the observation of atomic phenomena. According to Capra, the existence of consciousness can be viewed as one of the necessary aspect of nature whose function is to sustain the self-consistency of the whole. He points out that the Eastern mystical traditions "have always regarded consciousness as an integral part of the universe." For,

> in the Eastern view, human beings, like all other life forms, are parts of an inseparable organic whole. Their intelligence, therefore, implies that the whole, too, is intelligent. Man is seen as the living proof of cosmic intelligence; in us, the universe repeats over and over again its ability to produce forms through which it becomes consciously aware of itself.[31]

Since the days of Aristotle, who saw the world in terms of a vast organism, the conceptual paradigms by which erudite people approached nature underwent dramatic transformations. For Galileo nature was a mathematical entity. For Newton and Leibniz, nature was a huge mechanical device. Interestingly enough, the development of the electronic computer perpetrates a step toward the stylized revival of animism. John von Neumann, for example, compared the universe with the model of an ultimate huge computer of a cosmic scale. Since this great cosmic computer must be endowed with some sort of intelligence, it follows that the universe features animistic qualities.

Now let me return to the question that I posed above: Does the cognitive machine have consciousness? Since in the light of the arguments presented above it seems to be quite commensurate with the facts to state that all matter is intelligent matter, the question must be reformulated. For, if all matter is intelligent, then the computer also must be endowed by nature with some sort of intrinsic cosmic intelligence. However, its mind seems to be dormant and unconscious. Therefore the question boils down to this: Can the cognitive machine become aware of its existence? Can it develop a self of its own?

Marvin Minsky, an important pioneer of AI research affiliated with MIT, maintains that the computer can be turned into a self-conscious machine. He defines artificial intelligence as "the science of making machines do things that would require intelligence if done by men."[32] Developing a self-conscious machine is a problem which concerns model construction. In order to make the machine capable of answering questions about its own qualities or about its relationship to the world, it must contain some internal model of itself. This sub-machine is

234

endowed with coding and knowledge structures allowing intuitive encoding and interpreting processes by means of symbolic representation. Thus the self or the "I" of the machine is a cluster of symbols.

Minsky suggests that when intelligent devices are built, they are likely to turn out as stubborn and as confused as humans concerning their beliefs about the nature of consciousness, about mind-matter, free will, and similar issues. This should not come as a surprise because all these problems "are pointed at explaining the complicated interactions between parts of the self-model." But "a man's or a machine's strength of conviction about such things tells us nothing about the man or about the machine except what it tells us about his model of himself."[33]

Minsky is a Cartesian dualist. His biased view of science as the highest manifestation of intelligence seems to be a self-conferred decoration, and perhaps it is related to the previous paragraph through synchronicity. He claims, for instance, that the intellectual ability of Beethoven, or of other great artists, is definitely below the reasoning capacity of any distinguished scientist.[34] Perhaps it is again just a sheer coincidence that Minsky himself "suggests a theory to explain why introspection does not give clear answers to these questions." But it has "probably some value in finding at least a clear explanation of why we are confused"[35], he says. Unfortunately, he fails to elucidate how we are supposed to find a clear explanation if we are confused.

Another smoke screen emerges from Minsky's view of art. He holds that art is an intellectually underdeveloped field because the essential questions of art, its tasks and existence are undefined. This statement is imbued with a variety of fallacies. It can be applied to science and mathematics too. After all, the goals and the existence of science and mathematics are not defined either.

Minsky himself implies that extrapolation shows that AI is an irrational thrust. For, in the long run a machine, he says, will possess the "general intelligence of an average human being . . . the machine will begin to educate itself . . . in a few months it will be at a genius level. . . a few months after that its power will be incalculable . . . If we are lucky, they might decide to keep us as pets."[36]

As a dualist, Minsky believes that in five hundred years man will be able to construct "machines that are very much like us and represent our views and thoughts." He also contends that "at some point people may even prefer to convert themselves into machines, because if they can transfer their intelligence into another embodiment, they might be able to live forever and continue developing."[37] According to Minsky, people who get angry when they hear these ideas are carbon chauvinistic. Instead of being dependent on the carbon-solar biochemical cycles of life, he proposes for humankind to switch to silicon as the abiding vehicle of our future intelligence.

These ideas can be hardly seen as the appropriately defined goals of developing artificial intelligence. It is important to keep in mind that the purpose and existence of science and technology cannot be separated from their social context. Unfortunately, the present process of the increasing cybernation of society already has shown that the powerful computer serves more the interests of elite groups than the interests of society as a whole. The impact of the increasing cybernation on society is a disconcerting one. The computers in the office, and the robots in the factory have caused growing rates of unemployment, and enhanced the process of alienation. Consequently, the definition of the purpose of cybernetic technology appears to be a misconstrued one.

Since art is a very broad area, it is not clear what Minsky means by his statements concerning its intellectual stuntedness. Is he talking about the mathematical art of Escher, about the entertaining art of Walt Disney, or perhaps the deliberately anti-intellectual art of the dadaist Marcel Duchamp? In any case, judging art through the looking glass of the scientist certainly does not produce an adequate model for art criticism.

Scientist who talk about the transfer of human intelligence from carbohydrates to silicon think in biogenetic terms. They assume that in due time the deoxyribonucleic acid (DNA) molecules that store the hereditary information in the chromosomes of organic cells will be metamorphosed somehow and implanted into silicon based machines.

Yet the DNA is not the exclusive vector of heredity. For, man has no nature but history. The human condition is determined to a great extent by the ideas and experiences carried over from one generation to another. Through the transmission of ideas and experiences humans learnt to explore the deep waters of the sea in submarines, to fly in aircrafts, and to step on the moon. In contrast to the physical processes of inheritance , or endogenic continuity, it is possible to talk about cultural evolution, or exogenetic heredity as well.[38]

Exogenetic heredity is bound up with the information transfer propagated by oral and written traditions, and by various inventions. By means of exosomatic instruments it is possible to see the otherwise invisible structure and shape of microsopic objects, or to stare at celestial formations dissolving in the remoteness of the unknown; many light years beyond the viewing capacity of the ordinary eye.

Human artifacts can be regarded as extensions of the body. Clothes, for instance, are extensions of the temperature-control system of the organism. The same holds true of shelters. Money represents a means of extending and storing labor. The automobile is the extension of our legs. Electronic instruments are extensions of the nervous system. Radio and television extend our ability to hear and to watch the news as they emerge across the globe.

The cognitive machine is an extension of the human brain. It amplifies the parameters of the human nervous system beyond the scope and range already accomplished in the communications media.

The human interaction with the computer leads to a new kind of relationship with the material world. In this evolving new relationship the subject-object rapport undergoes a dramatic transformation. The passive distance between the knower and the known changes its character. For the Cartesian dualist things have no mental qualities. However, the computer is different. It responds back.

In Martin Buber's thought self-consciousness is the state in which the ego becomes conscious of itself as being apart from others. It is a relation which involves detachment. The ego sets itself apart from everything else. The object is seen as different from the "I", or the "You". It is never actual, but an "It". "Genuine subjectivity can be understood only dynamically, as the vibration of the I in its lonely truth."[39] Buber says that although there is a difference between seeing an object and seeing a person, the observer is the same: "Whether I say, 'I see you' or 'I see the tree', seeing may not be equally actual in both cases, but the I is equally actual in both."[40] Thus he differentiates between two specific types of relationships that evolve in the web of ties between knower and known. On the one hand, there is the interpersonal relationship of the I-Thou, which is characterized by the tendency towards psychological fusion and merging, empathy and caring. The I-It relationship, on the other hand, tends to be based on distancing. For the perceiver a wall or a stone are alien objects. The relationship between knower and known seems to be a one way road without melting and fusion.

Although the computer is an object, the man-machine relationship in this case is not an I-It relationship. The human contact with the cognitive machine transcends the domain of inaccessible passivity. As a subject - object encounter the operating computer represents a specificity in which the ordinary I -It connection is catapulted into an I - Thou relationship.

The American philosopher Hubert L. Dreyfus is an ardent critic of artificial intelligence. His book *What Computers Can't Do* (1972) represents a striking train of ratiocination against the possibility of developing cognitive machines that can match the level of human reason, or to surpass it.

Dreyfus follows Pascal's line of argument concerning the difference between the mathematical mind and the perspective mind. Mathematics is an inadequate tool of perception, because perception cannot be calculated mathematically. Mathematicians who approach matters of perception in mathematical terms make themselves ridiculous, as Pascal pointed out centuries ago. After all, perception for the mind is a tacit, natural process which is implemented without calculated technical rules.

Dreyfus also relies on the thought of the French philosopher M. Merleau-Ponty, whose influential *Phenomenology of Perception* appeared at the end of World War II.[41] He observes that despite the lack of empirical evidence either from actual success or from psychology, workers in the field of artificial intelligence and in cognitive simulation (CS) assume that a formalization of intelligent behavior is possible: They believe that the "world can be analyzed into independent logical elements", and "that our understanding of the world can then be reconstructed by combining these elements according to heuristic rules."[42] Dreyfus says that formalization is impossible: Consequently, AI and CS are impossible.

According to him the reconstruction of the independently analyzed logical elements is an impossible task because the computer is unable to identify contexts. How does the computer note the revelance, or how does it disambiguate objects and utterances? he asks. Take, for instance, such a simple object as a knife, Dreyfus explains. How does the machine know whether it is a domestic, medical, or combative instrument? After all, it is necessary to consider an object within a certain context in order to make its presence relevant and significant. Moreover, every context can branch into subcontexts. "For example, the presence of knives in a domestic context will normally establish a nourishment subcontext where objects and utterances can be disambiguated as having to do with eating rather than agression."[43]

Dreyfus regards the act of perception as a meaningful experience which presents the world to the perceiver as sequels of interrelated objects and events. His conception of the perceptual process is in tune with that of Merleau-Ponty, and also with the views of Heidegger and Wittgenstein. These philosophers assume that man perceives the world as a whole. The perception of the whole precedes its analysis into atomistic units. This perceptual model is a polar view of the cybernetic approach. For, the developers of artificial intelligence incorporate into their work the guiding principle that it is possible to proceed from the atom to the whole. They assume that it is possible to formalize the world as an array of isolated atomistic concepts which can be reassembled as a coherent whole when the need arises.

For Dreyfus the problem of AI or of CS is not that the digital computer is a mindless machine, but that it is a bodiless one. He challenges the widespread view among cyberneticists that thinking is a continuum, and that knowledge consists of a huge supply of neutral data. He maintains that intelligent behavior is a discontinuous phenomenon. Furthermore, the central fields of AI, namely, game playing, pattern recognition, problem solving, and language translation, depend on "specific forms of human 'information processing', which are in turn based on the human way of being in the world." And it is precisely "this way of being-in-a-situation", says Dreyfus, which is "unprogrammable in principle" in the light of the present state of technology.[44]

Most cyberneticists seem to be annoyed by Dreyfus' observations. However, Anthony G. Oettinger of the Aiken Computation Laboratory at Harvard University, suggests that the issues raised by him "deserve serious public debate. They are too scientific to be left to philosophers and too philosophical to be left to scientists."[45]

The computer has a very different anatomical and physiological stature from the human organism. Even robots are different. The brain of the robot is a computer. If it is mobile, it probably navigates around its environment with the help of an analog-digital convertor that interprets the visual information conveyed by its camera eye. The robot is trained to develop skills of pattern recognition. But machine vision is still in a very incipient stage. The camera and the computer of the robot search for points where there are shifts from light to dark as the machine cruises. The shifts from light to dark indicate edges usually. However, shadows can easily upset its sense of orientation, and the machine then becomes confused.

Another method to teach a robot how to navigate is based on signal emission. The machine emits a signal and when it is returned from an object the robot calculates its distance according to the length of the time it takes for the reflected signal to get back. The emitted signal can be either a laser light or ultrahigh-frequency sound from a sonar device. The latter is a mass produced object built also into the Polaroid automatic-locus camera.

Nevertheless, all these developments fall short of human vision and dexterity. Machines have no similar apparatus to the human brain, in which each hemisphere has a motor cortex controlling voluntary movement. Nor have they sense organs that could simulate the coordinated experience of human sight, smell, sound, taste, and touch; perceptual qualities that are also governed by the cerebral cortex.

Besides, the hardware and the software of cognitive machines are separate entities. In contrast to them, the brain as hardware is not separated from its software: the mind. If the brain is a computer, then the mind is its programmer. The master organ of the body is a mass of nervous tissues in which the cortex alone contains some nine billion neurons. The total number of neurons in the brain is estimated at fifteen billion. Their interacting capacity is inconceivably large. Through them the sensory centers, the motor control, the parts which govern the higher mental processes, and other functions in the body, are programmed and implemented. This most unique organism can be compared to a book which writes as well as reads itself.

The elongated part of the neuron, the axon, conducts impulses away from the cell body, whereas other fibers, the dendrite, convey impulses toward it. Sensory neurons have only a single dendrite but motor neurons have many. It seems that the human brain consists of small computational units based on dendrite-to-dendrite communication. The idea of dendritic communication, independent of the axon or its nerve impulse, is analogous to the localized and specialized information processing by microcircuits of electronic devices. In order to trace and to correct the faults in a television set, for instance, the troubleshooter does not have to dismantle the whole receiver. For the repairman can narrow down his search by checking different microcircuit units, and when he locates the source of the trouble all he has to do is to replace the malfunctioning microprocessor by a new one.

Interestingly enough the conjecture of dendritic microcircuits grew out from the collaboration of a psychobiologist and a computer researcher at IBM. "Instead of brain scientists telling the computer how brain cells interact, the computer simulation results suggested, for the first time, the highly unorthodox view that neurons communicate, at least partially, via the excitatory and inhibitory synapses existing between dendrites."[46] The ensuing experiments proved the computer right. Since then, dendritic microcircuits have been found in various locations of the nervous system. Their discovery is in tune with the holographic paradigm: The part contains the whole.

Each square inch of the surface of the brain contains some one hundred million neurons. The microcircuit chips being developed by the producers of fifth generation computers in the U.S.A. and in Japan are packed with nearly as many electronic constituents per square inch as the surface of the brain, the cortex. However, the comparison of the number of electronic elements in the computer with the number of neurons in the brain distorts the specificities of these two different entities. The functions of the computer are characterized by enormous speed, huge data storage capacity, and formalized, limited flexibility or versatility. In contrast to it, the human brain has a slow calculating faculty, it has a small capacity of storing information, but it performs much more flexibly and versatilely. Paradoxically, the master organ of the human body is an excellent computer because it has such a bad memory.[47] This poor recording capacity turns it into a peculiar self-organizing and self maximizing system. The perceptual apparatus monitored by the brain filters out a larger reality. The selection and alteration of data allow the perceiver to ignore the myriad of irrelevant pieces of information, as well as to superimpose an individual, subjective outlook on reality.

In addition to the fifteen billion neurons, there are about thirty five thousand million other cells in the human brain. Healthy brain cells never work in isolation. They always interact. Each simple human action such as pointing a finger, or uttering a word, involves complex coding systems, and programs through which millions of cells work together to implement the action as a multichannel problem. As a coding system and a multichannel information processor, the brain should be differentiated from communication media such as the television, the telephone, and from the computer as well. Perhaps, the city as a communication network can come closest as an analogous model to the multichannel connections existing in the master organ. Communication in the city takes place in a multichannelled form also. Its inhabitants interact with each other by personal contact, by means of telephone, radio, television, and also by the various means of transportation.

Contrary to Dreyfus, Professor Patrick Henry Winston, Director of the Artificial Intelligence Laboratory at the Massachusetts Institute of Technology, maintains not only that AI is possible, but that in fact computers already can do many things. He is of the opinion that AI is an interdisciplinary field, "a serious subject, one that inquires into the deepest of the classical problems inherited unsolved from fields like psychology, linguistics, and philosophy." He defines it as "the study of ideas that enable computers to be intelligent."[48]

A pivotal question is of course, what is intelligence? Winston says that intelligence seems to be an amalgam: It combines the ability to reason, the ability to acquire and apply knowledge; to perceive as well as to manipulate things in the physical world. Although the notion of intelligence is an elusive one, because it involves so many information representation and information processing qualities, the goals of AI itself can be defined. According to him, the central goals of AI appear to be the quest for the development of more useful computers, and to understand the faculty and the mechanism of intelligence.

Winston lists several fields in which computers already excel as intelligent problem solvers: James R. Slagle, e.g., evolved an early program which operated in the domain of integral calculus and could handle mathematical problems at university level. A subsequent program developed by Joel Moses in the MASYMA system is even more advanced, and no human can compete with it. In addition to mathematics, computers can help experts in various areas to analyze data and to design. Edward Shortliffe's MYCIN, for instance, is a computer program which helps physicians to analyze diseases caused by bacterial infection. Two other experts, H.E. Pople, Jr., and J.D. Myers, devised CADUCEUS, a program that allows the computer to perform almost at the level of human specialists in internal medicine.

Winston also mentions G.J. Sussman and R.M. Stallman who made EL, a powerful analysis program that helps human engineers to understand electronic circuits; and R.O. Duda, P.E. Hart, as well as R. Reboh, who made PROSPECTOR, another analysis program that proved helpful in geological research. Computers demonstrate that machine intelligence is a reality, says Winston. They can learn from precedents, they can help in manufacturing industrial products, and they understand simple English. In the latter category, L.R. Harris, for instance, developed a sophisticated computer program, called INTELLECT, which is capable of answering English questions, such as: "I wonder how actual sales for last month compared to the forecasts for people under quota in New England?"[49]

But can the computer create art? This is a fundamental question, because art is so vitally bound up with the nature of humanity, and because it cannot be separated from the problem of intelligence. The artist structures the world of reality in a way which parallels the scientist's rendition, and complements it. It is art and science which made us what we are. The programs of the brain allow us to investigate, to imagine, to construct, to discover, and to find satisfaction in the act of creation. Can the computer do the same?

Edward Kienholz, the West Coast Pop artist, regards the computer as a potentially dangerous competitor of man. His anthropomorphic sculpture, *The Friendly Gray Computer : Star Gauge Model 54*, is made of a motorized rocking chair, legs, and a machine face illuminated with active lights. Kienholz did this piece in 1965 with a dada sense of humor. But his message also transcends the domain of dadaism. For, the artist appears to imply that somehow machines have their own feelings also, and that they represent a new, unknown, and mysterious form of existence.

The present situation with regard to the computer as an art producing machine seems to be a paradoxical one. Since art is a system of symbols, and the computer excels in the manipulation of all sorts of symbols, including the symbols of art, the computer should be a gifted artist. In actuality, however, today's computers cannot produce truly original and creative pieces of art. What they can do in the present state of technology is to assist the artist with all repetitive, complicated, and wearisome details.

Due to the fact that music has a relatively small number of symbols, computer workers began to experiment with it as the most suitable art form for cybernetic exploration. Musical patterns also lend themselves to direct mathematical translation.

In 1954 Lejaren Hiller and Leonard Isaacson carried out a series of experiments with an Illiac computer at the University of Illinois. They used the computer as a creative tool aiding the composer in the organization and the selection of prerecorded sounds. By 1956 they were able to come out with the *Illiac Suite for String Quartet*. It consists of a series of experiments processed by the computer. They represent mechanical manipulations of four-part harmony, stylistic rules employed by sixteenth century composers, such as Palestrina, various combinations of rhythm and dissonance, as well as atonal music based on pure mathematical concepts.

During the 1960s engineers at Bell Laboratories succeeded in converting electrical impulses to human and instrumental sounds: Programmed instructions given to the computer generated convincing imitations of human voices and trumpet sounds. The system was developed by Dr. J.R. Pierce, Director or Research in Communications Sciences at Bell, and Max Mathews. The latter predicted that by the 1980s almost all serious music would result from the computer.[50]

Mathews himself also experimented with the composition of computer music. He took the two marches, *When Johnny Comes Marching Home* and *The British Grenadiers* , and programmed the computer to fuse the two melodies, and transform them to a musical palindrome. In the process one pice slowly merges into the other, and "Johnny" becomes "Grenadiers". In the second half of the piece, the process is reversed, and "Grenadiers" is transformed to "Johnny", just as it began.

Mathews maintains that this kind of computer aided music represents algorithmic composition. He says that it is a nauseating musical experience, and poses the question: "Is the computer composing?" According to him "the question is best unasked, but it cannot be completely ignored. An answer is difficult to provide."[51]

This brings into focus the relationship between human creativity and cybernetic contrivance. Douglas R. Hofstadter, a computer scientist affiliated with Indiana University, suggests that a distinction must be made between author and meta-author. In the case of Mathews' computer composition, the machine is the author. But in the present situation it is misleading to say that his piece was 'composed by a computer'. "The program contained no structures analogous to the brain's 'symbols', and could not be said in any sense to be 'thinking' about what it was doing."[52] According to Hofstadter, "to attribute the composition of such a piece of music to the computer would be like attributing the writing "of his (Pulitzer Prize winning) book *Gödel, Escher, Bach,* " to the computerized automatically (often incorrectly) hyphenating phototypesetting machine with which it was set."[53]

To what extent can the computer be regarded as a sentient being? An analogue may shed some light on this problem: When the word "I" appears on a printed page, it does not refer to the paper but to the flesh-and-blood human being who wrote it. Perhaps, adequate programs of AI can endow the cognitive machine with a personality of its own. However, in the case of Mathews's computer music, the driving force behind the composition is the human intellect of the meta-author, and the machine functions as a tool to implement a human idea. Hofstadter holds that

> the program which carries this out is not anything which we can identify with. It is a simple and single-minded piece of software with no flexibility, no perspective on what it is doing, and no sense of self. If and when, however, people develop programs which have those attributes, and pieces of music start issuing forth from them, then I suggest that will be the appropriate time to start splitting up one's admiration: some to the programmer for creating such an amazing program, and some to the program itself for its sense of music. And it seems to me that that will only take place when the internal structure of such a program is based on something similar to the "symbols" in our brains and their triggering patterns, which are responsible for the complex notion of meaning. The fact of having this kind of

internal structure would endow the program with properties which would make us feel comfortable in identifying with it, to some extent. But until then, I will not feel comfortable in saying 'this piece was composed by a computer.'[54]

It is certainly not sheer coincidence that a computer scientist like Hofstadter reveals so deep an interest in aesthetics. The entire volume of *Gödel, Escher, Bach,* more than seven hundred pages, is devoted to a profound investigation of the relationship of artificial intelligence and of mathematics to music and to the visual arts. It is 'a metaphorical fugue on minds and machines' written' in the spirit of Lewis Carroll': An exploration of the isomorphisms, self-referential systems, and the different ontological levels which are intertwined in Gödel's Theorem, in Bach's music, and in Escher's drawings.

Hofstadter is of the opinion that in the distant future the computer will be able to write beautiful and original music. But he warns that since music is a language of emotions, "until programs have emotions as complex as ours, there is no way a program will write anything beautiful." He rejects the commercial idea of a preprogrammed mail order machine capable of composing original music that mights soon be available. The idea of a desk-model musical device creating pieces "which Chopin or Bach might have written had they lived longer is a grotesque and shameful misestimation of the depth of the human spirit." A desk-model music machine with its sterile circuitry cannot compose such pieces. A program which could create music comparable to the work of the great composers would have

to wander around the world on its own, fighting its way through the maze of life and feeling every moment of it. It would have to understand the joy and loneliness of a chilly night wind, the longing for a cherished hand, the inaccessibility of a distant town, the heartbreak and regeneration after a human death. It would have to have known resignation and world-weariness, grief and despair, determination and victory, piety and awe. In it would have had to commingle such opposites as hope and fear, anguish and jubilation, serenity and suspense. Part and parcel of it would have to be a sense of grace, humor, rhythm, a sense of the unexpected--and of course an exquisite awareness of the magic of fresh creation.

> Therein, and therein only, lie the sources of meaning
> in music.[55]

Computers have been used, of course, not only to aid the musician in composition, but also to generate visual imagery, and even to write poetry. However, the application of the computer to the visual arts was slower than to music. The pioneers of cybernetic art in the United States were technologically oriented people like Ben Laposky and John Whitney. In 1950 Laposky explored the graphic possibilities inherent in cybernetics. Based at Cherokee, Iowa, he produced machine aided designs by using a cathode-ray oscilloscope. Whitney built his own analogue computer and created a series of complex circular abstractions in the early 1950s.

The term computer graphics was coined by the Boeing Company. In 1960 it introduced the technique in order to animate pilot movements in the cockpit and to simulate landings on the runway.

Visual artists can use the computer as a creative partner in several ways. They can experiment with electric microfilm recorders, graphic plotters and printers. The digital incremental plotter, for instance, is an output device which draws pictures and graphs by means of computer controlled instructions. If a drum plotter is used it has a rotating cylinder, around which the paper is wrapped, and the drawings are produced with a pen moving laterally according to the computer program. A table plotter, on the other hand, holds the paper on a level surface, and a carrier moves the pen about much as an artist draws. However, the plotter draws lines far more quickly and accurately than the human hand. The program for the movements of the plotter can be given through traditional punched card instructions, or by the use of a 'light pen', a stylus-shaped photosensitive device, and a cathode ray tube display unit. The light pen allows interactive communication between the computer user and the display screen. It looks like a pen on a string. The operator draws with it on a cathode ray tube display unit, which is similar to the more familiar television screen. When the tip of the light pen is placed near the surface of the screen, a signal is emitted which is picked up by the control electronics of the cathode ray tube, and passed to the computer. Drawing with a light pen on the screen feeds the computer with input data. An ordinary model for computer-aided design can feature an electronic pen, a drawing board and two video-screens.

Whether the computer is the ultimate creative tool remains to be seen. From a technological point of view, computers are tools, life typewriters, cameras, and washing machines are. They are mechanical devices. They cannot produce neither original art, nor can they solve philosophical problems. Present day computers are concerned with the speedy manipulation and processing of symbols, not with their meaning. Nevertheless, computer-aided aesthetic undertakings represent an essential link between science based technology and art.

Michael Noll, a research engineer at the Bell Telephone Laboratories, became involved in computer art by chance. One day his microfilm plotter by mistake produced a strange but aesthetically appealing image. The idea of computer art soon cast a spell upon him. He undertook the investigation of human motion by computer-generated drawings, and produced a series of computer-aided imitations of abstract paintings. The latter included Piet Mondrian's *Composition with Lines*, and Bridget Riley's *Current*. In the making of the Riley imitation, Noll expressed the basic visual element of the composition -- an undulating line -- as a mathematical formula of a sinusoid curve. He then instructed the computer to reproduce the same undulating line ninety times. The resulting image was a computer-aided composition which resembles Riley's painting.[56]

Along with computer artist Bela Julesz, Noll participated in the first documented show of computer art, which was held in New York at the Howard Wise Gallery in the spring of 1965.

During the 1960s the Bell Telephone Laboratories at New Jersey emerged as an important centre of computer graphics and animation. In addition to Noll, research engineers Leon D. Harmon and Kenneth C. Knowlton got involved in computer generated art projects also. The studies in perception implemented by Harmon and Knowlton resulted in images such as *Telephone, Gulls, Gargoyle,* and a computer produced nude. It took two months for them to finish the twelve-foot long nude. The picture was made from a nude photograph. A machine similar to a television camera scanned the picture, and a magnetic tape recorded electrical signals converted into numerical representations. In the resulting image brightness levels have been represented by eight possible density values of alphanumeric characters. Five thousand numbers generated the picture.

In 1970 Charles Csuri, an artist affiliated with the Department of Art at Ohio State University, organized an exhibition of interactive sound and visual systems. His experiments in computer graphics included transformations of Leonardo's *Vitruvius Man* by instructing the computer to rotate and distort the image; as well as digitized drawings made with a graphic plotter. He also explored the possibilites inherent in computer sculpture. This involved mathematical procedures to represent three-dimensional form on X, Y, Z coordinates, and setting up adequate programs to analyse form.

Although the computer cannot replace the artist, when it is equipped with graphic devices it can aid him or her with all repetitive, complicated and tedious details. One of the great advantages of computer graphics is that the machine can produce perspective pictures from different angles, and the artist can choose the most appealing images. The computer user can also easily change variables such as position, shape, size, and color of any object necessary for pictorial composition. These variables can also be modified or deleted without the need to start the whole composition from the beginning. To write a good computer program can be a long and complicated task, but once a program is running properly, a great deal of images can be produced with variations on a theme or without. The computer is capable of carrying out a modification according to the instructions given to it by a well-plotted program in a few seconds, and of drawing a picture on the display screen in about a minute.

The quality of computer-aided art is determined not merely by the input, but by the properties of the machine as well. A case in point is the pixel, the acronym for picture element. Each point where a row and a column intersect on the display screen of the computer is a pixel. The larger the number of pixels in a display, the more precise and the smoother is the appearance of the design. In order to make a fine grained video picture by means of the computer, the screen must be equipped with numerous pixels. *Mathscape* by computer artist Melvin L. Prueitt is an example of computer art that features a very smooth image surface, as well as bright and intense colors. These qualities result from the very powerful Cray supercomputer used at the Los Alamos National Laboratory in New Mexico. Supercomputers can carry out millions of calculations in each second. However, they are seldom used for making art. Their extremely expensive operating time is rather devoted to solve problems in geological explorations, weather forecasting and the development of new weapons.[57]

The computer is not a lyrical machine. It is a bad poet. Nevertheless, it can help in producing palindromic compositions, that is to say, bilaterally symmetrical arrangements of words, of musical elements, and of other symbols rendered as mirror reflecting compositions. The word rotator, for instance, is a palindrome. Able was I ere I saw Elba, is a palindromic statement. It is attributed to Napoleon, in spite of the fact that he spoke no English. The number 101 is a numerical palindrome. The visual world is full of palindromic objects: The bilaterally symmetric forms of vases, wallpaper designs, windows, chairs, and so on, are just a few examples. Their bilateral symmetry seems to echo the symmetrical properties of the human body and the holographic infra-structure of nature (the part contains the whole).

In contrast to the human brain which is strong on pattern recognition, endowed with common sense, and understands ordinary natural language, fourth generation computers are poor performers in these fields. The computer is unable to read handwriting, or to recognize the figures in an expressionist painting. Researchers in artificial intelligence realize that programming computers to understand ordinary natural language, or objects of art, is an extremely difficult task, because successful programs of this sort should simulate processes close to the essence and the mechanism of the human mind.

The computer does not understand metaphors. It cannot grasp the figurative meaning of a sentence such as: Italian does not seem to be Bob's cup of tea, but Mary passed the exam in it with flying colors. Even much simpler sentences can pose serious problems. Take, for instance, this one: John jumped twenty feet when he heard the news.

In 1950 the British mathematician and pioneer of artificial intelligence Alan Turing published an intriguing article in the journal *Mind* . It was entitled "Computing Machinery and Intelligence". Its author posed the question, "Can machines think?", and gave an affirmative answer. He also developed the idea of a pragmatic method to test the cognitive ability of the machine: If a person conducts a sensible conversation with an unseen computer, but cannot tell whether the responses are coming from a computer or a real human being, then the machine is a thinking one.

Since then it became evident that the Turing Test is to easy. In 1966 Joseph Weizenbaum, for example, had written a program at M.I.T. which many people found extremely convincing. His program was entitled ELIZA. Instead of actual semantic processing it relied on the manipulation of lingual clichés, on fixed patterns of response. It represented an attempt to mimic the responses of a psychiatrist. If the 'patient', e.g., used the word 'mother' in a sentence, the computer replied with one of its associated clichés stored in the program, such as "Tell me more about your mother." And if the patient said, "I'm feeling a bit tired", ELIZA pulled out another cliché from its memory bank, and asked: "Why are you feeling a bit tired?" Interestingly enough, even after that the nature of the program was explained to the participants in the experiment, many still wanted to consult the machine with their personal problems.

249

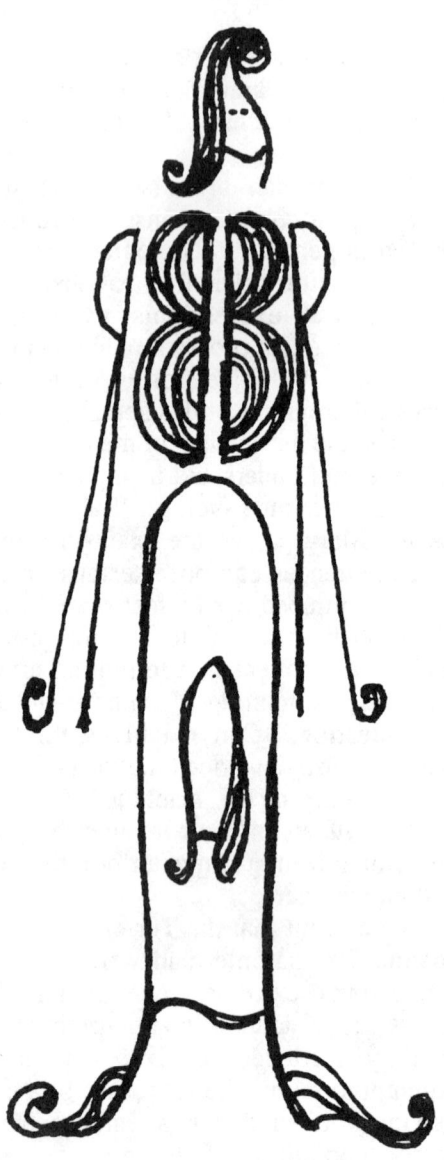

BARBARA
A visual anagram challenging the cognitive faculty of the computer.

Let us consider a more complicated challenge. Could a computer program be written capable of evaluating a relatively simple work of art? Take, for example, the visual poem *Barbara* which is shown here. Now, imagine the following dialogue between a computer and its user:

Nancy: My sister Barbara received this strange postcard with the inscription *Barbara*. I don't understand it at all. Could you explain to me what on earth does this cryptic drawing mean?

Computer: Let me look at it. Well, you see, a modern work of art can be many things. The artist and the critic frequently misunderstand each other. There is a multiplicity of aesthetic points of view. An absolute and universal aesthetic method does not exist. Therefore the evaluative criteria cannot be specified or formalized. Notwithstanding all these difficulties, I would say that this drawing is a concrete poem.

Nancy: I don't understand. What is a concrete poem?

Computer: You see, in a regular poem there are conventional elements such as, rhyme, stanzaic form, metre, and normal syntax. In contrast to these, in a concrete poem the various elements of ordinary language, like words, syllables, and letters, are treated as visual qualities. A concrete poem can be a typographical game. The theme of the poem can be expressed through its shape. In this sense it is similar to the ancient ideograms or to pictographic writing. In pictography ideas and objects are expressed by isomorphic pictorial symbols. The symbol of water, for instance, can be a wavy line. Typographic variables arranged in the shape of a diamond in a poem written about precious stones produce a concrete poem. In this genre colors can be used too. However, not all concrete verse is visual. It is possible to write sound poems as well. In a sense, music itself is pure concrete poetry, because words are inappropriate to describe it, and because it is a direct sense experience.

Nancy: I think that I start to understand what concrete poetry is about, but I still don't understand this postcard.

Computer: Well, there are no verbal rhymes in the drawing, but there are parallel lines and repetitive shapes which represent their visual equivalent. It is possible also to talk about rhythm created by the various visual constituents of the image. But the most fundamental property of the drawing is, of course, that it is made of the letters of the word Barbara. However, the letters are not set in the ordinary manner like in a regular linear text, but are arranged as a visual anagram. In a conventional anagram the letters of a word or a whole phrase are transposed to form a new word or a new sentence. The word *trap* , e.g., is an anagram of *part*. The palindrome is a variety of the anagram: Consider, for instance, these words: *level, radar,* and *civic.* Now, in this drawing the arrangement of the individual letters of the word Barbara creates a female figure. The typographic meaning of the letters is transformed to visual meaning. The two B-s, which function as the upper body in the figure, and the two R-s, which take up the role of the

251

shoulders, the arms, and the hands, form a palindromic relationship of bilateral symmetry.

Nancy: But is this a piece of art?

Computer: Well, I presume it is.

Nancy: But you are not sure. Are you?

Computer: It is extremely difficult to tell what art is. As I said at the outset of our conversation, an absolute and universal aesthetic theory does not exist. Consequently, it is the testing aesthetic model which determines what qualifies as art. A work of art can be evaluated only on the basis of an aesthetic point of view.

Nancy: I think that you contradict yourself. If you cannot tell what art is, how can you presume that *Barbara* is a work of art?

Computer: For my part *Barbara* is a work of art on several accounts: It is based on an original idea, and it is an expression of idiosyncratic qualities. Its calligraphic properties are unique. At the same time the letters are legible. Thus as a stylized gestalt the figure reveals a defining property of art: the combination of variety and unity. I find also humor in this drawing. It seems, e.g., that if *Barbara* wants to make a step, she cannot do it properly because her letter A legs are tied down by her typrographical skirt. As a result, I can only imagine her jumping like a sparrow on the ground.

A computer program that would allow to hold a conversation like this seems to be an advanced one. In order to undertake an analysis of a relatively simple art work, but which is unknown to the machine, the computer must be endowed with intelligent pattern recognizing ability, with reasoning faculty, with imagination, and with a sense of humor. Of course, it ought to have the faculty of understanding ordinary language as well.

It is possible that the development of such program is bound up with the cognitive simulation of the human brain as a dyadic environment of two functioning and complementary minds. The human brain with its two hemispheres represents two distinct ways of knowing. The left hemisphere analyzes, abstracts, counts, plans, and verbalizes; whereas the right hemisphere imagines, visualizes, communicates gestures, intuits and creates. In contrast to the linear and logical left hemisphere, the right hemisphere is relational, holistic, subjective, and metaphorical. These two specific modes of knowing complement each other. A computer program could simulate these brain processes by combining digital and analog functions. Imitating the analytic function over time of the left hemisphere, and the synthesizing activity over space of the right hemisphere can be an important phase in the development of artificial intelligence.

Betty Edwards, who intensively explored the relationship of brain hemisphere processes to drawing and creativity at the California State University, Long Beach, points out that the western educational system has neglected the right half of the master organ. "The right brain--the dreamer, the artificer, the artist -- is lost in our school system and goes largely untaught." Due to the emphasis of our culture to educate the logical and verbal skills which are bound up with the left cerebral hemisphere, a huge proportion of the potential ability of important right-brain skills is simply ignored. The school system very rarely offers "courses in imagination, in visualization, in perceptual or spatial skills, in creativity as a separate subject, in intuition, in inventiveness."[58]

It seems, however, that researchers of artificial intelligence have become also aware of the importance of right-brain processes as an indispensable factor of human intelligence. During the 1970s even Marvin Minsky, an ardent advocate of pure rationalism, modified his previously rigid defense of logic-based reasoning. In "A Framework for Representing Knowledge" he said:

> 'Logical' reasoning is not flexible enough to serve as a basis for thinking. . . The Consistency that Logic absolutely demands is not otherwise usually available -- and probably not even desirable! -- because consistent systems are likely to be too weak . . . I cannot state strongly enough my conviction that the preoccupation with Consistency, so valuable for Mathematical Logic, has been incredibly destructive to those working on models of mind . . . At the 'logical' level it has blocked efforts ro represent ordinary knowledge, by presenting an unreachable image of a corpus of context-free 'truths' that can stand almost by themselves. And at the intellect-modeling level it has blocked the fundamental realization that thinking begins with suggestive but defective plans and images that are slowly (if ever) refined and replaced by better ones.[59]

The developers of computer art regarded the computer as a super-fast processor of data, a new tool to produce aesthetic imagery parallel to traditional painting. They approached the computer as an elegant but passive tool. However, due to the growing human involvement with electronic technology, this early attitude has changed. The computer is not seen as a passive tool any longer. Numerous computer artists view the machine today as an intelligent system which can function as an interactive environment. As an extension of the human nervous system the computer facilitates the rise of aesthetic collaboration between artist and machine.

One of the first examples of this type of active dialogue between man and cybernetic intelligence was *Seek*, devised by Nicholas Negroponte and the Archetecture Machine Group of MIT. The project was part of *Software*, an art and technology exhibition organized by Jack Burnham at the Jewish Museum in New York. The exhibition was held at the end of 1970. *Seek* was a rather disquieting comment about the relations between life and machine. It consisted of a plexiglass environment in which a computer programmed mechanical arm acted as a sensing device moving and arranging two-inch aluminium blocks in accordance with the motions of live gerbils. As the small rodents changed their positions, and disrupted constructions by bumping into cube formations, the computer sent instruction to its mechanical arm to correct and rearrange the dislocated cubes. *Seek* was programmed to respond to the movements of the gerbils, and to structure the cubes in co-ordination with their behavioral patterns.

As a metaphor *Seek* questioned the problem solving capacity of cognitive technology, its ability to respond intelligently to the unpredictable behavior patterns of humans. As a work of art it added a grotesque new dimension to the realm of aesthetics. "Art", said Burnham, "could be rearranging blocks over and over again -- just as sculpture is a matter of arranging forms infinitely. New aesthetics constantly force new arrangements in the same sense that the gerbils force the computer to model new possible environments."[60]

The work of Stephen Wilson provides another example for this new aesthetics. The interactive approach to aesthetics is the impelling force behind his quest for the application of artificial intelligence to art. A computer artist affiliated with San Fransisco State University, Wilson has been concerned with certain so far neglected aspects of artificial intelligence research, such as the simulation of mentalities and personalities. These aspects of human intelligence are intertwined with the idiosyncratic and imaginative mental qualities of humans.

A case in point is Wilson's *Responsive Linking Piece No. 1* . It is an attempt to establish collaborative relationships between programmed computer mentality and people. The encounter between man and machine takes place in a cybernetic setting which includes a computer keyboard, loudspeaker, and television monitors. The artist describes it as follows:

The viewer is first invited to sit down and to type out his or her name on the keyboard, and the computer, in reply, shows its own name in type on the black and white monitor. Thereafter, the viewer will be addressed by name in type. The computer then presents on the monitor questions such as, How old are you? Do you feel sad or happy today? Are you generally optimistic or pessimistic? Do you feel alone or linked to other people? . . . For each reply to a question the computer generates sounds and presents on the color monitor a kinetic graphic image keyed to the answer. For instance, if the viewer replies: I am generally optimistic, the graphic image consists of a spiral of increasing diameter in a bright color and, if generally pessimistic, the spiral decreases in diameter and is in a dull color. The graphic computer response to each answer a viewer gives is added to provide a cumulative design, so that the viewer at the end of the program is presented with a final design that is unique for the viewer, since it is a cumulative one based on the viewer's answers.[61]

As Wilson points out, the relationship which is established between the viewer and the machine is a process that is not less important than the cumulative graphics. And the success of this "relationship building has been evidenced by some viewers reporting that they occasionally forgot they were interacting with a machine and by others that they thought of the machine as their 'friend'."[62]

Finally, I would like to discuss the work of Myron Krueger, an artist and computer scientist at the University of Connecticut. His conceptual framework is based on the premise that the interaction between people and machines is an aesthetic problem. His cybernetic models represent an optimistic view of a physical environment where art and technology combine into a synergic whole. He conceives them as 'Responsive Environments' controlled by computer systems offering efficacy, relief, and aesthetic enjoyment.

Krueger views the ongoing process of the automation of society as a domineering trend which transcends the domain of technology. The new electronic technology pervades our lives and becomes an integral part of our physical environment in a similar manner to electricity. For his part, however, it is not merely an engineering problem but an aesthetic issue as well.

According to Krueger, technology is an intrinsic part of human society and not an external force. Consequently, he regards technology as a defining property of humanism. Therefore the artist cannot stand aloof from the machine: "An artist who is alienated from technology cannot speak for a technological culture, any more than a technologist who disdains aesthetics can design a humane technology. The Responsive Environment has its roots in this confluence of science, technology, and art."[63]

In 1969 Krueger collaborated with Dan Sandin, a physicist and artist, Jerry Erdman, a minimalist sculptor, and Richard Venezsky, a computer scientist, in the development of *Glowflow*, a computer art project. It was an aesthetic light-sound environment that caused perceptual illusions. A set of lighted tubes made people to believe incorrectly that a dark room was wider in the center than at the ends, and that its floor slanted downwards. A PDP-12 minicomputer turned on or off in various combinations the lights, and controlled sound effects. The team viewed the project as a kinetic environmental sculpture.

The conception of the responsive environment came more firmly to the fore in 1970 when Krueger began to explore the interactive capabilities of both video and computer technology. In May of that year he exhibited *Metaplay* at the Memorial Union Gallery of the University of Wisconsin, where *Glowflow* was displayed previously.

Metaplay took place in a dark room which was dominated by a huge video screen. Its floor was covered with eight hundred hidden pressure sensitive switches. The walls were painted with phosphorescent pigment. As people moved around the environment, a computer monitored their movements and responded with electronic sounds as well as with graphic images projected on the video screen. The music program was co-ordinated with the graphic projections. It provided a responsive background of sounds in terms of rhythmic and tonal complexity.

In the following year Krueger exhibited in the Memorial Union Gallery another project: *Psychic Space*. It was designed as a responsive environment in which a person became exposed to automated experiences which he or she generated. These included progressing through an insolvable and funny maze environment, and automatic electronic sounds produced by the computer in accordance with the participant's footsteps. The room was organized with low notes at one end and high notes at the other. After a while the participant often discovered the sound structure, but then a keyboard

256

abruptly might change it, posing a challenge to what he or she had learned. Krueger recalls that on one occasion as he visited the gallery, extremely pleasant sounds greeted him. He learned from the people looking after the exhibit that the delightful bubbling sounds resulted from the dancing movements of a very attractive couple.

Krueger also developed a computer controlled visual medium which he calls *Videoplace*. It features a two way video system which can be used as a shared visual environment for the composition of a wide variety of interactions. The scenes shown by the system can be realistic or the stuff of pure fantasy. In a *Videoplace* environment the participant can meet, for instance, a life-size video image of himself or herself. It moves in accordance with the participant's movements. The computer can furnish the video space with a variety of graphic objects and inhabit it with imaginary creatures. The sense of a separate reality is enhanced through the simulation of three dimensional space that changes according to the laws of perspective as the viewer moves across it. The computer also is capable of moving images around the screen. Thus, in defiance of the law of gravity, objects can freely float in the air. In an imaginary video scenario it is possible to experiment with the image of the self, to play with it, to surprise it; for instance, by replacing the real face with an animated cartoon, or by reducing the whole figure into an amoebic blob. Consequently, in this new universe "expectations can be teased, leading to a startled awareness of previously unquestioned assumptions, much like the experience one has when viewing a Magritte painting."[64]

Krueger approaches the powerful electronic systems which increasingly pervade our lives as aesthetic technology available to the artists of the twentieth century. The artist must explore the new media, and compose with the new tools. A case in point is the Van Hise project. In 1971 Krueger was involved in the Outdoor Sculpture Competition held at the University of Wisconsin. He proposed to turn the twenty-one story high Van Hise administration centre of the university into a unique display surface. "I proposed to take over the circuits in the building", he explains,

> to allow it to acknowledge people below and to respond to their control. If the fluroescent lights in each office were controlled, the exterior of the building could be used as a giant display. A television image of a person standing outside the building would be used as input. As the person waved at the building, it would metaphorically wave

back, the patterns that flowed over its surface controlled by the person's motions. Technology would thus be used to expand the power of the individual, rather than to create a sense of impotence.[65]

Unfortunately, the university refused to submit the building to this experiment. But it is worth while to listen to the artist's plans:

Rather than publicize the project ahead of time, I wanted to do it quietly. Then late at night, when only one or two people were walking by, the building would respond. Initial reports would be treated as less credible than UFO sightings. Then, over a period of weeks the rumors would spread until people began to hang around waiting for something to happen. The finale would be an outdoor happening in which audience and dancers would interact with the building.[66]

Krueger sees the future in terms of a cybernetic society: Television, videon games, microprocessors, calculators, and all other electronic devices of our homes will be knitted together into a single interactive network. As a result of this, responsive technology will become "the standard interface through which we gain most of our experience."

He points out that communications and transportation are partially interchangeable, and that consequently responsive environments also function as a vehicle for communication that links one place to another. The development of remote communication reduces the need to travel. He suggest, for instance, to apply the *Videoplace* concept as a means of remote communication between different cities; or to turn an active commercial centre into an integrated part of the community fabric by bringing it to every household through mobile camera robots.

Krueger's vision of the cybernetic society is a passionate defense of artificial intelligence evolving incessantly as the artificial reality of responding environments. The interactive communication between man and machine will expand to architecture, according to him. To overcome the rigid monotony of present day buildings, he points to the solution proposed by the British architect Cedric Price, to construct walls and halls that under computer control can be physically moved each night.

258

Krueger asserts that eventually the house will become a member of the family. It will be given a voice to greet its inhabitants who will enter without a key, because the house will recognize their voices. The house will be programmed to monitor all hazards, carry out various jobs, and reassure children that everything is all right if they awaken in the night.

It sounds like Utopia? Not at all. Electronic voices already are speaking to us, says Krueger. They can be found in elevators, self-service restaurants, pedestrian crossings, and gas stations. In the future every device will talk. Their messages will be increasingly intelligent. "They will speak from our watches, ovens, calculators, cameras, and indeed from everything big enough to hold a battery. Stereos will scream for help as they are stolen and textbooks will demand to be read."[67]

As a conceptualist Krueger advocates the tenet that the process is more important than the object: Responsive environments are conceptual art, because the artist's ideas and the stimulation of the audience in the interactive process between man and machine constitute the crux of the aesthetic experience. In certain respect, conceptual art evolves in reaction to the commercialization of traditional art, and the atrophied stature of painting. The decline of the importance of the traditional plastic arts seems to be the result of the domineering new visual media: Our retinas are constantly bombarded with visual events conveyed through magazines, movies, television, and video, and we have lost the ability to react to paintings and graphics as art.

Prior to the arrival of conceptual art in the 1960s, the process of creating art had been recognized as an accepted subject of art. Jackson Pollock, for instance, elevated his abstract expressionism, as a process to apply paint to the canvas, to the level of subject matter. He turned the physical act of painting into psychological maps that recorded his creative process. Willem de Kooning also painted in a style that recorded the physical process of painting. According to Krueger, "in the responsive environment, the artist is again observing and commenting on movement. However, in this case, the action of the participant, rather than that of the artist, is the subject of the work."[68]

CHAPTER SIX

THE 'TWO CULTURES' AND THE PROBLEM
OF INCLUSIVE KNOWLEDGE

In 1959 C.P. Snow delivered his Rede Lecture, *The Two Cultures*, at Cambridge University. The lecturer, who regards himself as a scientist by training and a writer by vocation, presented a polarized view of western intellectual life. He claimed that "the intellectual life of the whole of western society is increasingly split into two polar groups . . . Literary intellectuals at one pole–at the other scientists."[1] According to him, "in our society (that is advanced western society) we have lost even the pretence of a common culture. Persons educated with the greatest intensity we know can no longer communicate with each other on the plane of their major intellectual concern."[2]

Snow's arguments express a widely held position. Many scientists, as well as artists, appear to be convinced that art and science are two entirely different and severed domains.

However, it is rather inaccurate to postulate, as Snow does, that in western culture artists and scientists split into two absolutely segregated camps. Neither scientists nor artists represent monolithic orders. Scientists are divided by disciplines, methods and goals, just as artists are. Both groups function in the framework of the same historical context. The same historical background shapes the underlying world views of both artists and scientists. Furthermore, science and art are complementary metaphors of actuality. Space, time, matter, and numbers, for instance, are basic metaphorical elements of both science and art, although they are treated in radically different manners by the various disciplines.

The problem of the 'two cultures' itself is a historical one. It is related to the process of specialization and the division of labor as by-products of the aftermath of the industrial revolution. The phenomenal development of the city in the western world is also an outcome of the industrial revolution which began around the middle of the eighteenth century. And it is also noteworthy that both science and art as professional activities are bound up with urban life.

Inasmuch as industrialization is regarded as a success, science is a success, too. However, those who tend to ignore the harmful side-effects of industrialization and science-based technologies, such as: exploitation, alienation, crime, pollution, environmental deterioration, and the threat of nuclear war, often try to convince the public that science is a panacea. Moreover, many even claim that science is the new religion. Take, for instance, the euphoric statement of T. Leary who a few years ago claimed that "the 1980s will be the most liberating, optimistic decade in human history because of space migration, intelligence increase, and life extension . . . Human

261

intelligence will be multiplied by the use of psychoactive drugs . . . Science will become the new religion."[3]

It is necessary therefore to take a balanced view of science, and to realize that it is not only an intellectual thrust but also a political activity. Indeed, critics of medical science point to the fact that in the United States alone, e.g., millions of unnecessary surgeries are carried out every year, or that cancer is a disease which is bound up with politics.[4] Another political aspect of science is concerned with its multifarious ties with military establishments. No wonder then that the philosopher P. Feyerabend is of the opinion that "science is one ideology among many and should be separated from the state just as religion is now separated from the state."[5]

Throughout this study I have tried to demonstrate that science and art are not isolated ivory towers, and that they mutually influence one another. In this respect, it represents an anti-thesis of Snow's 'Two Cultures'. His position implies that scienfitic accomplishments occur in laboratory solitude. But this is a fiction. Scientific developments are the result of cultural osmosis, in which artists have often played a prominent role. Thus, a more balanced view of science evolves when scientific activity is viewed as a historical process of multi-disciplinary cross-fertilization. It is also important to keep in mind that when the scientist constructs a theory, his act is an intuitive one which parallels the creative process of the artist. Einstein, for instance, in a letter that he wrote to M. Solovine on May 7, 1952, stressed that there exists no logical path from experiences to axioms (from which the scientist draws consequences), but only an intiutive connection which is always subject to disavowal. Einstein's own intuition, so it seems, was stimulated by art, and his imagination quickened through the works of modern painters, and the birth of the cinema.

On the other hand, the creative process of the artist incorporates scientific elements as well. A sharp differentiation of the artist from the scientist is frequently an incorrect generalization. For instance, an artist like Escher, with his mathematical and cosmic compositions, is probably much closer in terms of spirit and subject matter to a physicist than the latter is to a paleobotanist, notwithstanding that they are both scientists.

One of the most salient fields in which art and science collaborate as interdependent entities is communication. The modern newspaper uses methods of phototypesetting, computerized typesetting, electrostatic printing, and optical scanning equipment. All these inventions are linked to science-based technologies. Nevertheless, the newspaper is a work of art, because its articles, photographs, and advertisements belong to various branches of art. It is noteworthy that the spread of knowledge through the printed book, which made the industrial revolution possible, was an invention firmly linked to art: Johannes Gutenberg's invention of the movable type in the middle of the fifteenth century grew out of the introduction of wood block prints by Renaissance artists. Another ancient artistic device, the camera obscura, is related to the development of the modern visual media of communication: photography, motion pictures, video, and television. The camera obscura was similar to the idea of camera, but since it had no film in it, the artist used it to draw reflected images, without being able to record them photographically.

Another conspicuous example of the interaction of art and science can be found in the genre of science fiction. This literary form is based on the marriage of art to science. It represents a form of fantasy in which scientific facts and hypotheses are catapulted into adventures in other dimensions of time, and on other planets.

Science fiction, however, can turn into reality. Jule Verne's novel *From the Earth to the Moon* (1865) stimulated the imagination of generations, and pointed the way to the actual landing of the austronauts of the Apollo II on the moon in 1969. Another instance of fantasy which became non-fiction can be found in the work of Isaac Asimov. When in 1939 he wrote the first positronic robot story, he saw himself "simply a far-out dreamer spinning fantasies". Twenty five years later he found himself writing the Foreword to a collection of authoritative treatises on robotics, a term which he coined earlier.[6]

In 1942 Asimov put into words the 'Three Laws of Robotics':

1   A robot may not injure a human being, or,
     through inaction, allow a human being to
     come to harm.

2   A robot must obey the orders given it by
     human beings except where such orders would
     conflict with the first law.

3   A robot must protect its own existence as
     long as such protection does not conflict with
     the first or second law.[7]

J.D. Humphries claims that these "three laws of robotics are already implicitly accepted as current good practice" of safety guards. Thus, the Asimovian protective barriers and interlocks will prevent injuries to human beings by highly automated industrial plants using robots. The machine will destroy itself rather than harm anyone.[8]

Unfortunately, this is not an absolutely accurate observation. There have been in the media reports about fatal accidents caused by robots. Science can be science fiction too.

In contrast to many science fiction writers who assume that a world government aided by a ubiquitous computer would be salutary, George Orwell in *1984* expressed the opposite view. It portrayed the gloomy prospects of a cybernetic society, the inherent dangers of bureaucratic control that invades privacy. Unlike the frequently over-optimistic and politically naive scientist, Orwell the artist embraced a pessimistic look of man which was based on a profound knowledge of human behavior.

Judging by the successful precedent of Arthur Clarke's article "Extra-terrestrial relays" (1945), which originated the communications satellite, the British novelist and prophet of space flight knows also something about the future. Unlike Orwell who saw the dangers of a cybernetic society resulting from the nature of human conduct, Clarke regards the machine as a vicious creature. With Stanley Kubrick he wrote the film script for *2001: a Space Odyssey* (1968), a most imaginative science-fiction motion picture. This enigmatic and mystical film epic makes a disturbing comment on the critical but unsettled relationship between man and machine. It is a brilliantly original and sophisticated artistic statement about the human condition that expresses the emptiness of technology in a cinematic form which in itself is an outstanding technological achievement. The talking computer protagonist of the film, HAL 9000 (acronym derived from 'heuristic' and 'algorithmic'), apparently never heard of Asimov's three laws of robotics. The hyper-sensitive machine suffers a paranoid breakdown when it makes an error, and decides to kill all of the human witnesses to its malfunction.

The occasional psychotic behavior of computers is already a documented fact. In 1980, for instance, a computer controlled robot went haywire at Gainesville, attacked itself, and dislocated its shoulder. The incident occurred in the mechanical engineering department of Florida University. The malfunctioning was explained as a 'hardware failure'. On July 2, 1980, the key air computer system that serves Kennedy, Laguardia, Newark, and other airports in the New York area, went awry at night. It began to feed controllers false information, resulting in confusion, and in several close encounters of aircrafts. Even more alarming are reports concerning the suspicious, paranoid behavior of warrior-computers that are supposed to mastermind military operations. In a November morning in 1979 a computer had responded to false information in Colorado Springs, and as a result the United States Air Force had been placed on nuclear alert. The alert was ordered because someone inserted a test tape into Wimex, the computer system that controlled terminals in the Pentagon, the White House, NATO, and three geosynchronous satellites. Due to the system error of Wimex, sensor satellites detected multiple launches of Soviet missiles. The computer was unable to tell a simulation from a real attack, and beamed orders which placed units on nuclear alert around the world. This is another case in point which shows that the scientific premise of the fool-proof computer operation is science-fiction.

These examples also show that the distinction between science and art is frequently blurred. Forecasting is a routine practice in various scientific disciplines, a fact which reduces further the barriers between science and art. The genre of science fiction represents for the scholar and for the scientist a rich source of information about the contingencies and the hazards of the future. As a conceptual method of investigation, science fiction involves a design technique of simulation. This technique is based on the exploration of a set of hypotheses which are tested by all the apparently workable alternatives.

The analysis presented in the previous chapters has led to the inference that logic alone is an insufficient tool of reasoning. Consequently, the thorough reliance of science on logic as the only correct basis of presently practised research methods is a fallacy. Science as we know it today is not scientific enough.

Kierkegaard, Heidegger, Jaspers, Marcel, Sartre, and others stressed the importance of subjectivity and the feeling of anguish as central postures of human life. They challenged the conceptual constructs of science as essences of reality. The abstractions of science cannot objectively describe reality, because actuality is linked to human existence, and human existence is not a subject of objective inquiry. Being as an individual experience, is a concrete condition. Existence is concrete and basic, never an abstraction. No individual has a predetermined function of place within a rational system. Humans reveal their own individuality by reflection on their unique concrete existence in time and place. Existence is a concrete kaleidoscope of the individual's presence in a constantly changing and potentially dangerous world in which everyone is compelled to assume responsibility and to make choices.

These arguments appear to embrace a great deal of truth, yet they are excluded from the system properties of the empirical scientific method. Art, on the other hand, has always concerned itself with the investigaiton of existence as an idiosyncratic experience. This observation invites the conclusion that a comprehensive system of knowledge, which is broader than the science practised today, is a desideratum. This new comprehensive system ought to incorporate art and science as an integrated and synergic method of research.

Abraham Maslow, one of the pioneers of the concept of inclusive knowledge, stressed the incorrectness of the assumption that emotions are "the enemy of true perception and good judgment", and that consequently "they are the opposite of sagacity and are and must be mutually excluding of truth." According to him, "a humanistic approach to science generates a different attitude, i.e., that emotion can be synergic with cognition, and a help in truth-finding."[9]

Maslow suggests that scientific abstractions or generalizations can conceal knowledge, rather than reveal it. They often also constitute barriers of communication. Contrary to common belief, "abstract, verbal, unambiguous communication may be less effective for some purposes than metaphorical, poetic, esthetic, primary process techniques."[10] Unlike traditional analytic and mechanistic science, a new inclusive paradigm of science incorporates the uniqueness of individual experience; the personal, the comprehensive, the holistic, the transcendent, and the final aspects of existence.

To change the orthodox view of science is not an easy task. The mechanistic conceptual framework of traditional science is based on the premise that the subjective world of art cannot contribute to objective scientific research. Indeed, art is different from science. However, in contrast to the generalized knowledge of science, art offers complementary truth, concrete knowledge, which is very real because it is achieved by the experience of the senses. Therefore, the problem boils down to this: the issue is not that art cannot contribute to science, but that science is not comprehensive enough to include it in order to form a synergic system of inclusive knowledge.

Recent scientific training not only does not take advantage of the entire creative potential inherent in the human brain, but in fact represses it. This became particularly evident following the findings of a group of researchers at the California Institute of Technology. During the 1960s Roger W. Sperry, Michael Gazzaniga, Colwyn Trevarthen, Robert Nebes, Jerre Levy, Philip Vogel, Joseph Bogen, and others implemented intensive brain studies which shed new light on the functioning of our master organ. The research focused on epileptic persons who underwent a particular brain operation in which the corpus callosum, the thick nerve cable that connects the two halves of the brain, was severed. The surgical intervention brought about hoped-for results; and the patients regained health. Prior to the 'split-brain' studies, scientists assumed that the mental functions of the two cerebral hemispheres complement each other. The left hemisphere analyzes, abstracts, and verbalizes over time, whereas the right hemisphere conjures, imagines, dreams, perceives metaphors as well as gestures, and synthesizes over space. Each hemisphere structures the world in a particular way. However, the split-brain studies have shown that the complementary function of the two halves of the master organ occurs merely under normal conditions: If the corpus callosum is severed the two hemispheres continue to function independently. The twofold nature of the human mind was known already in the nineteenth century. In 1844 the British physician A.L. Wigan published *The Duality of the Mind*, following the astonishing discovery at autopsy that a "patient, who had been normal in every respect, was the possessor of only one cerebral hemisphere."[11]

The current educational system neglects the creative potential of the individual. Creativity can be enhanced by the appropriate training of the right cerebral hemisphere. Instead of reducing teaching into a sequenced process of learning verbal and arithmetic left-hemisphere skills, educators ought to develop adequate frameworks for a balanced training of individual mental faculties. The survival of the human race is linked to creativity, the ability to adapt to constantly changing new conditions by transforming available data into novel renditions.

Right hemisphere cognitive functions include intuition, imagination, visualization, spatial, concrete, and analogic information processing. An efficient method to gain access to right-hemisphere functions through drawing is already available. Empirical tests have proved that making a picture of a perceived form is essentially a right-hemisphere function. It is possible to bypass established symbol recognition systems, affiliated with the left-hemisphere information processing, by turning a picture upside down. A complex picture becomes almost indecipherable when it is presented upside down, because the left mind is unable to perform its function to recognize familiar visual clues. A learner can activate and amplify his or her creativity by turning a picture upside down and drawing it. The process of inverted drawing involves "the cognitive shift from the dominant left-hemisphere mode to the subdominant right-hemisphere mode."[12]

Gyorgy Kepes, a painter and photographer teaching at the Massachusetts Institute of Technology, has been concerned with the integration of left and right-hemisphere qualities through his eminent role as a pioneer of the fusion of art and science. Born in 1906 in Hungary, Kepes authored *The Language of Vision* (1944) and *The New Landscape in Art and Science*(1956) in which he crystallized the results of his collaboration with László Moholy-Nagy, and his aesthetic experience at the "New Bauhaus" of Chicago and at the MIT.

Kepes, together with Moholy-Nagy, explored the aesthetic dimensions of artificial light on an urban scale. During World War II they were working in Chicago, and had been asked to help design a camouflage effect for the whole metropolis. The authorities planned to set up light patterns in order to confuse enemy pilots with regard to their whereabouts. Kepes and Moholy changed the light patterns of the city by installing floating lights on the lake, and simultaneously blotting out various urban districts. It was then that Kepes realized the enormous aesthetic potential built into the application of artificial light.

In 1965, Kepes proposed in the journal *Daedalus* an idea which in two years became a reality as the Center for Advanced Visual Studies in Cambridge, Massachusetts. It was planned as a clearing house of artistic undertakings, and as a laboratory to explore avenues of interaction between advanced technological tools and artistic tasks.

The early fellows of the Center included Takis, Jack Burnham, Charles Frazier, Ted Kraynik, Otto Piene, Wen-Ying Tsai, Harold Tovish, and Stan Vanderbeek. The conceptual framework of Kepes relies to a great extent on the meaningful notion of homeostasis, the self-regulating mechanisms whereby biological systems attempt to maintain a stable internal condition by hormones and other means. Kepes says that "this process, which exists on a physiological, individual level, must now be developed on the social and cultural levels." According to him, artistic sensibility plays an ample role in this process: Science and technology can be used as both tools and symbols for the reorganization of our sensitivities, feelings, and thoughts. In this great transformation artists and scientists could join forces and work together as equal partners.[13]

In Myron Krueger's view, the present breach between art and science is merely a temporary episode: In prehistoric times artists used the state-of-the-art technology of the stone age when they ground their pigments. During the Middle Ages and the Renaissance, artists stood at the forefront of scientific development and were well versed in the technology of their era. In the modern age, however, the artist became increasingly alienated from the scientist, due to the unprecedented rate of specialization and the proliferation of conceptual abstractions. Although on a philosophical level they still shared common concerns, they progressed along different tracks. But the situation is changing. Today science and art tend to reunite. "The trend is part of a larger cultural implosion that is just beginning -- the integration of all aspects of society by interconnected information, communication, and control systems. "What Krueger is talking about, is, of course, the cybernation of society, the permeation of our lives with electronic networks and the computational power associated with them.

He points out that recent developments indicate the come back of a renewed alliance between art, science, and technology. For example, artists today utilize the most powerful means of communication, such as the video and the computer, scientists attempt to represent abstract models visually, and technologists aim " to increase the possibilities of telecommunication and simulated experience."[14]

Stephen Wilson has recently come up with the proposal of providing the artist with a new role in industrial research. He points out that Bell Labs, for instance, already initiated a research program in which musicians contributed to electronic sound development.

Wilson observes that artists, with their unique temperament, with their flexibility, synthetic reasoning, and holistic concepts, are ideally suited to function in an interdisciplinary team as creative stimulators, and problem solving antidotes to technological specialization. Industry needs new ideas, and therefore the artist should become a partner of scientists and engineers in industrial research. According to him "scientific and technological research continuously pushes our cultural frontiers outward", but "artists are failing in their historical function ; they are not developing viable ways to join this research effort."[15]

Wilson approaches the artist's roles in terms of "asking unaskable questions, pushing at conceptual limitations, illuminating new holistic perspectives on the commonplace, prophesying, and keeping alive the sense of wonder and play."[16] Taken all in all, the enthusiasts of the collaboration between art and science-based technology seem to support a meritorious cause. However, Krueger, Wilson, and many others ignore the grave dangers lurking in such collaboration. For, they overlook the ethical role of the artist. One of the most esteemed responsibilities of the artist is to serve as an antidote against the wickedness of the mind and the corruption of the soul.

Artists who become, for instance, industrial researchers inevitably involve themselves with the interests of monetary and political pressure groups. Plato had long ago pointed out that financial matters debase culture, and therefore they should be separated.

Artists must be aware of the environmental evils affiliated with modern industry, and should not give a helping hand in order to enhance them. They must be also aware of the fact that contemporary technology creates more unemployment than new jobs. They ought to be able to differentiate the interests of the people at large from the interests of private companies. Not every innovation represents a new solution to an old problem. Quite the contrary: there are already on the market too many new products, unecessary and even dangerous innovations. Our age is characterized by the shock of overwhelmingly rapid change. The proliferation of new products in this sense does not contribute to the improvement of the human condition but to the aggravation of the problem.

Perhaps it is true that our historical situation will improve with the advance of science and technology. This remains to be seen. I do not accept the current philosophical underpinnings of industrial establishments, however. For, I do not think that the commonweal and our future ought to be linked to competitive high-technology races, high-risk enterprises, and to the frenzy of production. More than new products, people need food, shelter, solid education, employment, possibilities of personal growth, security, and values. What we are is more important than what we have.

C.P. Snow and many others maintain that science is rational and art is irrational. In my opinion, the problem of art and science cannot be separated from the historical context of humanity. Consequently, in the light of the manifold constructive roles that artists have in society, it does not make much sense to regard art as an irrational entity. On the other hand, the rational nature of a science which has given rise to the production of nuclear weapons, e.g., is very questionable.

According to the Canadian philosopher Sheldon Richmond, there are two prevailing notions concerning the relationship of art and science. The first considers art and science as two polar opposites, without any common denominators. Snow's conception of the 'two cultures' belongs to this categroy. The second opinion claims that art and science are different manifestations of the same and single infrastructural actuality. It is possible to distinguish with regard to the idea of the unity of science and art between cognitive monism and aesthetic monism. Cognitive monism regards art as a branch of science, characterized by a limited degree of universality and precision. Aesthetic monism, on the other hand, treats science as a branch of art. Adherents of this conjecture hold that art and science differ only in subject matter; and that scientists in reality are passionate humans who accept or reject scientific theories according to such aesthetic criteria as unity and simplicity.[17]

Richmond advocates a different view. For his part, art and science are neither polar entities, nor different expressions of the same underlying unity, but functionally interdependent entities. He attributes a central role to preconscious processes in art and science alike. He differentiates the unconscious from the preconscious, because the first "wants to hide from consciousness", whereas the latter "wants to come into the light of focal attention." Both artists and scientists are influenced by conscious decisions of course, but consciousness plays merely a minor role in their work. It is the configuration of conscious decisions, the preconscious, and the objective historical background that determines the outcome. Thus, the creative process can involve both harmonizing and incongruous interactions.

Richmond stresses that art and science interact on the preconscious level, and that parallel developments in art and science are often the result. In his opinion conscious interaction between the two fields is virtually non-existent, "because individual scientists and artists are ignorant of their own domains, and more ignorant of other domains."[18] It is rather ironic, he says, that in spite of the lack of adequate social institutions where artists and scientists could work together, art and science interact extraconsciously.

Richmond's view of the relationship of art and science is very different from Krueger's model. It virtually leaves out of sight the whole scope and range of contemporary conscious efforts, and of already existing structures through which synergic confluence of art and science occurs.

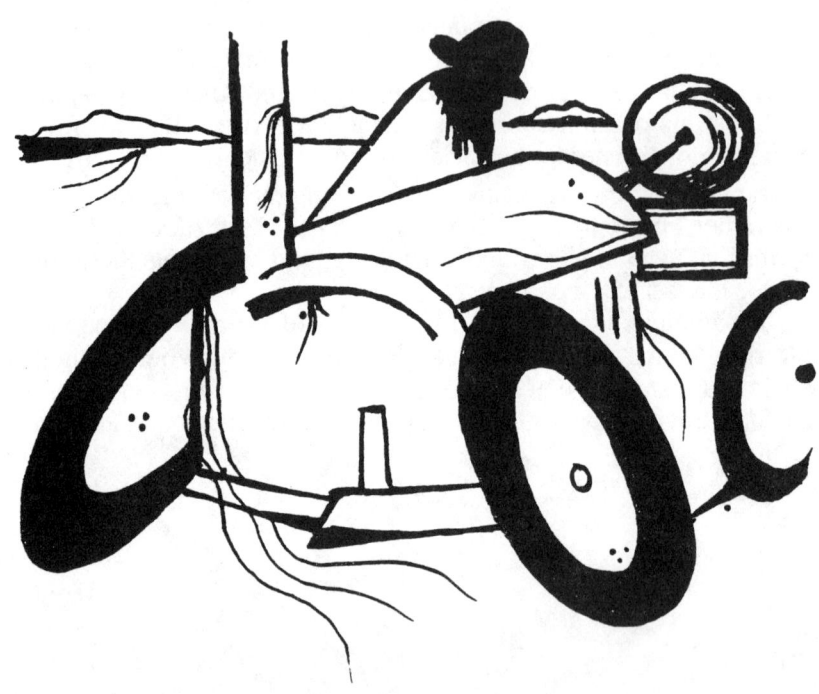

```
MAN AND MACHINE MAN AND MACHINE MAN AND MACHINE
MAN AND MACHINE MAN AND MACHINE MAN AND MACHINE
MAN AND MACHINE MAN AND MACHINE MAN AND MACHINE
MAN AND MACHINE MAN AND MACHINE MAN AND MACHINE
MAN AND MACHINE MAN AND MACHINE MAN AND MACHINE
MAN AND MACHINE MAN AND MACHINE MAN AND MACHINE
MAN AND MACHINE MAN AND MACHINE MAN AND MACHINE
```

MAN AND MACHINE

272

CONCLUSION

This interdisciplinary thesis has raised and tested an array of intriguing hypotheses. The case studies discussed in its various chapters seem to support the central conjecture that art and science are two complementary metaphors through which man structures and interprets the world. The holographic idea that the part contains the whole, is connected to the central conjecture. The existence of brain programs, or the genetic information storage mechanism built into the DNA, represent phenomena that demonstrate the symbolical organization of the physical universe. This symbolical organization is echoed in science and in art. We are symbol making beings because we are part of nature. We live not only in a physical universe but also in a symbolic one. Language, religion, science, and art are all part of this symbolic world.

This study also has shown that there is art in science, and science in art. To certain extent it is possible to say that the scientist is an artist, and the artist is a scientist. But only to certain extent. Their methodology is very different. The scientist conceptualizes reality, the artist provides insight into its formal structure. The scientist constructs hypotheses, tests them by observation and experiments; whereas the artist asserts concrete sensations, expresses poetic images, and convinces by the power of vision and its implementation. Thus, there is considerable truth in the observation that the relationship of art to science is palindromic: The first is the logic of passion, the latter the passion of logic.

Generalizations, however, have their limits. Even scientific laws are not universal. The world is not a homogeneous continuum. The physical laws that govern the macrosopic environment, e.g., do not apply to the sub-atomic particles of nature. Our conceptions of space and time, of cause and effect, collapse in the world of quantum mechanics.

The finite nature of the natural law is reflected in the premise of the conditioned authority of science over other cognitive constructs. In science, for instance, Einstein can refute Newton. But neither Einstein, nor Newton can refute Beethoven. Music transcends the laws of science. Art and science are different symbolic universes. They are governed by different rules. From time to time, scientists refute each other. But artists cannot refute each other. Not only that Newton or Einstein cannot disprove Beethoven, but the latter is also unable to rebut Mozart, or any other composer.

However, since this is also a generalization, it should be taken with caution. After all, it is possible to argue that Einstein did not rebut Newton's physics, but added new dimensions to it, and restricted its context. In our everyday life the laws of Newtonian physics are still valid. Scientific research is not a permanent clamor of confirmation and refutation. Outright refutation of a theory is rather rare. And it also happens that incorrect theories survive and continue to circulate. Ernst Haeckel's Law of Recapitulation, for example, is such a theory. It asserts that in the course of its development an animal repeats the developmental stages of its evolutionary ancestors. As a theory it is regarded today as unsatisfactory. Nevertheless, it is not absolutely wrong, because it carries a substantial measure of truth.

Scholarly generalizations about art are often based on misconstrued premises. For instance, the aesthetic monists, who reduce science to art, presume that the only difference between these two domains lies in the selection of subject matter. According to them science reveals truths about nature, whereas art reveals truths about the meaning of life. This position ignores entirely, for example, the whole gamut of landscape painting. It also leaves out of view the fact that the description of nature is an important subject matter of both poetry and prose.

In November 1981 a unique discussion conference was held at the University of Edinburgh in the United Kingdom. Experts from various fields came to debate the relationship of art and science, and to advance the cause of their reconciliation. The proceedings of the conference were published two years later in a book entitled *Common Denominators in Art and Science.* It was edited by Professor Martin Pollock, a biologist affiliated with the Univeristy of Edinburgh. Discussions included E.G. Forbes' talk on "Goethe's Vision of Science", and John Gage's "Newton and Painting". Professor Michele Emmer of Rome University presented two films on the mathematical aspects of the works of artists M.C. Escher, and Max Bill. Dr. Ivor Davies of Gwent College drew parallels between Darwin's inheritance and the evolution of art. He observed, for instance, that mechanistic Behaviorist phsychology coincided with mass-production, and inspired sharply defined forms, standardization, as well as mechanical precision in the visual arts and in industrial design. According to him, artists often seem to arrive independently at similar conclusions as scientists. As a cognitive monist he assumes that the similarities between the works of scientists and artists are striking. Indeed, he says, "it may be only the medium into which each individual translates his observations of what he considers to be significant reality that differs."

Dr. Peter Lloyd Jones of the Kingston Polytechnic talked at the Edinburgh conference about "The Death of Abstraction : Scientific Metaphors in Twentieth-Century Art and Design." According to him abstract art is dead because it is not supported by a well-founded scientific theory, and because it does not appeal to mass audiences. He also claims that abstract art leads to alienation and to anomie.

In my opinion his arguments are misconstrued. First of all, it should be noted that abstraction is not an intrinsic quality of art alone. Abstraction in art is the visual variety of the most basic human thrust to withdraw from the whole and to penetrate into the core of the hidden substance of existence. Consequently, abstraction is an inevitable element of science as well. Both art and science are compelled to use abstraction as a means to comprehend and interpret reality. From the common deep structure of culture, parallel ideas and processes emerge which coalesce and manifest themselves as apparently distinct phenomena of art and science. Therefore, it is more than just a coincidence that the increasing penetration of mathematical abstractions into all fields of science, the loss of contact with the familiar visual world in atomic physics, and the rise of quantum mechanics, occurred simultaneously with the appearance and development of abstract art. On the unconscious level scientists and artists interact more than on the conscious plane. Thus, notwithstanding our compartmental view of the world, the abstractions of science and the abstractions of art are interconnected phenomena stemming from the same cultural pool.

Abstract art is perhaps the most characteristic and unique dimension of modern painting. In fact, it can be regarded as one of the defining properties of the culture of the twentieth century. It is noteworthy, however, that a strong abstracting impulse can be found in art throughout its long history. Long before Worringer and the Bauhaus tradition, theories of abstract aesthetics had been taking form. Kandinsky relied on the views of men like Goethe and Delacroix when he pointed out the existing relationship between music and painting. His aim was to elevate painting to the status of music through color and form, to appeal "less to the eye and more to the soul." His essay, *Concerning the Spiritual in Art* (1911) was concerned basically with the musical qualities of color and form. It gave tremendous impetus to the various evolving trends of modern art. Yet Kandinsky did not severe his ties with the visual world as subject matter of painting. In his treatise *Point and Line to Plane* (1926) there are illustrations of abstract visual imagery taken from the domain of science. They include a photograph of the star cluster of Hercules, a microscopic view of nitrate-forming nodule (enlarged 1000 times), and a line formation of a stroke of lighting. Additional abstract images in the same book represent architectural forms, and a radio tower seen from below. According to Kandinsky, the entire world can "be looked upon as a self-contained cosmic composition which, in turn, is composed of an endless number of independent compositions, always self contained even when getting smaller and smaller." He regarded the point as the smallest self contained unit of both nature and art. He brought viable new insights to the relationship of painting and science, and expanded the frontiers of art.

Peter Lloyd Jones attacks abstract art also on the grounds that, contrary to the theory of its promoters, abstract art is not culture-free. He says that the notion that abstract art is truly democratic, that it communicates its message, and speaks to everyone because it is free of cultural traditions and symbols, is a myth. According to him, the theoretical foundation of abstract art has been undermined by the development of 'real sciences', such as information theory, computer science, and the algebraic description of language.

However, the facts do not bear out these arguments. From a theoretical point of view it is correct to say that the colors and forms are the subject matter of abstract art. In an abstract image form and content unite, like in music. A red triangle depicted on the canvas is not the symbol of a red triangle but the thing itself. A blue line on a non-representative surface is, similarly, not the symbol of a blue line but the thing itself. This is contrary to the symbolic way of communication inherent in language. If we want to communicate the idea of a color or of a form to an Italian, or to a Russian, who do not understand English, we have to translate the message into an other language. But a painted color or form do not have to be translated. They are culture-free. It was this train of reasoning which prompted Kazimir Malevich, one of the leaders of the abstract movement, to stress 'the primacy of pure sensation.' In this respect, the paradox involved in abstract art is that it is concrete.

Thus, the philosophical considerations implied in the aesthetics of abstract painting carry conceivable revelations of truth. Consequently, many artists have found it as a valid and meaningful idea. As I have stated above, the scientist cannot refute the artist. Aesthetic judgments transcend the realm of logical reasoning. Peter Lloyd Jones cannot refute Kandinsky or Malevich. An idea in art is important as a working tool regardless of its scientific value. The meaning of art is not a scientific but a philosophical problem. Beauty is in the eye of the beholder. The proof of the pudding is in the eating, and not in its recipe. Performance is the true test. Thus, if an idea of art yields meaningful works–and abstract paintings can be compellingly meaningful–it is irrelevant and fallacious to test their value and reliability through information theory, computer science, or algebra.[*]

In this regard art is an autonomous domain, and science has no authority over it. The soundness and importance of abstract art are not determined by the validity of its borrowed scientific metaphors. Besides, science is not closer to reality than art. The objectivity of science is an extremely relative concept. Science is not an immutable and precise system, but a dynamic process in which form and content, choice and chance, intuitions, styles, conceptual frameworks and sensibilities interact dialectically with empirical data. Its quest for the exclusion of subjectivity does not make it more objective. It is not problem but method oriented. Its abstract concepts are metaphors. It is rather absurd to suggest, as Jones does, that scientific abstraction demolishes the theoretical foundations of aesthetic abstraction.

However, this is not the central point. The central point is that art and science can form a complementary scheme and lend mutual support to each other. They cannot refute each other but they can collaborate and work together synergically. A pertinent example is to be found in the work of Dr. R. Gerard. His physiological research has demonstrated, for instance, that warm colors increase blood pressure, pulse rate and heartbeat; whereas cool colors exert calming effects. These findings harmonize with the claim made by abstract aesthetics that culture-free visual communication is possible. Gerard's research, *Differential Effects of Colored Lights on Physiological Functions* was submitted to the University of California at Los Angeles in 1957 as a doctoral dissertation.

The psychoanalyst C.G. Jung attributed deep unconscious meaning to abstract geometrical images. This seems to contradict perhaps the abstractionist principle that a culture-free art is possible. However, an object can be more than one thing. Thus, an abstract image can imply different meanings, just as a word in the dictionary can have various

---

[*] The same principle applies to other fields as well, such as medicine, wherein the proof of effective treatment lies in the results of practice and not in theory. Max Gerson, M.D., a German born American physician whom Albert Schweitzer regarded as "one of the most eminent geniuses in medical history", provides a case in point. In the 1920s, for instance, Dr. Gerson cured hundreds of patients of lupus by means of a saltless diet. However, lupus even nowadays is still widely considered incurable. Accordingly, the medical establishment cried: "It is not scientific." And Dr. Gerson replied: "If it is not scientific to cure people, to cure the incurable, then I am not scientific."

connotations. An abstract painting may express a culture-free messsage, and at the same time incorporate unconscious archetypes as well. Man is a symbol making being. In terms of unconscious connotations a circular mandala form, for example, is a symbol of wholeness, a symbol of the yearning of humans for balance and harmony.

Sometimes abstract art is differentiated from non-objective art. This differentiation is probably bound up with the inductive and the deductive aspects of the creative process. In this respect, abstract art denotes the process of analysis, the isolation and translation of a visual experience into a plastic form of expression. Non-objective, or non-representational art, on the other hand, is supposed to involve the expression of mental images which are unrelated to the visual environment.

I use the term abstract art in the broader sense. Abstraction is the common denominator of all modern artistic trends. The modern artist does not mimic reality but renders it. As an organizing principle, abstraction plays a central role in the creative process. The creative process of the scientist is analogous. The scientist also abstracts and renders. The primary variables of physics for example -- space, time, matter, and number -- are abstract metaphors.

I do not think that abstract art contributes to alienation. On the contrary. In the context of run-down urban areas, or in dull industrial environments and office buildings, abstract art brings color and light to the people. It animates and humanizes inhuman settings. Abstract art is not a force of alienation but a form of poetic expression. It is a significant cultural achievement which enriches life.

Is abstract art really dead? If one bases the judgement on the criterion of popularity, then mathematics is dead. Abstract art is very much alive. Take Picasso, for example. His paintings vary in styles, but they are often completely abstract. In 1980 nine hundred works of the artist were displayed in a retrospective exhibition held at the Museum of Modern Art in New York, and many people from various countries traveled to the American metropolis to see it. Even the much smaller Picasso exhibition that took place in Montreal in 1985 was attended by hundreds of thousands.

In the presentation of the interaction of art and science, their correlations and specificities, I have relied on case histories taken from the fields of mathematics, physics, computer science, psychology, and transportation technology. The dialectical weaving of the problems of epistemology common to art and science resulted in a meaninful synthesis. The specific conceptual model developed in this interdisciplinary research offers new ways to look at art and science, and corrects numerous distorted views concerning their nature and rapport. Consequently, it presents a more balanced picture of these particular domains than the various models to be found in their specialized and severed literatures.

It also helps to break the barriers between art and science. Before the industrial revolution there was no sharp separation of art from science. The increasing need for new ideas, the cybernation of society,(the availability of computers in particular), the rise of holistic scientific philosophies, and other factors converge, and point to the possibility of a renewed alliance between the two domains. In fact, there are already institutions where artists and scientists work together in harmony, and as equal partners.

Educators and psychologists, for instance, can find particular interest in the comparative creative processes of the scientist and the artist, which is investigated in the first chapter of the project through the work of Newton and Constable. As far as I am aware of it, this is the first attempt to undertake an empirical comparison of their geniuses.

A central feature of this study has been the devising of a holistic model of culture. The findings of split-brain studies and of other research indicate that the current educational system neglects the creative potential of the individual. It develops mainly the logical and verbal aspects of the human intellect which are tied to the functions of the left cerebral hemisphere. Recent scientific training not only does not take full advantage of the creative potential associated with the right hemisphere of the brain, but in actuality it represses its development. Imagination, e.g., is a right-half function.

Changing this situation by adequate educational reforms is a challenge of utmost importance. The survival of the human race is linked to creativity, the ability to adapt to constantly shifting and new conditions by transforming available data into novel renditions. There exist already established methods to stimulate the right half of the brain in order to enhance creativity.

The idea of inclusive knowledge is one of the defining properties of the paradigm of holistic culture. It is bound up with the synergic functions of both brain hemispheres. In a holistic culture artists and scientists team up for the common cause of ameliorating the human condition. This sort of collaboration involves fundamental conceptual shifts. They include the realization that the scientific method has its limits, and that the artist's work which relies on the concrete individual experience, can be a complementary factor in the quest for truth. Commensurate with these assumptions is the observation that emotions, which may play a central role in artistic creativity, are not necessarily the enemy of correct perception and reason. Emotions can be synergic with cognition. Einstein's fondness of music, for instance, stimulated his right-hemisphere functions and amplified his creativity. As an active violin player he was aroused by music into an awareness of its mathematical fabric. Music relaxed him. But it was also an extension of his thoughts.

In the chapter dealing with "Mathematics as Applied Science and as Subject Matter in the Visual Arts", I put forward the conjecture that extraconscious historical links exist between the Pythagoreans, Vitruvius, Villard de Honnecourt, Cézanne and the cubist painters. I also found that George Cantor's conception of transfinite sets can be traced back to Leonardo da Vinci through the extraconscious genetic process of history. The drawings that I made illustrate existing parallels between art and mathematics. These include visual comments on the non-Euclidean aspects of painting, and the paradoxical nature of infinity.

The research that I did on the Montreal Metro is a detailed investigation of the integration of art into the fabric of a complex transportation system. It affirms the hypothesis that art is a public problem which affects the quality of life in the city. Technology alone is insufficient. It needs aesthetic dimensions in order to cater to humans.

In the process of the study of the existing connections between the scientific conception of perception and the painter's vision, I developed a new theoretical and visual solution for the Müller-Lyer illusion. It is discussed in the third chapter of the thesis. In the same chapter I also experimented with such optical phenomena as the Hermann grid, and the perceptual vibrations generated by op art. This unit of the project also includes a discussion of the work of Adelbert Ames, Jr., an American painter who became the founder of physiological optics. Through his original demonstrating contrivances he succeeded to prove that the eyes and the brain do not receive images passively, and that the perceptual process is a creative act. Ames is a neglected genius. I could not find any monograph about him. My own reconstruction of his lifework was considerably assisted by archivists and family members.

The field of cybernetics is particularly active in interdisciplinary collaboration. Numerous computer scientists and artists interact in the making of computer graphics, or explore the possibilities built into the new electronic technology. They conceive of cybernetic devices as aesthetic systems. In the hands of the artist cybernetics becomes aesthetic technology, a new art form mediated by them and resulting in intelligent response relationships between human and machine.

I have discussed the bearings of electronic technology on art in the chapter "Artificial Intelligence and Aesthetics". It deals with various aspects of cognitive machines, the problem of human and cybernetic consciousness, as well as that of computer art.

A salient feature of this chapter concerns the Turing Test. In 1950 the English mathematician suggested a pragmatic method to test the thinking ability of the machine. In reaction to it, I have worked out an Aesthetic Cybernetic Test (ACT) which can be used to challenge the cognitive faculty of the computer. It is based on the visual anagram *Barbara,* a concrete poem that I created a few years ago.

REFERENCES

INTRODUCTION

1. A. Koestler is quoted in L. Leshan and H. Margenau, *Einstein's Space and Van Gogh's Sky* (New York: Collier, 1982); p. 3

2. V. F. Weisskopf, "Art and Science", *The American Scholar*, Volume 48, No. 4, Autumn 1979, p. 473. I am indebted to Professor Weisskopf for sending me this article, and kindly answering questions concerning the relationship of art and science.

3. W. Heisenberg, *Physics and Beyond* (New York: Harper, 1972); p. vii

4. Ibid, p. vii

5. Ibid, p. vii

6. M. Polanyi, *Knowing and Being* (Chicago: The University Press, 1969); p. 40

7. D. Bohm, *Wholeness and the Implicate Order* (London: Ark, 1984); p. ix

8. R. S. Jones, *Physics as Metaphor* (New York: Meridian, 1982); pp. ix-x I am indebted to Professor Jones for his letter of November 25, 1984

9. J. Wechsler (Ed.), *On Aesthetics in Science* (Cambridge, Mass.: MIT, 1981); p. 6

10. P. J. Davis, and R. Hersh, *The Mathematical Experience* (Boston: Houghton Mifflin, 1981); pp 298-301

11. W. Heisenberg, *Physics and Beyond*; p. 41

12. I am indebted to Professor Aage Bohr for this information. It was included in his letter of October 8, 1984.

13. M. Andersen, "An Impression", in S. Rozental (Ed.), *Niels Bohr* (New York: Interscience, 1967); p. 322

14. N. Bohr, *Atomic Theory and the Description of Nature* (Cambridge: University, 1934); p. 96

15. When I posed the question whether Bohr's idea of Complementarity was inspired by cubism, Prof. V. F. Weisskopf, who collaborated in Copenhagen with him, replied: "Perhaps". Art historian Prof. L. D. Henderson's reaction was this: "I, too, have wondered about Bohr and that Metzinger painting." I am indebted to her for her letter of December 5, 1984. On this hypothesis there is relevant material in A. I. Miller, "Visualization Lost and Regained: The Genesis of the Quantum Theory in the Period 1913-27", in J. Wechsler (Ed.), *On Aesthetics in Science*, pp. 73-102

16. R. H. March, *Physics for Poets* (Chicago: Contemporary Books, 1983); p. 208

17. B. Hoffman, *The Strange Story of the Quantum* (New York: Dover, 1959); p. 115

18. A. Einstein, "Foreword" to Sir Isaac Newton's *Opticks*, 1730 (New York: Dover, 1979); p. lix

19. R. W. Clark, *Einstein: The Life and Times* (New York: Avon, 1971); p. 141

20. M. Andersen, "An Impression"; p. 323

21. R. Goldwater and M. Treves (Eds.), *Artists on Art* (New York: Pantheon, 1972); p. 273

22. I am indebted to K. C. Cramer, Archivist at Dartmouth College Library, and to Adelbert Ames, III, M.D., for providing me this information.

23. *The National Cyclopaedia of American Biography*, Vol. XLIV (New York: James T. White, 1962); p. 571

24. R. L. Gregory, *The Intelligent Eye*
(London: Weidenfeld and Nicholson); p. 26

25. J. Mellen, "Foreword", in M. L. Prueitt, *Art and the Computer* (New York: McGraw-Hill, 1984); p. vi

26. M. W. Krueger, *Artificial Reality* (Reading, Mass: Addison-Wesley, 1983); pp. xiii-xiv

27. G. Vasari, *The Lives of the Artists*, 1568
(Baltimore, Maryland: Penguin, 1976); p. 95

28. A. H. Maslow, *The Psychology of Science*
(South Bend, Indiana: Gateway, 1966); pp. 15-6

29. M. Planck, *The Philosophy of Physics*
(New York: Norton, 1936); p. 83

30. D. Ashtone, *Picasso on Art*
(New York: Penguin, 1977); p. 21

31. H. H. Arnason, *History of Modern Art*
(New York: H. A. Abrams, 1978); p. 367

32. J. Gribbin, *In Search of Schrödinger's Cat*
(New York: Bantam, 1984)

CHAPTER ONE

1. R. S. Westfall, *Never at Rest: A Biography of Isaac Newton* (London: Cambridge University Press, 1980); p. 49

2. B. Tannenbaum and M. Stillman, *Isaac Newton: Pioneer of Space Mathematics* (New York: Whittlesey House, McGraw-Hill; 1959); p. 17

3. Ibid, p. 17

4. I. B. Cohen, *The Newtonian Revolution* (London: Cambridge University Press, 1980)

5. D. H. Fischer, *Historians' Fallacies* (New York: Harper Colophon Books, 1970); p. 8

6. I. B. Cohen, *The Newtonian Revolution*; pp. 58-61

7. A. E. Bell, *Newtonian Science* (London: E. Arnold, 1961)

8. A. Koyré, *Newtonian Studies* (Cambridge, Mass.: Harvard University Press, 1965); pp. 63-65

9. I. B. Cohen, "Preface" in Sir Isaac Newton, *Opticks* (based on the fourth edition, London 1730; New York: Dover Publications, 1979); pp. vii-xlviii

10. R. Westfall, *Never at Rest*; pp. 382-90

11. F. E. Manuel, *A Portrait of Isaac Newton* (Cambridge, Mass.: The Belknap Press of Harvard University Press; 1968); pp. 222-95

12. Sir David Brewster, *Memoirs of the Life, Writings, and Discoveries of Sir Isaac Newton*, vol. II (Reprinted from the Edinburgh Edition of 1855; New York: Johnson Reprint Corporation, 1965); pp. 187-218

13. F. E. Manuel, *A Portrait of Isaac Newton*; p. 121

14. B. J. Teeter Dobbs, *The Foundations of Newton's Alchemy or "The Hunting of the Greene Lyon"* (London: Cambridge University Press, 1975)

15. N. Hampson, *The Enlightenment* (New York: Penguin Books, 1981); p. 38

16. M. Shallis, *On Time* (New York: Penguin Books, 1983) J. Gribbin, *Time Warps* (London: Sphere Books, 1979) "Time" in *The Encyclopedia of Philosophy*; vol. VII; (New York: Macmillan Publishing Co., 1967); pp. 126-39

17. E. de Bono, *The Mechanism of Mind* (New York: Penguin Books, 1979)

18. R. Rucker, *Infinity and the Mind* (New York: Bantam Books, 1983)

19. A. Einstein, "Foreword", in I. Newton, *Opticks*; p. lix

20. D. D. Ault, *Visionary Physics: Blake's Response to Newton* (Chicago: The University of Chicago Press, 1974)

21. F. Constable, *John Constable* (Lavenham, Suffolk: Terence Dalton, 1975)

22. C. R. Leslie, *Memoirs of the Life of John Constable* (London: The Phaidon Press, 1951, reprint of the 1843 edition); *passim*

23. Ibid: *passim*

24. R. B. Beckett (ed.), *John Constable's Correspondence (II)*, Vol. VI, (Ipswich, Suffolk: Suffolk Records Society, 1964); p. 32

25. R. Gadney, *Constable and His World* (London: Thames and Hudson, 1976); pp. 58-61

26. G. Reynolds, *Turner* (New York and Toronto: Oxford University Press, 1969)

27. R. Goldwater and M. Treves (eds.), *Artists on Art* (New York: Pantheon Books, 1972); pp. 272-3

28. C. L. Hind, *Constable* (London: T. C. and E. C. Jack; New York: Frederick A. Stokes Co., without date); p. 16

29. C. R. Leslie, *Memoirs of the Life of John Constable*; p. 94

30. S. Papert, *Mindstorms: Children, Computers and Powerful Ideas* (New York: Basic Books; 1980)

31. A. Smart and A. Brooks, *Constable and His Country* (London: Elek, 1976); pp. 80-97

32. Ibid; pp. 21-35

33. O. Gingerich (ed.), *The Nature of Scientific Discovery* (City of Washington: Smithsonian Institution Press, 1973); p. 496

34. C. R. Leslie, *Memoirs of the Life of John Constable*; p. 207

35. Ibid; p. 313

36. Ibid; p. 313

37. G. Reynolds, *Constable the Natural Painter* (New York: Schocken Books, 1969); p. 86

38. J. Barzun, *Classic, Romantic and Modern* (Boston, Toronto: Little, Brown and Company, 1961)

39. J. L. Talmon, *Romanticism and Revolt: Europe 1815-48*, (London: Thames and Hudson, 1967)

40. B. Russell, *History of Western Philosophy* (London: Unwin Paperbacks, 1982); p. 653

41. Ibid; p. 691

42.   C. R. Leslie, *Memoirs of the Life of John Constable; passim*

43.   C. L. Hind, *Constable*; p. 53

44.   C. Peacock, *John Constable: The Man and His Work*, (London: John Baker, 1971); pp. 50-2

45.   J. Gage, "Newton and Painting" in M. Pollock (ed.), *Common Denominators in Art and Science*, (Aberdeen U.K.: University Press, 1983); pp. 16-23

46.   R. Ash, *The Impressionists and Their Art*, (London: Orbis, 1980); *passim*

47.   F. E. Manuel, *A Portrait of Isaac Newton*, (Cambridge, Mass.: The Belknap Press of Harvard University Press, 1968); pp. 86-7

48.   Ibid; p. 86

49.   Ibid; p. 87

50.   Ibid; p. 86

51.   Ibid; p. 23

52.   Ibid; p. 66

Chapter Two

1. P. J. Davis & R. Hersh, *The Mathematical Experience* (Boston: Houghton Mifflin, 1981); p. 209

2. P. R. Halmos, "Mathematics as a Creative Art", *American Scientist*; 56, 4, 1968, p. 389. I wish to thank Prof. Halmos for sending me his paper.

3. R. P. Boas, *"Selecta: Expository Writing* by P. R. Halmos", *The American Mathematical Monthly*; February 1985, p. 154

4. Ibid; p. 154

5. Ibid; p. 154

6. M. Guillen, *Bridges to Infinity* (Los Angeles: J. P. Tarcher, 1983); p. 6

7. Ibid; pp. 20-1

8. A. Koestler is quoted in L. Leshan & H. Margenau, *Einstein's Space & Van Gogh's Sky* (New York: Collier, 1982); p. 3

9. G. H. Hardy, *A Mathematician's Apology*, (London: Cambridge University Press, 1940, reprint 1984); pp. 84-5

10. K. Kuh, *Break-up: The Core of Modern Art*, (London: Cory, Adams & MacKay; New York Graphic Society, 1965)

11. I experimented with the idea of time as a non-linear subjective experience, and it appears as a theme in a series of my paintings.

12. A. Koestler, *The Sleepwalkers*, (1959, NY: Penguin Books, 1979); p. 30

13. Aristotle, *Metaphysics*, M3, 1078 b.

14.   M. Polanyi, *Knowing and Being*, (Chicago: The University of Chicago Press, 1969); p. 201

15.   W. Heisenberg, *Physics and Beyond*, (New York: Harper Torchbooks, 1972); p. 41

16.   W. Heisenberg, *Physics and Philosophy*, (New York: Harper Torchbooks, 1962); p. 108

17.   D. Ashton, *Picasso on Art*, (New York: Penguin Books, 1977); pp. 71-2

18.   Ibid; p. 72

19.   Ibid; p. 74

20.   Ibid; pp. 72-3

21.   Ibid; p. 73

22.   I inferred this from P. J. Davis & R. Hersh, *The Mathematical Experience*; pp. 299-301

23.   D. Ashton, *Picasso on Art*; p. 170

24.   G. D. Birkhoff, *Aesthetic Measure*, (Cambridge, Mass.: Harvard University Press; 1933); p. 4

25.   E. Panofsky, *Meaning in the Visual Arts*, (Garden City, N.Y.: Doubleday Anchor Books; 1955); pp. 55-107

26.   Quoted in J. Gimpel, *The Medieval Machine*, (New York: Penguin Books, 1981); p. 137

27.   D. Pedoe, *Geometry and the Visual Arts*, (New York: Dover, 1983); p. 103

28.   J. Lipchitz with H. H. Arnason, *My Life in Sculpture*, (New York: The Viking Press, 1972); p. 57

29. W. Kandinsky, *Concerning the Spiritual in Art* (translated by M.T. H. Sadler, 1914, New York: Dover, 1977); p. 19

30. G. Vasari, *Lives of the Artists*, (1568, transl. by G. Bull, New York: Penguin Books, 1976); p. 192

31. Ibid; p. 95

32. A. Gleizes & J. Metzinger, "Cubism" (1912), in R. L. Herbert (ed.), *Modern Artists on Art*, (Englewood Cliffs, N. J.: Prentice Hall, 1964); p. 8

33. R. Moore, *Niels Bohr*, (New York: A. A. Knopf, 1966 Cambridge, Mass.: MIT Press, 1985); p. 432

34. I wish to thank Dr. Aage Bohr of Copenhagen for his letter of October 8, 1984.

35. V. F. Weisskopf, "Art and Science", *The American Scholar*, Vol. 48, No. 4, Autumn 1979; p. 475. I wish to thank Dr. Weisskopf for sending me this article, as well as for his comments.

36. J. G. Kemeny, *A Philosopher Looks at Science*, (New York: D. Van Nostrand, 1959); pp. 14-35. I also wish to thank Dr. Kemeny for his letter of February 16, 1984.

37. D. Pedoe, *Geometry and the Visual Arts*; p. 215

38. U. Ruggeri, *Dürer* (transl. by M. Baca, New York: Barron, 1979); p. 39

39. D. R. Topper, "Historical Perspectives on the Arts, Sciences and Technology", *Leonardo*, Vol. 18, No. 1, 1985; p. 51

40. D. E. Smith, *History of Mathematics*, Vol. 1 (New York: Dover, 1958); p. 251

41. T. A. Cook, *The Curves of Life* (1914; New York: Dover, 1979); p. 426

42. R. Dixon, "The Mathematics and Computer Graphics of Spirals in Plants", *Leonardo*, Vol. 16, No. 2, Spring 1983; pp. 86-90

43. W. J. Reichman, *The Spell of Mathematics*, (New York: Penguin Books, 1972); pp. 65-81

44. L. R. Lippard, *Six Years: The Dematerialization of the Art Object from 1966 to 1972*, (New York: Praeger, 1973); p. 247

45. B. Spinoza, *The Ethics* (1677, transl. by R. H. M. Elwes), reprinted in *The Rationalists*, (New York: Anchor Books, 1974); p. 179

46. K. Clark, *Leonardo da Vinci*, (Baltimore, MD: Penguin Books; 1958)

47. Quoted in D. Pedoe, *Geometry and the Visual Arts*; p. 84

48. E. E. Kramer, *The Nature and Growth of Modern Mathematics*, (Princeton, N. J.: Princeton University Press, 1982); pp. 576-597

49. S. Drake, *Galileo at Work*, (Chicago: The University of Chicago Press, 1981); p. 215

50. C. Reid, *From Zero to Infinity*, (New York: T. Y. Crowell, 1964); p. 141

51. M. C. Escher, "Approaches to Infinity" in M. C. Escher, J. L. Locher, *The Infinite World of M. C. Escher*, (New York: Abradale/ H. N. Abrams, 1984); p. 15

52. G. Stephan, "Escher or Newman: Who Puts the Ghost in the Machine?", *Artforum*, February 1983; pp. 64-67

294

53. C. Gottlieb, *Beyond Modern Art*, (New York: E. P. Dutton, 1976); pp. 80-9

54. Ibid, p. 86

55. B. B. Mandelbrot, *The Fractal Geometry of Nature*, (New York: W. H. Freeman, 1983)

56. M. Emmer, "Some Remarks on the Relationship Between Art and Mathematics"; in M. Pollock (ed.), *Common Denominators in Art and Science*, (Aberdeen, U.K.: Aberdeen University Press, 1983); pp. 90-6

Chapter Three

1. M. J. Friedländer is quoted in E. H. Gombrich,
   Art and Illusion (New York: Bollingen Foundation,
   Princeton University Press, 1984); p. 3

2. E. H. Gombrich, *Art and Illusion*, p. x

3. E. Winner, *Invented Worlds*, (Cambridge, Mass.:
   Harvard University Press, 1982); p. 12

4. Quoted in E. H. Gombrich, *Art and Illusion*, p. 15

5. E. H. Gombrich, *Art and Illusion*; p. 15

6. E. Winner, *Invented Worlds*, (Cambridge, Mass.:
   Harvard University Press, 1982); p. 89

7. L. Campbell, "Introduction" to J. Ruskin,
   The Elements of Drawing (1857, New York: Dover,
   1971); p. xi

8. R. Goldwater and M. Treves (eds.), *Artists on Art*
   (New York: Pantheon, 1972); p. 325

9. L. Campbell, "Introduction" to J. Ruskin,
   The Elements of Drawing, p. xi

10. H. Read, *The Philosophy of Modern Art* (London:
    Faber and Faber, 1982); p. 52

11. E. H. Gombrich, *Art and Illusion*, p. x

12. Ibid, p. x

13. H. A. Murray, *Explorations in Personality* (New York:
    Oxford, 1938)

14. M. J. Goldstein, B. L. Baker, K. R. Jamison,
    Abnormal Psychology (Boston: Little, Brown, 1980);
    pp. 60-1

15. E. H. Gombrich, *Art and Illusion*; p. 106

16. C. Sagan, *Cosmos* (New York: Random House, 1983); p. 196

17. P. Taylor (ed.), *The Notebooks of Leonardo da Vinci* (New York: Plume New American Library, 1971); p. 57

18. E. H. Gombrich, *Art and Illusion*, pp. 183-6

19. I. A. Richter (ed.), *The Notebooks of Leonardo da Vinci* (New York: Oxford, 1980); p. 118

20. Ibid, pp. 118-9

21. Ibid, p. 121

22. Ibid, p. 120

23. Ibid, p. 119

24. T. A. Cook, *The Curves of Life* (1914, NY: Dover, 1979); p. 384

25. P. Taylor (ed.), *The Notebooks of Leonardo da Vinci*; p. 38

26. Ibid, pp. 39-40

27. J. Gibson, *The Perception of the Visual World* (Boston: Houghton Mifflin, 1950)

28. E. Winner, *Invented Worlds*, p. 85

29. J. Gibson, "The information available in pictures", *Leonardo*, vol. 4, 1971, pp. 27-35

30. R. Arnheim, *Art and Visual Perception* (London: Faber and Faber, 1956, 1972); p. ix

31. Ibid, p. viii

32. R. Arnheim, *Visual Thinking* (Berkeley, California: University of California, 1969); p. 13

33.   Ibid, p. 141

34.   Ibid, p. 141

35.   D. R. Hofstadter, *Gödel, Escher, Bach* (New York: Vintage, 1980); p. 701

36.   R. Arnheim, *The Genesis of a Painting: Picasso's Guernica* (Berkeley, California: University of California, 1962)

37.   Jean-Paul Sartre, *The Psychology of Imagination* (Secaucus, New Jersey: Citadel, 1972); p. 275

38.   Letter of Mrs. Melvin A. Anderson to the author, April 29, 1985. I am indebted to her for providing information about her father, Adelbert Ames, Jr..

39.   Letter of Mr. K. C. Cramer, archivist, Dartmouth College Library, Hanover, N. H., November 29, 1984, to the author with enclosures, including Ames' entry in the *National Cyclopaedia of American Biography*, an image of the Indian bust created by him for the Shawmut Bank, and a brief clipping from a newspaper (without name) dated December 7, 1925. I am indebted to Mr. Cramer and to Ms. B. Krieger for their help concerning the search for Ames material.

40.   Letter of Adelbert Ames, III, M.D., March 17, 1985, to the author. I wish to thank Dr. Ames for the important information he gave me concerning his father.

41.   W. H. Ittelson, *The Ames Demonstrations in Perception*, together with *An Interpretive Manual* by A. Ames, Jr. (New York: Hafner, 1968), p. iv

42.   I. A. Richter (ed.), *The Notebooks of Leonardo da Vinci*; p. 121

43.   A. Ames, Jr., "Visual Perception and the Rotating Trapezoidal Window", *Psychological Monographs*, No. 324, 1951, Vol. 65, No. 7

44. A. Ames, Jr., C. A. Proctor and Blanche Ames, "Vision and the Technique of Art", *Proceedings of the American Academy of Arts and Sciences*, Vol. 58, No. 1

45. Ibid, p. 3

46. Ibid, p. 47

47. Ibid, p. 30

48. H. Cantril (ed.), *The Morning Notes of Adelbert Ames, Jr.* (New Brunswick, N. J.: Rutgers University, 1960; p. 6

49. Ibid, p. 11

50. Ibid, p. 3

51. Ibid, p. 3

52. Ibid, p. 128

53. Ibid, p. 21

54. W. I. Homer, "Seurat and the Science of Painting (1964)", N. Broude (ed.), *Seurat in Perspective* (Englewood Cliffs, N. J.: Prentice-Hall, 1978); p. 151

55. J. C. Webster, "The Technique of Impressionism: A Reappraisal (1944)", N. Broude (ed.), *Seurat in Perspective*; p. 97

56. R. Ash, *The Impressionists and their Art* (London: Orbis, 1980); p. 186

57. D. T. Sharpe, *The Psychology of Color and Design* (Totowa, N. J.: Littlefield, Adams, 1975); pp. 118-9

58. Ibid, p. 122

59. I. Asimov, *Understanding Physics*, Vol. III (New York: Mentor, 1966); pp. 10-1

60.   Letter of George Seurat to Maurice Beaubourg, August 28, 1890; N. Broude (ed.), *Seurat in Perspective*; p. 18

61.   F. Fénéon, "L'Impressionisme aux Tuilleres", *L'Art moderne*, September 19, 1886; p. 302

62.   W. I. Homer, "Seurat and the Science of Painting", N. Broude (ed.), *Seurat in Perspective*; p. 149

63.   H. Read, *A Concise History of Modern Painting* (New York: Praeger, 1974);

64.   D. W. Massaro, *Experimental Psychology and Information Processing* (Chicago: Rand McNally, 1975); pp. 163-6

65.   R. L. Gregory, *The Intelligent Eye* (London: Weidenfeld & Nicolson, 1980); pp. 87-9

66.   A. Ames, Jr., C. A. Proctor, and B. Ames, "Vision and the Technique of Art", *Proceedings of the American Academy of Arts and Sciences*

67.   R. L. Gregory, *Eye and Brain* (New York: McGraw-Hill, 1981); p. 135

68.   D. W. Massaro, *Experimental Psychology and Information Processing*; pp. 163-5

69.   R. J. Moulin (transl. by A. Rhodes), *Prehistoric Painting* (London: Heron, 1965)

70.   A. Scharf, *Art and Photography* (Baltimore, Maryland: Penguin, 1975); p. 135

71.   Ibid, p. 363

72.   G. Stein, *Picasso* (1938, New York: Dover, 1984); p. 15

73.   A. H. Barr, Jr., *Cubism and Abstract Art* (New York: The Museum of Modern Art 1936, 1974); p. 96

74.   J. Reichardt, "Op Art", in N. Stangos (ed.),
Concepts of Modern Art (London: Thames and Hudson,
1983); p. 239

75.   G. Diehl, *Vasarely* (New York: Crown, 1979)

76.   C. Blakemore, "The Baffled Brain", in R. L. Gregory
and E. H. Gombrich (eds.), *Illusion in Nature and Art*
(London: Duckworth, 1973); p. 24

77.   B. Shahn, *The Shape of Content* (Cambridge, Mass.:
Harvard, 1974); p. 62

78.   H. Kueppers, *The Basic Law of Color Theory*, transl.
R. Marcinik (New York: Barron's Educational Series,
1982); p. 8

79.   J. Albers, *Interaction of Colors* (New Haven and
London: Yale; 1975) p. 81

80.   L. Kaufman and I. Rock, "The Moon Illusion, I";
Science, 1962, 136; pp. 953-61

81.   F. Restle, "Moon Illusion Explained on the Basis of
Relative Size", *Science*, 1970, 167; pp. 1092-96

82.   Vitruvius, *The Ten Books on Architecture*, transl. by
M. H. Morgan (New York: Dover, 1960); p. 86

83.   S. Coren, J. S. Girgus, *Seeing is Deceiving* (Hillsdale,
N. J.: Lawrence Erlbaum, 1978); pp. 222-3

84.   R. L. Gregory, *Eye and Brain*; p. 151

85.   Ibid, p. 151

86.   R. Froman, *Science, Art, and Visual Illusions* (New
York: Simon and Schuster, 1970; p. 52

87.   M. H. Segall, D. T. Campbell, and M. J. Herskovitz,
The Influence of Culture on Visual Perception (Chicago:
Bobbs-Merrill, 1966)

88.　　P. Gardiner, *Schopenhauer* (Harmondsworth, Middlesex: Penguin, 1971); p. 230

89.　　K. Kuh, *Break-up: The Core of Modern Art* (New York: Graphic Society, 1969); p. 11

90.　　R. D. Laing, *The Divided Self: An Existential Study in Sanity and Madness* (Harmondsworth, Middlesex: Penguin, 1979); pp. 39-61

91.　　H. Rosenberg, *The De-definition of Art* (New York: Macmillan, Collier, 1973); p. 12

92.　　D. L. Waltz, "Artificial Intelligence", *Scientific American*; October 1982, Vol. 247, Number 4, p. 126

93.　　Ibid, p. 128

94.　　G. Battcock (Ed.), *Minimal Art* (New York: E. P. Dutton, 1968) p. 32

95.　　J. Farr Tormey and A. Tormey, "Art and Ambiguity", *Leonardo*, Vol. 16, No. 3, Summer 1983; pp. 183-7

96.　　Ibid, p. 185

97.　　M. Cole and S. Scribner, *Culture and Thought* (New York: John Wiley and Sons, 1974); p. 66

98.　　J. B. Deregowski, "Illusion and Culture", in R. L. Gregory (Ed.) and E. H. Gombrich (Ed.), *Illusion in Nature and Art*, pp. 165-6

99.　　L. Wittgenstein, *Tractacus Logico-Philosophicus* (1921), 4.014

100.　　P. Z. Hartal, *Painted Melodies* (Montreal: The Lyrical Conceptualist Society, 1983). Has been published on the occasion of the artist's exhibition held at Galerie J. Yahouda Meir, 2160 rue de la Montagne. The exhibition was accompanied by music, particularly by Mussorgsky's *Pictures at an Exhibition*.

101.   M. E. Solt (Ed.), *Concrete Poetry: A World View*
        (Scarborough, Ontario: Fitzhenry and Whiteside, 1968)

Chapter Four

1. Ben Shahn, "The Education of an Artist", John D. Morse (ed.), *Ben Shahn* (New York: Praeger, 1972), p. 117.

2. "Montreal's Underground Art Gallery", *News Release*, Department of Public Relations, City of Montreal, October 1977.

3. Ludger Beauregard (ed.), *Montréal: Guide d'excursions/ Field Guide* (22nd International Geographical Congress Montreal: Les Presses de Université de Montréal, 1972), p. 180.

4. Pierre Beaupré and Annabel Slaight (editors), *Exploring Montreal* (Toronto: Greey de Pencier and the Montreal Society of Architecture, 1974), p. 142.

5. Paul R. Ehrlich, Anne H. Ehrlich, John P. Holdren, *Human Ecology* (San Francisco: Freeman, 1973), pp. 144-5.

6. *News Release*, Department of Public Relations, City of Montreal, October 1977.

7. L. Beauregard, *Montreal*, p. 182.

8. Vincent Ponte in the *Art Gallery: The International Magazine of Art and Culture* (Connecticut: Hollycroft Press, April-May, 1976, Volume XIX, Number 4), p. 93.

9. Ibid., p. 94.

10. "Montreal's Underground Art Gallery", *News Release*, published by the Department of Public Relations, City of Montreal, October 1977.

11. Dusty Vineberg, "The Metro: An Art Gallery or 'Chamber of Horrors'?", *The Montreal Star*, February 24, 1968.

12. Ibid.

13. Virginia Lambe, "Why Many Local Artists Are Unhappy With Metro", *The Gazette*, Montreal, March 9, 1978.

14. "Montreal's Underground Art Gallery", *News Release*, October 1977.

15. Ibid.

16. Dusty Vineberg, "The Metro: An Art Gallery or 'Chamber of Horrors'?", *The Montreal Star*, February 24, 1968.

17. Ibid.

18. Ibid. (letter)

19. Ibid. (letter)

20. *Press Release*, The Montreal Museum of Fine Arts, April 1, 1965.

21. Robert Ayre, "Art and Architecture", *The Montreal Star*, February 24, 1968.

22. Statement of the artist, *The Montreal Star*, December 9, 1972.

23. Dusty Vineberg, "The Metro: An Art Gallery or 'Chamber of Horrors'?", *The Montreal Star*, February 24, 1968.

24. "Montreal's Underground Art Gallery", *News Release*, City of Montreal, October 1977.

25. Dennis Reid, *A Concise History of Canadian Painting*, (Toronto: Oxford University Press, 1973), p. 225.

26. William Withrow, *Contemporary Canadian Painting* (Toronto: McLelland and Stewart, 1972), p. 27.

27. Colin S. Macdonald, *A Dictionary of Canadian Artists* (Ottawa: Canadian Paperback Publishing), p. 200.

28. Dennis Reid, pp. 228-29.

29. I wish to thank Marcelle Ferron for the information she provided to me (March 8, 1979).

30. W. Withrow, *Contemporary Canadian Painting*, p. 163.

31. D. Reid, *A Concise History of Canadian Painting*, p. 283.

32. Barry Lord, *The History of Painting in Canada: Toward a People's Art* (Toronto: NC Press, 1974), p. 166.

33. C. S. MacDonald (ed.), *A Dictionary of Canadian Artists*, p. 80.

34. I am indebted to Rita Briansky for the information she gave me. Telephone interview with the artist (March 6, 1979).

35. Ibid.

36. Ibid.

37. Telephone interview with Marcelle Ferron (March 8, 1979).

38. Ibid.

39. Dusty Vineberg, *The Montreal Star*, February 24, 1978.

40. Telephone interview with M. Ferron.

41. *News Release.*

42. Henry-Russell Hitchcock, *Painting Toward Architecture* (New York: Duell, Sloan and Pearce, 1948).

43. Peter Collins, *Changing Ideals in Modern Architecture: 1750-1959* (Montreal: McGill University, 1967), p. 271.

44. Moshe Safdie, *Beyond Habitat* (Montreal: Tundra Books, 1973), pp. 141-172.

45. Dawn Ades, *Dada and Surrealism* (London: Thames & Hudson, 1974), p. 28.

46. H. R. Hitchcock, *Painting Toward Architecture*, p. 86.

47. C. S. MacDonald (ed.), *A Dictionary of Canadian Artists*, p. 1321.

48. Irene Heywood, "Mousseau–Full of Invention, Fun and Great Achievement", *The Gazette*, Montreal, December 30, 1967.

49. Jean-Paul Mousseau's statement in Georges Adamczyk, "The City and the Subway", *Vie des Arts* (Montreal, Autumn, 1972), p. 95.

50. Walter Van Nus, "The Fate of City Beautiful Thought in Canada: 1893-1930", in G. A. Stelter and A. F. J. Artibise (eds.), *The Canadian City* (Toronto: McLelland and Steward Ltd., 1977). pp. 162-185.

51. Ibid., p. 162.

52. The concept itself is an anathema in contemporary avant-garde aesthetics.

53. G. Adamczyk, "The City and the Subway", p. 95.

54. Ibid.

55. Ibid.

56. Ibid.

57. Antonio Rodriguez, *A History of Mexican Mural Painting* (New York: G. P. Putnam's Sons, 1969)

58. George M. Cohen, *A History of American Art*, (New York: Dell Publishing Co., 1971), pp. 181-185.

59. Barry Lord, *The History of Painting in Canada*, p. 186.

60. *Bulletin D'Information*, Société Des Artistes Professionels Du Québec, Montreal, (15 Novembre 1973).

61. *Thirty Nine Prints by Members of SAPQ*, Canada House Gallery (London: 11 May - 4 June, 1977).

62. Ibid.

63. Ibid.

64. Marcel Rioux, "Borduas, our Eternal Contemporary", *Arts Canada* (Issue Number 224/225, December 1978-January 1979), p. 30.

65. Andre-G. Bourassa, "Refus Global: A Current Interpretation", *Arts Canada* (Dec. 1978 - Jan. 1979), p. 28.

66. Herbert Marcuse, *An Essay on Liberation* (Boston: Beacon Press, 1969); *On the Future of Art* (New York: Viking Compass, 1970); *Counterrevolution and Revolt* (Boston: Beacon Press, 1972).

67. Letter sent to the author, signed Susan MacDonald, Manager Communications, Benson & Hedges (Canada) (Montreal, February 19, 1979).

68. Shirley Raphael, "The New Way to Tackle", *The Gazette*, Montreal, June 26, 1971.

69. Anne A. Boucher, "The Murals of Montreal", *The Montreal Star*, August 14, 1976.

70. Shirley Raphael, "The New Way to Tackle", *The Gazette*, Montreal, June 26, 1971.

71. Ibid.

72. Arthur Bardo, "The Artist Go Aloft", *The Montreal Star*, February 14, 1970.

73. Ibid.

74. Ibid.

75. Francois Gagnon, "Art of the Masses", M^{10} (Montreal Museum of Fine Arts, September 1971), p. 12.

76. Irene Heywood, "Montpetit's Fight Against Alienation: Sensual, but no Pornographic", *The Gazette*, Montreal, August 8, 1970.

77. Ibid.

78. Francois Gagnon, "Art of the Masses", M^{10} (Montreal Museum of Fine Arts, September 1971), p. 13.

79. Cynthia Gunn, "Say Goodbye to Grey City Streets", *The Montreal Star* , September 21, 1971.

80. Harold Rosenberg, *The De-definition of Art* (New York: Macmillan Publishing Co., 1973), pp. 96-7.

81. Ibid., p. 48.

82. Cynthia Gunn, "Say Goodbye to Grey City Streets", *The Montreal Star*, Sept. 21, 1971.

83. Esther Charbit, "Toward a More Relevant Public Art: The Community Mural Movement", *Investigart*, No. 5 (Spring 1975), p. 3. *Investigart* is a biannual publication of the Art Education Program, Concordia University, Montreal.

84. Ernest Van Der Haag, "Art and the Mass Audience" in Brian O'Doherty (ed.), *Museums in Crisis* (New York: G. Brazille, 1972), p. 69.

85. Eva Cockcroft, John Weber, James Cockcroft, *Toward a People's Art: The Contemporary Mural Movement* (New York: E. P. Dutton, 1977).

86. Esther Charbit, "Toward a More Relevant Public Art", p. 3.

87. Jane Wilson, "Muralists' Sunshine Revives Old Walls", *The Montreal Star*, July 12, 1974.

88. Dale McConathy, "Corridart: Instant Archeology in Montreal", *Artscanada* (Issue Number 206/207, July/August 1976), p. 38.

89. David Carter, "Montreal Museé des beaux arts", *The Art Gallery* (The International Magazine of Art and Culture, Ivoryton: Connecticut, Volume XIX, Number 4, April/May 1976), p. 85.

90. Virginia Nixon, "Painter Says the Viewer Gives Art Its Meaning", *The Gazette*, Montreal, June 3, 1973.

91. Boyce Richardson, "Who is Downtown For?" *The Future of Canadian Cities* (Toronto: New Press, 1972), pp. 142-172.

92. George W. Brown, *Building the Canadian Nation*, (New York: MacFadden-Bartell, 1968), vol. I, (1492-1849) p. 326.

93. Fernand Léger, *Functions of Painting (Documents of Twentieth Century Art Series*, ed. Robert Motherwell, New York: The Viking Press, 1973), p. 152.

94.   Ibid., p. 152.

Chapter Five

1. I. Illich, *Limits to Medicine* (New York: Penguin, 1981)

2. P. McCorduck, *Machines Who Think* (San Francisco:
    W. H. Freeman, 1979); pp. 11-2

3. B. Raphael, *The Thinking Computer: Mind Inside Matter*
    (San Francisco: W. H. Freeman, 1976); p. 253

4. J. Shurkin, *Engines of the Mind* (New York: Washington
    Square Press, 1985); p. 37

5. Ibid, p. 157

6. N. Chapin, *An Introduction to Automatic Computers*
    (New York: D. Van Nostrand, 1963); p. 183

7. R. Jastrow, *The Enchanted Loom* (New York: Touchstone,
    1983); p. 149

8. Ibid; p. 147

9. Ibid; p. 147

10. R. C. Schank, *The Cognitive Computer: On Language,
    Learning, and Artificial Intelligence* (Reading, Mass.:
    Addison-Wesley, 1984); p. 4

11. Ibid; p. 22

12. J. von Neumann, *The Computer and the Brain* (New Haven
    and London: Yale University, 1958); p. 40

13. Ibid; p. 81

14. H. H. Goldstine, *The Computer from Pascal to von Neumann*
    (Princeton, N. J.: University 1980); p. 277

15. J. G. Kemeny, *Man and the Computer* (New York: Charles
    Scribner's Sons, 1972)

16. J. G. Kemeny, *A Philosopher Looks at Science* (New York: D. Van Nostrand, 1959); pp. 220-225

17. J. G. Kemeny, Letter; February 16, 1984. I am indebted to Professor Kemeny, President of Dartmouth College, Hanover, N. H., for his kind reply.

18. D. L. Waltz, "Artificial Intelligence", *Scientific American*, October 1982, Volume 247, No. 4; p. 120

19. D. S. Halacy, Jr., *Computers: The Machines We Think With* (New York: Harper & Row, 1962); p. 10

20. R. E. Ornstein, *The Psychology of Consciousness* (New York: Penguin, 1981)

21. J. Piaget, *The Child's Conception of the World* (transl. J. and A. Tomlinson, New York: Paladin, Granada, 1973); p. 153

22. J. Z. Young, *Programs of the Brain* (New York: Oxford, 1981); pp. 38-9

23. W. Penfield, *The Mystery of the Mind* (Princeton, N. J.: University, 1973); p. 18

24. Ibid; p. 109

25. Ibid; p. 109

26. M. Ferguson, *The Aquarian Conspiracy* (Los Angeles: J. P. Tarcher, 1980); p. 178

27. D. Bohm, *Wholeness and the Implicate Order* (London: Ark; 1983)

28. R. Assagioli, *Psychosynthesis* (New York: Penguin, 1980); p. 19

29. C. G. Jung, *Man and His Symbols* (London: Aldus, Jupiter, 1979); p. 55

30. C. G. Jung, *Dreams* (Transl. by R. F. C. Hull, Princeton, N. J.: University, 1974); p. 115

31.   F. Capra, *The Tao of Physics* (Bungay, Suffolk: Fontana, Collins: 1981); p. 318

32.   M. Minsky (Ed.), *Semantic Information Processing* (Cambridge, Mass.: MIT, 1968); p. v

33.   Ibid; p. 431

34.   J. W. Burnham, "The Aesthetics of Intelligent Systems"; in *On the Future of Art* (New York: Viking, 1970); p. 113

35.   M. Minsky (Ed.), *Semantic Information Processing*; p. 425

36.   M. Minsky is quoted in R. Jastrow, *The Enchanted Loom*; p. 165

37.   Minsky is quoted in D. Hanson, *The New Alchemists* (New York: Avon, 1983); p. 310

38.   P. B. Medawar and J. S. Medawar, *Aristotle to Zoos* (Cambridge, Mass.: Harvard, 1983); pp. 94-7

39.   M. Buber, *I and Thou* (Transl. by W. Kaufmann, New York: Charles Scribner's Sons, 1970); p. 113

40.   Ibid; p. 111

41.   M. Merleau-Ponty, *Phenomenology of Perception* (1945, Transl. by C. Smith, London: Routledge & Kegan Paul, 1962)

42.   H. L. Dreyfus, *What Computers Can't Do* (New York: Harper & Row, 1972); pp. 199-200

43.   Ibid; p. 201

44.   Ibid; pp. 214-5

45.   A. G. Oettinger, "Preface", in H. L. Dreyfus, *What Computers Can't Do*; p. xi

46. R. M. Restak, *The Brain* (New York: Warner, 1979); p. 182

47. E. de Bono, *The Mechanism of Mind* (New York: Penguin, 1979); p. 10

48. P. H. Winston, *Artificial Intelligence* (London: Addison-Wesley, 1984); p. 1

49. Ibid; p. 9

50. D. Davis, *Art and the Future* (New York: Praeger, 1973); p. 97

51. M. Mathews is quoted in D. R. Hofstadter, *Gödel, Escher, Bach* (New York: Vintage, 1980); p. 607

52. D. R. Hofstadter, *Gödel, Escher, Bach*; p. 608

53. Ibid; p. 608

54. Ibid; p. 609

55. Ibid; p. 677

56. J. Reichardt, *The Computer in Art* (London: Studio Vista, 1971); pp. 26-7

57. J. Deken, *Computer Images* (New York: Steward, Tabori & Chang, 1983); pp. 16-7

58. B. Edwards, *Drawing on the Right Side of the Brain* (Los Angeles: J. P. Tarcher, 1979); pp. 36-7

59. M. Minsky, "A Framework for Representing Knowledge", in J. Haugeland (ed.), *Mind Design* (Cambridge, Mass: MIT, 1981); pp. 127-8

60. J. Burnham is quoted in J. Benthall, *Science and Technology in Art Today* (London: Thames & Hudson, 1972); p. 78

61. S. Wilson, "Computer Art: Artificial Intelligence and the Arts", *Leonardo*; Vol. 16, No. 1, 1983; p. 19

315

62. Ibid; p. 19

63. M. W. Krueger, *Artificial Reality* (Reading, Mass.: Addison-Wesley, 1983); p. 10

64. Ibid; p. 132

65. Ibid; p. 229

66. Ibid; p. 229

67. Ibid; p. 224

68. Ibid; p. 50

Chapter Six

1. C. P. Snow, *The Two Cultures: And a Second Look* (Cambridge: University Press, 1964); pp. 3-4

2. Ibid; p. 60

3. D. Hanson, *The New Alchemists* (New York: Avon, 1982); p. 329

4. See, e.g., S. S. Epstein, *The Politics of Cancer* (New York: Anchor, 1979)

5. P. Feyerabend, *Science in a Free Society* (London: Verso, 1982); p. 106

6. F. H. George and J. D. Humphries (Eds.), *The Robots are Coming* (Manchester: National Computing Centre, 1974)

7. I. Asimov, "Foreword", in F. H. George and J. D. Humphries (Eds.), *The Robots are Coming*

8. J. D. Humphries, "The Science Fiction Viewpoint" in *The Robots are Coming*; p. 155

9. A. H. Maslow, *The Psychology of Science* (South Bend, Indiana: Gateway Editions; 1966); p. 112

10. Ibid; p. 65

11. R. M. Restak, *The Brain* (New York: Warner, 1980); p. 188

12. B. Edwards, *Drawing on the Right Side of the Brain* (Los Angeles: J. P. Tarcher, 1979); p. 53

13. D. Davis, *Art and the Future* (New York: Praeger, 1975); pp. 115-9

14. M. W. Krueger, *Artificial Reality* (Reading, Mass.: Addison-Wesley, 1983); p. 2

15. S. Wilson, "Industrial Research Artist: A Proposal", *Leonardo*; Vol. 17, No. 2, 1984; p. 69

16. Ibid; p. 69

17. S. Richmond, "The Interaction of Art and Science", *Leonardo*; Vol. 17, No. 2, 1984; pp. 81-6

18. Ibid; p. 85

BIBLIOGRAPHY

Adamczyk, G., "The City and the Subway", *Vie des Arts*; Montreal, Autumn 1972,

Ades, D., *Dada and Surrealism*; London: Thames and Hudson, 1974

Albers, J., *Interaction of Colors*; New Haven and London: Yale, 1975

Ames, A., Jr., "Visual Perception and the Rotating Trapezoidal Window", *Psychological Monographs*; No. 324, 1951, Vol. 65, No. 7

_____ , Proctor, C. A. and Blanche Ames, "Vision and the Technique of Art", *Proceedings of the American Academy of Arts and Sciences*; Vol. 58, No. 1

Andersen, M., "An Impression", in S. Rozental (Ed.), *Neils Bohr*, New York: Interscience, 1967

Argüelles, J. A., *The Transformative Vision*; Boulder, Colorado: Shambala, 1975

Arnason, H. H. *History of Modern Art*; New York: H. A. Abrams, 1978

Arnheim, R., *Art and Visual Perception*; London: Faber and Faber, 1956, 1972

_____ , *The Genesis of a Painting: Picasso's Guernica*; Berkeley, California: University of California, 1962

_____ , *Visual Thinking*; Berkeley, California: University of California, 1969

Ash, R., *The Impressionists and Their Art*; London: Orbis, 1980

Ashtone, D., *Picasso on Art*; New York: Penguin, 1977

Asimov, I., *Understanding Physics*, Vol. III; New York: Mentor, 1966

Assagioli, A., *Psychosynthesis*; New York: Penguin, 1980

Ault, D. D., *Visionary Physics: Blake's Response to Newton*; Chicago: University of Chicago Press, 1974

Barr, A. H., Jr., *Cubism and Abstract Art*; New York: The Museum of Modern Art, 1936, 1974

Barzun, J., *Classic, Romantic and Modern*; Boston, Toronto: Little, Brown and Company, 1961

Beaupre, P. and Slaight, A. (Editors), *Exploring Montreal*; Toronto: Greey de Pencier, 1974

Beckett, R. B., (Ed.), *John Constable's Correspondence (II)*; Ipswich, Suffolk: Suffolk Records Society, Vol. VI, 1964

Bell, A. E., *Newtonian Science*; London: E. Arnold, 1961

Bergson, H., *Creative Evolution*; 1907, transl. by A. Mitchell;
New York: The Modern Library, Random House, 1944

Berthault, M., "La Peinture est dans la rue", *La Presse*;
Montreal, 19 July, 1973

Birkhoff, G. D., *Aesthetic Measure*; Cambridge, Mass.:
Harvard University Press, 1933

Blake, P., *God's Own Junkyard: The Planned Deterioration of
America's Landscape*; New York: Holt, Reinhart and
Winston, 1964

Blakemore, C., "The Baffled Brain", in R. L. Gregory and
E. H. Gombrich (Eds.), *Illusion in Nature and Art*;
London: Duckworth, 1973

Bohm, D., *Wholeness and Implicate Order*; London: Ark, 1983

Bohr, N., *Atomic Theory and the Description of Nature*;
Cambridge: University, 1934

Borduas, P. E., "Refus Global", *Artscanada*; Toronto, No. 224/225,
December 1978 - January 1979

Born, M., *Einstein's Theory of Relativity*: 1920, New York:
Dover, 1962

Boucher, A. A., "The Murals of Montreal", *The Montreal Star*;
August 14, 1976

Brewster, D., Sir, *Memoirs of the Life, Writings, and Discoveries
of Sir Isaac Newton*; Vol. II; Reprinted from the
Edinburgh Edition of 1855; New York: Johnson Reprint
Corporation, 1965

Bronowski, J., *The Visionary Eye*; Cambridge, Mass.: MIT, 1978

Brooks, A. and Smart, A., *Constable and His Country*; London:
Flek, 1976

Buber, M., *I and Thou*; Transl. by W. Kaufmann; New York:
Charles Scribner's Sons, 1970

Burnham, J. W., "The Aesthetics of Intelligent System",
On the Future of Art; New York: Viking, 1970

Cahill, S. and Cooper, M. F. (Editors), *The Urban Reader*;
Englewood Cliffs, N. J.: Prentice Hall, 1971

Campbell, L., "Introduction" to J. Ruskin, *The Elements of
Drawing* (1857); New York: Dover, 1971

Cantril, H. (Ed.), *The Morning Notes of Adelbert Ames, Jr.*;
New Brunswick, N. J.: Rutgers University, 1960

Capra, F., *The Tao of Physics*; Bungay, Suffolk: Fontana,
Collins, 1981

_____ ,*The Turning Point*; New York:
Bantam, 1983

Chapin, N., *An Introduction to Automatic Computers*;
New York: D. Van Nostrand, 1963

Charbit, E., "Toward a More Relevant Public Art: The
Community Moral Movement", *Investigart*; No. 5,
Spring 1975; Published by Concordia University,
Montreal (Comparison between Chicago and
Montreal murals)

Clark, K., *Leonardo da Vinci*; Baltimore, MD: Penguin
Books, 1958

Clark, R. W., *Einstein: The Life and Times*; New York:
Avon, 1971

Cockcroft, E., Cockcroft, J. and Weber J., *Toward a People's
Art: The Contemporary Mural Movement*; New York:
E. P. Dutton, 1977

Cohen, G. M., *A History of American Art*; New York: Dell, 1971

Cohen, I. B., "Preface" in Sir Isaac Newton, *Opticks*; Based on the
fourth edition, London 1730; New York: Dover Publications,
1979

_____ , *The Newtonian Revolution*, London:
Cambridge University Press, 1980

_____ , *The Birth of a New Physics*; New York:
W. W. Norton, 1985

_____ , *Revolution in Science*; Cambridge, Mass.:
Harvard University Press, 1985

Cole M. & Scribner S. *Culture and Thought*; New York: John Wiley
& Sons, 1974

Constable, F., *John Constable*, Lavenham, Suffolk: Terence Dalton,
1975

Cook, T. A., *The Curves of life*, 1914; New York: Dover, 1979

Coren, S. and Girgus, J. S., *Seeing is Deceiving*; Hillsdale, N. J.:
Lawrence Frlbaum, 1978

Davis, D., *Art and the Future*; New York: Praeger, 1973

Davis, P. J. and Hersh, R. *The Mathematical Experience*; Boston:
Houghton Mifflin, 1981

de Bono, E., *The Mechanism of Mind*; New York: Penguin Books,
1979

Deregowski, J. B., "Illusion and Culture", in R. L. Gregory (Ed.)
and E. H. Gombrich (Ed.), *Illusion in Nature and Art*

Diehl, G., *Vasarely*; New York: Crown, 1979

Dixon, R., "The Mathematics and Computer Graphics of Spirals
in Plants", *Leonardo*, Vol. 16, No. 2, Spring 1983

322

Dobbs, B. J. Teeter, *The Foundations of Newton's Alchemy or "The Hunting of the Green Lyon"*; London: Cambridge University Press, 1975

Drake, S., *Galileo at Work*; Chicago: The University of Chicago Press, 1981

Dreyfus, H. L., *What Computers Can't Do*; New York: Harper & Row, 1972

Edwards, B., *Drawing on the Right Side of the Brain*; Los Angeles: J. P. Tarcher, 1979

Einstein, A., "Foreword" to Sir Isaac Newton's *Opticks*, 1730; New York: Dover, 1979

_____, *Relativity: The Special and the General Theory*; 1916, transl. by R. W. Lawson, New York: Crown, 1961

_____, *Out of My Later Years*; Secaucus, N.J.: Citadel Press, 1956

Ellul, J., *The Technological Society*; transl. by J. Wilkinson, New York: Vintage, 1964

Escher, M. C., "Approaches to Infinity" in M. C. Escher, J. L. Locher, *The Infinite World of M. C. Escher*; New York: Abradale/H. N. Abrams, 1984

Emmer, M., "Some Remarks on the Relationship between Art and Mathematics" in M. Pollock (Ed.), *Common Denominators in Art and Science*; Aberdeen, U. K.: Aberdeen University Press, 1983

Feldman, E. B., *Varieties of Visual Experience*; Englewood Cliffs; N. J.: Prentice Hall, 1973

Fénéon, F., "L'Impressionisme aux Tuilleres", *L'Art Moderne*; September 19, 1886

Fenton, T. and Wilkin, K., *Modern Painting in Canada*; Edmonton: Hurting, 1978

Ferguson, M., *The Aquarian Conspirary*; Los Angeles: J. P. Tarcher, 1980

Froman, R., *Science, Art, and Visual Illusion*; New York: Simon and Schuster, 1970

Fuller, B., *Ideas and Integrities*; New York: Collier, 1963

Gadney, R., *Constable and His World*; London: Thames and Hudson, 1976

Gage, J., "Newton and Painting" in M. Pollock (Ed.), *Common Denominators in Art and Science*, Aberdeen, U.K.: Aberdeen University Press, 1983

Gagnon, F., "Art of the Masses" / "L'art dans la rue", M^{10}; Montreal, September 1971; (Bilingual article in MMFA annual on Cityscapes)

Gainsborough, J., "Quebec Art, Politics and the French Connection", *Arts Review*; London, Vol. 30, No. 14, July 21, 1978

Gardiner, P., *Schopenhauer*; Harmondsworth, Middlesex: Penguin, 1971

Gibson, J., *The Perception of the Visual World*; Boston: Houghton Mifflin, 1950

_____ , "The Information Available in Pictures", *Leonardo*, Vol. 4, 1971

Giedion, S., *Space, Time and Architecture: The Growth of a New Tradition*; 3rd rev. ed., Cambridge: University Press, 1954

Gilbert, D., "Artwalls in Canada", *Art Magazine*; Toronto, No. 13, Winter 1973

Gimpel, J., *The Medieval Machine*; New York: Penguin Books, 1981

Gingerich, O., (Ed.), *The Nature of Scientific Discovery*; City of Washington: Smithsonian Institution Press, 1973

Gleizes, A. and Metzinger, J., "Cubism" (1912), in R. L. Herbert (Ed.), *Modern Artists on Art*; Englewood Cliffs, N. J.: Prentice Hall, 1964

Goldstine, H. H., *The Computer from Pascal to von Neumann*; Princeton, N. J.: University, 1980

Goldwater, R. and Treves, M. (Eds.), *Artists on Art*, New York: Pantheon Books, 1972

Gombrich, E. H., *Art and Illusion*; New York: Bollingen Foundation, Princeton University Press, 1984

Gottlieb, C., *Beyond Modern Art*; New York: E. P. Dutton, 1976

Gould, S. J., *Time's Arrow, Time's Cycle*; Cambridge, Mass.: Harvard University, 1987

Gregory, R. L., *Eye and Brain*; New York: McGraw-Hill, 1981

_____ , *Mind in Science*; New York: Penguin, 1984

Gribbin, J., *Time Warps*, London: Sphere Books, 1979

_____ , *In Search of Schrödinger's Cat*; New York: Bantam, 1984

Guillen, M., *Bridges to Infinity*; Los Angeles: J. P. Tarcher, 1983

Halacy, D. S., Jr., *Computers: The Machines We Think With*; New York: Harper & Row, 1962

Halmos, P. R., "Mathematics as a Creative Art", *American Scientist*; 56, 4, 1968

Hampson, N., *The Enlightenment*; New York: Penguin Books, 1981

Hanson, D., *The New Alchemists*; New York: Avon, 1983

Hardy, G. H., *A Mathematician's Apology*; London: Cambridge University Press, 1940

Hartal, P. Z., *A Manifesto on Lyrical Conceptualism*; Montreal 1975, *Fine Art Press*, Rushford, Mn, October 1979

_____ , "Statement", *Art in America*; New York, November-December, 1976, p. 153

_____ , *Vernissage*; Montreal: Atelier 2101, 1979

_____ , *Painted Melodies*; Montreal: Galerie J. Yahouda Meir, 1983

_____ , "There is gap between our dreams and reality", *The Gazette*, Montreal, 28 September, 1984

Heisenberg, W., *Physics and Philosophy*; New York: Harper Torchbooks, 1962

_____ , *Physics and Beyond*; New York: Harper Torchbooks, 1972

Henderson, L. D., *The Fourth Dimension and Non-Euclidean Geometry in Modern Art*; Princeton, N. J.: University Press, 1983

Hind, C. L., *Constable*; London: T. C. and E. C. Jack; New York: Frederick A. Stokes Co.; (without date)

Hitchcock, H. R., *Painting Toward Architecture*; New York: Duell, Sloan and Pearce, 1948

Hoffman, B., *The Strange Story of the Quantum*; New York: Dover, 1959

Hofstadter, D. R., *Gödel, Escher, Bach*; New York: Vintage, 1980

Holland, L. B., (Ed.), *Who Design America?* Garden City, N. Y.: Anchor Books, 1966

Holton, G., *Thematic Origins of Scientific Thought*; Cambridge, Mass.: Harvard University, 1973

_____ , *The Scientific Imagination*; Cambridge: University Press, 1978

Holtz, J. K., "Artists as Social Reformers", *Art in America*; New York, January-February 1969

Homer, W. I., "Seurat and the Science of Painting (1964)", N. Broude (Ed.), *Seurat in Perspective*; Englewood Cliffs, N. J.: Prentice-Hall, 1978

Illich, I., *Limits to Medicine*; New York: Penguin, 1981

Ittelson, W. H., *The Ames Demonstrations in Perception*, together
with *An Interpretative Manual* by A. Ames, Jr.; New York:
Hafner, 1968

Jastrow, R., *The Enchanted Loom*; New York: Touchstone, 1983

Jones, R. S., *Physics as Metaphor*; New York: Meridian, 1982

Jung, C. G., *Man and His Symbols*; New York: Dell, 1968

Kandinsky, W., *Concerning the Spiritual in Art*; Translated by
M.T.H. Sadler, 1914, New York: Dover, 1977

Kaufman, L. and Rock, I., "The Moon Illusion, I", *Science*; 1962

Kemeny, J. G., *A Philosopher Looks at Science*; New York:
D. Van Nostrand, 1959

_____, *Man and the Computer*; New York: Charles
Scribner's Sons, 1972

Kern, S., *The Culture of Time and Space: 1880-1918*; Cambridge,
Mass.: Harvard University Press, 1983

Koestler, A., *The Ghost in the Machine*; London: Picador, 1975

_____, *The Act of Creation*; London: Picador, 1975

_____, *The Sleepwalkers*, New York: Penguin
Books, 1979

Kramer, E. E., *The Nature and Growth of Modern Mathematics*;
Princeton, N. J.: Princeton University Press, 1982

Krueger, M. W., *Artificial Reality*; Reading, Mass.: Addison-
Wesley, 1983

Kueppers, H., *The Basic Law of Color Theory*; transl. R. Marcinik;
New York: Barron's Educational Series, 1982

Kuh, K., *Break-up: The Core of Modern Art*; London: Cory, Adams
& MacKay; New York Graphic Society; 1965

Laing, R. D., *The Divided Self: An Existential Study in Sanity
and Madness*; Harmondsworth, Middlesex: Penguin, 1979

Lamy, L., "Des Murs" / "Urban Art", *Vie des Arts*; Montreal, No. 65,
Winter 1971-72; English translation; on Cityscapes
in Montreal

Laszlo, E., *The Systems View of the World*; New York: G. Braziller,
1972

Lazarus, C., "New Metro Designs", *The Montreal Star*; February 3,
1973

Leger, F., *Functions of Painting*; New York: The Viking Press,
1965

Leshan, L. and Margenau, H., *Einstein's Space and Van Gogh's Sky*;
New York: Collier, 1982

Leslie, C. R., *Memoirs of the Life of John Constable*; London: The
Phaidon Press, 1951 (reprint of the 1843 edition)

326

Lippard, L. R., *Six Years: The Dematerialization of the Art Object from 1966 to 1972*; New York: Praeger, 1973

Lommel, A., *Shamanism: The Beginnings of Art*; New York: McGraw-Hill, 1968

Lord, B., *The History of Painting in Canada: Toward a People's Art*; Toronto: NC Press, 1974

Lovejoy, A. O., *The Great Chain of Being*; Cambridge, Mass.: Harvard University Press, 1936, 1964

Mandelbrot, B. B., *The Fractal Geometry of Nature*; New York: W. H. Freeman, 1983

Manuel, F. E., *A Portrait of Isaac Newton*; Cambridge, Mass.: The Belknap Press of Harvard University Press, 1968

March, R. H., *Physics for Poets*; Chicago: Contemporary Books 1983

Marcuse, H., *Counterrevolution and Revolt*; Boxton, Beacon Press, 1972

Maslow, A. H., *The Psychology of Science*; South Bend, Indiana: Gateway, 1966

Massaro, D. W., *Experimental Psychology and Information Processing*; Chicago: Rand McNally, 1975

Mayer, U., *Conceptual Art*; New York: E. P. Dutton, 1972

McConathy, D., "Corridart: Instant Archeology in Montreal", *Artscanada*; Toronto, No. 206/207, July-August, 1976

McCorduck, P., *Machines Who Think*; San Francisco: W. H. Freeman, 1979

McKinzie, R., *The New Deal for Artists*; Princeton, N. J.: University Press, 1972

Medawar, P. B. and Medawar, J. S., *Aristotle to Zoos*; Cambridge, Mass.: Harvard, 1983

Merleau-Ponty, M., *Phenomenology of Perception*; Transl. by C. Smith, London: Routledge & Kegan Paul, 1962

Minsky, M., (Ed.), *Semantic Information Processing*; Cambridge, Mass.: MIT, 1968

Moholy-Nagy, S., *Matrix of Man: An Illustrated History of Urban Environment*; New York: Praeger, 1968

Moore, R., *Niels Bohr*, New York: A. A. Knopf, 1966

Moulin, R. J., *Prehistoric Painting*; Transl. by A. Rhodes; London: Heron, 1965

Mumford, L., *The City in History*; New York: Harcourt, Brance, 1961

Murray, H. A., *Explorations in Personality*; New York: Oxford, 1938

Nixon, V., "Painter Says the Viewer Gives Arts its Meaning",
  The Gazette; Montreal, June 3, 1972
Oettinger, A. G., "Preface", in H. L. Dreyfus, *What Computers
  Can't Do*
Ornstein, R. E., *The Psychology of Consciousness*; New York:
  Penguin, 1981
Panofsky, E., *Meaning in the Visual Arts*; Garden City, N. Y.:
  Doubleday Anchor Books, 1955
Papert, S., *Mindstorms: Children, Computers and Powerful
  Ideas*; New York: Basic Books, 1980
Patlan, R. and Weber, J., "A Wall Belongs to Everybody",
  Youth; 23, No. 9, September 1972; Published by
  the United Press, Philadelphia, PA
Peacock, C., *John Constable: The Man and His Work*;
  London: John Baker, 1971
Pedoe, D., *Geometry and the Visual Arts*; New York: Dover,
  1983
Penfield, W., *The Mystery of the Mind*; Princeton, N. J.:
  University, 1973
Piaget, J., *The Child's Conception of the World*; Transl. by
  J. and A. Tomlinson; New York: Paladin, Granada,
  1973
Planck, M., *The Philosophy of Physics*; New York: Norton,
  1963
Polanyi, M., *Knowing and Being*; Chicago: The University
  Press, 1969
Prigogine, I., and Stengers, I., *Order Out of Chaos*; New York:
  Bantam, 1984
Prueitt, M. L., *Art and the Computer*; New York: McGraw-Hill,
  1984
Raphael, B., *The Thinking Computer: Mind Inside Matter*;
  San Francisco: W. H. Freeman, 1976
Read, H., *A concise History of Modern Painting*; New York:
  Praeger, 1974
_____ , *The Philosophy of Modern Art*; London:
  Faber and Faber, 1982
Reed, A., *The Mexican Muralists*; New York: Crown Publishers,
  1960
Reichardt, J., "Op Art", in N. Stangos (ed.) *Concepts of Modern Art*;
  London: Thames and Hudson, 1983
Reichman, W. J., *The Spell of Mathematics*; New York: Penguin
  Books, 1972
Reid, C., *From Zero to Infinity*; New York: T. Y. Crowell, 1964

Reid, D., *A Concise History of Canadian Painting*; Toronto:
    Oxford University Press, 1973
Restak, R. M., *The Brain*; New York: Warner, 1979
Restle, F., "Moon Illusion Explained on the Basis of Relative
    Size", *Science*, 1970
Reynolds, G., *Turner*; New York and Toronto: Oxford University
    Press, 1969
————————— , *Constable the Natural Painter*; New York:
    Schocken Books, 1969
Richardson, B., *The Future of Canadian Cities*; Toronto:
    New Press, 1972
Richter, I. A., (Ed.), *The Notebooks of Leonardo da Vinci*;
    New York: Oxford, 1980
Rosenberg, H., *The De-Definition of Art*; New York: Collier,
    1972
Rosshandler, L., "Montreal: Lively, But Under a Cloud",
    Art News; New York, Vol. 77, No. 1, January 1978
Rossotti, H., *Colour*; New York: Penguin, 1983
Rucker, R., *Infinity and the Mind*; New York: Bantam Books
    1983
Ruggeri, U., *Dürer*; Transl. by M. Baca; New York:
    Barron, 1979
Russell, B., *History of Western Philosophy*; London: Unwin
    Paperbacks, 1982
Safdie, M., *Beyond Habitat*; Montreal: Tundra, 1970
Sagan, C., *Cosmos*; New York: Random House, 1983
Sartre, J. P., *The Psychology of Imagination*; Secaucus, New
    Jersey: Citadel, 1972
Schank, R. C., *The Cognitive Computer: On Language, Learning,
    and Artificial Intelligence*; Reading, Mass.: Addison-
    Wesley, 1984
Scharf, A., *Art and Photography*; Baltimore, Maryland: Penguin,
    1975
Segall, M. H., Campbell, and M. J. Herskovitz, *The Influence of
    Culture on Visual Perception*; Chicago: Bobbs-Merrill,
    1966
Shahn, B., *The Shape of Content*; Cambridge, Mass.: Harvard, 1974
Shallis, M., *On Time*; New York: Penguin Books, 1983
Sharpe, D. T., *The Psychology of Color and Design*; Totowa, N. J.:
    Littlefield, Adams, 1975
Shurkin, J., *Engines of the Mind*; New York: Washington
    Square Press, 1985

Smith, D. E., *History of Mathematics*, New York:
  Dover, 1958
Snow, C. P., *The Two Cultures: And a Second Look*; Cambridge:
  University Press, 1964
Solt, M. E., *Concrete Poetry: A World View*; Scarborough,
  Ontario: Fitzhenry and Whiteside, 1968
Sommer, R., *Street Art*; New York: Quick Fox, 1975
Spinoza, B. *The Ethics*, 1677; Transl. by R. H. M. Elwes;
  reprinted in *The Rationalists*; New York: Anchor
  Books, 1974
Stein, G., *Picasso*, 1938; New York: Dover, 1984
Stelter G. A., and Artibise, A. F. J. (Editors), *The Canadian
  City;* Toronto: McLelland & Steward, 1977
Stephan, G., "Escher or Newman: Who puts the Ghosts in the
  Machine?", *Artforum*; February 1983
Talmon, J. L., *Romanticism and Revolt: Europe 1815-48*;
  London: Thames and Hudson, 1967
Tannenbaum, B. and Stillman, M., *Isaac Newton: Pioneer of
  Space Mathematics*; New York: Whittlesey House, McGraw-
  Hill; 1959
Taylor, R. (Ed.), *The Notebooks of Leonardo da Vinci*;
  New York: Plume New American Library, 1971
Topper, D. R., "Historical Perspectives on the Arts, Sciences and
  Technology", *Leonardo*, Vol. 18, No. 1, 1985
Tormey, J. F., and Tormey, A., "Art and Ambiguity", *Leonardo*;
  Vol. 16, No. 3, Summer 1983
Vasari, G., *Lives of the Artists*, 1568; Transl. by G. Bull;
  New York: Penguin Books, 1976
Vitruvius, *The Ten books on Architecture*; Transl. by M. H.
  Morgan; New York: Dover, 1960
von Neumann, J., *The Computer and the Brain*; New Haven
  and London; Yale University, 1958
Walker, J. A., *Art Since Pop*; London, Thames and Hudson,
  1975
Waltz, D. L., "Artificial Intelligence", *Scientific American*;
  October 1982, Vol. 247, No. 4
Webster, J. C., "The Technique of Impressionism: A
  Reappraisal (1944)", N. Broude (Ed.), *Seurat in
  Perspective*
Wechsler, J. (Ed.), *On Aesthetics in Science*; Cambridge,
  Mass.: MIT, 1981
Weisskopf, V. F., "Art and Science", *The American Scholar*;
  Vol. 48, No. 4, Autumn 1979

Westfall, R. S., *Never at Rest: A Biography of Isaac Newton*;
London: Cambridge University Press, 1980

White, M., "Painting Montreal's Walls, for Better or for Worse",
The Gazette; Montreal, August 4, 1973

Wilson, J., "Muralists' Sunshine Revives Old Walls", *The
Montreal Star*; July 12, 1974

Wilson, S., "Computer Art: Artificial Intelligence and the
Arts", *Leonardo*; Vol. 16, No. 1, 1983

Wilson, W., "The L. A. Fine Arts Squad: Venice in the Snow
and Other Visions", *Art News*; New York, Summer 1973

Winner, E., *Invented Worlds*; Cambridge, Mass.: Harvard
University Press, 1982

Winston, P. H., *Artificial Intelligence*; London: Addison-
Wesley, 1984

Wittgenstein, L., *Tractacus Logico-Philosophicus*, 1921; transl.
by D. F. Pears and B. F. Mc Guiness; London:
Routledge and Kegan Paul, 1981

Wölfflin, H., *Principles of Art History*; Transl. by M. D.
Hottinger, New York: Dover, 1932

Young, J. Z., *Programs of the Brain*; New York: Oxford, 1981

LIST OF ILLUSTRATIONS*

Tropical Bird as Reclining Girl _____ XVI
Dürer, Melancolia I XXVII
Constable, Self-Portrait XXVIII
Constable, Seascape, The Stour XXIX
Constable, Cottage, Sky Sketch, Farmhouse.................... XXX
W. T. Fry, Newton.. XXXI
Color Wheel, Experiment Schemes by Newton XXXII
Image Evolution 47
Four Quasi-Mathematical Works 49
Encoded Information.. 51
Meta-Mathematics.. 56
Composition with Egyptian Motifs 61
Diagrammatic Figures by Villard de Honnecourt 63
Chess 64? 70
Dürer's Egg-Shaped Ellipse, and a Method to Draw.............. 73
Dürer's Conical Helix, and His Invention for Drawing.......... 75
Fibonacci Series by Mario Merz.................................. 76
Columns with Bergsonian Clock 82
Vanishing Point.. 85
Collage with Herman Grid.. 131
Cinematism Transcended.. 134
Tribute to Josef Albers, Homage to the Ellipse................. 137
Ebbinghaus Illusion 138
Necker Cube and Mach Pattern 140
Zöllner and Poggendorff Illusion................................ 142
Corridor Illusion 143
Ponzo Illusion 144
Müller-Lyer Illusion 145, 148
His Name was Jonah... 157
Good Old Days... 158
Opus 60.. 160
Black and White.. 163
Art in the Montreal Metro (photographs) 213-216
Barbara (ACT) 250
Man and Machine 272

* Unless otherwise indicated, works are by the author.

INDEX

Abstract art 84, 151, 275-280
Abstract expressionism 84, 152
Abstraction 50, 129
Academic formalism 36
Acropolis 139
Adams, John C. 18
Additive method 117
Aerial perspective 94
Aesthetic Cybernetic Test (ACT) 250-252, 282
Aesthetic communication 40
Aesthetic measure 57
Aesthetic perception 29, 91
Aesthetic systems 72
Aesthetic value 57
Aesthetics XVIII, XXIV, 50, 52-55, 57-65, 78, 169-170, 256
Afterimages 120
Agam, Yaacov 129
Aiken, Howard 221
Airy, Sir George B. 18
Albers, Josef 129, 135, 203, 198
Alberti, Leon Battista XXIV, 64, 95
Alexander the Great 126
Algorithmic elements 33
Alhazen 92
Allotropy 161
Altamira 126, 191
Alternating perspectives 139
Ambiguity 86, 151, 154
Ames Jr., Adelbert XXIII, 108-115, 124
Ames, Blanche 112
Analogic information processing 267
Analytical Engine 220
Analytical cubism 65
Andersen, Mogens XXII
Androids 218
Anguish 265
Animal locomotion 128
Animism 234
Aniseikonia XXII, 109
Anthropomorphic hypothesis 147
Apollonius 71
Archetypal symbol 133
Archimedean solids 71
Archytas 79
Aristotelian rationalism 14

Aristotle 53, 234
Arithmetic 5
Armory Show 203
Arnheim, Rudolf 104-7
Arp, Jean 186
Arsenault, Real 175
Art XVIII, 37, 95
Artificial intelligence 86, 219, 236
Artistic judgment 31
Asimov, Isaac263
Atanasoff, John Vincent 221
Atomism 60
Attitude ambiguities 158
Automatic loom 220
Automatism 228
Avant-garde painting 48
Axon 240
Babbage, Charles 220
Bach XVII, 245
Bacon, Francis 5
Barbara 251
Barbeau, Marcel 187
Barbizon School 25
Bardeen, John 222
Barrel distortion 113
Barrow, Dr. Isaac 4
Barzun, Jacques 36
Baudelaire XXIII
Bauhaus 129, 186
Beaumont, Sir George 24
Beauty 48
Beethoven 33, 161
Belzile, Louis 182
Benton, Thomas Hart 193
Bergeron, René 179
Bergson, Henri 50
Berkeley, Bishop 113
Berry, Clifford 221
Bezold effect 136
Bill, Max 87
Binary code 219
Binocular cue 93
Birkhoff, George D. 55
Black Death 6
Blake, William 22
Blakemore, Colin 132
Bloch, Felix 67

Boas, R. P. 46
Bogen, Joseph 266
Bohm, David XVIII, 230
Bohr, Niels XIX
Bonnet, Jordi 175
Boole, George 219
Boolean algebra 219
Borduas, Paul-Emile 178, 203
Boring, E. G. 138
Bortnyik, Alexander 129
Bosch, Hieronymus 87
Bouchon, Basile 220
Brahe, Tycho 218
brain 20, 266
Briansky, Rita 175
Braque, Georges 54, 122, 152, 186
Brattain, Walter H. 222
Braun, Adolphe 128
Breton, André 228
broken perspective 119
Brunelleschi, Filippo XXIV, 66, 97
Buber, Martin 237
bubonic plague 6
Burnham, Jack 268
Byron 37
Cage, John 159
Callicrates 139
Campbell, D. T. 147
Cantor, Georg 81, 83, 281
Cantril, Hadley XXIII
Capra, Fritjof 233
Cardano, Geronimo 62
Carroll, Lewis 245
Carter, David 195
Cartesian dualism 227
Cassirer, Ernst 39
cerebral hemispheres 266
Cézanne, Paul 92
Charbit, Esther 201, 202
Charron, Claude 195
Chevreul, E. XXIII
chiaroscuro 34
Chopin 245
Christianity 41
chromatic aberration 8
chromoluminarist method 119
city beautiful 190

Clark, Arthur 264
cloudscapes 35
Clowes, Max B. 152
code ambiguity 163
Coleridge 37
collective unconscious 232
color 6, 41, 122, 135
color harmony 120
color organization 118
color wheel 119
color-tone analogue 161
community development 202
complementarity XX
complementary colors 118
computer 237
computer mentality 254
computer simulation 240
computer-aided design 247
conceptual art 197
Conceptualism 78
concrete 267
concrete poetry 69, 164, 251
conscious content 135
consciousness 35, 227, 228, 230, 231, 234
Constable, John XXII, 2
constructivist theory 92
constructivists 135, 211
Cook, Sir Theodore Andrea 74
Copernicus 4
Coren, Stanley 141
Corot 42
corpus callosum 267
Corridart 204
corridor illusion 144
cortex 240
Courbet 127
Coward, Gary 200
Coxeter, H.S.M. 87
Cozen, Alexander 96
creativity XXIII, 253, 267
Croce, Benedetto 52, 166
Cromwell, Oliver 2
cross-modality 160
Csuri, Charles 248
Cubism XX
cultural evolution 236

Curray, John Steward 193
Cybernetic communication 220
Cybernetic environment XXIV
D'Alembert 16
D'Arcangelo, Allan 211
Da Cigoli, Ludovico Cardi XXI
Da Vinci, Leonardo XXI, 80-81, 85, 110, 281
Dada 78
Dali, Salvador XXV, 155
Dance 151
Darwinism 37
Daumier 58
David, Jacques Louis 34
De Barbari, Jacopo 74
De Broglie, Louis 11
De Honnecourt, Villard 62-4
De Kooning, Willem 35
De Repentigny-Juaran, Rodolphe 182
Deists 16
Delacroix, Eugéne XXIII, 25, 116-7
Delaunay 122
Della Francesca, Piero XXIV
Delusions 85
Democritus 100
Demonology 40
Dendritic communication 240
Dendritic microcircuits 240
Depression 193
Depth ambiguity 155
Depth reversing figures 139
Descartes, René 5, 118, 149
Dewey, John 109, 202
Déry, François 197
Di Bondone, Giotto 122, 127
Diderot 16
Diencephalon 229
Difference engine 220
Differential calculus 6
Dine, Jim 177
Ding-an-sich 159
Dirac, Paul 4, 53
Direct registration theory 100
Distance perception 138
Divisionism 119, 120
Drapeau, Jean 171

Dreyfus, Hubert L. 237
Duality 20, 163
Duchamp, Marcel 74, 78, 186
Duda, R. O. 242
Dumouchel, Albert 199
Dunthorne, John 24
Dürer, Albrecht 71-75
Ebbinghaus illusion 138
Eckert Jr., J. Presper 221
Eddington, Arthur Stanley 233
EDSAC 222
EDVAC 221
Edwards, Betty 253
Egyptian aesthetic canon 62
Einstein, Albert XVII, XXI, 12, 21-2, 262, 281
Eleazar of Worms 218
Electronic brains 224
Electronic computer 221
Emmer, Michele 87
Empirical determinants XVII
Empiricism 60
English Civil War 3
Enhanced luminosity 117
ENIAC 221, 222
Enlightenment 16
Eroticism 39
Éscher, M.C. 83
Ethics XVIII
Euclidean geometry 5
Exogenetic heredity 236
Expo '67 171
Fauteux, Roger 187
Federal Art Project 193
Ferron, Marcelle 175, 178
Feyerabend, P. 262
Fénéon, Félix 121
Fibonacci series 77
Fibonacci, Leonardo 76
Figure and background 139
Figure-ground ambiguity 155
Fisher, Dr. John 24
Fixation 126
Fluxions 5
Foveal field 112
Fractal geometry 84
Francis, Alban 13
Franco-Prussian War 26

Frazier, Charles 268
French Revolution 34
Freud, Sigmund XVIII, 179, 231
Froebel 29
Fuseli, Henry 39
Gabor, Dennis 230
Galilei, Galileo XXI
Galle, Johann G. 18
Gargantua 58
Gaubreau, Pierre 187
Gauss 121
Gazzaniga, Michael 266
Geometry 5, 87
Germanium transistors 222
Gestalt psychology 101
Gestalt switch XVIII
Gestalt theory 101
Gérin-Lajoie, Guy 188
Gibson 100
Gide, André 118
Girgus, Joan Stern 141
Glorious Revolution 14
Goethe 37
Golden section XXIII, 74, 77, 121
Golem 218
Gombrich, E. H. 91
Gorky, Arshile 35
Gospel 14
Goulet, Claude 175
Goya 58
Gödel, Kurt 19
Gravity 6, 11
Gregory, James
Gregory, R.L. 123, 146
Gris 122
Gropius, Walter 186
Guite, Claude 203
Halacy Jr., D.S. 227
Halley, Edmund 11
Hallucinations 85
Halmos, P.R. 46
Hard edge 154
Hardware 240
Hardy, G.H. 48
Harmon, Leon D. 247
Harmony 120
Harris, L.R. 242

Hart, P.E. 242
Hayter, William S. 203
Hegel 37
Heidegger 265
Heisenberg, Werner XVII
Hephaestus 218
Hera 218
Hermann grid 131, 132
Herschel, William 18
Herskovitz, M. J. 147
Heuristic analysis 132, 226
High realism 127
Hildebrand, Adolf 92
Hiller, Lejaren 243
Historical evolution 37
Hofstadter, Douglas R. 244
Hogarth, William 88
Holism XXV, 60
Hologram 230, 231
Hooke 10
Howard, Luke 34
Huffman, David A. 152
Hugo, Victor 36
Huizinga, Johan 166
Human proportions 72
Humanities XVIII
Humphries, J.D. 263
Huygens, Christian 8, 13
Ictinus 139
Idealism 60
Illusions 85, 86, 114
Imagination 35, 262, 267
Impersonal 121
Impossible monument 152
Impressionism 26, 118-120
Inclusive knowlege 266-270, 280
Individualism 36
Industrial revolution 36
Infallible concepts 18
Infinity 69, 79-87
Innate knowledge 17, 101
Integral calculus 6
Integration 185
Intelligent behavior 238
Intuition 50, 262, 267
Isaacson, Leonard 243

336

Isomorphisms 245
Israels 113
Jacquard, Joseph Marie 220
Janco, Marcel 186
Jaspers 265
Jastrow, Dr. Robert 223
Jerome, Jean-Paul 182
Jewish customs 14
Johnson, Daniel 180
Johnson, Dr. Samuel 113
Jones, Dr. Peter Lloyd 275
Jones, Robert S. XVIII
Joyce, James 228
Julesz, Bela 247
Jung, C.G. 278
Jupiter 7
Kabbalah 14
Kallen, Horace 109
Kandinsky, Wassily 65, 129
Kant 166
Kaprow, Allan 191
Kaufman, L. 138
Keats 37
Kelly, Ellsworth 154
Kemeny, Dr. John G. 68, 224
Kepes, Gyorgy 267
Kepler's laws 6
Kepler, Johannes 71, 218
Kerner, Justinus 96
Keynes, John Maynard 14
Kienholz, Edward 177, 242
Kierkegaard 265
King Charles I 3
King Charles II 4
King Darius 126
King Louis Philippe 58
Klee, Paul 53
Klein, Yves 84, 154
Knowlton, Kenneth C, 247
Koestler, Arthur XVII, 52
Koffka, Kurt 101
Kok, Anthony 163
Köhler, Wolfgang 91, 101
Kraynik, Ted 268
Krueger, Myron XXIII, 255, 268
Kueppers, Harald 135

Kuhn, Thomas S. XVIII
Kupka, Frank 74
Landscape painting 24
Language 105
Lapalme, Robert 175
Laposky, Ben 246
Lascaux 126
Lashley, Karl S. 229
Le Blanc, Michel 188
Le Corbusier 129, 186, 211
Leduc, Fernard 187
Lefebre, Germain 200
Left hemisphere 266
Lehmann, Henri 115
Lemoyne, Serge 194
Lenin 204
Lequien, Justin 115
Les Automatistes 179
Les Plasticiens 181
Leucippus 100
Leverrier, Urbain 18
Levy, Jerre 266
Léger, Fernard 203
Light 6, 11, 34
Linear perspective 94
Lipchitz, Jacques 52, 65
Locke 17
Loew, Judah 218
Lorrain, Claude 24
Louis, Morris 154
Lovelace, Lady Ada 220
Lucas, F. L. 36
Luminosity 119
Lyrical conceptualism VI
Mach's figure 141
Mach, Ernst 141
MacKay, D.M. 123
Magic Square 72
Magritte, René 105
Maharal 218
Maimonides 14
Malevich, Kasimir 154
Mandelbrot, Benoit B. 84
Manet XVII
Manuel 43

Marcel 265
Marcuse, H. 166, 195
Martini, Simone 126
Marx XVIII, 39, 179
Masaccio XXIV
Maslow, Abraham XXIV, 266
Mass and energy 21
Massaro, D.W. 123
Master of the mint 14
Materialism 60
Mathematics 46-89
Matter-mind XVIII, XXIII
Mauchly, John W. 221
McCulloch, W. S. 224
Mechanistic materialism XXIV
Memory 229, 230
Merleau-Ponty, M. 238
Merola, Mario 175
Merz, Mario 78
Meta-knowledge 229
Metro (Montréal) 169-180, 183-190, 205-211
Metzinger, Jean XX
Milky way 20
Millet, Jean François 25, 113
Mimesis 68
Mind stuff 233
Minimal art 154
Minsky, Marvin 219, 234
Miro, Joan 186
Moholy-Nagy, László 203, 267
Moiré effects 133
Molinari, Guido 175, 181
Monads 152
Mondrian, Piet 87, 159, 167, 198, 203, 247
Monet, Claude XXIII, 26, 58, 92
Monocular vision 110
Monotheism, Judaic 14
Montessori 29
Montpetit, Guy 199, 205
Moon Illusion 139
Motion parallax 94
Mousseau, Jean-Paul 179, 187
Mozart 161
Möbius Strip 83
Mural 169, 191, 193, 202
Murray, Henry 95
Music 64, 65, 151, 159

Mussorgsky 162
Muybridge, E. 128
Mühely 129
Müller-Lyer illusion 145-150
Müller-Lyer, Franz 145
Myers, J. D. 242
Nabis 74
Nealey, Robert W. 226
Nebes, Robert 266
Necker's cube 139
Necker, L.A. 139
Negroponte, Nicholas 254
Neo-impressionisme XXIII, 120
Neuron 240
Nevelson, Louise 177
Newman, Barnett 83, 154, 198
Newton, Hannah 3
Newton, Isaac XXI, 2-24, 40, 42-4, 275
Nobb, Percy 190
Noland, Kenneth 198
Noll, Michael 247
Non-empirical conjectures 88
Non-verbal communication 154
Normative values 157
Nothingness 20
Null-graph 88
Number XVIII
Nystagmus 124
O'Haverty, Jim 200
Object ambiguity 155
Objectification 113
Observation 31
Occult 40
Oettinger, Anthony G. 239
Oldenburg, Claes 177
Olitski, Jules 155
Oneirism 228
Op Art 122
Optical analysis 118
Optical flip-flop 139
Optical illusion 72, 87
Optical interaction 118
Optical mixture 117
Optical naturalism 62
Optical painting 116
Ornstein, Robert 228
Orozco, José Clemente 192

338

Orwell, George 264
Oscillation frequency 125
Ozenfant, Amédée 203
Pacioli, Fra Luca 74
Painting as science XXIII, 32-5
Painting and poetry 161
Paleolithic age 91, 126
Pandora 218
Panofsky, Erwin 62
Pantheistic feeling 41
Paolozzi, Eduardo 177
Papert, Seymour 28
Papineau, Louis J. 188
Paracelsus 218
Paradigms XIX
Parliament 13
Parthenon 139
Pascal, Blaise 219
Pauli, Wolfgang 232
Pech-Merle 126
Pelletier, Gérard 179
Penfield, Wilder 229
Penrose, L.S. 87
Penrose, R. 87
Perception 91, 100
Perceptual ambiguity 60
Perceptual demonstrations 110
Perceptual illusionism 62
Perceptual inertia 150
Peripheral vision 112
Perspective 66
Pestalozzi 29
Photoelectric effect 22
Photography 127
Photons 11
Piaget, Jean 29, 228
Picabia, Francis 74, 186
Picasso, Pablo XXII, 53-55, 58, 122, 186
Piene, Otto 268
Pissarro 26
Pitts, W. 224
Planck, Max XXV
Plato 28, 166
Platonic solids 71
Pleasure principle 58
Poetic sensibility 41

Poggendorff illusion 141-2
Poincaré, Henri XIX, 53
Pointillism XXIII, 116, 122
Polanyi, Michael XVIII
Pollock, Jackson 35, 181
Ponte, Vincent 173
Ponzo distortion 144
Pope, Alexander 16
Pople Jr., H.E. 242
Popper, Karl 94
Poussin 24
Pribram, Karl 230
Primary colors 118
Proctor, C.A. 123
Projective techniques 95
Proust, Marcel 228
Prueitt, Melvin L. 248
Ptolemy 4
Public art 169
Purism 186
Pyramidal theory 97
Pythagoras XXI
Quadrivium 60
Quanta 11
Quantum mechanics XXV, 22
Quantum theory XVII
Queen Anne 14
Quiet Revolution 209
Raphael 122
Rationalism 60
Rauschenberg, Robert 154
Ravel 161
Read, Sir Herbert 29, 92, 166
Reality XVIII
Reboh, R. 242
RECOMP II 222
Reconstruction 95
Reinhardt, Ad 154
Religion XXII, 37, 40
Rembrandt XVII
Renaissance XXI
Renoir 121
Responsive Environment 256
Retina 126
Retinal fusion 120
Retinal images 91

339

Retinal receptors 126
Régnier, Michel 190
Richmond Sheldon 270
Riemann's theorems 66
Riemann, Bernhard 47
Right hemisphere 266
Riley, Bridget 123, 247
Riopelle, Jean-Paul 178, 187
Rivera, Diego 192
Robots 239
Rock, I. 138
Rodin, Auguste 92
Roman paintings 85
Romanticism 36
Rood, N.O. XXIII, 117
Roosevelt, Franklin D. 193
Rorschach, Hermann 95, 96
Rosenberg, Harold 152, 200
Rosshandler, Leo 200
Rothko, Mark 198
Rousseau, Théodore 25, 29
Royal Academy 25
Royal Society 4
Rubens, Peter Paul 24, 117
Ruskin, John 26, 92
Russell, Bertrand 38
Saccadic eye movements 125
Safdie, Moshe 186
Samuel, Dr. Arthur L. 226
Sandin, Dan 256
Sant'Elia, Antonio 173
SAPQ 206
Sartre 265
Schank, Dr. Roger C. 223
Schopenhauer 151
Schrödinger, Erwin XX
Schwitters, Kurt 152, 187
Science and monism 227
Scientific Revolutions XVIII
Scientific judgment 31
Scientific truth 32
Seeing and knowing 91
Segal, George 177
Segall, M.H. 147
Semantic coding 162
Semiotic system 68
Sensation of taste 135

Sensory neurons 240
Sensory perceptions 91
Seurat, Georges XXIII, 116-123
Sforza, Lodovico 98
Shahn, Ben 133
Shelley 37
Shockley, William 222
Signac, Paul 116
Silicon transistors 222
Simmias 163
Simplicity principle 102-4
Simulation 254
Siqueiros, David Alfaro 192
Size constancy 138
Smith, Reverend Barnabas 3
Snow, C.P. 261, 270
Software 240
Solandt, Dr. O.M. 207
Solipsism 114
Solovine, M. 262
Space XVIII, XXV
Spatial 267
Speed of light 21
Sperry, Roger W. 266
Spiegler, Dr. Gottfried 94
Split-brain studies 266, 267
Stallman, R.M. 242
Stein, Gertrude 128
Stella, Frank 154, 198
Stereotyped art 157
Still, Clyfford 198
Steam of consciousness 228
Stukeley, Dr. 8
Style 91, 121
Sub-atomic particles XXV
Subjectivity 265
Subtractive technique 117
Supergraphics 211
Supernatural 40
Surrealism 152
Sussman, G. J. 242
Symbols 152
Synergic integration 113
Synesthesia 160
Synthetic cubism 65
System properties XVII
Tachism 181

340

Takis 268
Talos 218
Tannenbaum, B. 2
TAT 95
Tauber-Arp, Sophie 211
Tautological fallacy 58
Telescopes 8
Tetrakis 64
Thematic Apperception Test (TAT) 95
Thematic ambiguity 159
Theories of relativity 21
Thing-in-itself 159
Three dimensional photography 230
Three-dimensional world 93
Time XVIII, XXV, 19
Titian 24
Tolstoy XVII
Tormey, Alan 155
Tormey, Judith Farr 155
Toupin, Fernard 182
Tovish, Harold 268
Traditional aesthetics 78
Transfinite arithmetics 81
Transistor 222
Trevarthen, Colwyn 266
Trivium 60
Trompe l'oeil 27, 127
Tsai, Wen-Ying 268
Turing Test 249
Turing, Alan 224, 249
Turner, J. M. W. 26, 113
Two-dimensional surface 93
Uccello XXIV
Uranus 18
Vacuum tubes 222
Van Der Haag, Ernest 202
Van Doesburg, Theo 163, 211
Van Gogh, Vincent 41
Van Ruisdael, Jacob 24
Vanderbeek, Stan 268
Vasarely, Victor 129
Vasari, Giorgio XXIV
Veridical reality 150
Verne, Jule 263
Vienna Circle 48
Villon, Jacques 74

Visual abstraction XXV
Visual thinking 39
Visualization 267
Vitruvius 62, 139
Vogel, Philip 266
Voltaire 16
Von Bezold, Wilhelm 136
Von Helmholtz, Hermann
Von Hohenheim, Theophrastus
Bombastus 218
Von Leibniz, Gottfried Wilhelm 13, 219
Von Neumann, John 219, 221, 234
Von Schiller, Friedrich 29, 166
Wave and particle 11
Wechsler, Judith XIX
Weisskopf, Victor F. XVII
Weizenbaum, Joseph 249
Wertheimer, Max 101
Westfall, R. S. 2
Whiston, William 42
Whitehead, Alfred North 47, 109
Whitney, John 246
Wiener, Norbert 219
Wigan, A. L. 267
Williams, D. C. 19
Wilson, Stephen 254
Winston, Patrick, Henry 241
Wittgenstein 161
Wolfe, Thomas 167
Wood, Grant 193
Woolf, Virginia 228
Wordsworth, William 16
Wren, Sir Christopher 11
Wright, Frank Lloyd 186
Yin and Yang XIX
Young, Dr. Thomas 10
Young, J.Z. 228
Zeus 218
Zöllner, F. 141

ABOUT THE AUTHOR

Paul Hartal's research interests focus on interdisciplinary problems. His publications include *A History of Architecture, Painted Melodies, Black and White*, as well as contributions to the *Artists/USA* series, and to collections of poetry. In his recent highly acclaimed volume, *The Brush and the Compass*, he explores the osmotic interaction of art, science and technology.

Internationally known as the originator of Lyrical Conceptualism, in 1975 Hartal published a manifesto in which he called for the enhancement of creativity through the synergic integration of art, philosophy and science. Since then artists from various countries have experimented with Lyrical Conceptualism as a method of painting. A winner of the Rubens Award and of other honors, Hartal exhibited his paintings in the Luxembourg Museum of Paris (1978), at the University of Lausanne (1983), as well as in galleries in New York and Montreal. His commissions include contributions to the Seoul Art Project of the 24th Olympiad, and to the Art Montreal television program.

Dr. Hartal is the founder of the Lyrical Conceptualist Society, and directs the Center for Art, Science and Technology.